The Law of Poetry
Studies in Hölderlin's Poetics

LEGENDA

LEGENDA is the Modern Humanities Research Association's book imprint for new research in the Humanities. Founded in 1995 by Malcolm Bowie and others within the University of Oxford, Legenda has always been a collaborative publishing enterprise, directly governed by scholars. The Modern Humanities Research Association (MHRA) joined this collaboration in 1998, became half-owner in 2004, in partnership with Maney Publishing and then Routledge, and has since 2016 been sole owner. Titles range from medieval texts to contemporary cinema and form a widely comparative view of the modern humanities, including works on Arabic, Catalan, English, French, German, Greek, Italian, Portuguese, Russian, Spanish, and Yiddish literature. Editorial boards and committees of more than 60 leading academic specialists work in collaboration with bodies such as the Society for French Studies, the British Comparative Literature Association and the Association of Hispanists of Great Britain & Ireland.

The MHRA encourages and promotes advanced study and research in the field of the modern humanities, especially modern European languages and literature, including English, and also cinema. It aims to break down the barriers between scholars working in different disciplines and to maintain the unity of humanistic scholarship. The Association fulfils this purpose through the publication of journals, bibliographies, monographs, critical editions, and the MHRA Style Guide, and by making grants in support of research. Membership is open to all who work in the Humanities, whether independent or in a University post, and the participation of younger colleagues entering the field is especially welcomed.

ALSO PUBLISHED BY THE ASSOCIATION

Critical Texts
Tudor and Stuart Translations • *New Translations* • *European Translations*
MHRA Library of Medieval Welsh Literature

MHRA Bibliographies
Publications of the Modern Humanities Research Association

The Annual Bibliography of English Language & Literature
Austrian Studies
Modern Language Review
Portuguese Studies
The Slavonic and East European Review
Working Papers in the Humanities
The Yearbook of English Studies

www.mhra.org.uk
www.legendabooks.com

GERMANIC LITERATURES

Editorial Committee
Chair: Professor Ritchie Robertson (University of Oxford)
Dr Barbara Burns (Glasgow University)
Professor Jane Fenoulhet (University College London)
Professor Anne Fuchs (University College Dublin)
Dr Jakob Stougaard-Nielsen (University College London)
Professor Annette Volfing (University of Oxford)
Professor Susanne Kord (University College London)
Professor John Zilcosky (University of Toronto)

Germanic Literatures includes monographs and essay collections on literature originally written not only in German, but also in Dutch and the Scandinavian languages. Within the German-speaking area, it seeks also to publish studies of other national literatures such as those of Austria and Switzerland. The chronological scope of the series extends from the early Middle Ages down to the present day.

APPEARING IN THIS SERIES

10. *Comedy and Trauma in Germany and Austria after 1945*, by Stephanie Bird
11. *E.T.A. Hoffmann's Orient*, by Joanna Neilly
12. *Structures of Subjugation in Dutch Literature*, by Judit Gera
13. *Isak Dinesen Reading Søren Kierkegaard: On Christianity, Seduction, Gender, and Repetition*, by Mads Bunch
14. *Yvan Goll: The Thwarted Pursuit of the Whole*, by Robert Vilain
15. *Foreign Parts: German and Austrian Actors on the British Stage 1933-1960*, by Richard Dove
16. *Paul Celan's Unfinished Poetics*, by Thomas C. Connolly
17. *Encounters with Albion: Britain and the British in Texts by Jewish Refugees from Nazism*, by Anthony Grenville
18. *The Law of Poetry: Studies in Hölderlin's Poetics*, by Charles Lewis
19. *Georg Hermann: A Writer's Life*, by John Craig-Sharples
20. *Alfred Döblin: Monsters, Cyborgs and Berliners 1900-1933*, by Robert Craig
21. *Confrontational Readings: Literary Neo-Avant-Gardes in Dutch and German*, edited by Inge Arteel, Lars Bernaerts and Olivier Couder

Managing Editor
Dr Graham Nelson, 41 Wellington Square, Oxford OX1 2JF, UK
www.legendabooks.com

The Law of Poetry

Studies in Hölderlin's Poetics

CHARLES LEWIS

Germanic Literatures 18
Modern Humanities Research Association
2019

Published by Legenda
an imprint of the Modern Humanities Research Association
Salisbury House, Station Road, Cambridge CB1 2LA

ISBN 978-1-78188-729-5 (HB)
ISBN 978-1-78188-730-1 (PB)

First published 2019
Paperback edition, with minor corrections, 2021

All rights reserved. No part of this publication may be reproduced or disseminated or transmitted in any form or by any means, electronic, mechanical, photocopying, recording or otherwise, or stored in any retrieval system, or otherwise used in any manner whatsoever without written permission of the copyright owner, except in accordance with the provisions of the Copyright, Designs and Patents Act 1988, or under the terms of a licence permitting restricted copying issued in the UK by the Copyright Licensing Agency Ltd, Saffron House, 6–10 Kirby Street, London EC1N 8TS, *England, or in the USA by the Copyright Clearance Center, 222 Rosewood Drive, Danvers MA 01923. Application for the written permission of the copyright owner to reproduce any part of this publication must be made by email to legenda@mhra.org.uk.*

Disclaimer: Statements of fact and opinion contained in this book are those of the author and not of the editors or the Modern Humanities Research Association. The publisher makes no representation, express or implied, in respect of the accuracy of the material in this book and cannot accept any legal responsibility or liability for any errors or omissions that may be made.

Trademark notice: Product or corporate names may be trademarks or registered trademarks, and are used only for identification and explanation without intent to infringe.

© *Modern Humanities Research Association 2019*

Copy-Editor: Dr Birgit Mikus

CONTENTS

	Acknowledgments	ix
	Note on Editions and Translations	x
	Abbreviations and Conventions	xi
	Introduction	1
	PART I: ESSAYS	
1	Hölderlin and the Dialogue of Genres	9
2	Hölderlin's Ode 'Natur und Kunst oder Saturn und Jupiter' and Cleanthes' 'Hymn to Zeus'	37
3	The One-Sided Surface and the *Wechsel der Töne*	57
4	Boileau and 'Longinus' in Hölderlin's *Sophokles-Anmerkungen*	83
5	Hölderlin on Tragedy and Paradox	101
6	The Tragic and the Anti-tragic: *Pindarfragmente* and *Nachtgesänge*	121
	PART II: TRANSLATIONS	
	The *Sophokles-Anmerkungen*	147
	'Notes on *Oedipus*'	153
	'Notes on *Antigone*'	169
	Die Bedeutung der Tragödien ...	185
	Bibliography	187
	Index	205

ACKNOWLEDGEMENTS

This project would have been impossible without the superb resources of the British Library. Thanks are also due to the London Library; the Philologische Bibliothek of the Free University, Berlin; and the Staatsbibliothek (Preußischer Kulturbesitz) at Berlin.

In the very earliest stages of this project I enjoyed the benefit of a Fellowship from the Alexander von Humboldt Foundation, which is here gratefully acknowledged.

For comments and advice on parts of the manuscript I am grateful to Felix Christen, Christopher Gill, Ritchie Robertson, John Sellars and Juliane Zachhuber. And special thanks to Irmelind Kirchner.

I am grateful to Graham Nelson and Birgit Mikus at Legenda, and the anonymous referee; and also to all those (including journal editors and referees) who commented on the previously-published material incorporated in Chapters 2 to 5:

Chapter 2 is a substantially revised and corrected version of 'Hölderlin's Ode "Natur und Kunst oder Saturn und Jupiter" and Cleanthes' "Hymn to Zeus": A Note on Hölderlin's Stoicism', *Hölderlin-Jahrbuch*, 35 (2006–2007), 375–96. With kind permission of the editors. <https://www.hoelderlin-gesellschaft.de>

Sections 1–4 of Chapter 3 are a revised version of 'Hölderlin and the Möbius Strip: The One-Sided Surface and the "Wechsel der Töne"', *Oxford German Studies*, 38:1 (2009), 45–60, DOI: 10.1179/007871909x429888. With kind permission of Taylor & Francis. <https://www.tandfonline.com>

Chapter 4 is a revised version of 'Boileau and 'Longinus' in Hölderlin's "Sophokles-Anmerkungen"', *The Germanic Review: Literature, Culture, Theory*, 86:2 (2011), 114–33, DOI: 10.1080/00168890.2011.564521. Again with kind permission of Taylor & Francis. <https://www.tandfonline.com>

Chapter 5 is a revised version of 'Hölderlin On Tragedy and Paradox: "Die Bedeutung Der Tragödien [...]"', *Modern Language Review*, 109.1 (2014), 139–59.

Thanks are also due in respect of the illustrations:

The cover picture shows a view of Homburg vor der Höhe from the south west. Gouache on paper by Conrad Wolf (?), ca. 1825–30. Museum im Gotischen Haus, Bad Homburg v. d. Höhe. With kind permission of the municipality of Bad Homburg v. d. Höhe. © Städtisches historisches Museum, Bad Homburg v. d. Höhe.

Figure 1.1. Württembergische Landesbibliothek, Hölderlin-Archiv, Der gefesselte Strom, Signatur: Cod.poet.et.phil.fol.63, I, 30, 11 (Natur und Kunst oder Saturn und Jupiter).

Figure 3.1. Württembergische Landesbibliothek, Hölderlin-Archiv, Stuttgarter Foliobuch, Signatur: Cod.poet.et.phil.fol.63, I, 6, 58v (Wechsel der Töne).

Figures 1.1 and 3.1 with kind permission of the Hölderlin Archive of the State Library of Württemberg, Stuttgart. © Württembergische Landesbibliothek.

C.L., August 2019

NOTE ON EDITIONS AND TRANSLATIONS

There is no entirely satisfactory complete edition of Hölderlin. That is not so much a criticism, as a reflection of the fact that the task of editing him has inspired ever higher standards of textual scholarship and editorial presentation. The landmarks are the 'historical-critical' editions of Hellingrath, Beißner, and most recently Sattler; but the current state of the art may be represented by editions of individual poems such as Groddeck 2012 and Christen 2013. For convenience and consistency I have cited throughout Michael Knaupp's widely-used readers' edition (in which the theoretical essays in vol. II were edited by Michael Franz), supplemented where necessary by reference to others. Jochen Schmidt's edition for the Deutscher Klassiker Verlag is indispensable above all for its informative commentary. For the complete poetry, Luigi Reitani set a new benchmark with his bilingual German-Italian edition; and for the poetics, the (mostly bilingual) edition of Jean-François Courtine deserves a special mention.

For translations, in the case of the odes I refer principally to the versions of Nick Hoff, on the basis that they tend to be a better guide to the literal meaning of the original. Otherwise, and in particular in the case of the hymns, I refer as appropriate to Michael Hamburger, David Constantine or Richard Sieburth. For *Hyperion* I refer to Ross Benjamin; the excellent recent version by Howard Gaskill came too late for systematic use. In the case of the hymns, it is perhaps Sieburth's versions that best capture Hölderlin's idiom. But that terminology itself requires some preliminary explanation. By Hölderlin's 'odes' is meant an important group of (relatively short) poems based on classical metres, and dating mostly from 1797–1800. The term 'hymn' is often used for the later long poems (or incomplete drafts) in free verse, which were also in part inspired by a classical example — namely the 'victory songs' (*epinikia*) of Pindar. The accuracy of the term 'hymn' can be debated, and Hölderlin himself seems to have used it only in an earlier period. In the case of the theoretical essays and the letters I have used the edition of Adler and Louth, except for the texts translated here in Part II. Any other unattributed translations are my own.

ABBREVIATIONS AND CONVENTIONS

The following abbreviations will be used for Hölderlin editions and translations (where in the case of the latter, 'ed.' indicates that the German text is also included):

AL	*Essays and Letters*, trans. by Jeremy Adler and Charlie Louth (London: Penguin Books, 2009).
FHA	*Sämtliche Werke: Historisch-kritische Ausgabe ('Frankfurter-Ausgabe')*, ed. by D. E. Sattler, 20 vols with 3 supplements (Frankfurt a.M.: Stroemfeld, 1976–2008).
Hamb	*Poems and Fragments*, ed. and trans. by Michael Hamburger, 4th edn (London: Anvil Press Poetry, 2004; rev. 2007).
Hell	*Sämtliche Werke: Historisch-kritische Ausgabe*, ed. by Norbert von Hellingrath, Friedrich Seebaß and Ludwig von Pigenot, 6 vols (Munich: Müller, for vols I, IV and V; Berlin: Propyläen, for vols II, III and VI; 1913–23).
HF	*Hymns and Fragments*, ed. and trans. by Richard Sieburth (Princeton, NJ: Princeton University Press, 1984).
KA	*Sämtliche Werke und Briefe*, ed. by Jochen Schmidt, 3 vols (Frankfurt a.M.: Deutscher Klassiker Verlag, 1992–94).
MA	*Sämtliche Werke und Briefe*, ed. by Michael Knaupp, 3 vols (Munich: Hanser, 1992–93).
OE	*Odes and Elegies*, ed. and trans. by Nick Hoff (Middletown, CT: Wesleyan University Press, 2008).
RB	*Hyperion or the Hermit in Greece*, trans. by Ross Benjamin (Brooklyn, NY: Archipelago Books, 2008).
SP	*Selected Poetry*, trans. by David Constantine (Hexham: Bloodaxe Books, 2018).
StA	*Sämtliche Werke: Große Stuttgarter Ausgabe*, ed. by Friedrich Beißner, Adolf Beck and Ute Oelmann, 8 vols (Stuttgart: Kohlhammer, 1946–1985).
TL	*Tutte le liriche*, ed. and trans. by Luigi Reitani (Milan: Mondadori, 2001).

Other abbreviations:

AA, AO	Respectively the 'Anmerkungen zur Antigonä' [Notes on *Antigone*] and 'Anmerkungen zum Oedipus' [Notes on *Oedipus*], with paragraph numbers as inserted in Part II below.
Analecta	Bennholdt-Thomsen and Guzzoni 1999 etc.
Brill	*The Brill Dictionary of Ancient Greek*, by Franco Montanari, English Edition ed. by Madeleine Goh and Chad Schroeder (Leiden: Brill, 2015).

EGP   *Early Greek Philosophy*, ed. and trans. by André Laks and Glenn W. Most, 9 vols, LCL 524–32 (Cambridge, MA: Harvard University Press, 2016).
Grimm   *Deutsches Wörterbuch von Jacob und Wilhelm Grimm*, 16 vols (Leipzig: Hirzel, 1854–1961).
LCL   Followed by a number, the corresponding volume in the Loeb Classical Library.
Littré   *Dictionnaire de la langue française*, by E. Littré (Paris: Hachette, 1873–74; supplement 1878), electronic version by François Gannaz.
LS   *The Hellenistic Philosophers*, ed. and trans. by A. A. Long and D. N. Sedley, 2 vols (Cambridge: Cambridge University Press, 1987); and where followed by a number and capital letter, the corresponding source text in that collection.
LSJ   *A Greek-English Lexicon*, by Henry George Liddell and Robert Scott, 9th edn 1940, rev. by Henry Stuart Jones and others (Oxford: Clarendon Press, 1996).

Quotations from foreign languages are translated where they first occur, except on occasion in the footnotes. Ancient Greek is left in the original where an exact quotation is intended, and is otherwise transliterated; but in the case of names I have generally used English equivalents. A modification of a cited translation is not expressly indicated where it relates solely to punctuation or capitalization.

Secondary literature is cited according to the author–date system. Except where an abbreviation defined above is used, a full reference for primary literature is given when the work is first cited within a chapter, but may be omitted from the bibliography of primary literature where it is not cited more than once. An edition or translation of a primary text may be included under secondary literature where it is cited for its commentary or an alternative translation (e.g. Kahn 1979).

Titles not deriving directly from Hölderlin himself are put in italics (e.g. *Sophokles-Anmerkungen*); where followed by an ellipsis they form the opening words of the corresponding manuscript (e.g. *Wenn der Dichter* ...). All emphases in citations are in the original unless otherwise indicated.

INTRODUCTION

What follows is neither a complete nor a systematic treatment of Hölderlin's poetics. There will, however, be found a number of interconnected themes — for instance, the relation between poetry and philosophy; Hölderlin's conception of a poetic 'law', 'calculus' or 'logic', and poetic method generally; and his account of tragedy, and of what I shall call the 'anti-tragic'. And the idea of a 'law' enters, directly or indirectly, into each.

As Chapter 1 recalls, the relation between what may be called the genres of poetry and philosophy is a problem as old as philosophy itself. It is true that it was particularly important in that golden age of German literature and philosophy, the *Goethezeit* of 1770–1830. One has only to think of such figures as Schiller, Friedrich Schlegel and Friedrich von Hardenberg (Novalis) — and of course Hölderlin himself. It is a central problem even in Hegel, and has a bearing on the form that was taken by his philosophy, most notably in his *Phenomenology of Spirit* of 1807.[1] And the question remains central to later German thought, as exemplified by such otherwise contrasting figures as Adorno and Heidegger.

There is no doubt that Hölderlin made a significant contribution to the development of German philosophy after Fichte. Some of its complex conceptual apparatus persists in his theoretical writings, even after their focus had, it seems, shifted decisively towards poetics. A final account would have to grapple, more adequately than is attempted here, with the longer texts of Hölderlin's first Homburg period (1798–1800). They are approached more obliquely in Chapter 3, which considers only one facet of that Homburg poetics. And rather than attempting another exposition of Hölderlin's relation to German Idealism — there is fortunately no shortage of such accounts — my first two chapters concentrate on his reception of ancient philosophy.[2] It is difficult, in fact, to exaggerate the intensity of Hölderlin's engagement with both the literature and the philosophy of ancient Greece. If that involved a dialogue with philosophical ideas, rather than merely their application, it was also (in the terms of Nightingale 1995) a 'dialogue of genres', one where the relation between two kinds of discourse was at issue.

Chapter 1 considers first of all his (initially enthusiastic) response to Platonism, and then his engagement with ancient Stoicism. I suggest that, in the course of

---

[1] *Phänomenologie des Geistes*, ed. by Hans-Friedrich Wessels and Heinrich Clairmont; Philosophische Bibliothek, 414 (Hamburg: Meiner, 1988). On the peculiar narrative structure of the work see the comments in Chapter 3.5 below.

[2] On Hölderlin in the context of German Idealism see e.g. A. Bowie 2003: 69–88, and Frank 1998: 715–53.

the composition of *Hyperion*, the Stoics replace Plato as privileged philosophical interlocutors. That novel was completed in Homburg, and it was there too that he worked on a drama based on the life (or the death) of the Presocratic philosopher Empedocles — a figure who can himself be described as both philosopher and poet, and whose status in that regard had been a matter of controversy from the time of Aristotle. The discovery of the importance of Stoicism for Hölderlin belongs above all to Jochen Schmidt.[3] But despite that author's eminence, it is one that has perhaps been too little appreciated. There is a no doubt justified suspicion of using philosophical sources to explain a body of poetry: after all, such sources can hardly account for the process of poetic creation. They might of course more readily explain the process of poetological reflection, and here the case examined in Chapter 2 may be particularly significant.[4] There I claim that Hölderlin was in dialogue with an ancient philosophical poem, Cleanthes' famous 'Hymn to Zeus'. On the evidence of that hymn Cleanthes too was a poet as well as a philosopher, and his own memorable observation has been preserved: 'As our breath produces a louder sound when it passes through the long and narrow opening of the trumpet [...] even so the fettering rules of poetry clarify our meaning.'[5] On that view, poetry is a vehicle for the expression (or amplification) of a content provided by philosophy. Accordingly, Cleanthes' hymn is an inspiring allegory of a fundamental Stoic doctrine, namely that the cosmos is governed by universal reason embodied in law. This is the 'law of Zeus', who is better regarded as a pantheistic creative force than as a personal god (the Stoics gave allegorical accounts also of other mythological figures). A related doctrine is expressed by the slogan that was in vogue in late eighteenth-century Germany: the *hen kai pan* or 'One and All'. In one well-known episode it was cited by Jacobi as the epitome of Lessing's Spinozism, the latter being a philosophy that has many striking Stoic affinities.[6] But Hölderlin's creative transformation of his ancient source leads to a poetics quite distinct from the doctrine of Cleanthes' trumpet.

---

3   See Schmidt 1978: 104–10, and also Schmidt 1996 and 2008b. And see already Montgomery 1923: 212–17.
4   Although the term 'poetology' may not be firmly established in English, it is useful as an equivalent of the German 'Poetologie', which can apply both to a theoretical poetics and to the reflection (or self-reflection) embodied in a poetic work itself. For instance, Chapter 2 considers one of Hölderlin's most obviously 'poetological' odes, namely 'Natur und Kunst oder Saturn und Jupiter'.
5   Seneca, Epistle 108.10, in *Epistles*, 3 vols, trans. by Richard M. Gummere, LCL 75–77 (Cambridge, MA: Harvard University Press, 1917–1925), III (1925), 234–35. The thought commended itself to Montaigne: see *The Complete Essays*, ed. and trans. by M. A. Screech (London: Penguin Books, 1993), p. 164.
6   For a vivid account of the episode (and ensuing 'Pantheism controversy') see Beiser 2004; and on Spinoza and the Stoics, see Brooke 2012: 136–39, and Miller 2015. Hölderlin's excerpt of Jacobi's report can be found at MA, II, 39. The thought derives ultimately from Heraclitus, although the expression itself from Xenophanes (see Hölscher 1965a: 48–50, and cf. Bremer 1998: 182). In *Hyperion*, Hölderlin offers a development of it that is also to some degree Heraclitan in origin: *hen diapheron heautōi* [the One divided in itself]. Some of the ambiguities attaching to both formulae are discussed in Chapter 1.2.

The *Meditations* of Marcus Aurelius are another Stoic source that is relatively easy to document in the case of Hölderlin. Beyond those specific examples, however, I also suggest some broader affinities with Stoic thought. The Stoic doctrine of the 'incorporeal' is one of the more difficult and technical areas of their system. In Chapters 2 and 3 I explore, more speculatively, some possible connections between such a doctrine and Hölderlin's thoughts on the distinction between 'Natur' [Nature] and 'Kunst' [Art, or Culture]. Going beyond the consideration of sources and influences, it provides a framework within which some of his ideas might be understood. Furthermore, the Stoic ideal of 'tranquillity' has a broader significance for Hölderlin, both in his life and in his work. From one point of view, it is the ultimate achievement of the narrative process recounted in *Hyperion*. It also has a biographical significance in relation to Hölderlin's often precarious state of mind. As he in effect says in a letter to his mother: the repose or tranquillity that others may find in philosophy, he finds only in the act of poetic creation (MA, II, 736; AL, 127). The theme returns with a new force in the latest phase of his poetics, where concepts of 'repose' [Ruhe] and 'sanctuary' [Asyl] are themselves linked to the notion of 'law' [Gesez].[7] This is the 'anti-tragic' aspect of Hölderlin's late poetics, which as I suggest in Chapter 6 serves as a counterpart to his reflections on ancient and modern tragedy.

The earlier poetics of his first Homburg period is considered in Chapter 3, which as already observed deals with only one of its facets. But by concentrating on the most formal features — those embodied in Hölderlin's curious 'tone tables' — I attempt to bring a difficult and complex area into more narrow focus. I show how those tables can be seen to describe a particular kind of surface, the one-sided (or 'non-orientable') surface now known as the 'Möbius strip'. Despite appearances, however, this chapter is not about Hölderlin's relation to mathematics; indeed, the Möbius strip did not figure in the mathematics of his day. To that extent my enquiry is distinct from those who trace mathematical themes in Novalis, say, or Heinrich von Kleist.[8] Hölderlin's argument is driven not by a mathematical analogy, but by a particular poetological problem. And that problem can itself be traced to his early philosophical investigations concerning the relation between 'subject' and 'object' and the possibility of self-reflection.

The rules, or algorithms, embodied in Hölderlin's tone tables are a striking example of a poetic law, and Hölderlin refers expressly to the notion of a 'calculable law' in the Sophocles commentary translated here in Part II (the *Sophokles-Anmerkungen*). There is an equally remarkable reference to what he calls the 'law of this song' [Gesez dieses Gesanges], in a prefatory note to his great hymn 'Der Rhein' [The Rhine].[9] In some respects the 'law' sketched there recalls the procedures of the earlier Homburg poetics, as both Ryan and Böschenstein noted. But as Albrecht Seifert observed, it might also be regarded as the outcome of an analysis of one

---

7   I follow MA throughout in preserving Hölderlin's orthography; modernized spellings can be found in KA.
8   See e.g. respectively Bomski 2014, and Pourciau 2015.
9   The note is to an earlier draft of the hymn: see MA, III, 191; and for a translation HF, 259.

of Pindar's 'victory odes' or *epinikia* (the Third Pythian). What would then be remarkable is Hölderlin's insight into the formal structure of a Pindaric ode — an understanding far removed from the image of Pindar as the poet of 'leaps', 'disorder' and 'lyrical digressions'.[10] Seifert also noted how Hölderlin's conception of those matters would have been influenced by his reading of a famous work of ancient poetics, the treatise *On the Sublime* formerly attributed to Longinus.[11] The treatise was given wide circulation as a result of Boileau's translation of 1674, although Hölderlin's own acquaintance with it began before he is likely to have consulted the latter. If, as I claim in Chapter 4, he in effect cites that translation at the beginning of his Sophocles commentary, this is interesting for the context it provides for his notions of a 'calculable law' of poetry, on the one hand, and the complementary idea of poetic 'enthusiasm' on the other. And there is one passage, relevant to the notion of a 'law of poetry', that Hölderlin alludes to in one of the earliest documents of the Homburg poetics:

> We must remember [...] that mere grandeur runs the greatest risk if left to itself without the stay and ballast of scientific method [...]. For genius needs the curb as often as the spur. [...] And [...] the very fact that in literature some effects come of natural genius alone can only be learned from art.[12]

As James Porter has recently emphasized, the author of the treatise mobilizes a wide range of rhetorical devices in the service of what by definition cannot be prescribed by rule, but for which a reflection on poetic method is nonetheless essential.[13]

The argument in Chapter 4 rests on what may seem to be a minor detail, namely Boileau's translation of the two Greek terms *methodos* and *ekstasis*. But again, it is such details that can help to bring Hölderlin's difficult and often elliptical theoretical writings into sharper focus. Those difficulties are well illustrated by the brief text considered in Chapter 5. This may possibly be a fragment of the planned 'introduction' to Hölderlin's Sophocles translations, which was promised to his publisher as a supplement to the *Sophokles-Anmerkungen*. If so, it is regrettable indeed that the manuscripts have been lost, for his thoughts in those *Anmerkungen* are compressed in the extreme. Such difficulties also inspired the work of translation and commentary undertaken in Part II. While several translations already exist — three into English alone — there can be no doubt that Hölderlin's commentary to Sophocles itself calls for elucidation. And if many obscurities will inevitably remain, the work may at least help to measure the extent of our understanding. Thus both translation and commentary in Part II are best regarded as work in progress.

---

10   The words of Charles Batteux (1764) cited in Chapter 4.1. It is true that the history of the reception of Pindar prior to Hölderlin is more complex than this may suggest (cf. Vöhler 2005: 180–81).
11   For the above points, see respectively Böschenstein 1959: 135–38; Ryan 1960: 249–55; Seifert 1983; and Seifert 1982: 69–79.
12   *On the Sublime*, ed. and trans. by W. H. Fyfe, rev. by Donald Russell, in Aristotle, XXIII, LCL 199 (Cambridge, MA: Harvard University Press, 1995; corrected repr. 1999), pp. 165–67 (from chapter 2 of the treatise). And cf. MA, II, 58; AL, 240.
13   See generally Porter 2016: 57–177. On the continuing relevance of the rhetorical tradition, cf. Groddeck 2008.

Some of the most hair-raising difficulties of the *Sophokles-Anmerkungen* concern the differences drawn there between Greek and modern forms of poetic representation, and more specifically between ancient and modern tragedy. The reflections in question are found in the second set of *Anmerkungen*, the 'Notes on Antigone', apparently in the form of a last-minute interpolation. It also seems to have been at this late stage that Hölderlin modified his translation practice, with a view to making his version more 'lively', to expose more 'boldly' the original or 'oriental' spirit of the Greek, in the direction even of 'eccentric enthusiasm'.[14] Here the 'oriental' stands in contrast to what, in the *Anmerkungen*, is sometimes called the 'Hesperian' (from the Greek *hespera*, meaning 'evening' or 'west'). We modern Europeans are 'Hesperian' in comparison with the ancient Greeks. But there is also a polarity within Greek culture itself, between its oriental foundation and its development towards the Hesperian — or (in the words of the first letter to Böhlendorff) its 'Fortschritt der Bildung' [process of civilization].[15] This is reflected, for instance, in an at first sight startling observation on Sophocles' tragedy *Ajax*. There Hölderlin suggests that Ajax and Ulysses (or Aias and Odysseus) are related as 'Nationelles', on the one hand, and 'Antinationelles' or 'Gebildetes', on the other (see AA [2.13]). That is to say: as natively Greek, and what subsequent cultural development has brought into opposition to the Greek. It may appear odd to say that Odysseus is not truly a Greek. But the observation can be related to more recent discussions of Sophocles. Thus Charles Segal observes that for the 'tragic dimension' of the play 'what is important is not so much the emergence of civilized values per se as the clash between those values and the unbending epic heroism [of Ajax]' (1981: 110). The tragedy records a conflict, and by implication a transition, between an older set of heroic aristocratic values and the new democratic values of the Greek polis (see also Burian 2012: 81). And conversely, as Leslie Kurke has suggested, the Pindaric *epinikion* is 'aimed at the defusion and resolution [of tensions] inherent in civic ideology', amounting to the 'antitype' of a tragedy that 'pitted the realm of the mythic heroes against the civic community' (2013: 6–7). Hölderlin's theory of tragedy sometimes anticipates such modern accounts more than it recalls the analyses of Aristotle. There are other points of contact with modern commentators, in particular his analysis of the tragic process as a transgression of the boundary that separates the human from the divine, and his resulting emphasis on 'das Ungeheure'. That word, difficult enough in itself to translate — the 'prodigious', the 'fearful', the 'monstrous' — corresponds to Hölderlin's more 'lively' translation of the Greek term *deinos* that is central to the most famous choral song (the first stasimon) of *Antigone*.[16] That is not to say that Hölderlin's account of these matters is necessarily correct, or sufficiently clear in its details. But it does, I think, help us to understand a text whose difficulty arises in part from its very untimeliness.

---

14 See, in the letters to his publisher Wilmans at MA, II, 925, 930 (AL, 215–16, 220): 'dadurch lebendiger, als gewöhnlich dem Publikum darzustellen, daß ich das Orientalische [...] mehr heraushebe'; 'nicht lebendig genug'; 'kühner exponieren [...] gegen die exzentrische Begeisterung'.
15 MA, II, 912; AL, 207. See the celebrated analyses of Peter Szondi (1978c).
16 See in Part II below the commentary to AO [3.1].

Kurke's contrast between Greek tragedy and its 'antitype' in the victory ode sheds retrospective light on Hölderlin's relation to Pindar, in particular in his commentaries to nine translated Pindaric fragments (the *Pindarfragmente* discussed in Chapter 6). We might say that Greek tragedy for Hölderlin is structured by an internal opposition between the originally Greek (or 'oriental'), and the more Hesperian, one that is reflected in a passage from one to the other. But that opposition also corresponds to our own relation to Greek tragedy, for we too are Hesperian after our own fashion. This seems to be why he wishes in his translation to bring out the strangeness and intensity of the Greek original, for instance by forgoing the names of the Greek gods that by now have grown too familiar to us. We can better see our difference from Greek antiquity, even as its origins are brought closer.[17] But the relation to Pindar established in the *Pindarfragmente* is of a different kind. There the poet is inscribed in a continuum that begins with Pindar, and ends with Hölderlin's reflections on Pindar (which turn out also to be reflections on his own process of interpretation). If Pindar's athletic aristocrats, with their heroic values, are restored by the victory ode to a place in the democratic polis, so modern poets too need not always be opposed to their Greek forebears. This may also explain why Hölderlin can find in his later hymns a continuity with the Pindaric model, after the attempt to compose a tragedy had been abandoned.

But the question then remains: what significance could the idea of a modern tragedy still have for Hölderlin, once that *Empedocles* project had been abandoned? The *Anmerkungen* themselves seem to envisage such a possibility, precisely in their emphasis on the difference between tragedy in a 'Greek' and a 'Hesperian' mode. In Chapter 6, I attempt to sketch a possible solution to that problem. It is unlikely that Hölderlin himself reached final clarity here. But his tantalizingly brief indications can be compared with his actual practice in composing a series of nine (mostly short) poems, probably the ones described to his publisher as 'Nachtgesänge' [Nightsongs]. Were these a variation on the theme of 'modern tragedy'? It seems, in any event, that they were the last poems he saw into publication.

---

17   Here too, however, Hölderlin's practice can give rise to difficult questions: see in Part II the introductory note to the translation of the *Sophokles-Anmerkungen*.

PART I

Essays

CHAPTER 1

Hölderlin and the Dialogue of Genres

1. An Ancient Quarrel?

The 'ancient quarrel between poetry and philosophy' may have been Plato's own invention.[1] But by finding such a quarrel, and ascribing to it an illustrious antiquity, Plato was the better able to define 'philosophy' as a newly authoritative form of discourse — albeit one that laid claim to ancient pedigree. As Nightingale has suggested, the subject thereby emerged 'as the powerful adversary of the giant that is poetry'.[2] Still, Plato's own dialogues are full of literary devices and effects. These are by no means purely decorative; indeed they are often central to the presentation of the argument.[3] And there is not only a confrontation of speakers or arguments in Plato's dialogues, but also a veritable 'dialogue of genres' in which other kinds of discourse — poetic, rhetorical, political — are engaged, parodied and usually trumped by Plato's new master-discourse.[4]

That is not to say that there was no philosophical thought before Plato; but a question does arise as to the meaning of the familiar expression 'Presocratic philosophy'.[5] Thinkers before Plato had their own strategies to affirm their authority, although again these seem to raise the question of genre. Prose had already been invented by the time of Empedocles and Parmenides: what then is the significance of their choice to compose in epic hexameters, or to frame their discourse in terms of initiatory ceremonies or the discourse of a banished god?[6] If Empedocles is

---

1   Plato, *Republic*, trans. by Robin Waterfield (Oxford: Oxford University Press 1993; repr. 1998), 607b (p. 361). See Most 2011: 19–20 (but suggesting that it was not a conscious fabrication); and cf. Ford 2002: 46–49, and Sassi 2018: 139.
2   Nightingale 1995: 60–67 (p. 67); but for a different view see Halliwell 2011: 231–32.
3   See generally Kahn 1996, and also Goldhill 2002: 80–98. Praise of Plato as at once 'philosopher' and 'poet' was commonplace from Cicero onwards, and in particular during Hölderlin's period at the Tübingen Protestant seminary or *Stift*: see Matuschek 2002a: 83, and Kurz 2002: 64.
4   On philosophy and tragedy, see Nightingale 1995: 60–92; on philosophy and the rhetoric of praise 93–132; and on the *Phaedrus* as an exceptional case in which other discourses are 'granted full semantic autonomy' 131–71 (p. 133). The mixture of genres in Plato was already an important theme in the early German Romantics, especially Friedrich Schlegel (see Kurz 2002: 74–75).
5   See Laks 2001. On the question whether thinkers before Plato or Socrates can be regarded as 'philosophers', cf. M. Frede 2000: 5–9. Conversely, on the development of the idea of 'poetry' as a genre distinct from performance in the 5th century BCE, see Ford 2002: 131–57; and cf. Sassi 2018: 139–40.
6   On poetic form in Presocratic philosophy, see Laks 2001: 303–04, and Most 1999; and cf. Long

regarded essentially as a natural philosopher, or Parmenides as a logician, do we thereby lose an important dimension of their thought? Such questions affect the very establishment of a text, given that editorial conjectures are influenced by such presuppositions or prejudices.[7]

In the history of reflection on the relation between philosophy and poetry, Empedocles is a particularly important case. He figures at the outset in Aristotle's *Poetics*, where Aristotle follows Plato in proposing 'mimesis' as a distinguishing criterion of poetry. This has the interesting result that Plato's own dialogues fall within the category of poetry, whereas Empedocles (notwithstanding the hexameters) is better regarded as natural philosopher than poet.[8] But more is at stake than the relevance of metrical form as a criterion of poetry. What we would now regard as the poetic qualities of a thinker such as Empedocles go beyond the choice of a particular metre, and are related to the intended function of his poems. What can now be appreciated as poetry may have belonged originally to the discourse of religion or myth. Conversely, it may be equally one-sided to regard Empedocles or Parmenides simply as poets, magicians or healers, rather than as transitional figures who used archaic means of expression to express new forms of thought.[9] In the case of Empedocles, the surviving poetic fragments most probably belong to two distinct poems: *On Nature* [Περὶ φύσεως, or Φυσικά] and *Purifications* [Καθαρμοί]. It might at first be supposed that the former is simply a philosophy of nature, while the latter has a mythological and initiatory character (narrated as it is from the perspective of a banished god). *On Nature* would then be a natural philosophy in verse form, *Purifications* a religious text. But as recent manuscript discoveries have confirmed, there is a striking parallelism between those two dimensions of Empedocles' thought. The four elements whose separation and combination is central to *On Nature* correspond to divine beings, whose story of exile (separation) and return (reunification) is narrated in a different manner in the *Purifications*. Indeed, the parallelism emerges in the poem *On Nature* itself, as does the full divinity of the elements at one stage of Empedocles' cosmic cycle (where they become 'pure masses' or 'roots' rather than simply constituent elements).[10] One

---

2011. On initiation in Parmenides cf. Kingsley 1999: 61–76, and for Empedocles' banished god see Primavesi 2008: 262–63. The question of Empedocles' poetics is the subject of a major recent study (Gheerbrant 2017).

7   On the interaction between editorial conjecture and assumptions about genre, cf. Kingsley 2002.

8   Aristotle, *Poetics*, ed. and trans. by Stephen Halliwell, in Aristotle, XXIII, LCL 199 (Cambridge, MA: Harvard University Press, 1995; corrected repr. 1999), 1447b (pp. 30–33); on which see especially Primavesi 2013. Aristotle notwithstanding, in the later reception of the Presocratics Empedocles was seen as the supreme poet among them (Kraye 2003: 341); and Empedocles may qualify even on Aristotle's own criterion (Primavesi 2014: 19).

9   For Empedocles and Parmenides as essentially magicians and shamanistic healers, see Kingsley 1995 and 1999 (Kingsley is himself a mystic as well as a scholar). But for an allegorical reading of such aspects of their poems see Primavesi 2005, contrasting Kingsley 2002: 372. On the one-sidedness of 'hyporational' as much as 'hyperrational' interpretations cf. Sassi 2018: 158; and on Parmenides as a transitional figure who, as a philosopher, is 'obliged to leave the sanctuary of revelation', Detienne 1996: 130–34 (p. 133).

10 Following the lucid account in Primavesi 2008: 256–61; cf. Sassi 2018: 129–30. On the divinity

of Hölderlin's most important, if uncompleted, projects was a tragedy based on the legend of the death of Empedocles.[11] Primavesi has shown how Hölderlin's drafts demonstrate an almost prescient awareness of those parallels in Empedocles' natural philosophy.[12] In summary, therefore: the relationship between the genres of poetry and philosophy is a long-standing problem in the Western philosophical tradition; and the extent to which it turns on poetic form, such as the use of metre, or on some other feature such as mimesis or the invocation of myth, is a matter of long controversy. It is hardly surprising that Hölderlin had an uncommon sensitivity to those concerns. More surprising, perhaps, is the depth and precocious modernity of his insight.

In the modern era, the first collection of surviving Presocratic philosophical fragments in their original Greek was published by Henri Estienne in 1573. It is not for nothing that he entitled his collection *Poesis philosophica* [*Philosophical Poetry*]: for a renewed interest in Plato's predecessors was connected with an appreciation of their poetic qualities.[13] But it is not only the title of Estienne's collection that is significant. The work's prefatory letter of dedication was itself a contribution to the long-standing debate regarding the poetic status of philosophical texts.[14] And the collection is likely to have been a source for Hölderlin's own *Empedocles* project.

It is also clear that, at least for a time, Hölderlin was intimately involved in contemporary philosophical debates. He was close to both Schelling and Hegel, from the time of their student days in the Tübingen *Stift*, and in 1794–95 he attended Fichte's seminal lectures at the University of Jena. At this point he even harboured ambitions to be an academic philosopher; and both letters and manuscript fragments from the period testify to his contribution to those debates. Dieter Henrich's ambition has been to find in Hölderlin a body of thought that would place him

---

of the elements in *On Nature*, see also Primavesi 2005: 87; and for a comprehensive analysis of the evidence for two distinct poems, Primavesi 2007.

11 MA, I, 761–903; or for an alternative reconstruction of the various drafts KA, II, 277–445. There are English translations of the second and third versions in Hamb, 339–454. For translations of all three versions, see *The Death of Empedocles: A Mourning-play*, trans. by David Farrell Krell (Albany: State University of New York Press, 2008).

12 'Hölderlins Vorstellung einer vertrauten *Gemeinschaft* mit den Elementargöttern [...] nähert sich in erstaunlichem Maße einem naturphilosophischen Gedanken des historischen Empedokles an, dessen originale Formulierung erst zweihundert Jahre nach Hölderlin wiederentdeckt wurde' (Primavesi 2014: 40).

13 Ποίησις φιλόσοφος. *Poesis philosophica, Vel saltem, Reliquiæ poesis philosophicæ, Empedoclis, Parmenidis, Xenophanis, Cleanthis, Timonis, Epicharmi* [...], ed. by Henr. Stephanus [Henri II Estienne] ([Geneva]: 1573). On the epoch-making character of Estienne's collection, see Kraye 2003: 340, and Primavesi 2011a: 156. Not all of the fragments included by Estienne are in verse form, although the poetic qualities of the prose fragments of Heraclitus can now be more easily appreciated (Kahn 1979: 7–8; Most 1999: 335, 350; Laks 2001: 303–04). His collection also contains a striking example from a later period, namely Cleanthes' 'Hymn to Zeus' (on which see section 4 below and Chapter 2).

14 See Primavesi 2011a and 2011b. Note that the celebrated Horatian dictum *Aut prodesse volunt aut delectare poetae* ... forms the epigraph to that dedicatory letter: *Poesis philosophica*, p. 3 (and on that dictum see further section 2 below). In the preface Estienne attempts, not always convincingly, to refute or reconcile the different positions of Horace, Plutarch and Aristotle. It seems that Estienne's immediate response to the poetic quality of the Empedocles fragments was more significant than any arguments for or against their status.

alongside Hegel and Schelling as a representative of what he calls 'classical German philosophy'.[15] And it is true that, thanks to Henrich and his followers, the history of German Idealism can no longer be written without taking Hölderlin's contribution into account.[16] However, an undue concentration on Hölderlin's involvement in those controversies can distort our understanding of his thought, and above all of its development.[17] His relationship to philosophy was a complicated one, and ambivalent even at a personal level. Hölderlin's abrupt departure from Jena, at the end of May 1795, was in part a flight from the ferment of philosophical speculation. On the way back home to Nürtingen he stopped off at Heidelberg, an episode recalled in the ode of the same name. Lines from an earlier draft of 'Heidelberg' — perhaps omitted as too autobiographical from the final version — remember the poet as 'Ein vertriebener Wandrer | Der vor Menschen und Büchern floh' [A wanderer driven out, | Fleeing from people and books]; although, as the lines indicate, his flight was as much from the overpowering presence of his mentor Schiller.[18] Writing from Frankfurt to his friend Hegel on 20 November 1796, he celebrates his freedom from 'die Luftgeister, mit den metaphysischen Flügeln, die mich aus Jena geleiteten' [the ethereal spirits with metaphysical wings that accompanied me out of Jena].[19] It may in the end be more fruitful to regard Hölderlin as engaging in his own kind of 'dialogue of genres'. It is true that this is in part a dialogue with his own earlier self. But as Bremer has observed (1998: 184–90), it is as much one with ancient philosophy as with the speculative systems of his contemporaries. This can be seen in the case of the first undoubted masterpiece of Hölderlin's maturity, his novel *Hyperion*.

2. 'Holy Plato, forgive!'

The importance of Plato for the composition of *Hyperion* has frequently been noted.[20] The novel is in the form of a series of letters written by Hyperion (a contemporary

---

15 Henrich 1992: 17, 36. For Hölderlin's academic ambitions, see e.g. the letter to his brother of 13 April 1795 (MA, II, 579; AL, 52).
16 As well as Henrich 1992 (and, more concisely, Henrich 1993), cf. Hanke 2015: 102.
17 For doubts concerning Henrich's approach, see Strack 2013: 24–25; Hornbacher 1995: 31–32, 53–54, and 2001: 28.
18 MA, III, 133; see Louth 2000: 1045.
19 MA, II, 635; AL, 81. See also the letter to Niethammer, his 'philosophical mentor', of 24 February 1796: 'Die Philosophie ist eine Tyrannin, und ich dulde ihren Zwang mehr, als daß ich mich ihm freiwillig unterwerfe' [Philosophy is a tyrant, and I suffer its rule rather than submitting to it voluntarily] (MA, II, 614; AL, 68). Strauß aptly refers to the 'ursprünglich[e] Gebrochenheit von Hölderlins Verhältnis zur Philosophie' (1927: 682).
20 *Hyperion oder der Eremit in Griechenland* [*Hyperion or the Hermit in Greece*] (MA, I, 609–760; RB). The novel was published in two volumes in 1797 and 1799, but went through a number of drafts, parts of which have been preserved in manuscript. An early extract was published as 'Fragment von Hyperion' in Schiller's journal *Thalia* in 1794 (MA, I, 489–510). On the Platonic sources for *Hyperion*, see in particular Billings 2010; Bassermann-Jordan 2008; von Perger 2004; Roche 2002; Lampenscherf 1993; Düsing 1981; and on Hölderlin and Platonism see further Gaier 2014a, and Franz 2012: 73–123. See also Beiser 2002: 383–84. An early enthusiastic response to the reading of the dialogues *Phaedrus*, *Timaeus*, and *Symposium* is recorded in a letter to Neuffer from July 1793 (MA, II, 499; AL, 14–15).

Greek) to a German correspondent ('Bellarmin'). They tell both of Hyperion's experiences as protagonist and, crucially, of the development of Hyperion's own self-understanding in the course of his narration. Platonic references and allusions abound in parts of the final version of the novel, as they do in early drafts from Hölderlin's Jena period, and above all in the preface to the so-called 'Vorletzte Fassung' [penultimate version] from the second half of 1795 in Nürtingen (MA, I, 557–71). In that preface Hölderlin appears to subscribe to a full-blown version of what Düsing (1981) has called 'Aesthetic Platonism', inspired above all by the discourses about love and beauty found in Plato's *Symposium* and *Phaedrus*. And at the end Plato is even addressed directly, in a curious plea for forgiveness:

> [E]s wäre überhaupt gar nichts, (für uns) wir wären selbst nichts, (für uns) wenn nicht dennoch jene unendliche Vereinigung, jenes Seyn, im einzigen Sinne des Worts vorhanden wäre. Es ist vorhanden — als Schönheit; es wartet, um mit Hyperion zu reden, ein neues Reich auf uns, wo Schönheit Königin ist. —
>
> Ich glaube, wir werden am Ende alle sagen: heiliger Plato, vergieb! man hat schwer an dir gesündigt.
>
> [There would be absolutely nothing, (for us) we would ourselves be nothing, (for us) if that infinite unification, that Being in the only true sense of the word, were not nonetheless present. It is present — as Beauty; to speak with Hyperion, a new realm awaits us, where Beauty is queen. —
>
> I believe we will in the end all say: holy Plato, forgive! you have been much sinned against.] (MA, 1, 558–59)

The preface is signed in the name of the author or supposed editor ('Der Herausgeber'), who professes to echo the words of the novel's protagonist, Hyperion ('um mit Hyperion zu reden'); and Hyperion, as supposed author of the novel's constituent letters, is also its narrator. In the final version of the novel, the distinctions between author and protagonist, and between protagonist and narrator, become increasingly important. But if they are signalled in this earlier version, it is only to be overcome — as it were in a moment of joint Platonic enthusiasm.

It is worth pausing to consider what that 'sin' against Plato might be. The word suggests a distortion or misinterpretation of Plato's doctrine, rather than mere disagreement. Accordingly the apology might be on behalf of those who have represented Platonism as involving a rigorous dualism of the empirical and intellectual realms. An obvious candidate here is Kant, who used the Platonic 'Forms' or 'Ideas' as a foil in his critique of metaphysics: 'Plato [verließ] die Sinnenwelt, weil sie dem Verstande so enge Schranken setzt, und wagte sich jenseits derselben, auf den Flügeln der Ideen, in den leeren Raum des reinen Verstandes' [Plato forsook the world of the senses, because it set such narrow limits to the intellect, and dared to venture beyond it on the wings of the Ideas, in the empty space of pure intellect].[21] As Dorothea Frede has observed, such a dualism is tempered in the *Phaedrus* and the *Symposium*. In these works the physical world is no longer one that is simply to be

---

21 Immanuel Kant, *Kritik der reinen Vernunft*, ed. by Ingeborg Heidemann (Stuttgart: Reclam, 1966; repr. 1980), B9 (p. 57); see also B369–B375 (pp. 394–99). Cf. Summerell 2003: 162–63.

fled; and in them there can be found a kind of 'education through enchantment' in which the phenomena of beauty and love provide a ladder of ascent to the world of the Forms, and embody a reflection of the latter in the world of empirical reality.[22] Of course, in the final analysis even the Plato of the *Symposium* remains a dualist; and as in the *Republic*, the path to be taken is the one that leads out of the cave of sensory experience.[23] But the experience of beauty at least provides a means of passage to the super-sensible world of the Forms.

If such phenomena as beauty provide a bridge to the world of the Forms, enabling a passage from a temporal to a timeless realm, such a passage is also a return to a pre-existing condition. As Kahn puts it, for Plato 'the domain of unseen reality is the place of origin from which the human spirit or the rational psyche has come, and to which it may under favourable circumstances return' (1996: 66). Similarly, for the Hölderlin of the preface to the 'penultimate version', time is abolished in so far as an original 'blessed unity' can be regained. It is true that the preface is equivocal as to whether such a unity can indeed be restored, as opposed to merely being the object of striving:

> Die seelige Einigkeit, das Seyn, im einzigen Sinne des Worts, ist für uns verloren und wir mußten es verlieren, wenn wir es erstreben, erringen sollten. Wir reißen uns los vom friedlichen Εν και Παν der Welt, um es herzustellen, durch uns Selbst. [...]
>
> Aber weder unser Wissen noch unser Handeln gelangt in irgend einer Periode des Daseyns dahin, wo aller Widerstreit aufhört, wo Alles Eins ist.
>
> [The blessed unity, Being in the only true sense of the word, is lost to us, and we had to lose it if we were to strive for it and win it. We tear ourselves free from the peaceful *Hen kai Pan* [One and All] of the world, in order to establish it through our own efforts. [...]
>
> But neither our knowledge nor our action reaches any period of existence where all conflict ceases, where All is One.] (MA, I, 558)

The question therefore is whether such an original blessed unity is of this world or — as in Plato — belongs to a world of the Forms known prior to our birth. There is a degree of syncretism in this passage, where the formula 'One and All' (the hallmark of a pantheistic monism) can stand for the undivided unity of Nature as much as the world of the Forms. But note the qualification 'peaceful': this is a unity that belongs only to certain privileged moments of our existence, of which the encounter with beauty is the most important. What then is the ultimate guarantor of such 'peace'?

The thoughts expressed in that preface are closely parallel to the more rigorous

---

22   D. Frede 1993: 409, and see also 402–03, 410–12, 416. On the ladder of ascent from the experience of the beautiful to the knowledge of 'the beautiful itself', see *Symposium*, trans. by Michael Joyce, 211b-d, in *The Collected Dialogues of Plato including the Letters*, ed. by Edith Hamilton and Huntington Cairns; Bollingen Series, 71 (Princeton, NJ; Princeton University Press, 1961; repr. 1978), pp. 526–74 (pp. 562–63).
23   See Kahn 1996: 384–86. And as Belfiore observes, when Plato clothes the rigour of his doctrine with mythic and poetic elements, he is himself providing his audience with a seductive kind of access to a more austere wisdom (2012: 150–60).

— or at least more abstract — discussion contained in Hölderlin's most celebrated theoretical text, often cited as a seminal contribution to contemporary philosophical debate (MA, II, 49–50; AL, 231–32). The text has been edited under various titles, and I shall refer to it here as *Being and Judgment* or 'BJ'. Further essential context is provided by the letter to Schiller of 4 September 1795.[24] Thus the '*Seyn schlechthin*' [Being as such] of BJ is easily identifiable as the 'Seyn, im einzigen Sinne des Worts' of the preface; and in the letter to Schiller 'die Vereinigung des Subjects und Objects' [the union of subject and object] is said to be possible 'ästhetisch, in der intellectualen Anschauung' [aesthetically, in an act of intellectual intuition], which is no doubt the same 'intellectual intuition' that, in BJ, is said to yield the most intimate unity of subject and object. And conversely, the 'ewig[er] Widerstreit zwischen unserem Selbst und der Welt' [eternal conflict between our self and the world] of the preface corresponds to the 'ursprüngliche Trennung' [primal separation] or 'Ur=Theilung [sic]' [original division] of BJ. If the discussion in BJ is more abstract, this might be explained by the circumstances of its composition; for it seems to be a direct response to his friend Schelling's contemporary philosophical treatise *Vom Ich*.[25]

The idea of a return to a state of original unity provides another link with the preface to the 'penultimate version'. In BJ it takes the form of a logical conundrum. Hölderlin suggests that it is only through the separation involved in Judgement that object and subject first become possible; yet Being is defined precisely as 'die Verbindung des Subjects und Objects' [the connection of subject and object]. As he puts it in the 'Judgment' section of the manuscript: '*Urtheil*. ist [...] die ursprüngliche Trennung des in der intellectualen Anschauung innigst vereinigten Objects und Subjects, diejenige Trennung, wodurch erst Object und Subject möglich wird' [*Judgment*. is [...] the primal separation of the object and the subject that are most intimately united in intellectual intuition, that separation by which object and subject first become possible]. Which therefore comes first, Being or Judgment, unity or division? The function of 'intellectuale Anschauung' seems to be to as much to restore the integrity of a whole that has already been damaged by division, as to express an original state of wholeness that precedes conscious reflection.[26] In that sense it corresponds to the function of 'beauty' in the preface, as the guarantor

---

24   See MA, II, 595–96; AL, 62–63. See also the letter to Niethammer of 24 February 1796 (MA, II, 614–15; AL, 67–68). On the need to read BJ in context, cf. Strack 2013: 47.
25   *Vom Ich als Princip der Philosophie* [Of the 'I' as Principle of Philosophy] (1795), in Friedrich Wilhelm Joseph Schelling, *Historisch-kritische Ausgabe*, ed. by Hans Michael Baumgartner and others (Stuttgart: Frommann-Holzboog, 1976–), Series I, *Werke*, II, ed. by Hartmut Buchner and Jörg Jantzen (1980), pp. 64–175. See Strack 2013, noting in particular Hölderlin's adoption of Schelling's unusual spelling 'intellektuale Anschauung', rather than Kant and Fichte's 'intellectuelle' (2013: 12); and see also Frank 1998: 716–17.
26   For Strack there is accordingly no place for Henrich's interpretation of Hölderlin's 'Seyn' as a 'Grund' inaccessible to consciousness (see Strack 2013: 54, and contrast Henrich 1992: 263). That may be to gloss over the circularity inherent in Hölderlin's argument; but Henrich may indeed place undue emphasis on the idea of a pre-reflective 'Grund' (a term that figures in Henrich's title but not in Hölderlin's manuscript). See also Friedrich 2007: 72–73; and on the relation between 'intellectuale Anschauung' and Aesthetic Platonism, and its subsequent fate in Hölderlin's thought, see Kreuzer 2003.

of a return to unity. It may seem curious to describe the aesthetic experience of beauty as an 'intellectual' intuition, as Hölderlin does in his letter to Schiller. If the terminology is explained by his wish to respond to Schelling, it is also a symptom of the Platonic background that the preface makes so explicit.

The paradox remains that the unity to be regained — the 'blessed unity' of the preface — is one that is essentially lost, and that cannot be restored at least in this world. In practice it is a goal to be achieved 'in unendlicher Annäherung' [in infinite approximation]. We can have an intimation of it, in the beauty of the world; but in the end the latter must be conceived as an imperfect reflection of the intelligible beauty of the Forms.[27] For that lost unity to be fully restored, the soul would have to return to its pre-incarnate condition. And short of that Platonic consummation, the return to a condition of 'blessed unity' corresponds to a wish for death. Hölderlin confesses as much in a letter to his brother of 2 June 1796: 'Freilich sehnen wir uns oft auch, aus diesem Mittelzustand von Leben und Tod überzugehn *in's unendliche Seyn* der schönen Welt, in die Arme der ewigjugendlichen Natur, *wovon wir ausgegangen*' [I admit that we often long to pass out of this middle state of life and death over *into the infinite being* of the world in all its beauty, into the arms of eternally youthful Nature, *which is where we began*] (MA, II, 621; AL, 71; my emphasis).

That Platonic ideal is, however, subjected to an exacting scrutiny in the final version of the novel. Hyperion, the modern Greek protagonist of the work, is inspired above all by two incarnations of the idea of beauty: that of his lover Diotima, and that of the ruined beauty of ancient Greece. And Diotima of course shares her name with the wise 'Mantinean woman' whose discourse on beauty and love is recalled by Socrates in the *Symposium*. Animated by that ideal, Hyperion decides to re-establish the Athenian polis by liberating his homeland from Ottoman occupation. In the end, however, the novel recounts the failure of that project; as Billings puts it: 'the first volume ends with the vision of a reunification of what history has divided. [...] The second volume radically undermines Hyperion's dream of renaissance' (2010: 18). But it is not simply the failure of Hyperion's war of Greek liberation that leads to an abandonment of the ideal. If the problem lay only in the means, a better and more righteous struggle could be prepared. It is the ideal that falls short, in so far as it is based on an inadequate conception of nature (not to mention a questionable view of history).

The 'vision' to which Billings refers follows (and echoes) the discourse that Hyperion pronounces on a journey with friends to see the ruins of Athens, the so-called 'Athenerrede' (MA, I, 681–87; RB, 104–12). It is important to note that this is a discourse of Hyperion the protagonist, rather than Hyperion the narrator or (above all) Hölderlin the author. One should therefore be wary of citing it as a source for a philosophical 'theory of beauty' that is still to be attributed to Hölderlin.[28] As the climax to the first volume of *Hyperion*, it prepares the way for

---

27 Cf. the letter to his brother of March 1796: 'das reine Ideal alles Denkens und Thuns, die undarstellbare, unerreichbare Schönheit' [the pure ideal of all thought and action, unrepresentable and unattainable beauty] (MA, II, 617; AL, 69). The expression 'unendlich[e] Annäherung' is used in both the preface and the letter to Schiller.

28 As in Kurz 2015b: 72, referring without distinction to early hymns from 1790–91, the letter to

the process of disillusionment and renunciation in the second — and as Hölderlin warns us in his preface, the evaluation of his overall plan must await the publication of the latter. In contrast to the 'penultimate version', the preface now no longer expounds a philosophical thesis — say 'Aesthetic Platonism' — that is to be exemplified in the novel that follows. The purpose of the novel may rather be to put any such position to the test, and perhaps to overcome it. It is illuminating therefore to compare the forms taken by the earlier and the later preface.[29] For it is clear that in the final version it now belongs to a different genre — as it were to Poetics rather than Philosophy:

> Wer blos an meiner Pflanze riecht, der kennt sie nicht, und wer sie pflükt, blos, um daran zu lernen, kennt sie auch nicht.
> Die Auflösung der Dissonanzen in einem gewissen Charakter ist weder für das bloße Nachdenken, noch für die leere Lust.
>
> [Who merely sniffs my flower does not know it, and who plucks it merely so as to learn from it also does not know it.
> The resolution of dissonances in a certain character is neither for mere thought nor for empty pleasure.] (MA, I, 611; RB, 9, trans. modified)

As Schmidt observes, there is an allusion here to the Horatian dictum: 'Poets aim either to benefit, or to amuse, or to utter words at once both pleasing and helpful to life'.[30] Famous as it is, Horace provides only a few clues as to how pleasure and instruction are to be united (as they must be) in a successful work. We have already seen the prominent place it occupied in Estienne's *Poesis philosophica*. After the completion of the first volume of *Hyperion*, Hölderlin had already turned his attention to a drama based on the death of Empedocles; and as noted, the Empedoclean fragments assembled by Estienne may well have been a source for that project.[31]

In a similarly poetological mode, the new preface then invokes the category of the 'elegiac': 'Der Schauplatz, wo sich das Folgende zutrug, ist nicht neu, [...] aber ich überzeugte mich, daß er der einzig Angemessene für Hyperions elegischen Charakter wäre' [The setting where what follows occurred is not new, [...] but I convinced myself that it was the only setting appropriate to Hyperion's elegiac character]. And as already noted, it concludes with the regret that, until the second volume appears, 'die Beurtheilung des Plans noch nicht jedem möglich ist' [the

---

Schiller of 4 September 1795, the preliminary versions of *Hyperion*, and Hyperion's 'Athenerrede', as Hölderlin's 'Theorie der Schönheit'. However, Kurz's purpose here is not the interpretation of *Hyperion*. For Düsing it is clear that 'Aesthetic Platonism' is still exemplified in the final version of the novel, and superseded only with the *Empedocles* project (1981: 109–12). For Lampenscherf, the preface to the 'penultimate version' embodies the whole lesson of *Hyperion* (1993: 150–51).

29 On the differences between the prefaces to different versions of the novel — the *Thalia* fragment of 1794, the 'penultimate version', and the final version — see also Reitani 2015: 35–42.
30 *Ars Poetica* ll. 333–34: 'Aut prodesse volunt aut delectare poetae aut simul et iucunda et idonea dicere vitae', in Horace, *Satires* etc., ed. and trans. by H. Rushton Fairclough, LCL 194 (Cambridge, MA: Harvard University Press, 1926; rev. and repr. 1929), pp. 478–79. See KA, II, 970–71.
31 See MA, III, 328 (and for the chronology, pp. 318, 331 and 846); see also Primavesi 2014: 34, n. 88, and Chapter 2.1 below

evaluation of the book's plan is not yet possible for everyone].[32] It is true that the earlier preface makes a similar point about the first volume being unlikely to 'please' [gefallen] in the absence of the completed whole (MA, I, 558). But the emphasis is precisely on the lack of pleasure, in contrast to the 'evaluation' or 'judgement' required in the case of the final version.

With the preface to the final version, the author is no longer offering a philosophical key to the work that follows. The key, rather, is provided by the construction of a narrative framework that is only fully revealed at the end. The second volume will conclude as Hyperion is on the point of returning from Germany to Greece, where he will begin writing the letters that compose the narrative of the work. Thus the 'plan' of the work lies in the process by which Hyperion finally becomes the author of his own narrative. And Hyperion's development does not end there, since the process of narration is accompanied by the narrator's deepening insight into the significance of his story.[33]

None the less, we should not be surprised to find themes from the preface to the 'penultimate version' recurring in final version, in the thoughts of Hyperion as protagonist and even of Hyperion as narrator. At one point the narrator exclaims:

> Ich hab' es Einmal gesehn, das Einzige, das meine Seele suchte, und die Vollendung, die wir über die Sterne hinauf entfernen, [...] die hab' ich gegenwärtig gefühlt. [...] [W]ißt ihr seinen Nahmen? den Nahmen deß, das Eins ist und Alles?
> Sein Nahme ist Schönheit.
>
> [I have seen it one time, the unique thing that my soul sought, and the perfection that we project far upward above the stars, [...] I felt its presence. [...] [D]o you know its name? the name of that which is One and All?
> Its name is beauty.] (MA, I, 657; RB, 70–71, trans. modified)

Hyperion is here about to relate his first encounter with Diotima, who embodies the ideal of beauty celebrated in the preface to the 'penultimate version', with its telling reference to the 'One and All' or Εν και Παν (MA, I, 558). Who is speaking at this point in the novel? In one sense it is Hyperion as narrator, who has already lived through the entire sequence of events and is now looking back in order to recount them. But at this point there is little gap between the experiences recalled, and the narrator's current consciousness. Hyperion's reflection on his encounter with Diotima is itself inhabited by thoughts and feelings revived in the process of narration.[34] And we too, as captivated readers, will share in the same feelings and thoughts, which might be placed in their proper perspective only on a second reading.

---

32 The second volume finally appeared at the end of October 1799. See also the letter to Schiller of 20 June 1997, in which Hölderlin regrets the separate publication of the two volumes (MA, II, 656; AL, 88).
33 See Ryan 1965: 223–26, and 2002: 177; also Constantine 1988: 88–89, and Bay 2003: 359.
34 See Ryan 1965: 111, 118–19. As Ryan observes, it is only at the end of the novel that the narrator is able to achieve full independence from the narrated events (1965: 105–06). The development of the lived experience of the narrator is an aspect emphasized by Gaskill in the 'Afterword' to his translation: *Hyperion, or the Hermit in Greece* (Cambridge: Open Book Publishers, 2019).

The 'Athenerrede' episode is undoubtedly the high-water mark of Aesthetic Platonism as it features in *Hyperion*. It is narrated in the final letter of the first volume, a volume that concludes by citing the following ringing declaration of the protagonist: 'Es wird nur Eine Schönheit seyn; und Menschheit und Natur wird sich vereinen in Eine allumfassende Gottheit.' [There will be but one beauty; and humankind and nature will unite in one all-embracing divinity] (MA, I, 693; RB, 121, trans. modified). How might such an ideal be realized? In the 'Athenerrede' itself Athenian culture is praised as its embodiment, while it in turn guarantees the harmonious unity of a culture at its zenith. But when Hyperion and friends actually arrive at Athens, and witness its ruins, he is cast down by the thought of the transience of that world of perfection. He then turns to Diotima's beauty as substitute incarnation of his ideal, but is admonished by her, and told to seek a more enduring solution by becoming the educator of their nation. Hyperion's hopes are revived, and he looks forward to achieving the rejuvenation of what has gone before and fallen into ruin — in accordance, as we seen, with the ideal of 'Eine Schönheit'.

In the 'Athenerrede', a connection with Plato is also signalled by means of a philosophical quotation — of Heraclitus — drawn from the *Symposium*. To complicate matters, however, this is an inexact and partial quotation of a formula that is itself an inexact citation. Furthermore it is cited not by Socrates but by one of the other guests (the medic Eryximachus), and even then with less than wholehearted approval.[35] On both of the occasions on which it is cited by Hyperion, its function is to explain the relationship between philosophy and poetry:

> Die Dichtung, sagt' ich, [...] ist der Anfang und das Ende dieser Wissenschaft. [...] Das große Wort, das εν διαφερον εαυτῳ (das Eine in sich selber unterschiedne) des Heraklit, das konnte nur ein Grieche finden, denn es ist das Wesen der Schönheit, und ehe das gefunden war, gabs keine Philosophie.
>
> [Poetry, I said [...] is the beginning and the end of this science. [...] The great word of Heraclitus, εν διαφερον εαυτῳ (the One differentiated in itself), this only a Greek could find, for it is the essence of beauty, and before this was found, there was no philosophy.] (MA, I, 685; RB, 108–09, trans. modified; see also MA, I, 687; RB, 112)

Here poetry and philosophy stand in a reciprocal and mutually validating relationship. The essence of beauty (and hence of poetry) is captured by a philosophical motto, extracted by Hyperion (via Plato) from a Heraclitan fragment. And, it is implied, the motto in turn reflects the aesthetic perfection of a vanished Greek world.

If earthly beauty could be expressed in a philosophical formula, that might be because it is the reflection of an intelligible realm — a world that is the proper

---

35 See *Symposium*, trans. by Michael Joyce, 187a: 'The one in conflict with itself is held together, like the harmony of the bow and of the lyre' (p. 540). Eryximachus then objects that 'it is absurd to speak of harmony as being in conflict, or as arising out of elements which are still conflicting'. But as Belfiore observes, the doctor 'not only misquotes, but also radically misinterprets Heraclitus' (2012: 129). On the *Symposium* as Hölderlin's source for the Heraclitus citation, cf. Bremer 1998: 187–89. For the more authentic version of the fragment see EGP, III, 160–61 (D49 = Diels-Kranz B51); and on its interpretation, Kahn 1979: 197–200.

object of philosophy, and as such an image of timeless unity.[36] Such a conception belongs to the Platonist that Hyperion may still be at this stage, rather than to Heraclitus. More complete and authentic versions of the fragment go beyond the image of musical consonance or harmony, and include not only a reference to the 'bow' — already present in Plato's version, although not discussed by Eryximachus — but also the notion of a 'backward-turning' (or 'back-stretched') fitting-together.[37] The latter applies to the bow as well as the lyre. But however congruent those instruments may be, in construction and operation and as twin attributes of the god Apollo, their combination also suggests a paradoxical relation between harmony and discord, peace and war, life and death.[38] Note also that the image of a backward-turning 'arc' or 'bow' of life is present in a short ode from 1798, that was later expanded into a four-stanza version. Both versions have the title 'Lebenslauf' [The Course of Life] (MA, I, 190 and 325; OE, 25 and 95). The image recalls another, now equally-famous, Heraclitan fragment, one which exploits the ambiguity in a Greek term for 'bow' (*bios*). For, depending upon the position of the accent, the name of that bringer of death can also mean 'life'.[39] Whether or not he was acquainted with that fragment, the author of the novel — as opposed to the protagonist of its first volume — was in a position to appreciate its lesson. And it is one that has a bearing on the form of his discourse as much as on its content. For the language of such Heraclitan fragments can itself be taken to express a tension between poetry and philosophy, whose unity is held in a precarious and ambiguous balance. In any event, one can see how a formula such as 'the One differentiated in itself' — like the earlier motto of the 'One and All' — is self-explanatory only to the extent that its presuppositions remain unexamined. For Hyperion at Athens it may amount to a definition of 'the essence of beauty', but he cannot yet be aware of its full implications. The citation allows us to measure the gap between Hyperion's present understanding and the one that he will eventually attain.[40]

36 Cf. Shelley's lines (1822) relating to a later phase of the Greek war of independence: 'But Greece and her foundations are | Built below the tide of war, | Based on the crystalline sea | Of thought and its eternity'. See *Hellas: A Lyrical Drama*, ll. 696–99, in Percy Bysshe Shelley, *The Major Works*, ed. by Zachary Leader and Michael O'Neill (Oxford: Oxford University Press, 2003), pp. 548–87 (p. 572).
37 παλίντροπος (or παλίντονος) ἁρμονίη; the former version is preferred by most recent editors. It is difficult by translation to do justice to παλίντροπος ἁρμονίη. As Kahn argues (1979: 199–200), the fragment's multiple meanings themselves resonate and fit together in tension and opposition (as παλίντροπος resonates, through Homeric association, with παλίντονος). EGP has 'a backward-turning fitting-together', while Kahn (1979: 195) offers both 'attunement' and 'fitting together'.
38 See Sassi 2015: 17–22, and Kahn 1979: 200.
39 Respectively βιός and βίος: see EGP, III, 162–63 (D53 = Diels-Kranz B48). It is not known for certain whether Hölderlin was directly acquainted with the fragment, which is not found in Stephanus (see the concordance in dos Santos Gomes 2004: 316–17). Cf. Reitani in TL, 1364, and Bremer 1998: 177.
40 For a similar conclusion see Stiening 2005: 355. Note Hyperion's own immediate self-doubts (MA, I, 687), and also how the formula is embedded in a series of at least five nested citations. Thus Hölderlin as author (1) cites Hyperion as narrator, who (2) cites the protagonist's 'Athenerrede', which (3) cites Plato, who (4) cites his own character Eryximachus, who (5) cites Heraclitus. And the framing narrative of the *Symposium* adds two additional levels, given that Plato cites Apollodorus who cites Aristodemus: cf. Belfiore 2012: 110.

If the 'Athenerrede' in the first volume of *Hyperion* marks the high point of the protagonist's Aesthetic Platonism, the 'Schiksaalslied' episode of the second volume introduces its final abandonment (MA, I, 744–45; RB, 192–93). The episode is remarkable in a number of respects.[41] To begin with, it is the only place in which Hölderlin's highly poetic novel breaks into verse. This 'song of destiny' is a lyric remembered from Hyperion's youth, and which he now sings at his deepest moment of sorrow. The song was taught to him by his mentor Adamas: 'einst in glüklicher unverständiger Jugend meinem Adamas nachgesprochen' [once, in happy, ignorant youth repeated after my Adamas]; it is accordingly again a kind of citation. It describes an unbridgeable dichotomy between the world of the gods — free from the vicissitudes of temporality — and a world of mortals burdened by the restless uncertainty of fate:

> Schiksaallos, wie der schlafende
>   Säugling, athmen die Himmlischen;
> [...]
> Doch uns ist gegeben,
>   Auf keiner Stätte zu ruhn,
>   Es schwinden, es fallen
>   Die leidenden Menschen
>   Blindings von einer
>   Stunde zur andern.
>
> [Free of fate, like the sleeping
>   Infant, the heavenly breathe;
> [...]
> Yet to us is given
>   No place to repose,
>   They dwindle and fall
>   The suffering mortals
>   Blindly from one
>   Hour to the next.] (trans. modified)

This in effect revokes the optimistic Platonism of the preface to the 'penultimate version'. The link has been severed between our temporal, fate-bound world and the 'eternal clarity' [[e]wig[e] Klarheit] of the divine. It marks a point of deepest disillusionment, which in the narrative is confirmed by the receipt of Diotima's letter containing news of her mortal illness, and a subsequent letter from his friend Notara with the news of her death. But by framing the lyric as a song from Hyperion's youth, Hölderlin is careful to distinguish it from the position reached by Hyperion as protagonist — and even more so, by Hyperion as narrator. It functions rather as a counterpoint to Hyperion's highest point of narrative self-reflection:[42]

---

41 See also Groddeck 1998: 183–84.
42 On the contrast between the 'Schiksaalslied' and that high-point of reflection, see Ryan 2002: 191. See also Schmidt 2008b: 948, and Gaskill 1984: 42 (albeit with a theological gloss).

> So schrieb Notara; und du fragst, mein Bellarmin! wie jetzt mir ist, indem ich diß erzähle?
> Bester! ich bin ruhig, denn ich will nichts besser haben, als die Götter. Muß nicht alles leiden? Und je treflicher es ist, je tiefer! Leidet nicht die heilige Natur? [...] Aber die Wonne, die nicht leidet, ist Schlaf, und ohne Tod ist kein Leben. Solltest du ewig seyn, wie ein Kind und schlummern, dem Nichts gleich?
>
> [So Notara wrote; and you ask, my Bellarmin! how I am now, while I tell you this?
> Dearest friend! I am calm, for I want nothing better than the gods. Must not everything suffer? And the more excellent it is, the more deeply? does not holy nature suffer? [...] But the bliss that does not suffer is sleep, and without death there is no life. Should you be eternally like a child and slumber like nothingness?] (MA, I, 751; RB, 202)

Here it is not only the strong form of Platonic dualism that is being rejected — the version for which the preface to the 'penultimate version' may have begged forgiveness — but also any doctrine that would find images of a lost unity immanent in certain privileged moments or places, whether in the oneness with nature of the slumbering infant, or the perfect harmony of a beautiful form. Instead, the narrator finds a way of affirming all aspects of nature, including its suffering and imperfections. For the alternative is an illusory ideal of infantile bliss: 'be eternally like a child and slumber like nothingness'. This position is one achieved by Hyperion, as narrator, and as a result of his narration: it is achieved, that is, in the course of the process of poetic reflection embodied in *Hyperion*.[43] Indeed, it is expressly declared to be such a result ('indem ich diß erzähle'). This result has justifiably been described as one of 'philosophic calm' (Roche 1987: 74; Ryan 2002: 192). Or more precisely, there is a philosophical counterpart to the position reached by the narrator. But it is not to be found in Platonism, 'Aesthetic' or otherwise; it is found rather in a different philosophical school, one with which Hölderlin engages in a different kind of dialogue.

---

43 Note that the position is anticipated at MA, I, 706, where the narrator already explains the purpose of his narration in terms of 'Ruhe' and observes 'du solltest sogar meinen Briefen es ansehn, wie meine Seele täglich stiller wird und stiller.' On the episode as a high-point of narrative reflection and the articulation of a new conception of Nature, see Ryan 1965: 222–23, and 2002: 192, and cf. Engel 1993: 351–52. Stiening rejects what he concedes is the usual view that the episode represents the novel's high-point of reflection, on the unconvincing ground that Hyperion himself (by writing a despairing letter) had inadvertently contributed to Diotima's death (2005: 464, n. 121, and 471). Thus Stiening appears to find the narrative high-point in the subsequent letter, with its impassioned critique of the Germans (ibid. p. 484), the so-called 'Scheltrede'. A different perspective (qualifying the significance of the narrator's final position and emphasizing that of the 'Scheltrede') is also offered in Bay 2003: 359–402. It is no doubt true, in any event, that the ultimate significance of the novel is not exhausted by the theme of narrative self-reflection, important as it is for our present purposes.

3. 'I am ever unfitted to be a Stoic'

'Ich bin zum Stoiker ewig verdorben. Das seh' ich wol. Ewig Ebb' und Fluth.' [I am ever unfitted to be a Stoic. That well I see. Perpetual ebb and flow.] — In that self-diagnosis of the student Hölderlin, an ideal of Stoic repose is contrasted with the violent swings of emotion that he recognized in himself, symptoms of the bipolar disorder known to the time as Melancholia.[44] There is a connection between that diagnosis, and the syndrome of Aesthetic Platonism. The Platonist finds in beauty the reflection of an unattainable ideal — at least unattainable in this world — and is accordingly condemned to oscillate between the enthusiasm for that ideal, on the one hand, and the sentiment of personal unworthiness and lack on the other.[45] On the one hand: 'Eines zu seyn mit Allem, das ist Leben der Gottheit, das ist der Himmel des Menschen.' [To be one with all — that is the life of the divinity, that is the heaven of humankind.] (MA, I, 614; RB, 12, trans. modified). But on the other: 'O ein Gott ist der Mensch, wenn er träumt, ein Bettler, wenn er nachdenkt, und wenn die Begeisterung hin ist, steht er da, wie ein misrathener Sohn, den der Vater aus dem Hause stieß' [O man is a god when he dreams, a beggar when he thinks, and when enthusiasm is gone, he stands there like a wayward son whom the father has driven out of the house] (MA, I, 615; RB, 13). Here Hyperion the narrator is speaking of himself at the beginning of the novel, before he has begun to recount his earlier life. And he begins by lamenting the loss of a union with divine Nature, in terms that are similar to the preface to the 'penultimate version'. At this stage a blissful return 'in's All der Natur' [into the All of nature] is still half-imagined, and with it 'der Ort der ewigen Ruhe' [the place of eternal repose] — before being unmasked as an all too transient illusion: 'Auf diese Höhe steh' ich oft, mein Bellarmin! Aber ein Moment des Besinnens wirft mich herab.' [I often stand at this height, my Bellarmin! but a moment of reflection hurls me down] (MA, I, 615; RB, 13). Where can a true, a lasting repose be found, a relation to the 'All of nature' that is not confined to certain transient privileged moments (say the bliss of the slumbering child)?

The same alternation of exultation and despair is evident in Hyperion's relation to Diotima, and accurately diagnosed by Diotima herself. As she points out, it is intrinsic to all of Hyperion's relationships, and a symptom of an underlying metaphysical need — the need for the return of what is irretrievably lost:

---

44   Letter to Neuffer, Tübingen 8 November 1790 (MA, II, 461); as Seifert observes (1983: 92), the image recurs in the letter to Neuffer of March 1796 (MA, II, 615–16) and corresponds to 'die Eigenart der psychischen Konstitution des Dichters'. On Hölderlin's melancholic disposition see generally Gaier 2014b (and on 'Ebb' und Fluth' pp. 52, 95). Gaier is surely correct to approach the question of Hölderlin's mental illness in terms of the categories current at the time, and which Hölderlin applied to himself. However, the diagnosis of Hölderlin's condition after his collapse in September 1806 raises more difficult questions.

45   See Gaier 2014b: 100–04; and cf. Engel 1993: 350 ('Schwärmersyndrom'), and Deleuze 1969: 152 ('L'idéalisme est la maladie congénitale de la philosophie platonicienne et [...] la forme maniaco-dépressive de la philosophie même'). The dilemma has the same structure, whether the ideal is conceived pantheistically as a union with the All of nature, or in transcendent terms as a return to an intelligible world of the Forms: for as already noted, it is vitiated by the inability of the supposed 'One and All' to encompass suffering and division.

> Du wolltest keine Menschen, glaube mir, du wolltest eine Welt. Den Verlust von allen goldenen Jahrhunderten, so wie du sie, zusammengedrängt in Einen glüklichen Moment, empfandest [...]. Siehest du nun, wie arm, wie reich du bist? [...] warum so schröcklich Freude und Laid dir wechselt?
>
> [You wanted no human beings, believe me, you wanted a world. The loss of all golden centuries, as you felt them, compressed into one happy moment [...]. Do you see now how poor, how rich you are? [...] why joy and sorrow alternate so terribly for you?] (MA, I, 671; RB, 90; trans. modified)

Or in an image used slightly earlier by the narrator, describing his reaction to Diotima's presence (MA, I, 670; RB, 88): 'wie der Schwimmer aus reißenden Wassern hervor, rang und strebte mein Geist, nicht unterzugehn in der unendlichen Liebe' [like a swimmer in raging waters, my spirit struggled and strove not to go under in infinite love]. We might be reminded of the 'perpetual ebb and flow' of the student Hölderlin, noting also Diotima's capacity to discern in Hyperion 'die Ebb' und Fluth des Herzens' [the ebb and flow of my heart] (MA, I, 666; RB, 83).[46] It is true that, by the time of the 'Athenerrede' episode, a more structured conception of beauty has been obtained, one that may provide a more stable basis for the ideal. When that ideal is embodied in a culture such as that of ancient Athens, a certain reconciliation is achieved between 'unity' and 'difference', between the reflection of the timeless world of the Forms and the vicissitudes of the temporal sphere. In terms of Hölderlin's two philosophical slogans, it is a progress from the *hen kai pan*, the 'One and All' celebrated in the preface to the 'penultimate version', to the *hen diapheron heautōi*, the 'One differentiated in itself' of the 'Athenerrede'. But in the absence of such a cultural guarantee, itself historically questionable, a different conception of Nature is required that makes no apologies for movement, suffering and change. It is that revised conception that allows the narrator to experience a certain kind of calm. Not the transient calm experienced at the beginning of the novel, the temporary feeling of oneness with the natural world: for that was a unity which had no room for the narrator's own self-consciousness and its attendant conflicts. If a philosophical model is required for such 'Ruhe', the Stoic idea of 'tranquillity' is the one that lies nearest to hand.[47] But the narrator's calm is in the end made possible by the process of narrative reflection: it is attained 'indem ich diß erzähle'. Accordingly it is the result of a poetic rather than a philosophical activity — the result, in effect, of the composition of the novel.

While therefore the twenty-year old Hölderlin could only lament his failure to be a Stoic, this is a judgment that must be revisited in the case of the poet who

---

46 See also the first version of the ode 'Dichtermuth' discussed below, where poets are compared to a swimmer 'in silberner | Immertönender Fluth' [through the silver and ever-sounding | Tide] (MA, I, 275, ll. 9–10; OE, 232, which however follows the earlier variant 'Fernhintönender' [far-sounding] as in KA, I, 302).

47 As Schmidt has argued: see KA, II, 1060–63, 1066; and 2008b. Cf. Seneca's concept of 'tranquillitas', in Epistle 92.3: *Epistles*, 3 vols, trans. by Richard M. Gummere, LCL 75–77 (Cambridge, MA: Harvard University Press, 1917–1925), II (1920), 448–49 (also in LS 63F); and see generally Striker 1996, who notes the corresponding or cognate Greek expressions *euthumia*, *ataraxia*, *galēnē* and *hēsukhia* (ibid. pp. 183–84). On the place of that Stoic concept in German literature, see Roche 1987: 163–71; although in the case of Hölderlin, Roche prefers to highlight the influence of Spinoza (1987: 95).

has completed *Hyperion* and begun to the lay the foundations for a new poetics in Homburg.[48] One index of this change is the increasing importance of the notions of 'Asyl' [sanctuary] or 'Ruhestätte' [place of repose], or more exactly a change in their significance. Again, it is not that the study of philosophy will provide such a sanctuary. It will be sought instead in the poetic work, as something that can alone contain the 'ebb and flow' of the heart and put to rest the swings between enthusiasm and despair.[49] In *Hyperion* it was the 'Schiksaalslied' that corresponded to the deepest moment of such despair, where a humanity separated from the divine is granted no place of repose ('uns ist gegeben, | Auf keiner Stätte zu ruhn'). And to repeat the point, it was the process of narrative reflection that finally provided such a sanctuary ('Bester! ich bin ruhig'). This contrasts with Hyperion's position at the beginning of his narration, where an oblivious union with the 'All of nature' banished thought and provided an all-too temporary 'asylum of my heart' [meines Herzens Asyl] (MA, I, 615; RB, 13). Now a more lasting refuge is found in the sanctuary of the poetic work.

4. Homage to Marcus Aurelius

The *Meditations* of Marcus Aurelius must be counted among Hölderlin's most important philosophical sources. The work was found in his personal library, and he alludes to its Greek title in an epigrammatic poem from November 1799 entitled Προς εαυτον, i.e. 'To himself'.[50] As the epigram begins: 'Lern im Leben die Kunst, im Kunstwerk lerne das Leben' [In living learn about art, in the artwork learn about life] (MA, I, 236; OE, 67, trans. modified); this in itself recalls the genre of Marcus' work, in which Stoic philosophy is applied as a guide to life, or an 'art of living'. The act of writing the *Meditations* was itself a way of assimilating philosophical doctrines and using them to form the character of the author, so that he may conduct his life according to Stoic precepts.[51] Literary self-reflection becomes a kind of ethical self-constitution.

Philosophical reflection as providing a sanctuary — or to use Hadot's expression, 'inner citadel' — is itself a central theme in the *Meditations* (Hadot 1998). That might

---

48 Link curiously draws the opposite conclusion, discounting on the basis of the letter of 8 November 1790 any future significance of Stoicism for Hölderlin (1999: 17, n. 18). Seifert has sounder judgment, referring to Hölderlin's relationship to Stoicism as both 'gründliche Auseinandersetzung mit dem gedanklichen Gesamtsystem' and 'persönliche Lebensgestaltung nach stoischem Ideal' (1982: 293, n. 15).
49 Note the letter to his mother from Homburg, January 1799, confessing that 'Ruhe' comes to him precisely from poetry rather than philosophy (MA, II, 736; AL, 127).
50 See the list of Hölderlin's books found in Nürtingen at StA, VII.3, 388–91 (p. 388), and cf. the title traditionally given to the work: τὰ (or τῶν) εἰς ἑαυτόν. Hölderlin's was the bilingual Greek and Latin edition (Leipzig, 1775) that can be viewed at http://digitale.bibliothek.uni-halle.de/vd18/content/titleinfo/2921849 [accessed 29 May 2019]. References below are to *Ad se ipsum* [Τῶν εἰς ἑαυτόν], ed. by Joachim Dalfen, 2nd edn (Leipzig: Teubner, 1987); and *Meditations*, trans. by Martin Hammond (London: Penguin Books, 2006). References to chapters will include the sub-divisions (usually corresponding to complete sentences) given by Dalfen, rather than the broader ones given by Hammond: e.g. 4.3.2 corresponds to the second sentence of Book 4, Chapter 3.
51 On Stoic philosophy as an 'art of living' see Sellars 2009 (and on the significance of the act of composition in Marcus, ibid. p. 165).

even shed light on the subtitle to Hölderlin's novel: 'der Eremit in Griechenland' [the Hermit in Greece]. Its initial sense is clear enough: at the beginning of the book Hyperion has returned to his native land after an unhappy period in Germany, having meanwhile lost his closest friends: 'Fern und todt sind meine Geliebten' [Distant and dead are my loved ones] (MA, I, 614; RB, 11). He has also despaired of his projects and ambitions, finding solace only in nature — and even there only when reflection can be put aside: 'Ich denke nach [...] und meines Herzens Asyl, die ewigeinige Welt, ist hin' [I reflect [...] and the asylum of my heart, the world's eternal unity, is gone] (MA, I, 615; RB, 13). Thus at this stage a union with nature can provide only a transient refuge, one that is immediately banished by reflection. But on the other hand, the entire novel consists in nothing less than Hyperion's autobiographical self-reflection; and in that sense its programme was already anticipated by Marcus:

> They seek retreats for themselves — in the country, by the sea, in the hills — and you yourself are particularly prone to this yearning. But all this is quite vulgar [ἰδιωτικώτατόν], when it is open to you, at any time you want, to retreat into yourself. No retreat is more tranquil [ἡσυχιώτερον] or untroubled [ἀπραγμονέστερον] than that into one's own mind. (*Meditations* 4.3.1–2; trans. modified)

Hyperion's starting-point is precisely such a 'vulgar' — or in Hammond's version 'unphilosophic' — retreat, one that does not provide him with a secure refuge from his despair. The more enduring peace that he will eventually find is within the shelter of his narrative self-reflection: a citadel constructed in this case by the activity of poetry, rather than the practice of Stoic philosophy.

The theme of a 'refuge' or 'asylum' emerges with poignant clarity in an ode of the Homburg period entitled 'Mein Eigentum' [What is Mine] (MA, I, 237–38; OE, 69–71). This is one among several 'poetological' odes from the period 1799–1800: that is to say odes in which Hölderlin reflects upon his poetic mission or vocation.[52] The poem is itself said to be a sanctuary — a place of refuge, in particular, against the impulse to transcend the mortal sphere:

> Und daß auch mir zu retten mein sterblich Herz
> Wie andern eine bleibende Stätte sei
> Und heimathlos die Seele mir nicht
> Über das Leben hinweg sich sehne
>
> Sei du, Gesang, mein freundlich Asyl!

---

52 The ode has been dated late September 1799 (FHA, v, 611), hence as contemporary with Προς εαυτον. For later references to the notions of 'Asyl' or 'Ruhestätte', see the letter to his sister of 11 December 1800, explaining his need for a 'stillere Ruhestätte' [quieter place of rest] (MA, II, 880; AL, 186); and above all two of the late commentaries to fragments of Pindar — namely 'Die Asyle', referring to 'die *Asyle des Menschen*, die stillen Ruhestätten' (MA, II, 383; AL, 338), and 'Von der Ruhe' (MA, II, 380; AL, 335) — discussed in Chapter 6.2 below. Note that the title 'Von der Ruhe' corresponds to a rubric *de tranquillitate* given in the edition used for his translations of the fragments (see n. 9 to Chapter 6). The corresponding Greek term *hēsukhia* in the body of the fragment is similarly rendered by Hölderlin as 'Ruhe', as it is in his translation of Pindar's Eighth Pythian Ode (MA, II, 230, l. 1). And as we have just seen, the adjective *hēsukhios* figures in *Meditations* 4.3.2.

> [And so that for me too, as there is for others,
>   To save my mortal heart there will be a place
>   To abide and the soul not leave my life
>   And go beyond me, longing and homeless,
>
> May you, O song, be my friendly refuge!]
> (MA, I, 238, ll. 37–41; OE, 71, but for ll. 37–40 following SP, 43)

The poem keeps at bay the wish to transcend, to be pulled up by the 'heavenly heights' (l. 29), so that the poet's soul may remain. And the poem itself is figured as place of refuge, a garden tended by the poet (ll. 41–43), with an allusion to another destabilising threat (ll. 45–48):

> [...] wenn draußen mir
>   Mit ihren Wellen alle die mächtge Zeit
>   Die Wandelbare fern rauscht und die
>   Stillere Sonne mein Wirken fördert.
>
> [when outside, far away,
>   Mighty time rolls its changes
>   In wave upon wave and the
>   Quieter sun looks after my work.]

The poem is a refuge from the annihilating forces of Time, and the poet stands under the guardianship of a more benign cosmic principle — the sun, which can also be identified with Apollo as patron god of poetry. And unlike the roses that stand for the transience of the poet's previous happiness (ll. 17–18), the words of the poem can have a more enduring bloom.[53]

The poem builds a kind of sanctuary in the present — the here and the now — which guards against two sources of instability: the impulse to transcend the mortal sphere (as it were the threat of Platonic enthusiasm), but also the annihilating forces of Time. Indeed there is a connection between the two, in shape of the 'powers' consuming the poet from within, as it were the perpetual ebb and flow of the heart: 'Fühl ich verzehrend euch im Busen | Wechseln, ihr wandelnden Götterkräfte' [I feel you changing, | Consuming in my breast, O mutable godly powers] (ll. 31–32). The connection is also clear at a biographical level, to the extent that the ode reflects the anguish of Hölderlin's separation from Susette Gontard.[54] The stability of the present moment is threatened by passage of time, experienced in the form of a traumatic loss, as much as by an impulse to transcend that amounts to a rejection of this mortal life. What role might the Stoic philosophy have in articulating this predicament?

Here it will be useful to consider two further 'poetological' odes from this

---

53   On Apollo as sun-god, see Schmidt in KA, I, 772–73 and 778–79. On the poem as garden, see Böschenstein 2004; and, on words as flowers in the garden of song, Bennholdt-Thomsen 1967: 79–88.
54   Thus compare 'im Busen | Wechseln, ihr wandelnde Götterkräfte' with 'die mächtige Zeit | Die Wandelbare' (ll. 46–47) (my emphasis); and on the biographical background, see Schmidt in KA, I, 631. For the revolutions of the sun as exemplifying a 'stille[r] Wechsel' see 'Ermunterung', second version (MA, I, 278, l. 23). See also the formulation 'stille Sonne' in the first version of that ode (MA, I, 277, l. 19). Thus the periodic return of the sun contrasts with the annihilating force of boundless change.

period. As Schmidt has suggested, Stoic themes are particularly prominent in the second version of the ode 'Dichtermuth' [The Poet's Courage], further revised in 1803–04 under the new title 'Blödigkeit' [Timidity]. And as I shall also argue in Chapter 2, the relation to Stoicism may be clearer still in the case of 'Natur und Kunst oder Saturn und Jupiter' [Nature and Art or Saturn and Jupiter].[55] Both 'Dichtermuth' and 'Natur und Kunst' date from the second half of 1800. Hölderlin was now in Stuttgart rather than Homburg, but still apparently preoccupied with poetological questions. Both poems figure in a fair copy of seven odes that seem to have been intended as a group or a cycle (cf. Gaier 2002a). In that copy 'Dichtermuth' was originally to be followed by the ode 'An Eduard', as is shown by the crossed-out title (see Figure 1.1, and FHA, IV, 340–41). Instead it was followed by 'Natur und Kunst' and only then by 'An Eduard'. That might in itself suggest a close relation between 'Dichtermuth' and 'Natur und Kunst' (or indeed between all three odes). 'Blödigkeit' represents a final phase in the evolution of 'Dichtermuth', with a new title befitting its inclusion in a published cycle of nine 'Nachtgesänge' — as Hölderlin described them to his publisher — that is to say 'Night Poems' or 'Nightsongs' (see MA, II, 927; AL, 217; OE, 245).

The evolution of the ode 'Dichtermuth' was particularly complex. Apart from the two distinct versions edited under that title, and the subsequent revision under the title 'Blödigkeit', a still earlier version has been constituted with the title 'Muth des Dichters' (MA, I, 240–41). That version ends with an allusion to the fate of Orpheus, who was torn limb from limb by the Maenads of Dionysus (Graves 1958: 112–13). According to Ovid, as Orpheus' severed head and lyre were carried to the sea — and eventually to the shore of Lesbos — they continued to give forth music. Thus Hölderlin can justifiably conclude that the singer fell in the course of his noble calling ('edel | Starb in edlem Beruf'). The theme of a singer or poet being exposed to danger recurs in different forms throughout the several versions. In the second version of 'Dichtermuth' the exhortation to courage takes on a more particularly Stoic character.[56]

For the purposes of that second version, the dangers to which the poet is exposed are of two different, but related, kinds. The first arises from his apparent lack of a defined social position.[57] That danger is addressed by a reflection on the poet's

---

55 MA, I, 285; hereafter simply 'Natur und Kunst'. For English translations of 'Dichtermuth', and 'Blödigkeit', see OE, 232, 113 and 177, SP, 70–71 and 78, and Hamb, 261–65; and for 'Natur und Kunst' Hamb, 223–25. Note that Hamburger translates the first version of 'Dichtermuth' only (MA, I, 275–76), and translates the longer version of 'Natur und Kunst' given in KA, I, 297–98 (the additional stanza after line 16 can also be found at MA, III, 159). Unless otherwise indicated, references below to 'Dichtermuth' are to the second version (MA, I, 284–85), and in the case of 'Natur und Kunst' line references are to the shorter version.

56 Note that 'Muth' or 'Mut' can mean not only courage, but also mood or state of mind (and specifically a cheerful one).

57 Like 'Mein Eigentum', 'Dichtermuth' is also a reflection of the poet's personal circumstances (justifying the use here of the masculine pronoun). See for example Hölderlin's letter to his mother of 16 November 1799, in which he refers to someone who, like himself, lacks a defined sphere of social activity, and who 'nur dadurch bestehen kann, daß er mit *Muth* in seiner Art sich festsezt, und sein *Schiksaal* einsieht und trägt, wie andre das ihrige' [can only survive by having the *courage* to affirm

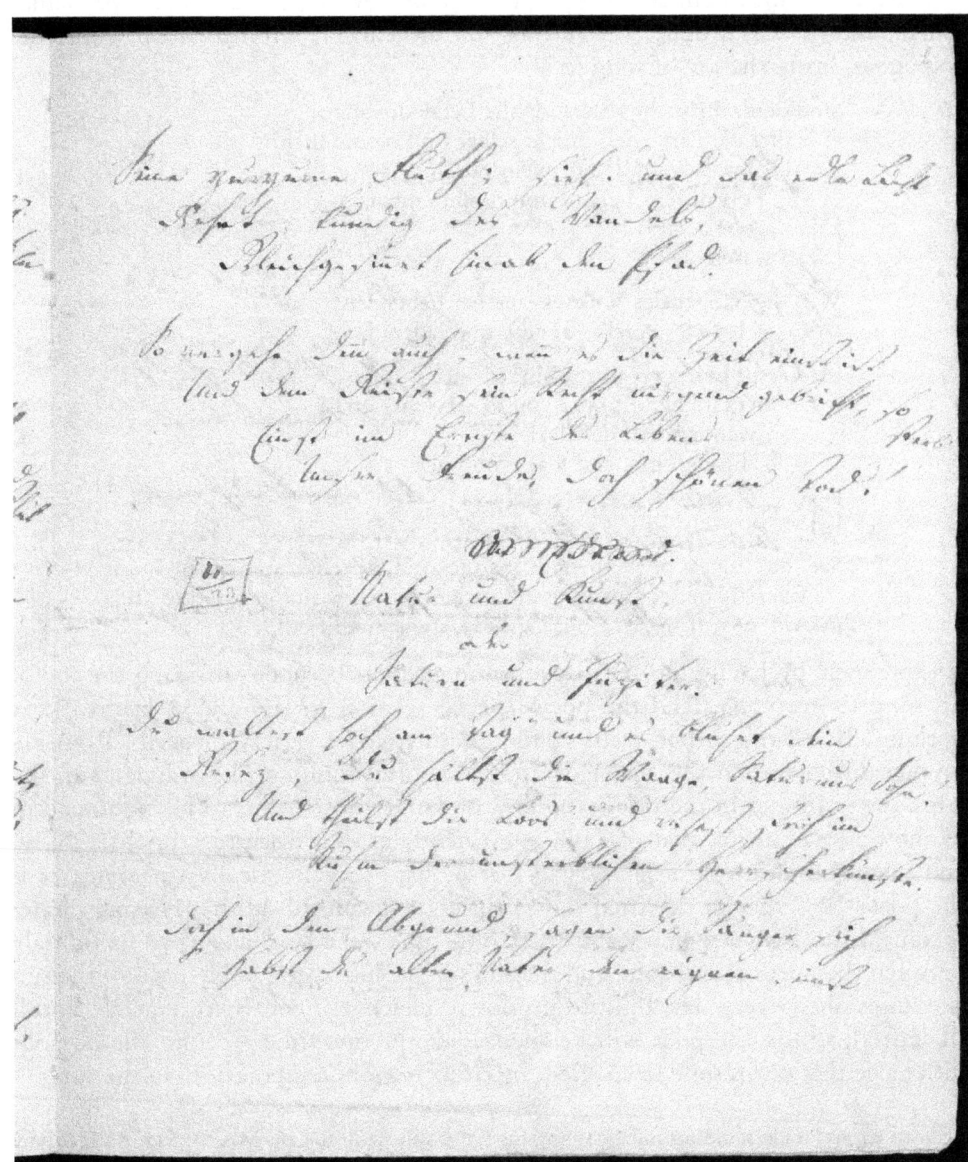

FIG. 1.1. End of a fair copy of the ode 'Dichtermuth', followed by the beginning of 'Natur und Kunst oder Saturn und Jupiter'; between the two, the title of the ode 'An Eduard' has been crossed out. © Württembergische Landesbibliothek

kinship with all living creatures, and his special relation to destiny. Thus the poet's role derives from a connection with the totality of life, rather than a particular sphere, and he stands under the tutelage of 'die Parze'.[58] From that can come the courage to bring the joy of song to all:

> Sind denn dir nicht verwandt alle Lebendigen,
>   Nährt die Parze denn nicht selber im Dienste dich?
>   Drum, so wandle nur wehrlos
>   Fort durchs Leben, und fürchte nichts!
> […]
> […] so waren auch
>
> Wir, die Sänger des Volks, gerne bei Lebenden
>   Wo sich vieles gesellt, freudig und jedem hold.
>
> [Aren't all living creatures kin to you?
>   Doesn't fate herself raise you to serve her ends?
>   So wander then defenceless
>   Through life, and fear nothing!
> […]
> […] so too were
>
> We, the singers of the people, glad to find ourselves among the living
>   Where many companions are gathered, joyful and inclined to all.]
>   (MA, I, 284, ll. 1–4, 12–14; OE, 113, trans. modified)

It is precisely by having no narrow attachment that the poet can bring the joy of his song to everyone. And the poet's special relation to fate allows him to 'fear nothing'. But if the earlier drafts of the ode invoked a variety of perils, from the mythic (Orpheus and the Maenads), to the natural-sublime (the wanderer in the Alps, the swimmer in the tides), the idea of danger now seems to be embodied in its most abstract form, that of Time — 'flüchtig[e] Zeit' [fleeting time] (l. 18) — and inevitable death (l. 25).[59] Strictly (or perhaps metonymically) speaking, it is the poet's 'joy' that in the final stanza suffers a 'beautiful death'. The ode draws a comparison between poets and their 'forefather' the sun, and correspondingly between the poet's joyful song and the sun's light. Just as the noble light of the sun is extinguished every day, only to go down 'gleichgesinnet' [with equable mind] (ll. 21–24), so too the poet will be silenced at the due time — with the obvious difference that our respite from 'fleeting time' is more temporary than the sun's.[60]

---

his own nature, understanding and assuming his *fate* as others do theirs] (MA, II, 842; AL, 167; my emphasis).
58   I.e. one of the three Fates (*Parcae*, or Greek *Moirai*), among whom Clotho (literally 'the Spinner') has the function of spinning the thread of life (Graves 1958: 48). See also the ode 'An die Parzen' [To the Fates] (MA, I, 188; OE, 27).
59   For the poet as 'ein muth'ger | Alpenwandrer', and then as Orpheus, see 'Muth des Dichters' (MA, I, 241, ll. 17–20, 29–33). For the poet as a swimmer who entrusts himself to the tide, only to be dragged under by the waves, ibid. ll. 26–28, and the first version of 'Dichtermuth' (MA, I, 276, ll. 17–20). As Indlekofer suggests, the latter danger could be regarded as a metaphor for the perils of poetic enthusiasm (2007: 38).
60   Cf. the earlier ode 'Sonnenuntergang', with its assimilation of sunset to Apollo's 'Abendlied' [evensong] (MA, I, 226, l. 5; OE, 37).

It is in this version that the resonances with Marcus Aurelius are particularly striking (albeit prefigured to some extent in the earlier versions).[61] Recall, for example, the idea of the poet being in the service of fate, more precisely one of the three Fates, and compare: 'Willingly surrender yourself to Clotho: let her spin your thread into whatever she wills' (4.34). This is the interconnected 'web and mesh' of the universe (4.40), the 'thread of destiny spun for you from the first by the most ancient causes' (5.8.12). For the 'common nature' of all things, from which one must not stand aside, see 4.29.3 (and cf. 6.38 and 9.9); and for the proposition in the second stanza of the ode, that everything that happens should be welcome to the poet, see 5.8, 8.23 and 10.6. Compare the emphasis in the fifth and sixth stanzas, on 'fleeting time' and continual 'change', with 4.43, 5.24, 6.59 and 9.19; for the reference in Hölderlin's sixth stanza to the quality of being '[g]leichgesinnet' [equable], compare the calm [*galēnē*] recommended in 5.2, 7.28 and 12.22.[62] And for the final stanza, on the acceptance of death, see the concluding chapters of Marcus' work (12.34 to 12.36).

There is accordingly no doubt as to the abundance of Stoic themes evoked in 'Dichtermuth'. But what exactly are we to make of them?[63] One could say that the initial consolation offered to the poet — that his place is assured precisely by an affinity with universal nature and his relation to the tapestry of fate — is the obverse of the reconciliation offered in the final stanza. The same cosmic sympathy that gives the poet his unique role in society also reconciles him to the transience of all things, the victory of 'fleeting time' that is only temporarily arrested by the daily rising of the sun. The difficulty is that the poet's courage here seems, if anything, too dependent upon a Stoic philosophy of nature, as if Marcus had gained the upper hand in the dialogue of genres.

Turning to the final revision of 'Dichtermuth', under its new title 'Blödigkeit', the dialogue with Stoicism can be seen to continue in a new form (MA, I, 443–44; OE, 177). From the opening lines, the images of cosmic sympathy and service to fate give way to ones associated with knowledge and truth: 'Sind denn dir nicht bekannt viele Lebendigen? | Geht auf Wahrem dein Fuß nicht, wie auf Teppichen?' [Aren't many living creatures known to you? | Don't your feet tread the truth as they do on soft carpet?]. But rather than being entirely new, those images seem to have been derived by transformation of the earlier version. A relationship of kinship ('verwandt') becomes one of acquaintance ('bekannt'); and a reference to the spinner of fate ('die Parze') becomes one to the woven fabric of truth ('wie auf Teppichen').[64] The day itself is now said to be 'pensive' rather than 'joyful' (l. 17).

---

61   See Schmidt 1978: 104–11 (substantially identical with 2008a); and see also KA, I, 768–76. Schmidt notes that the mode of Hölderlin's self-address in 'Dichtermuth' can itself be compared with the literary form of that work, referring to the ode's 'lyrisch-stoisch[e] Selbstzuwendung' (2008a: 953).
62   As Schmidt suggests (KA, I, 775) 'gleichgesinnet' may also be a reference to the virtue, mentioned in 10.8.1–2, of being 'in agreement' [σύμφρων] with the course of things. Hammond renders this as 'cooperative'; in German it can also be rendered as 'gleichmütig' (Wittstock 1949: 148). See also Reitani in TL, 1697, pointing to a possible 'play' on the two meanings.
63   Their poetological significance is doubted by Indlekofer (2007: 44, n. 79).
64   Cf. Stanitzek 1989: 249. We have seen that the corresponding places in Marcus Aurelius refer to

But the most striking transformation is in the new final stanza, which replaces the last two stanzas of the previous version, and refers to the poet's 'art' and 'skill' rather than to tranquillity of mind and the acceptance of death:

> Gut auch sind und geschikt einem zu etwas wir,
>   Wenn wir kommen, mit Kunst, und von den Himmlischen
>   Einen bringen. Doch selber
>   Bringen schikliche Hände wir.
>
> [We too are good, sent to serve someone, and useful
>   For something when we bring forth one of the gods
>   With our art. Yet we ourselves
>   Bring our skilful and suitable hands.]

Schmidt traces the term 'schiklich' to the Stoic notion of *kathēkon* or 'decorum': that which it is necessary or appropriate to do in a given circumstance, and thus to a notion of duty taken at once in an ethical and aesthetic sense (KA, I, 831–32). But it can also mean 'skilled', and it seems clear that such a meaning also resonates in the closing lines of the poem. Hölderlin is playing on the phonetic and etymological connections between 'geschikt' (in the sense of being 'sent', but also in the sense of being 'useful', 'fitted' or 'skilled'), and 'schiklich' (in the sense of 'appropriate', but also again 'skilled'), not to mention 'Geschick' (in the sense of 'fate').[65] However, a connection between fate, skill and appropriate action is also a cardinal feature of Stoic philosophy. The Stoic notion of 'fate' was intrinsically connected to the idea of 'skill', in that the universe was ordered as if by a craftsman by means of creative fire, or *pneuma* (fire blended with air). The universe is the locus for the expert activity of an immanent divine principle ('Zeus'), and Stoicism accordingly finds a relation between what is 'fated', as belonging to the order of a cosmos governed by law, and the exercise of human expertise. Marcus himself is true to this tradition when he cites the example provided by the 'gardener, the vine-dresser, the breaker of horses, the dog trainer'.[66] But if the closing lines of 'Blödigkeit' establish a similar relationship between 'fate' and 'skill', this is not by the exercise of philosophical

---

Clotho, the spinner among the Fates. But the image also belongs to the shift, in this version, from the world of universal nature to the realm of culture and art (cf. André 2000: 59–60).

65 See also Hamburger: 'fitting, skilful hands' (Hamb, 265); Reitani: 'mani esperte nel decoro' (TL, 295, with his commentary at TL, 1483). Schmidt himself points to the play on 'geschikt' and 'schiklich' (KA, I, 831). The implicit presence of the term 'Geschick' echoes the invocation of 'die Parze' in the first stanza of 'Dichtermuth', and 'Schiksaalsgöttin' in the earlier version 'Muth des Dichters) (cf. TL, 1483, and Frey 1990: 96–97). See also the exactly contemporary letter to Wilmans of 8 December 1803 (MA, II, 925–26; AL, 216), with the density of its uses of 'schiken' or 'zuschiken' (in the sense of 'send' a manuscript or book) and 'schiklich' or 'unschiklich' (in the sense of 'suitable' or '(in)appropriate'); Hölderlin even concludes the letter, somewhat over-optimistically, by celebrating his contact with Wilmans as 'ein wahr und glüklich Geschik'. On this complex of terms see further Chapter 6.3 below, as well as AA [2.13] and [3.2].

66 *Meditations*, 6.16.5; see also 6.35. And see Diogenes Laertius, *Lives of eminent philosophers*, II, ed. and trans. by R. D. Hicks, LCL 185 (Cambridge, MA: Harvard University Press, 1925; repr. 1979), 7.156 (pp. 260–61): 'Nature in their view is an artistically working fire [πῦρ τεχνικόν]'. See also LS 46A, and LS, I, 286–89; and see generally Bénatouïl 2009, and Meyer 2009. Brouwer (2014: 49) observes that 'Wisdom [for the Stoics] is not only the most useful of the kinds of expertise, it also fits the expert-like structure of the universe', with a corresponding 'consistency of human and cosmic reason'.

reason or the application of a philosophical doctrine; rather, it is by an ostentatious employment of poetic technique. The assonance and ambiguity in the expressions connoting fate, vocation and skill seems intended, therefore, to mark a distinction of genre. And what appears to be the willed clumsiness of line 21 ('Gut auch sind und geschikt einem zu etwas wir') might itself regarded as the ironical display of poetic prowess.[67] In 'Dichtermuth' the poet was assumed to have a special relation to fate, and hence to the order established by the divine craftsman; but such a relation is now demonstrated by an exhibition of poetic skill.

Turning now to the ode 'Natur und Kunst', the dialogue is not so much with Stoic philosophy as with a specific philosophical poem, namely Cleanthes' 'Hymn to Zeus'. I have already noted how the latter was included in Estienne's epoch-making collection *Poesis philosophica*, a work that itself belonged to a long-standing debate on the relation between philosophy and poetry. Hölderlin's ode can be seen as a further intervention in that debate.

Cleanthes' hymn is addressed to Zeus, and recites reasons for praising him that are founded on the Stoic philosophy of nature.[68] It begins by praising Zeus as the 'prime mover of nature, who with your law steer all things', later referring to 'the universal reason which runs through all things', and concluding that there is no greater privilege than 'to sing for ever in righteousness of the universal law'. Thus the idea of Zeus as supreme law-giver figures prominently at the beginning and the end of the hymn. That law is the one governing nature, the corporeal cosmos that (for the Stoics) alone had full independent reality.[69] Hölderlin's ode similarly begins and ends with a reference to the law-giving of Zeus (ll. 1–2 and 23). The god is addressed initially as the Roman Jupiter, or 'Saturn's son', but in the end under the Greek epithet 'Kronion' (i.e. Zeus, or 'son of Cronus'). As the full title to the ode makes clear, Jupiter and Saturn — or Zeus and Cronus — represent for Hölderlin two distinct domains: Art and Nature respectively. That might seem already to be an attack on Cleanthes' premise, namely the identity of the 'reason' or 'law' of Zeus with the laws governing universal nature. But from another point of view, Hölderlin gives voice to an idea that we have already encountered — namely Zeus as divine craftsman. Zeus can represent the principle of Art, to the extent that his action upon the universe is analogous to that of a human designer. Both impose shape on the formless, but in doing so leave an aspect of nature out of account — or so Hölderlin will argue. In mythological terms, this is represented by the overthrow by Zeus of his father Cronus, the god of a golden age in which no legislation was

---

67 On the artful obscurity of this line, see Franz 2013: 194–96. See also Analecta 2004: 21; and on the self-reference involved in 'Wenn wir kommen, mit Kunst' (l. 22), cf. André 2000: 72.
68 I cite the hymn in Long and Sedley's translation (LS, I, 326–27). See Chapter 2 below for a more detailed discussion.
69 As Plutarch reports the doctrine of Cleanthes' successor Chrysippus, the universe was governed by a strict causal nexus identified with the 'reason' or 'rationale' of Zeus [τοῦ Διὸς λόγον], which is identical to 'destiny' or 'fate' [τῇ εἱμαρμένῃ]. See *On Stoic Self-contradictions* 1056C, in *Moralia*, XIII, Part 2, trans. by Harold Cherniss, LCL 470 (Cambridge, MA: Harvard University Press 1976), pp. 594–95; and also LS 55R. The latter term literally means 'the lot assigned by fate' (Brill, s.v. μείρομαι, 2A), which can be compared with 'Natur und Kunst', l. 3 ('[du] theilst die Loos"). On the distinction between 'corporeal' and 'incorporeal' in the Stoic system, see Chapters 2.3 and 3.5 below.

necessary, and who now stands for a Nature banished by Art:

> Doch in den Abgrund, sagen die Sänger sich,
>   Habst du den alten Vater, den eignen, einst
>   Verwiesen [...]
> [...]
>   Einst mühelos und größer, wie du, wenn schon
>   Er kein Gebot aussprach und ihn der
>   Sterblichen keiner mit Nahmen nannte.
>
> [Yet to the abyss, the singers tell themselves,
>   You once the old father, your own,
>   Consigned [...]
> [...]
>   Once effortless and greater than you, although
>   He uttered no command, and none among
>   The mortals named him with names.]
> (MA, I, 285, ll. 5–12; Hamb, 223, trans. modified)

Cronus, or Saturn, represents the aspect of Nature that is not captured by the law of Zeus, and would correspondingly remain unspoken by human language, at least to the extent that human name-giving is a reflection of Zeus' law. The purpose of the ode is to remind Zeus of this limitation, and demand that poets be allowed to name the silent and hidden realm (ll. 15–16).[70] Only then will Zeus, in turn, be deemed worthy of praise. Furthermore, in a manner to be more closely analysed in Chapter 2, the ode associates the law of Zeus with a particular temporal order, the flux of 'changing Time': 'wandelnde Zeit' or (in the longer version of the ode) 'wechselnde Zeit'.

By the ode's final stanza, poet and Stoic god stand side by side, almost as equals:

> Und war in ihrer Wiege mir, in
>   Wonne die wandelnde Zeit entschlafen,
>
> Dann hör' ich dich, Kronion! Und kenne dich,
>   Den weisen Meister, welcher, wie wir, ein Sohn
>   Der Zeit, Geseze giebt.
>
> [And if in his cradle changing Time has, for me,
>   Fallen asleep in rapture,
>
> I'll know you then, Kronion! and hear you then,
>   The wise master who, like ourselves, a son
>   Of Time, gives laws.]
> (ll. 19–23, trans. modified).

How does the name-giving to which the poet now aspires differ from the one that has previously been allowed? Is there a law of poetry, one that is no longer simply a reflection of the order of Zeus? I would argue that the ode not only lays claim to such a poetic law; it also provides an object-lesson in its application. The procedure is similar to the one we have already seen in the case of 'Blödigkeit'. We saw there

---

70 On the problem of naming a banished silent realm, see the related ode 'Ermunterung' (MA, I, 277–79), with Frey's commentary (1990: 78–88).

how the final stanza of the ode invoked the idea of appropriate poetic skill or 'Schicklichkeit', while at the same time putting it to work in the form of a play on the words 'Schicksal' and 'Geschick'. The last two stanzas of 'Natur und Kunst' embody a similarly self-reflexive lesson in poetic technique. In staking his claim to a poetic law, Hölderlin exploits a distinctively poetic device of ambiguity — one both lexical and syntactic.

To take the syntactic ambiguity first: this turns precisely on the scope of the notion of law-giving, or on the question whether law-giving belongs only to Zeus. As we have just seen, the final stanza contains a comparison between the poet, on the one hand, and a god on the other 'welcher, wie wir, ein Sohn | Der Zeit, Geseze giebt'. As I have translated it above, this describes a god 'who, like ourselves, a son | Of Time, gives laws'. But the scope of that comparison is ambiguous. It can be understood as meaning either: (1) that the god, like the poet, is a son of Time and gives laws, or (2) that the god, who like the poet is a son of Time, gives laws. Hamburger eliminates the ambiguity, with the version 'like ourselves, a son | Of Time, gives laws *to us*' (my emphasis), and other translators in effect adopt the same solution.[71] But what if both alternatives are intended, and the ambiguity deliberate? A poet must of course have the right of ambiguous utterance. Indeed how else can the realm of Cronus be 'named' in the way that the poet now demands? For that to be possible, a language is required that does justice to the previously unspoken aspect of nature, one that escapes the order of Zeus:

> Und hab' ich erst am Herzen Lebendiges
>   Gefühlt und dämmert, was du gestaltetest,
> [...]
> Dann hör' ich dich, Kronion!
>
> [And once my heart has felt that life
>   Most living, and things that you shaped grow dim,
> [...]
> I'll know you then, Kronion!]
> (ll. 17–21, trans. modified).

According to meaning (2) distinguished above, it is only Zeus and not the poet who is truly the law-giver. Poets might be allowed to give names to their obscure feelings, but without making possible a new order that would rival the reign of Zeus. It is clear that this is a possible alternative — after all, it is the one adopted by Hamburger and other competent interpreters. But the other possibility exists, and in giving voice to it the poem can demonstrate all the better the possibility of a uniquely poetic law. Poetry does not only give voice to feeling; it can reflect on the conditions of law-giving (including its own). In that sense the ambiguity between alternatives (1) and (2) is if anything a confirmation of the validity of the first. The interpretation can be upheld not despite, but because of, an ambiguity that leaves room for the second.[72]

---

71   See e.g. Robert Rovini, in Hölderlin, *Œuvres* (Paris: Gallimard, 1967), p. 777: 'fils comme nous | Du Temps, toi le législateur'. But the alternative interpretation is certainly possible (see Staiger 1961: 36).
72   On the relation between the unequivocal law of Zeus, and a poetic regime of ambiguity, see

Turning now to the second, lexical or semantic, ambiguity: this is one that involves the notion of Time.[73] The term '[die] Zeit' occurs three times in the ode (ll. 9, 20 and 23). It is on the last occasion that it carries a double meaning. In the first two, any potential ambiguity is eliminated by a qualifying adjective. Thus in line 9, Saturn is referred to as 'der Gott der goldenen Zeit' [the god of the golden age], which is no doubt a reference to the mythic period ruled by Cronus, an epoch of perpetual youth and immunity from change.[74] On the second occasion the reference is to 'wandelnde' or 'wechselnde Zeit'. This would be a temporal order associated with Zeus, rather than Cronus: for it is when such 'changing Time' is rocked to sleep in its cradle that the 'things [he] shaped grow dim' (ll. 17–20). But what are we to make of the third reference? There Zeus ('Kronion', or son of Cronus) is said to be a son of Time. Hölderlin is evidently playing on the false etymology that identifies Cronus or *Kronos* [Κρόνος], with time or *khronos* [χρόνος].[75] But if Cronus thereby becomes a god of Time, it is clear that Hölderlin also regards Zeus as such a god — as the ode 'An Eduard' in particular makes clear.[76] It seems, therefore, that each presides over a distinct regime of temporality. We have already seen the comparison between ourselves and Zeus, as sons of Time ('wie wir, ein Sohn | Der Zeit'). But such a comparison can only work if 'Time' is taken in this double sense. We mortals are children of Time, but only in the sense of being subject to the law of Zeus. Immortal Zeus, for his part, is a son of Cronus. It is the law of Zeus that is celebrated in the Stoic hymn, which places its hexameters in the service of philosophy. A poetic law, by contrast, allows two senses to be uttered in the same breath — so that a dialogue with a Stoic hymn becomes a veritable dialogue of genres.

---

also Chapter 6.4 below. And cf. Tang 2007 on the relation between notions of poetic and political law-giving in Hölderlin's *Empodocles* project.
73 For a fuller treatment see Chapter 2 below.
74 See Hesiod, *Works and Days*, ll. 109–20, in Hesiod, I, ed. and trans. by Glenn W. Most, 2nd edn, LCL 57 (Cambridge, MA: Harvard University Press, 2018), pp. 94–97.
75 On a Stoic source for that etymology, see Chapter 2.1 below.
76 See 'An Eduard', ll. 33–36, contrasting wisdom's old 'lullaby' [Wiegengesang] with the 'admonishing flame' of the thunderbolt of Zeus, the 'god of Time': 'es flammt | Aus fernetönendem Gewölk die | Mahnende Flamme des Zeitengottes' (MA, I, 287). A similar contrast, between the lightning of Jupiter and the thunder-cloud of Saturn, is made in the longer version of 'Natur und Kunst'. And as already noted, the shorter version is closely related to 'An Eduard' in the manuscript.

CHAPTER 2

Hölderlin's Ode 'Natur und Kunst oder Saturn und Jupiter' and Cleanthes' 'Hymn to Zeus'

1. A Stoic Hymn

It is above all Jochen Schmidt who has drawn attention to the significance of Stoicism for Hölderlin's thought. In a survey of the subject, he suggests three phases in Hölderlin's reception of the Stoics: an early phase, represented by the poem 'Das Schiksaal' [Fate], inspired by Seneca's concept of virtue and influenced by Schiller; a second phase influenced above all by the Stoic philosophy of nature; and, more debatably perhaps, a final phase dominated by the Stoic notion of cosmic conflagration or *ekpurōsis*.[1] The presence of Marcus Aurelius in Hölderlin's ode 'Dichtermuth' has already been noted, as well as the Stoic tenor of the narrator's ultimate position in *Hyperion*.[2] In this chapter I shall argue that one of Hölderlin's most important poems, the programmatic ode 'Natur und Kunst oder Saturn und Jupiter' [Nature and Art or Saturn and Jupiter],[3] was inspired — or provoked — by an ancient Stoic text, namely Cleanthes' 'Hymn to Zeus'.[4]

Such a claim may appear paradoxical to some. Hölderlin's ode is sometimes read as a simple critique of Jupiter (or Zeus), a rejection of his law-giving in favour of the benign lawlessness of feeling, the realm of Saturn (or Cronus).[5] In his own

---

1   Schmidt 1996: 48; but contrast Bennholdt-Thomsen 1998: 29–30, and Martens 2008: 28–29. On Stoicism in 'Das Schiksaal', see also Reitani in TL, 1320–21.
2   See Chapters 1.3 and 1.4 above. On 'Dichtermuth' cf. Schmidt 1978: 104–10; Schmidt 2008a; KA, I, 768–76; and similarly Reitani in TL, 1694–98. On *Hyperion* see Schmidt 2008b. Furthermore, on Stoic sources for the hymn 'Der Einzige', see Schmidt 1990: 111–15. As mentioned in Chapter 1, a copy of the *Meditations* of Marcus Aurelius was found in Hölderlin's personal library and its Greek title will have inspired that of the epigram Προς εαυτον (MA, I, 236; OE, 67).
3   MA, I, 285; Hamb, 223–25; hereafter cited simply as 'Natur und Kunst'. In KA, I, 297–98 Schmidt gives a longer version of the ode (which is also the version translated by Hamburger). Apart from containing a significant additional stanza (for which see also MA, III, 159), the differences between the two versions are minor. Reitani (TL, 1698–99) provides arguments for including both versions in TL, 798–803.
4   See LS 54I, at LS, I, 326–27 (English) and LS, II, 326–27 (Greek). For a detailed commentary to the hymn see Thom 2005. Thom observes that the hymn is the only complete surviving text of an early Stoic philosopher (2005: 2).
5   Hölderlin tends to refer without distinction to the Roman and Greek names of the two gods:

commentary to the ode (KA, I, 752–56) Schmidt emphasises the critique of Zeus's law-giving that it contains, and perhaps for that reason does not consider the Stoic sources.[6] Such an exercise might also appear to be of merely antiquarian interest, deflecting attention from more contemporary influences on Hölderlin.[7] But it is more than a question of sources and influences. The possibility must be considered that, in composing a poem addressed to Zeus, Hölderlin was engaging in a dialogue with Cleanthes' poem. If that is the case, the Stoic hymn will be essential to our appreciation of the ode.

The differences between the two poems cannot of course be ignored. At first sight, Cleanthes' hymn appears to have a cultic as well as a philosophical significance. Long and Sedley observe that it conveys 'the depth and power of his religious sentiments, presenting in the traditional clothing of the Greek hymn a god who is at once the Zeus of popular religion, the ordering fire-god of Heraclitus, and the Stoic providential deity'.[8] But it also seems that Cleanthes employs the poetic form of the cult hymn as a vehicle for his philosophy. The allegorical interpretation of myth was a central innovation of the early Stoics, and the poem can be said to have been the first allegorical hymn by a Greek philosopher.[9] Cleanthes uses the hymn to broadcast a philosophical doctrine, namely the universality of a divine reason immanent in the cosmos. Similarly, the allegorical nature of Hölderlin's ode is already evident from its title. But the ode is a vehicle neither of religious piety nor of Stoic rationalism. In addressing Zeus, Hölderlin is reflecting upon the role of the poet and the law-giving peculiar to poetry; which is to say that the ode is a key text of Hölderlin's poetics.

It is overwhelmingly likely that Hölderlin was familiar with the 'Hymn to Zeus'. Before the composition of 'Natur und Kunst', Hölderlin had been working on his tragedy based on the death of Empedocles.[10] The sources for that *Empedocles* project have been analyzed by Hölscher, who observes that Hölderlin will have had

see e.g. the reference to Jupiter as 'Kronion' in the final stanza of the ode, and see also his translation of Pindar's Second Olympian Ode (MA, II, 187–93, ll. 4, 22, 49, 106, and 126–28).

6   Schmidt concentrates instead on Proclus and Plotinus (KA, I, 753–55); see also Schmidt 2003: 87–88. Hölderlin's ode has attracted numerous other commentaries — see in particular Ryan 1960: 213–17; Staiger 1961: 25–39; Binder 1963: 110–12; Ryan 1973; Szondi 1975: 389–94; Beyer 1993: 81–82; Mögel 1994: 136–38; Gaier 1996; Raulet 1996; Bothe 1998; Reitani in TL, 1698–1706; Honold 2005: 102–13; and Tang 2010: 566–69.
7   Cf. Link 1999: 12–19.
8   LS, I, 332. See also Thom 2005: 24. Note that the title to the hymn is 'of modern provenance' but the genre of a 'traditional cult hymn' is clearly indicated by its structure and content (ibid. 7–8). On Cleanthes as an interpreter of Heraclitus, see Dilcher 1995: 178 and Long 1996a; and on the affinity of Stoic and Heraclitan thought see Kahn 1979: 4–5 and Bréhier 1971: 141–42, 176–77.
9   See Most 2010: 27, 34; or at least the first 'to a single anthropomorphic god of the traditional pantheon' (p. 34). Note also Cleanthes' observation, reported by Seneca: 'As our breath produces a louder sound when it passes through the long and narrow opening of the trumpet and escapes by a hole which widens at the end, even so the fettering rules of poetry clarify our meaning'; see Seneca, Epistle 108.10, in *Epistles*, 3 vols, trans. by Richard M. Gummere, LCL 75–77 (Cambridge, MA: Harvard University Press, 1917–25), III (1925), 234–35.
10 The beginning of November 1800 has been suggested as the date for the composition of the ode: see FHA, V, 789. The *Empedocles* project occupied Hölderlin between summer 1797 and the beginning of 1800: see MA, III, 329, 352.

access to the Empedoclean fragments included in Estienne's *Poesis philosophica*.[11] But Estienne's collection also includes texts of Cleanthes, among which the most substantial is the 'Hymn to Zeus'.[12] Assuming that Hölderlin made use of the anthology, Cleanthes' poem — which is by any standards a striking work — cannot have escaped his attention, not least on account of its literary qualities. It was in any case well-known, being reproduced (together with a Latin translation) in Cudworth's widely-read *The True Intellectual System of the Universe*. As Cudworth observes:

> But because many are so extremely unwilling to believe that the Pagans ever made any religious address to the supreme God as such, we shall here set down an excellent and devout hymn of the same Cleanthes to him, the rather because it hath been but little taken notice of.[13]

An annotated Latin translation of Cudworth's book was first published in Germany in 1733, and the work will have been familiar to Hölderlin from his student days in the Tübingen *Stift*. Cudworth will also have been a source for Hölderlin's reception of Empedocles.[14]

Hölderlin could also have found an account of the Stoic deity in Diogenes Laertius, which was another important source for him in this period:

> God is one and the same with Reason, Fate and Zeus; he is also called by many other names. [...] The world, in their view, is ordered by reason and providence [...] inasmuch as reason pervades every part of it, just as does the soul in us. [...] The deity, say they, is a living being, immortal, rational, perfect or intelligent in happiness, admitting nothing evil into him, taking providential care of the world and all that therein is, but he is not of human shape. He is, however, the artificer of the universe and, as it were, the father of all, both in general and in that particular part of him which is all-pervading, and which is called by many

---

11 Ποίησις φιλόσοφος. *Poesis philosophica, Vel saltem, Reliquiæ poesis philosophicæ, Empedoclis, Parmenidis, Xenophanis, Cleanthis, Timonis, Epicharmi* [...], ed. by Henr. Stephanus [Henri II Estienne] ([Geneva]: 1573). See Hölscher 1965a: 10–13, and 1965b: 23–24; and similarly MA, III, 328, and Primavesi 2014: 34, n. 88. On Estienne's collection see Primavesi 2011a and 2011b, and Chapter 1.1 above; and for the collection as a source also for Hölderlin's reception of Heraclitus see Bremer 1998: 174, 197. For a more cautious assessment see dos Santos Gomes (2004: 306), who points out nonetheless that the work was frequently used and cited in this period. Given Hölderlin's interest in both poetry and philosophy, it seems unlikely that he would have refrained from opening the pages of a well-known work with that title.
12 *Poesis philosophica*, pp. 49–50; the source is the anthology of Stobaeus (the latter probably 5th century CE).
13 Ralph Cudworth, *The True Intellectual System of the Universe* [...] *With a Treatise concerning Eternal and Immutable Morality* [1678]. *To which are added, the notes and dissertations of Dr. J. L. Mosheim*, translated by John Harrison [...], 3 vols (London: 1845), II, 117–19 (p. 117). The cited passage is an intervention in a contemporary debate on whether the Stoics were to be regarded as theists or atheists (see Brooke 2012: 135–36).
14 See *Systema intellectuale hujus Universa, seu de veris Naturae rerum originibus*, trans. with commentary by J. L. Mosheim, 2nd edn, 2 vols (Leiden, 1773), I, 662–65. For the importance of Cudworth in the reception of Empedocles, and as a source for the formula *hen kai pan* [One and All] later popularised by F. H. Jacobi, see Hölscher 1965a: 13–14, 48–49, and MA, II, 39; and cf. MA, III, 328, and Primavesi 2014: 24. On Cudworth in the Tübingen *Stift*, see further dos Santos Gomes 2004: 25–30. For some other possible sources for Hölderlin's knowledge of the hymn, see Brandt 2002: 226–28.

names according to its various powers. They give the name Dia [Δία] because all things are due to [διά] him; Zeus [Ζῆνα] in so far as he is the cause of life [ζῆν] or pervades all life.[15]

Thus Zeus, for the Stoics, is a divine principle of reason immanent in the universe, expressing itself in a cosmic order that is accessible to the human intellect. As a principle of reason and order, it founds both human action and understanding, on the one hand, and the natural world on the other. And the Stoic universe is a deterministic one, in which everything that happens necessarily happens, according to a chain of causation identified with fate or the reason of Zeus.[16]

According to the myth reported in Hesiod, Zeus was the son of Cronus (*Kronos*), whom he dethroned and imprisoned in Tartarus along with his fellow Titans.[17] The Stoics gave the two figures an allegorical interpretation, founded it seems upon a speculative etymology. As Cicero reports it:

> By Saturn [...] they [i.e. the ancient myths] denoted that being who maintains the course and revolution of the seasons and periods of time, the deity actually so designated in Greek, for Saturn's Greek name is *Kronos* [Κρόνος], which is the same [sic] as *khronos* [χρόνος] a space of time. The Latin designation 'Saturn' on the other hand is due to the fact that he is 'saturated' or 'satiated with years' (*anni*); the fable is that he was in the habit of devouring his sons — meaning that Time devours the ages and gorges himself insatiably with the years that are past. Saturn was bound by Jove [i.e. Jupiter] in order that Time's courses might not be unlimited, and that Jove might fetter him by the bonds of the stars.[18]

Here the figures of Jupiter and Saturn seem to represent a distinction between two temporal orders. Saturn devours his sons, the years to which he in turn gives birth: as it were a recurring cycle of periods and seasons. Jupiter intervenes in this endless

---

15   Diogenes Laertius, *Lives of eminent philosophers*, II, ed. and trans. by R. D. Hicks, LCL 185 (Cambridge, MA: Harvard University Press, 1925; repr. 1979), 7.135, 138 and 147 (pp. 240–51); see also 7.88 (pp. 196–97): 'the law common to all things, that is to say, the right reason [ὀρθὸς λόγος] which pervades all things, and is identical with this Zeus [Διί], lord and ruler of all that is.' In its epic form, the name declines Ζηνός, Ζηνί, Ζῆνα, rather than Διός, Διί, Δία: see Brill, s.v. Ζεύς; on the Stoic fondness for speculative etymology see further below. Hölderlin mentions the deep impression made by his reading of Diogenes Laertius in the letter to Sinclair of 24 December 1798 (MA, II, 722–23; AL, 117). It will also have provided a source for his *Empedocles* drama (cf. MA, III, 327).
16   See Plutarch, *On Stoic Self-contradictions* 1056C, in *Moralia*, XIII, Part 2, trans. by Harold Cherniss, LCL 470 (Cambridge, MA: Harvard University Press 1976), pp. 594–95. On fate as a chain of causes, and identified with Zeus as 'the *pneuma* that unifies the cosmos', see Meyer 2009: 79–80, 85.
17   *Theogony*, ll. 711–33, in Hesiod, I, ed. and trans. by Glenn W. Most, 2nd edn, LCL 57 (Cambridge, MA: Harvard University Press, 2018), pp. 60–61.
18   Cicero, *On the Nature of the Gods*, 2.64, in Cicero, XIX, ed. and trans. by H. Rackham, LCL 268 (Cambridge, MA: Harvard University Press,1933; repr. 1972), pp. 184–85. Similarly 'Jupiter' is to be interpreted as the heavens, and 'Juno' as the air (2.65–66, pp. 186–87). On Hellenistic allegory see Most 2010, and on the connection between the allegorical interpretation of myth and Stoic etymology see Long 1996b: 69–84. As Franz has noted (1987: 96), Hölderlin possessed an edition of Cicero's collected works; furthermore, his attendance of Flatt's lectures on that work in the Tübingen *Stift* is recorded in the 'Magisterium' notice of September 1790 (MA, III, 574). Note also that the report was included in Hederich's widely-consulted mythological lexicon: Benjamin Hederich, *Gründliches mythologisches Lexikon*, rev. by Johann Joachim Schwaben (Leipzig: 1770), s.v. Saturnus, cols. 2163–64.

cycle, imposing a different order that might be identified with the reason or will of Zeus.

If Hölderlin employs the Latin versions of the gods' names in the title to his ode, that may be because he is concerned to emphasise the peaceful aspects of the older god, in contrast to the ferocious reputation of Cronus (who is nonetheless evoked in Hölderlin's final stanza).[19] The Latin name is also used, somewhat anachronistically, in the first version of Hölderlin's *Empedocles* drama: as he prepares to hurl himself into the crater of Etna, Empedocles cries 'Jupiter Befreier!' [Jupiter Liberator!]. Those were also the dying words attributed to the Roman Stoic philosopher Seneca — a connection which is not without interest in the present context.[20] In the ode Jupiter is identified with Art, that is to say culture in its widest sense, including reason, law and language; Saturn with the Nature that precedes Art, but which also forms the basis for the latter. It also seems clear that, for Hölderlin, it is Zeus who imposes the iron law of temporal succession that contrasts with the peaceful reign of Cronus. All this has been explained frequently in the commentaries to the ode.[21] Furthermore, Szondi has suggested that a related distinction is drawn in the hymn 'Friedensfeier' [Celebration of Peace] between '[d]er stille Gott der Zeit' [the quiet god of Time] and the god of 'historical' Time, for whom Hölderlin uses the epithet 'Herr der Zeit' [Lord of Time].[22]

At first sight, Hölderlin's ode may appear to be a trenchant critique of the sovereignty of Zeus, and a plea for the rights of the older god. But as several commentators have seen, the ultimate message of the poem is more balanced, giving each of the two divine powers its due.[23] And it would be surprising if it were otherwise. The ode is contemporary with his elaboration of his theory of the 'Wechsel der Töne' [alternation of tones], and the idea that the life of a poem consists in the constant alternation or modulation of its elements is one of Hölderlin's basic insights. It is revealing that, in the manuscript sources, the poem is found next to the poetological tables in which Hölderlin gave an algebraic formulation of that theory, which is itself based on an opposition between the unexpressed 'Grundton' [basic tone] of a poem and its articulated 'Kunstkarakter' [art-character]. The element of change and transformation — 'Wechsel' and 'Wandel' — is just as essential to Hölderlin's poetics as the all-encompassing unity of the 'One and All'; and both elements can be traced to the Stoic conceptions of a unified cosmos ruled by divine providence, which (at least for us) is subject to the vicissitudes of time. This is the lot of human kind as dispensed by Zeus: unceasing change under divine law.[24]

---

19   Cf. Gaier 1996: 129–30; Honold 2005: 103–04; Vöhler 1993a: 425.
20   MA, I, 833, l. 1768; see Franz 1991.
21   See e.g. Schmidt in KA, I, 755–56; Binder 1963: 110–11.
22   Szondi 1975: 394: see MA, I, 364, ll. 89, 79; Hamb, 529. See also the ode 'Der Zeitgeist' (MA, I, 228; OE, 57).
23   See especially Ryan 1973: 74–75; and cf. Raulet 1996; Bothe 1998: 233–34.
24   Cf. Schmidt 1996: 36–37, referring to the concept of unceasing change in Seneca and Marcus Aurelius; and see Ryan 1960: 95, n. 57, 214–16. On the Stoic concept of time see further section 3 below; and on the *Wechsel der Töne* see Chapter 3.

One feature of 'Natur und Kunst' should be evident from the outset: the ode, as much as Cleanthes' hymn, is addressed directly to Zeus. But unlike Cleanthes, Hölderlin does not offer up a simple song of praise; in his case, praise of Zeus depends upon the fulfilment of a prior condition. Hölderlin will acknowledge the wisdom of Zeus, but only if Zeus grants him in return the right to sing of Cronus, the deposed god of a vanished golden age. And to the extent that such wisdom corresponds to the 'right reason' of the Stoics, Hölderlin's reception of a philosophical hymn will become a poetological dialogue with philosophy.

2. From Cleanthes' Hymn to Hölderlin's Ode

In Long and Sedley's translation the hymn begins as follows (and in this section certain terms will be italicized for the purpose of comparison):

> *Most majestic* [κύδιστ'] of *immortals, many-titled* [πολυώνυμε], *ever omnipotent Zeus*, prime mover of nature, who *with your law* [νόμου μέτα] steer all things, hail to you.[25]

It is also useful to compare the eloquent German version of Wilamowitz, which begins:

> *Höchster* der *Unsterblichen*,
> *viele Namen* nennen dich,
>   ewig *allmächtiger Zeus*,
> dich, den Urquell alles Werdens,
> der nach *ewigen Gesetzen*
>   *herrschest* im All, ich grüße dich, *Zeus*.[26]

Like Cleanthes' hymn, Hölderlin's ode begins with a direct address to Jupiter (or Zeus) as supreme lawgiver:

> Du *waltest hoch* am Tag' und es blühet *dein*
>   *Gesez*, du hältst die Waage, *Saturnus Sohn*!
>   Und theilst die Loos' und ruhest froh im
>   *Ruhm* der *unsterblichen Herrscherkünste*.
>
> [*High up* in the day *you govern*, and *your law* flourishes
>   You hold the scales of judgment, O *Saturn's son*,
>   Hand out our lots and well-contented
>   Rest on the *fame* of *immortal kingship*.] (trans. modified)

Thus the note of praise for an immortal god who is most 'high', 'majestic' or 'famous' — all these are possible translations of Cleanthes' opening κύδιστ[ος] — is sounded from the beginning in Hölderlin's ode. For both authors, Zeus is declared

---

25 Long and Sedley divide the hymn into four sections, corresponding to lines (1) 1 to 6, (2) 7 to 14, (3) 15 to 31, and (4) 32 to 39 of the Greek original. In what follows line-number references to Hölderlin's ode correspond to the six-stanza version; the longer version includes an additional four-line stanza after line 16. The ode is cited in Hamburger's translation.
26 Wilamowitz-Moellendorff 1925: 325–27 (p. 325). See also the German prose translations by Steinmetz (1994: 577–78), and Zuntz (2005: 32–33).

to be a supreme god who governs the universe by means of his 'law'.[27] However, by addressing Jupiter as 'Saturn's son' Hölderlin already hints that his praise may be less absolute; and it may also be significant that (with 'hoch') he avoids Cleanthes' use of the superlative. As for the image of a 'many-titled' god, this is present by converse implication in ll. 11–12 of the ode, which regarding Saturn observe that no mortal 'ihn [...] mit Nahmen nannte' [named him with names] (trans. modified). Here — especially if one follows Reitani in construing 'Nahmen' as plural (TL, 799) — the language is close to the Wilamowitz version of the hymn ('viele Namen nennen dich'). The ode (ll. 15–16) accordingly demands that Zeus grant the poet the right to 'name' Cronus before 'all others' [vor Allen, | [...] nenne].

In his final stanza Hölderlin promises to acknowledge Zeus, provided only that certain conditions are fulfilled:

> *Dann hör' ich dich*, Kronion! und *kenne dich*,
> Den weisen Meister, welcher, wie wir, *ein Sohn*
>   *Der Zeit, Geseze giebt* und, was die
>   Heilige Dämmerung birgt, verkündet.
>
> [*I'll know you then*, Kronion! and *hear you then*,
> The wise master who, like ourselves, a *son*
>   *Of Time, gives laws*, and uncovers
>   That which lies hidden in holy twilight.]
> (ll. 21–24; trans. modified)

'Kronion' (as in Κρονίων or 'son of Cronus') echoes the epithet 'Saturnus Sohn' in l. 2 and confirms the identity of Saturn and Cronus, Jupiter and Zeus. At the end of his hymn, Cleanthes too reaffirms his intention to honour Zeus; but here also this will be possible only if a prior condition is fulfilled:

> so that *by winning honour we may repay you with honour* for ever *singing* [ὑμνοῦντες] of your works, as it befits a *mortal* [θνητὸν] to do. For neither mortals nor gods have any greater privilege than this: *to sing* for ever in righteousness [ἐν δίκῃ ὑμνεῖν] of the universal *law* [νόμον]. (ll. 36–39; trans. modified)

Hence both poems begin by singing the praise of Zeus, and end by reaffirming that praise, and in each case single out his *majesty, power* and *law*.[28] In both cases, too, that reaffirmation is made subject to a condition. For Cleanthes, the singer will be able to praise Zeus when, by forsaking the example of 'the bad among mortal men, the wretched' (ll. 22–23), he has achieved the power of judgment:

> [D]evoid of intelligence, they rush into this evil or that [...]. Scatter this from our soul, Father. Let us achieve the power of judgment by trusting in which you steer all things with justice [δίκης], so that by winning honour [...]. (ll. 26, 34–36)

---

[27] Long and Sedley's 'with your law' is closer to Hölderlin's 'dein | Gesez', and arguably to the original, than Wilamowitz's 'nach ewigen Gesetzen' (as is Steinmetz's 'mit deinem Gesetz'). Similarly Zuntz's 'mit dem Gesetz' conveys the instrumental sense of νόμου μέτα: 'with' (and not merely 'in accordance with') the law. On κύδιστος as 'most famous', cf. Zuntz's 'Berühmtester der Unsterblichen' with Hölderlin's 'im | Ruhm' (l. 4), and see Brill, s.v. κυδρός, A.

[28] The significance, for Hölderlin, of the association of the 'law' (*nomos*) of the Stoic Zeus with 'righteousness' or 'justice' (*dikē*) is explored in Chapter 6.4 below.

It is true that in Hölderlin the condition is startlingly different. According to his fourth stanza (ll. 13–16), the poet will only acknowledge Zeus if Zeus, in turn, acknowledges the right of his deposed father Cronus:

> Herab denn oder schäme des Danks dich nicht!
>   Und willst du bleiben, diene dem Aelteren,
>   Und gönn' es ihm, dass ihn vor Allen,
>   Göttern und Menschen, der *Sänger* nenne!
>
> [So down with you! Or cease to withhold your thanks!
>   And if you'll stay, defer to the older god
>   And grant him that above all others,
>   Gods and mortals, the *singer* name him!] (trans. modified)

This is of course a reversal of the position in the hymn. For Cleanthes, we win the ability — or the right — to praise Zeus, by putting aside error and achieving the power of judgment: 'so that by winning honour we may repay you with honour'. For Hölderlin, it is Zeus who wins the right to be acknowledged, by granting Cronus his due and allowing the poet to name the older god: 'I'll know you then, Kronion!' Zeus has to become deserving of praise, just as the poet has to become able to praise.[29] By the end of the ode, the reversal is complete: poet and god now stand side by side, embraced in a puzzling formula that is made to apply to them both. Each is said to be 'ein Sohn | Der Zeit' [a son | Of Time]. As applied to the poet, that too might correspond to the words of the hymn ('for ever singing of your works, as [...] befits a *mortal*'). Mortals are perhaps sons and daughters of Time. But how can the formula apply to immortal Zeus?

Before returning to that question, it will be useful to note some further points of comparison between Hölderlin's poetological ode and Cleanthes' Stoic hymn. The stanza omitted in the shorter version of the ode explains why Jupiter should pay homage to Saturn. This is because all power, including his, ultimately derives from Saturn's peaceful realm, an argument that is made concrete in the image of the thunderbolt: 'Denn, wie aus dem Gewölke dein Bliz, so kommt | Von ihm, was dein ist' [For as from clouds your lightning, from him has come | What is yours] (trans. modified). The thunderbolt is of course a traditional attribute of Zeus, and it also plays a prominent role in the hymn. For Cleanthes, as for Heraclitus, it is through the thunderbolt that 'all the works of nature are accomplished'; and with it Zeus directs 'universal reason' (ll. 11–12).[30] Accordingly the thunderbolt is an

---

29 The form of both hymn and ode can be compared to the 'threefold structure' of the traditional cult hymn, as described by Thom — namely 'Invocation' (the opening address to the god); 'Argument' (description of the attributes of the god that are worthy of praise); and concluding 'Prayer' (2005: 8). However, the Argument of the ode includes a description of Zeus' mistreatment of Cronus, and the Prayer is conditional on a demand to allow the older god to be named — only then bestowing praise on Zeus 'the wise master'.

30 On fire and the thunderbolt in Heraclitus, see Kahn 1979: 271–76. This passage is included as a 'Stoic appropriation' of Heraclitus in EGP, III, 258–59 (R52). But note that there is a lacuna in the manuscript here. Laks and Most (with Stephanus) read ἐρρίγασιν [shudder] rather than Long and Sedley's ἔργα βέβηκεν [works accomplished]; Zuntz has τελεῖται (translated as 'vollendet'); Thom (2005: 83) prefers νέμεται, which he renders 'guided'.

image of the god's power, in particular his power to create order: for Zeus 'know[s] how to make things crooked straight and to order things disorderly' (ll. 18–19). Cleanthes then refers to Zeus 'of the dark clouds and gleaming thunderbolt' (l. 32) — the image that Hölderlin uses to convey the emergence of Jupiter's reason and law from the twilight realm of Saturn. But for Hölderlin the coexistence of cloud and thunderbolt becomes a genealogy of Zeus' power, which can now be seen to issue from the obscure realm of Cronus.

Then there is the idea that poet and god are from a common stock. Thus the opening lines of the hymn, cited above, continue: 'For it is proper for any mortal to address you: we are your offspring' (l. 4).[31] And Zeus is later described as 'father' [πάτερ] (l. 34). As we have already seen, Hölderlin's final stanza itself declares a kind of kinship between the poet and Zeus:

> [...] welcher, wie wir, ein Sohn
>   Der Zeit, Geseze giebt und, was die
>   Heilige Dämmerung birgt, verkündet.

It is that comparison which gives rise to certain difficulties, including the one already noted concerning the formula 'Sohn | Der Zeit'. The first point to note is an ambiguity in the scope of the comparison. It is normally construed as one between poet and god as respective 'son[s] of Time' (raising the question of the sense to be given to such a comparison). As argued in Chapter 1.4, however, it can also be read as extending further — namely as including the attribute of law-giving (and by extension of uncovering what 'lies hidden').[32] The comparison of the poet to a lawgiver is not inappropriate. Poets are expressly described as such in the ode 'An unsre großen Dichter' [To Our Great Poets].[33] And conversely, in an earlier phase of 'Natur und Kunst', Hölderlin describes Zeus as '[der] Künstler Kronion | Der alles scheidet und ordnet' [Kronion the artist | who divides and orders everything], before replacing 'artist' with 'master' as in the last stanza of the final version (FHA, IV, 390). The title of the ode is of course itself relevant: as the god who brings order and law, Jupiter (like the poet) belongs to the realm of 'Kunst'. And it is clear that the concept of a poetic 'law' is central to Hölderlin's poetics, both in the first Homburg period and in the later Sophocles commentary.[34] But that also raises the question of what kind of laws may be intended. If the poet is construed as a lawgiver, the

---

31 Here Long and Sedley emend ἐκ σοῦ γὰρ γένος ἐσμὲν to read [...] γενόμεσθα, but as Thom observes either reading can be translated 'we have our origin in you' (2005: 64).

32 The ambiguity tends to be elided by translators, as in Hamburger: 'who, like ourselves, a son | Of Time, gives laws *to us*' (Hamb, 225, emphasis added). See also Rovini, in Hölderlin, *Œuvres* (Paris: Gallimard, 1967): 'fils comme nous | Du Temps, toi le législateur' (p. 777); and Reitani: 'che, figlio, come noi, | Del tempo, dai le leggi' (TL, 803). Note how both of the latter transpose the word-order of the original: '[1] wie wir, [2] ein Sohn | Der Zeit, Geseze giebt'. But for the other alternative, see Staiger 1961: 36.

33 'O wekt, ihr Dichter! [...] | [...] gebt die Geseze' [Wake them, O poets! [...] | [...] hand down the laws] (MA, I, 197, ll. 5–6; OE, 35). The poem is a two-stanza precursor to the great poetological ode 'Dichterberuf' [The Poet's Calling] (MA, I, 329–31; OE, 103–07). On the poet as lawgiver cf. Tang 2007.

34 See Chapter 3 below (for the Homburg period), and Chapter 4.1 (for the *Sophokles-Anmerkungen*).

laws in question must differ from the bright commandments of the Stoic god. They must also share in the character of Saturn's twilight realm, as exemplified in the very ambiguity of these lines. The peculiar resources of poetic language enable the poet to 'name' the silent world of Saturn, and — in this thoroughly poetological ode — to reflect upon that act of naming.

As we also saw in Chapter 1.4, there is a second (and more obvious) ambiguity in the final stanza, this time lexical rather than syntactic. Thus the term '[die] Zeit' in line 23 is semantically ambiguous. Both the poet and the god are said to be 'a son of Time'. If we are Time's children, this is presumably in the sense of being mortal; and as already noted, in that sense Hölderlin echoes Cleanthes: 'for ever singing of your works, as it befits a *mortal* to do' (ll. 37–38). On the other hand, if Zeus is a 'son of Time', this is evidently in a different sense — that presumably of being the son of Cronus, *Kronos* being identified with *khronos* in accordance with the false etymology. When 'die Zeit' is taken in the first sense, it is Zeus who is the god of Time. For it is Zeus who presides over 'die wandelnde Zeit' [changing Time], in l. 20 of the ode, and who dispenses to mortals their allotted fate: '[du] theilst die Loos" (l. 3).[35] This is the Zeus of Cleanthes' ordering thunderbolt, 'die | Mahnende Flamme des Zeitengottes' [the god of Time's admonishing flame] ('An Eduard', MA, I, 287, ll. 35–36).

It is only by virtue of an ambiguity, therefore, that god and mortal poet can both be described as 'sons of Time'. And as in the case of the syntactic ambiguity already noted, such a technique is a privilege of poetry and its peculiarly ambivalent 'law'. In the end, Hölderlin can claim a closer affinity of god and mortal poet than any asserted by Cleanthes. Both for him are legislators, even if each brings a different kind of order to a previously hidden realm. By the end of the ode, the Stoic god can be addressed as equal rather than simply as benevolent father.

3. The Stoic Theory of Time

As we have seen, the most straightforward explanation of the formula 'ein Sohn der Zeit' is in terms of the equation of *Kronos* with *khronos*.[36] We saw too that the formula can be taken in a different sense, one in which it applies to mortals rather than to Zeus. It is now Zeus, not Cronus, who is the god of Time, and 'die Zeit' accordingly has a different meaning — namely that of 'wandelnde Zeit'. The relationship between those species of Time is expressed in the evocative image of the penultimate stanza: 'Und war in ihrer Wiege mir, in | Wonne die wandelnde Zeit entschlafen' [And in its cradle changing Time has, for me | Blissfully fallen

---

35 In the longer version of the ode, l. 20 (now l. 24) reads 'die wechselnde Zeit'. Cf. the closely-related 'flüchtig[e] Zeit' [fleeting time] of the ode 'Dichtermuth', there expressly linked to mortality: 'die Vergänglichen' [the transient ones] (MA, I, 284, l. 18; OE, 113). On fate as the 'reason' or 'rationale' of Zeus see LS 55R, where (as already noted in Chapter 1.4) τῇ εἱμαρμένῃ literally means 'the lot assigned by fate'.

36 A similar explanation is accepted by Schmidt in KA, I, 758–59, referring to the Neoplatonic tradition; see similarly Schmidt 2003: 89, and cf. Gaier 1996: 129. By contrast, Staiger is insistent that no such equation is intended: 'Im Gegenteil!' (1961: 27); and see similarly Mögel 1994: 137.

asleep] (ll. 19–20, trans. modified). Where changing Time has fallen asleep, we are left with a Time which is older than that of Zeus, and which provides as it were the cradle for the latter.[37] The clue is in the rocking rhythm of the cradle. Rather than hurrying over the present moment, and turning the present into a fleeting instant, Time is now associated with the rhythm of natural periods and seasons. And if for Hölderlin Zeus is the god of a temporal order that belongs to the realm of language, law and conscious reflection ('Kunst'), the Time of Cronus belongs to the natural order of a corporeal realm ('Natur'). But in what sense exactly does it so belong? And is there a Stoic analogue for such a distinction?

The Stoic conception of time is one of the most remarkable, if also most difficult, features of that philosophy. The concept plays a prominent role in the *Meditations* of the later Stoic Marcus Aurelius, a work that will have been an important source for Hölderlin.[38] Although Marcus' discussion of these matters is relatively free from technicalities, it will still be useful to look at the Stoic ontology that apparently underlies it: namely the distinction between the 'corporeal' and the 'incorporeal'.[39] However, a note of caution must be sounded at the outset. The sources for early Stoic doctrine are fragmentary or indirect, and sometimes hard to reconcile with one another. Ancient Stoicism spanned the Greek and Roman worlds, and several centuries separate the founder of the school, Zeno of Citium (332–262 BCE), from Marcus himself (121–80 CE). And if the interpretation of the Stoic doctrine of the incorporeal is much disputed, that is particularly the case with their concept of incorporeal time.

For the Stoics, only physical body was fully real. But there were in addition at least four species of incorporeals (*asōmata*). These, while not independently existing, were nonetheless to be classified as 'something': the void; place; time; and the *lekton* (corresponding roughly speaking to the meaning of a linguistic expression). This may seem at first to be a disparate collection of things; but there also appear to be connections between them. Take for instance 'the void' and 'place' (LS 49A). For the Stoics the physical cosmos was a finite plenum surrounded by the void (empty space). Thus space is divided into parts that are occupied by body ('places'), and the infinite remainder that is unoccupied ('the void'). Time too is infinite, stretching endlessly back into the past, or forward into the future. It is also, like space, infinitely divisible, so that any present interval can be further subdivided into a portion that is past, and one that is still to come, separated by an extensionless

---

37 See also 'An Eduard' (MA, I, 286–87, ll. 29–36), where the peace of nature is linked to the wisdom of an old lullaby ('die Weisheit | Singt dir den alten Wiegengesang'), and contrasted with the admonishing thunderbolt of the god of Time. As noted in Chapter 1.4, the two odes (together with 'Dichtermuth') are closely related in Hölderlin's fair copy: see Figure 1.1.

38 See Chapter 1.4 above. As in that chapter, the *Meditations* will be cited according to book and chapter number, including any further sub-divisions given by Dalfen (rather than the broader sub-divisions in Hammond's translation). See *Ad se ipsum* [Τῶν εἰς ἑαυτόν], ed. by Joachim Dalfen, 2nd edn (Leipzig: Teubner, 1987); and *Meditations*, trans. by Martin Hammond (London: Penguin Books, 2006). Hölderlin will also have been familiar with reports of Stoic doctrine given for example by Cicero, Plutarch and Diogenes Laertius.

39 On the Stoic doctrine of 'incorporeals', see LS, I, 162–65; Bréhier 1970; Brunschwig 1994; de Harven 2012; and Totschnig 2013.

point. But just as a body can occupy a part of space, and thereby delineate a 'place' within the infinite incorporeal continuum, so too it seems that a physical process can delineate a finite interval of time. In so far as it is related to such an ongoing process or event, a region of the 'present' can be regarded as forming a distinct part of infinite time. Such a process may have a greater or lesser extent. For the Stoics the world both begins and ends in a cosmic conflagration, and the period between such conflagrations can accordingly be said to be the largest possible 'present'.[40]

Among the most important testimonies of the doctrine is the following from the anthology of Stobaeus (LS 51B):

> Chrysippus said time is the dimension [διάστημα] of motion according to which the measure of speed and slowness is spoken of; or the dimension [διάστημα] accompanying the world's motion.[41] And (he says) every single thing moves and exists [εἶναι] in accordance with time; *unless time is spoken of in two senses [διττὸς λέγεται ὁ χρόνος], just as the earth, the sea and the void: the whole or its parts.*[42] Just as the void in its totality is infinite in every respect, so time in its totality is infinite on either side. For both the past and the future are infinite. He says most clearly that no time is wholly present. For since continuous things are infinitely divisible, on the basis of this division every time too is infinitely divisible. Consequently no time is present exactly, but it is broadly said to be so. He also says that only the present belongs [ὑπάρχειν]; the past and the future subsist [ὑφεστάναι], but belong in no way, just as predicates which are (actual) attributes are said to belong, for instance, walking around belongs to me when I am walking around, but it does not belong when I am lying down or sitting.

As well as establishing a connection between incorporeal time and infinite space, the passage also brings in the remaining category of incorporeal. For the 'predicates' mentioned would be examples of the *lekton*, which again can be regarded from two perspectives: either as applying or 'belonging' to an existing body (when

---

40 On the extent of the 'present' as being relative to the corporeal process that occupies it, see Schofield 1988: 357. There may appear to be an argument against the comparison of infinite time with the infinite void that surrounds the physical cosmos (cf. Brunschwig 1994: 141). For although the cosmic cycle was finite in extent for the Stoics, they also envisaged a series of endlessly repeating cycles, beginning anew after each conflagration — the famous doctrine of the 'eternal return'. But to the extent that each cycle is identical with the preceding one, and therefore distinguished only by its position in incorporeal time, in physical terms there may be said to be only one such cycle. See LS, I, 310–13, and Totschnig 2013: 137.

41 Note that διάστημα can be translated as 'interval' rather than 'dimension', which would be more consistent with the parallel theory of 'void' and 'place': cf. LS 49B, and for that parallel see also LS 49A ('Just as anything corporeal is finite, so the incorporeal is infinite, for time and void are infinite'). For a similar reason, de Harven uses 'extension' (2012: 33, n. 161, and passim).

42 Oddly the second part of the sentence, given here in italics, is omitted from Long and Sedley's translation, although the full Greek text is at LS, II, 301, ll. 4–5. The beginning phrase εἰ μὴ ἄρα is translated by Goldschmidt as '[t]outefois' (1977: 31), which is perhaps too strong: cf. Brill, s.v. ἄρα, C ('unless perhaps'), although that in turn may here be too weak; cf. Plato, *Apology*, 38b, in *Euthyphro* etc., ed. and trans. by Chris Emlyn-Jones and William Preddy, LCL 36 (Cambridge, MA: Harvard University Press, 2017), pp. 180–81. The phrase may be a qualification of the definition of time as the interval of movement, suggesting that it applies to the parts but not the infinite extent of time: for all movement, like body itself, is finite (see notes 40 and 41 above). For the discussion below, note that the same elision is made by Sellars (2007: 185).

I am walking), or as not so belonging (when I am lying down or sitting). The terminology here is of some significance. The passage suggests that 'time' can be considered from two points of view: as simply a past or a future, which only 'subsist' (*huphestanai*); and that of a present which 'belongs' (*huparkhein*). Both terms can be distinguished from the more usual term for 'exist' (*einai*), which would apply only to corporeal things. Thus for the Stoics only a corporeal thing has full reality, or is an 'existent' (*on*). Incorporeals are merely 'something' (*ti*). But an incorporeal may do more than merely 'subsist' as a possible object of thought, when considered in relation to an underlying corporeal reality.[43]

The fullest treatment of the Stoic conception of time must still be that of Victor Goldschmidt (1977), who also argues for its central place in Stoic ethics (in particular those of Marcus Aurelius). His starting-point is the text that has just been cited, with its suggestion — elided in the Long and Sedley translation — that time is, or at least may be, spoken of in two senses. Goldschmidt suggests that two distinct notions of time can indeed be found in Stoicism, one corresponding to the potentially infinite time of past and future, and one to a finite moment or interval corresponding to the 'present'. Thus the first notion would be that of an infinite (and infinitely subdivisible) temporal continuum, in which the present is merely a vanishing instant: time as a 'pure' incorporeal. But the second is that of a present which has a derivative degree of reality of the kind that has just been discussed (*huparkhein*).[44] Goldschmidt's thesis has been disputed, in particular by John Sellars who points out that the original founders of Stoicism did not employ two distinct terms for those allegedly different notions (2007: 194).

For Goldschmidt the question is no doubt one of substance rather than terminology; but he suggests that the distinction is marked later, and by none other than Marcus Aurelius. Thus he observes that Marcus reserves the term *aiōn* for the boundless flux of infinite time; and one could add, conversely, that Marcus tends to use *khronos* when referring either to present time or time as a finite interval.[45] *Aiōn* (in the sense of time as a potentially infinite whole) would be a pure incorporeal, while *khronos* (in the sense of a finite part) could amount to something more. It is true that *khronos* in the *Meditations* is not used with the same consistency as *aiōn*; but that is hardly surprising given that it is the ordinary Greek word for 'time'. For Sellars, on the other hand, 'a careful reading [...] makes clear that Marcus uses neither term in any technical sense to refer to a specific conception of time' (2007: 195).

It is true also that the *Meditations* is not a technical metaphysical treatise, and that Marcus is concerned above all with the moral (and indeed practical) implications

---

43   The term *huparkhein* in this context can also be rendered as 'obtain', as suggested by Schofield (1988: 354); or even as 'being present' or 'being there' (M. Frede 1994: 117), which brings out still more clearly the relation with the problem of time.

44   Although Goldschmidt translates *huparkhein* as 'existe', and at one point says that only infinite time is 'incorporel' (1977: 40), it is clear that he distinguishes infinite time as a 'pure' incorporeal, from a present that is also incorporeal, but derives a certain degree of reality from the corporeal process that occupies it (1977: 40–41).

45   See Goldschmidt 1977: 39, noting that 'eternity' is among the ordinary meanings of *aiōn*. To which one can add that 'period' or 'duration' are among the ordinary senses of *khronos*: see Brill, s.vv. αἰών, C ('infinite or indefinite period of time, eternity'); χρόνος, 1.B.

of Stoic doctrine. That raises a question that is analogous to the one we have been concerned with in the case of Hölderlin: namely the relation between a philosophical concept or doctrine, and a work belonging to a different genre in which it may be reflected. As we saw in Chapter 1.4, there is even a sense in which Marcus was himself composing a literary work, albeit one that is closely informed by the teachings of the Stoic philosophy. It is in that spirit, therefore, that I propose to pursue Goldschmidt's thesis a little way further. As regards *aiōn* at least, it seems possible to argue that a particular conception of time is being invoked, one that corresponds to its potential infinity. Here time is considered as the locus of ceaseless change, in which the present moment is lost as in an abyss. Both the infinite extent and the infinite divisibility of *aiōn* seem to be relevant, as each tends to annihilate the significance of the present. So for example in *Meditations* 6.36.1: 'The whole of present time [πᾶν τὸ ἐνεστὼς τοῦ χρόνου] is a pin-prick of eternity [τοῦ αἰῶνος]. All things are tiny, quickly changed, evanescent'. Note here the contrasting uses of *khronos* and *aiōn*, and the thought that any present time is an instant in comparison with the latter. Elsewhere in the *Meditations aiōn* is used, almost invariably, in a similar sense: either as a time that is literally infinite, or as a stretch of past or future time extending beyond, and eclipsing, the present.[46] Such passages can readily be seen as a source for Hölderlin's image of a 'fleeting', 'changing' or 'tearing' time, in 'Natur und Kunst' and elsewhere.[47] For it is from the point of view of *aiōn* that the present moment is reduced to nothing, so soon is it swallowed up by endless time. But is there another perspective from which the present has a greater degree of reality?

As far as *khronos* is concerned, it is true that Marcus' usage is less consistent: as already noted, the term is after all the ordinary word for 'time'. Still, in a clear

---

46 In the following examples, I have italicized 'time' and 'eternity' where they correspond (in Hammond's translation) to *aiōn*. — 2.12.1: 'all things quickly vanish, our bodies themselves lost in the physical world, the memories of them lost in *time*'; 4.3.7: 'Look at the speed of universal oblivion, the gulf of immeasurable *time* both before and after'; 4.21.1–2: 'from everlasting [ἐξ ἀϊδίου] [...] over the same *eternity*' (trans. modified); 4.43: '*time* is a violent stream. As soon as one thing comes into sight, it is swept past'; 4.50.5: 'Look behind you at the huge gulf of *time*, and another infinity [ἄπειρον] ahead'; 5.24: 'think of the whole of *time*, in which you have been assigned a brief and fleeting moment'; 5.32.2: 'cycles through all *eternity*'; 6.59.2: 'How quickly *time* will cover everything'; 7.10: 'the memory of everything is rapidly buried in *eternity*'; 7.19.2: 'How many [...] has *eternity* already swallowed?'; 7.70.1: 'throughout all the length of *eternity*'; 9.28.1: 'The recurrent cycles of the universe are the same [...] from *eternity* to *eternity*'; 9.32.2: 'contemplating the eternity of *time*' [τὸν ἀΐδιον αἰῶνα] [...] how brief the gap from birth to dissolution'; 9.35.1: 'Similar things have happened from *time everlasting* [ἐξ αἰῶνος]'; 10.5 'Whatever happens to you was being prepared for you from *everlasting* [ἐξ αἰῶνος]'; 11.1.3: 'the infinity of *time*' (note also the reference to the universe's 'surrounding void'); 12.7: 'the shortness of life; the immensity of *time* future and past'; 12.32.1: 'What a tiny part of the boundless abyss of *time* has been allotted to each of us'. For 6.15.1 and 10.17, where both terms are used, see note 48 below; and for 6.36.1 see main text above.

47 Apart from 'Natur und Kunst' itself, see as already noted 'Dichtermuth' ('in flüchtiger Zeit'); 'Mein Eigentum' ('die mächtige Zeit | Die Wandelbare': MA, I, 238, ll. 46–47); 'Der Archipelagus' ('das Wechseln | Und das Werden [...] die reißende Zeit': MA, I, 304, ll. 292–93). See also AO [2.3], '[die] reißend[e] Zeit' (MA, II, 312), and compare Wittstock's translation of *Meditations* 4.43: 'Die Zeit ist ein Fluß, ein ungestümer Strom, der alles fortreißt' (1949: 54). There the connection with Heraclitus seems evident, and the latter is expressly cited for other purposes in 4.46.

majority of cases it is used by Marcus to denote a limited period — whether the span of a human life, a brief moment within it, or a larger historical epoch. It is true that this is not an invariable rule, and in particular such a meaning can be displaced when the term is qualified by other expressions. Nonetheless, there are relatively few instances in which *khronos* and *aiōn* are used interchangeably.[48]

It seems difficult to deny that some kind of distinction is being drawn between two notions of time, even if the extent to which these are two distinct metaphysical conceptions can perhaps be disputed. Recall again the report of Chrysippus (LS 51B), with its suggestion that 'time' may be spoken of 'in two senses'. Those two senses might relate to two modes of temporal existence mentioned later in the report: a present that can 'belong' (*huparkhein*) to a corporeal process, the extent of which will be limited to the duration of that process; and a potentially unlimited past or future that can only 'subsist' (*huphestanai*). A recent commentary to the *Meditations* refers to this as 'the idea that the present is radically different in conceptual status from the future and the past', and observes (with appropriate caution) that both Seneca and Marcus Aurelius 'seem to build on this point' (Gill 2013: 99).

For Sellars the only relevant difference in Marcus is 'between the *khronos* of a human life and the *aiōn* of the cosmos', and its function 'is merely to draw a contrast between the limited amount of time allotted to each human life and the infinite time of which it is an insignificant part' (2007: 196). That is indeed the first step in Marcus' analysis; but it surely represents only one half of his argument. If a life depended solely upon its duration or extent, then it would indeed be insignificant when measured against the twin immensities of time and space. But if Marcus dwells frequently on the transience of things (as in 6.15), that does not prevent him from going on to ask what may nonetheless be of value (6.16). Whatever that is will not depend upon the extent of the time available, but on an activity that occupies the present (cf. 6.32.3). And Hadot has identified the need to 'delimit' or 'circumscribe' such a present as one of the central themes of the *Meditations*:

> This indissoluble link between the delimitation of the self and the delimitation of the present moment is extremely significant. It is only when I am active, either within myself or upon the outside world, that I am truly myself and at liberty; and it is only in the present moment that I can be active.[49]

---

48 As Sellars points out (2007: 195) both 2.14.5 and 10.31.3 refer to an 'infinity of time' [τῷ ἀπείρῳ χρόνῳ]; but there the qualification might be said to remove the normal presumption that *khronos* denotes a limited stretch of time (see also 7.35, although this is a citation of Plato). And contrast the following, where I have italicized the expression that translates *khronos*. — 1.17.4: 'the proper *time* [for a first experience]'; 2.4.2: 'a limit circumscribed to your *time*'; 2.17.1: 'In man's life his *time* is a mere instant'; 3.7.3: '[to live] for a longer or a shorter *time*'; 3.11.3: 'how *long* [πόσον χρόνον] [...] will it last?'; 4.6.2: 'in a very brief *time*'; 4.32.3: 'the histories of other *eras* [ἄλλας ἐπιγραφὰς χρόνων]'. And see similarly 4.48.4; 6.18.1; 6.23.2; 6.25; 6.36.1; 6.49; 7.29.3; 7.46 (twice); 8.5.1; 8.7.2; 8.11; 8.44.1; 9.25; 10.1.2; 12.18; 12.35. It is true that there are some exceptions, as well as neutral or ambiguous cases, e.g. 5.10.5; 6.15.1 (where both terms are used); 9.14; 12.3.4. Both are also used in 10.17, but note how this contrasts the 'whole of time' [τοῦ ὅλου αἰῶνος] with a measurement 'on the scale of time' [πρὸς χρόνον]. — In a clear majority of cases *khronos* refers to a brief instant, a limited interval or a circumscribed present.

49 Hadot 1998: 119, and see also pp. 120, 131–37 and 196. On the need to attend only to the present, see e.g. *Meditations* 12.3.4.

Similarly Goldschmidt identifies in Stoicism an imperative to attend to the exigencies of the present moment. If passion enslaves us to the unreal — that is to say purely incorporeal — time of the past or the future, moral action inhabits the present: 'le seul temps réel, le présent, [...] le seul où puisse se placer l'initiative morale' [the only real time, the present [...] the only one in which moral initiative can be situated].[50] On this view, Marcus dwells upon the potential immensity of past and future time, the better to prepare us to seize the present: 'leave all the past behind, entrust the future to Providence, and direct the present solely to reverence and justice' (12.1.2). Such a present has to be actively 'defined' or 'delimited', carved out of the infinite expanse of incorporeal *aiōn* by the active pursuit of Stoic philosophy: 'Stop the puppet-strings of impulse. Define [περίγραψον] the present moment of time [τοῦ χρόνου]' (7.29.2–3).[51] And within that imperative, *perigrapson*, one can find *graphein*: to 'inscribe' or 'write'.

For both Hölderlin and Marcus, therefore, there seems to be a distinction between 'fleeting' or 'changing Time', the instant that is swallowed by eternity, and a Time that is brought to rest in the present. And if, for both authors, that distinction may ultimately relate to Stoic metaphysics, the relation will be complicated in each case by their different ambitions and purposes. If we now return to Hölderlin's ode, we may recall how the ode employs the image of a rocking cradle in which 'changing Time' is lulled to sleep. It will be useful to consider other places in Hölderlin where that image is associated with an experience of the present. But we must also bear in mind the conclusions reached in Chapter 1.2 concerning the argument of *Hyperion*. We saw how, in the course of the novel, the idea of a peaceful oneness with nature gives way to that of the sanctuary created by a poetic work. Such a moment of bliss would, at best, be a prelude to the activity of poetic creation: an activity that, in the light of the preceding discussion, might be said to inscribe a present within the flux of fleeting time.

We can begin with 'Andenken' [Remembrance], where a moment of balance or repose at the March equinox is described:

> Zur Märzenzeit,
> Wenn gleich ist Nacht und Tag,
> Und über langsamen Stegen,
> Von goldenen Träumen schwer,
> Einwiegende Lüfte ziehen.

---

50 Goldschmidt 1977: 193; and see further pp. 194–210. Hadot objects that Goldschmidt sees the present as an instant rather as having extension (Hadot 1998: 137). But it might be better to say that Goldschmidt opposes the unreal instant obtained by mathematical division, from the plenitude of a 'now' given reality by the activity of a moral agent. Thus 'La décision de "délimiter l'instant présent" [7.29.3] parvient à s'opposer efficacement au flux qui emporte tout, à le stabiliser' (Goldschmidt 1977: p. 199).
51 On the two stages of Marcus' argument, respectively destructive and affirmative of the reality of the present, see Goldschmidt 1977: 196–99. The relevant distinction is not so much between 'human life' and 'the cosmos', as between a purely incorporeal time of past and future and the plenitude of a time seized in the present.

> [In the month of March,
> When night and day are equal
> And over slow footpaths,
> Heavy with golden dreams,
> Lulling breezes drift.]
> (MA, I, 474, ll. 20–24; Hamb, 577)

There 'lulling' translates 'einwiegende', which in its primary meaning connotes the rocking of an infant. One could say that the period of the equinox is a moment when night and day are temporarily brought into balance, as a cradle must be to rock the infant to sleep. And if the lengthening or shortening of the days represents the progress of 'changing Time', the equinox represents a point at which that progression is temporarily halted (while still being a moment within the temporal continuum).[52] Ulrich Gaier has made a connection between those lines of 'Andenken', and the following from 'Mnemosyne':

> Vorwärts aber und rükwärts wollen wir
> Nicht sehn. Uns wiegen lassen, wie
> Auf schwankem Kahne der See.
>
> [Forward, however, and back we will
> Not look. Be lulled and rocked as
> On a swaying skiff of the sea.]
> (MA, I, 437, ll. 15–17; Hamb, 587)

As Gaier observes, the lines recall the famous passage in Rousseau's 'Cinquième promenade' describing the sensation of plenitude in the present moment that he experienced at the Lac de Bienne (or 'Bielersee').[53] Looking neither 'forwards' nor 'backwards' therefore also means: looking neither to the future nor the past, experiencing instead the presence of nature with its rhythms and seasons. As we saw in Chapter 1.4, in 'Mein Eigentum' (another poem of the Homburg period) Hölderlin sees the sanctuary established by the poem as a refuge from the ravages of changing Time ('die mächtge Zeit | Die Wandelbare'); there too one can detect a reference to Rousseau. And on a wider scale this can apply to the sphere of world-historical events, the tearing succession of wars and revolutions. In that sense, the great hymn 'Friedensfeier' concerns not only the celebration of peace indicated in its title, but also the momentary incarnation of a different temporal order and its inscription in the act of writing.[54]

---

52 See also 'Der Rhein' [The Rhine], 'Und ausgeglichen | Ist eine Weile das Schiksaal.' [And Fate for a while | is levelled out, suspended.] (MA, I, 347, ll. 182–83; Hamb, 509). Or in Sieburth's version, 'And for a while | Fate achieves a balance' (HF, 79). Note that Hölderlin has alluded earlier to the Lake Biel (or Bienne) passage in Rousseau's *Rêveries*, discussed below ('Im Schatten des Walds | Am Bielersee', ll. 162–63).
53 Gaier 1989: 181–82, and similarly Link 1999: 40–41, 156. See Jean-Jacques Rousseau, *Les Rêveries du promeneur solitaire*, in *Œuvres complètes*, ed. by Bernard Gagnebin and Marcel Raymond, 5 vols (Paris: Gallimard, 1959–95), I (1959), 993–1099 (pp. 1043–44). A connection between the cradle reference in 'Natur und Kunst' and the Rousseau allusion in 'Mnemosyne' is also made in Bothe 1998: 232–33. And on the *Rêveries* as a 'blending of Stoic and Epicurean themes', see Brooke 2012: 200.
54 For 'Mein Eigentum', see MA, I, 237–38, ll. 41–47 (OE, 71); and on the place of Rousseau in that poem see Böschenstein 2004. On the hymn 'Friedensfeier' as the poetic analogue of a peace

However, in demanding that Jupiter acknowledge the rights of the older god, Hölderlin is not proposing a return to a golden age, one blissfully free from the vicissitudes of 'changing Time'. The poet, as legislator in the realm of 'Kunst', must pay homage to Zeus as much as to Cronus. Just as Zeus' thunderbolt brings order and illumination to a world that would otherwise be lost in darkness, the poet claims on Saturn's behalf the right to 'name' his realm (ll. 12, 16). By definition, a poem belongs to the realm of Art rather than Nature. But it can also be a sanctuary against the ravages of 'fleeting' or 'changing' Time. It is as if a Stoic imperative — to seize the present within the endless flux of *aiōn* — becomes the task of constructing the unity of the poem. And if the goal of Marcus Aurelius is to establish an 'inner citadel', a sanctuary of thought in which the philosopher can take refuge, Hölderlin sought such a sanctuary in the practice of his craft.[55]

4. Other Sources for the Ode

Returning finally to Cleanthes' hymn, we can note that it concerns a Zeus who gives laws to the entire cosmos. Only human wickedness falls outside the ambit of Zeus' ordering thunderbolt:

> With it you direct the universal reason which runs through all things [...]. No deed is done on earth, god, without your offices, nor in the divine ethereal vault of heaven, nor at sea, save what bad men do in their folly. (ll. 12–17)

The hymnist's prayer is to achieve that same 'power of judgment' by which Zeus 'steers all things with justice' (ll. 34–35). Leaving folly aside, there can be no conflict between the realms of 'Natur' and 'Kunst', and Cleanthes' praise is unqualified by any tribute to a silent, lawless domain. In what way, then, is the hymn essential for the understanding of Hölderlin's ode?

There were undoubtedly other, more contemporary, sources that might have prompted Hölderlin's treatment of the figures of Saturn and Jupiter, and his use of them as an allegory of the relation between Nature and Art. For example, in his elegy 'Der Genius' (1800) Schiller portrays genius in terms of a return to the harmony of a golden age, the resurrection of a lost unity of law and feeling.[56] A still more interesting precedent is provided by Friedrich Schlegel's 'Rede über die Mythologie' [Discourse on Mythology], also from 1800, which forms part of his 'Gespräch über die Poesie' [Dialogue on Poetry]. There Schlegel uses the myth of the dethronement of Saturn to represent the fate of Spinoza at the hand

---

treaty (and its subsequent festival) see Tang 2010: 558–64. As Tang observes, a peace festival 'happens in the present, in which the ordinary flow of time from the past to the future is broken' (2010: 560); he suggests that '[t]he sense of time evoked by the poem is the ecstatic present of the festival' while being 'inexorably caught up in the medium of writing' (2010: 562). See also Stierle 1989: 505.

55 For the theme of 'refuge' or 'sanctuary' in Hölderlin, see also the *Pindarfragment* 'Die Asyle' (MA, II, 383; AL, 338), discussed in Chapter 6.2 below.

56 'Freund, du kennst doch die goldene Zeit, es haben die Dichter | Manche Sage von ihr rührend und kindlich erzählt': Friedrich Schiller, *Sämtliche Gedichte und Balladen*, ed. by Georg Kurscheidt (Frankfurt a.M.: Insel, 2004), pp. 16–17, ll. 15–16. Note that this is a revised version of the poem of 1795 entitled 'Natur und Schule' (ibid. pp. 337–39).

of Kant and his successors. As both Reitani and Gaier have observed, Schlegel may well have been the immediate stimulus for Hölderlin's own use of the same myth.[57] Of more interest still, perhaps, is the curious expression used in the opening paragraph of that 'Rede'. For in connection with the rule of 'Kunst' over the 'Geist der Liebe' [spirit of love], Schlegel refers to something he calls: '[die] nothwendig[e] Willkühr' [the necessary arbitrariness]. The same expression occurs in one of Hölderlin's poetological essays from the same year, where it is connected with the figure of Zeus: '[die] nothwendig[e] *Willkür des Zevs*' (MA, II, 106; AL, 305). There the formula designates the principle of division of a primordial unity. Thus (for Hölderlin at least) both Jupiter and Saturn are present in Schlegel's text, representing an opposition between principles of unity ('Nature', or Spinozism) and division ('Art', or Kant's Critical Philosophy).

However, none of this explains why Hölderlin should have responded by writing a poem addressed directly to Zeus: one which both begins and ends with such an address, and which lays down the conditions under which the god can be praised. This aspect of the ode is particularly striking when one compares it with other poetological odes of this period. It is in effect the poet who is addressed in 'Ermunterung' [Exhortation] (MA, I, 278–79; Hamb, 219–21), a poem with several striking thematic correspondences with 'Natur und Kunst'; and similarly in the already-mentioned odes 'Dichtermuth' and 'Dichterberuf'. It is true that, in 'Dichterberuf', the address to the poet is followed by a veiled reference to the patron god Apollo, while the poet is compared more expressly with Bacchus.[58] But if the triumph of the latter god is indeed portrayed in the poem's opening stanza, the god himself is not directly addressed. 'Dichterberuf' is not an ode to Bacchus, or even to Apollo, in the way that 'Natur und Kunst' is so evidently an ode to Zeus.[59]

It seems that we are entitled to regard the ode as a dialogue with Cleanthes' hymn, albeit one in which its meaning is transformed. And the transformation is of course radical. By identifying Cronus as the god of Nature, and confining the law-giving of Zeus to the realm of Art, a Stoic harmony is broken. But the same operation permits the poet to recognize himself in the younger god. As with Zeus,

---

57 'Rede über die Mythologie', in *Athenaeum*, ed. by August Wilhelm Schlegel and Friedrich Schlegel, 3 vols (Berlin: 1798–1800; repr. Darmstadt: Wissenschaftliche Buchgesellschaft, 1992), III (1800), 94–105 (pp. 99–100). For these sources in Schiller and Schlegel, cf. TL, 1700–01; and Gaier 1996: 126–27, 138–40.
58 See Schmidt in KA, I, 778–79.
59 For completeness I should mention various shorter odes addressed mostly to minor deities: 'An die Parzen' (MA, I, 188; OE, 27), where the Fates are begged for a summer and an autumn so that the poet's song may be brought to fruition; 'Dem Sonnengott' (MA, I, 194; OE, 35), in which the poet mourns the setting sun (who, having departed, is mainly referred to in the third person); and 'Die Götter' (MA, I, 252; OE, 77), praising both the Aether and the Sun (Helios). Only 'Der Zeitgeist' (MA, I, 228; OE, 57) is truly comparable to 'Natur und Kunst': again addressed to Zeus in his capacity as 'Gott der Zeit', its prayer is unqualified by the reservations contained in the latter ode. It will have been sent to Neuffer in July 1799, for publication in the same year; Reitani notes the connection with both 'Natur und Kunst' and 'An Eduard' (TL, 1396–97). Moreover, in the case of 'Der Zeitgeist' Brandt discerns 'eine entfernte Verwandtschaft zwischen der Ode Hölderlins und dem Zeus-Hymnos des Kleanthes' (2002: 229); my thesis, obviously, is that in the case of 'Natur und Kunst' the kinship is much more than 'remote'.

a poet's law-giving may be in danger of forgetting the ground from which it arises. If a prayer to Zeus becomes a criticism of that god, that critique in turn amounts to an act of poetic self-examination.

CHAPTER 3

The One-Sided Surface and the *Wechsel der Töne*

1. Introduction

The emphasis on the 'calculable law' is one of the most remarkable features of Hölderlin's poetics. Hölderlin not only asserts the need for such a law in poetry; there is a period in which he formulates one with a degree of almost algebraic rigour that is not often found in the realm of poetics. That law is embodied in the set of poetic rules contained in what has been called his theory of the 'alternation' or 'modulation of tones' [Wechsel der Töne], referred to below as 'WT'.[1] The theory is found in manuscript sources dating from the years 1799 and 1800. For most of that time, Hölderlin was resident in Homburg vor der Höhe; hence his theoretical writings of the period are sometimes called the 'Homburg poetics'.[2] Among the most striking features of those writings are the schematic sequences in which Hölderlin sets out his theory, sometimes called his 'poetological tables' [Poetologische Tafeln]. The meaning of Hölderlin's tables, which were not published until the early years of the twentieth century, has been unlocked above all in the exemplary work of Lawrence Ryan.[3] One of the virtues of his approach — apart from the clarity and rigour lacking in some other treatments — lies in his refusal to see the tables as

---

[1] On Hölderlin's concept of the calculable law, and a possible contemporary source for his interest in formulating precise rules in algebraic notation (Gottfried Ploucquet), see Franz 2005, and 1987: 97–98. The expression 'Wechsel der Töne' is used only incidentally at MA, II, 64, but has become a standard designation for the corresponding theory (see e.g. Ryan 1960). The 'alternation' concerned is between three, rather than merely two elements, but I follow Adler and others in using 'alternation' in this arguably extended sense (AL, 248). For a concise introduction to the theory, see Adler and Louth in AL, xxxviii–xli.

[2] The relevant period (September 1798 to June 1800) was in fact the first of two that Hölderlin spent in Homburg (now 'Bad Homburg'): he returned there in June 1804, and remained until his break-down in September 1806. Furthermore he spent the second half of 1800 in Stuttgart and Nürtingen, and some of the relevant manuscripts may have been composed there (see FHA, XIV, 329 and 343). For the sake of simplicity I use 'Homburg poetics' to include all the poetological work of the period 1798–1800.

[3] Ryan 1960 and 1963. See MA, II, 109, and FHA, XIV, 340–41 ('Poetologische Tafeln'); cf. *Theoretische Schriften*, ed. by Johann Kreuzer (Hamburg: Meiner, 1998), pp. 66–67 ('Poetologische Schemata'); StA, IV, 238–40, and KA, II, 524–26 ('Wechsel der Töne'). Their first publication, in the form of a facsimile of the manuscript shown in Figure 3.1, was by Lange (1909: 153) under the rubric 'Katatonische Spielerei mit Stereotypien' and misattributed to 1802–06.

rigid schemata to which all poems are supposed to conform, or as inspired (in the words of one recent commentator) 'by the desire to secure the success of any poetic enterprise in advance' (Eldridge 2015: 55). Building on Ryan's approach, I shall attempt to shed further light on these at first sight puzzling notations.

Hölderlin's tables can in fact be seen to embody a set of simple mechanical rules, or what we would today call 'algorithms'. Thus a poem is analyzed as expressing a series of 'tones' (or more exactly, as we shall see, a double series), and the tones follow one another in a prescribed sequence. Not that every poem follows the sequences laid down; it is more that the rules embody an ideal case, one which clearly had a special significance for Hölderlin. The varying exemplification of Hölderlin's algorithms can often be seen in successive versions of the same poem, as shown for instance in Ryan's analysis of the three versions of the ode 'Dichtermuth'. The first version does not yet exemplify the full theory (although the 'tones' themselves are certainly present); the last (renamed 'Blödigkeit') no longer does so, and corresponds to a distinct and later phase of Hölderlin's poetic thought.[4] In a strict sense, WT comprises the complete set of rules governing the sequence of tones in a poem. In that sense, the theory belongs to the relatively short period of the Homburg poetics. In a broader, or looser, sense, the theory had a more lasting presence in Hölderlin's poetic thought. Thus the requirement for an alternation of tones in a poem, and the central idea that (as we shall see) a poem's outward expression stands in opposition to its underlying meaning, do not in themselves depend on the full rules for the sequences of tones, and survive into later phases of Hölderlin's poetics. And in 1804 Hölderlin began the *Sophokles-Anmerkungen* with his most striking statement of the need for a 'calculable law' in poetry.[5]

I shall concentrate here on the strict theory of the 'alternation of tones'. The rules of alternation will be analyzed in their most rigorous form, in an attempt to answer the question of what *structure* those rules describe.[6] It will be suggested that this question has an at first sight surprising answer: namely that Hölderlin's rules describe what became known later to mathematics as a 'one-sided' or 'non-orientable' surface (also called the 'Möbius strip' or 'Möbius band'). That surface did not come to the attention of mathematicians until the middle of the nineteenth

---

4   See Ryan 1960: 198–203; the three versions are at MA, I, 275–76, 284–85 and 443–44 respectively (see further Chapter 1.4 above). On the presence of the tones in the first version see also Indlekofer 2007: 29–32. Ryan similarly contrasts the ode 'Der blinde Sänger', exemplifying the strict succession of tones, and its later version 'Chiron' (1960: 209). While those examples could be said to illustrate the evolution of Hölderlin's poetic technique, Ryan's more general point is that 'der Hölderlinsche Tonwechsel kein starres Schema ist, sondern einem dem Geist des Dichters innewohnenden "Rhythmus der Vorstellungen" [MA, II, 310] entspringt' (1960: 205).
5   See MA, II, 309, and AO [1.1]–[1.2] in Part Two below. See also Nägele 2005: 133–48, and Chapter 4.1 below.
6   As already mentioned, my account relies heavily on Ryan 1960. Although this has not I think been superseded by a comparable monograph, important work has also been done on the sources and context of the theory in contemporary theories of poetic genre, and theories of musical tonality and expression. On WT and the theory of genre, see Szondi 1978a; on the relation to musical theory, Gaier 1998: 43–48, and Gaier 2000, and cf. Donelan 2002 and Martens 2008: 42–45. For an account of Hölderlin's poetic thinking in Homburg, see Louth 1998: 69–102; and for a general survey of WT, Schmid 2002.

century, more than fifty years after Hölderlin's poetological tables and an equally long period before their publication.

A connection between the poetics of the period and a mathematical figure is not in itself surprising. Thus the ellipse was a favourite image of Hölderlin's during the earlier stages of the composition of *Hyperion* (MA, I, 489, 558). In the poetics of Friedrich Schlegel an important role is played not only by the ellipse, but also by related geometrical figures such as the hyperbola and parabola.[7] And in Schlegel one can find an analogy between the intellectual operation of 'reflection' and the arithmetical operation of raising a number to a higher power, as well as an often fantastical use of algebraic abbreviations and symbols.[8]

However, my claim is not that Hölderlin makes inventive use of an image or analogy, but rather that by means of rigorous poetological rules he formulates what amounts to a precise description. And the structure so described is not one that had previously been investigated by mathematicians. Those two differences are not unrelated. It is true that, since its popularization in the second half of the twentieth century, the Möbius strip has become a commonly used image among artists, writers and others: so much so, in fact, that it is now in danger of becoming a cliché.[9] One now refers to the Möbius strip in much the same spirit as Schlegel appealed to the ellipse or the hyperbola: as a pre-existing figure that can be used as the material for a more or less exact analogy. But before it had been defined by mathematicians, the Möbius strip was not available as a ready-made term of comparison. Hölderlin therefore had no existing model to draw upon.

A suggested connection between Hölderlin's poetics and the Möbius strip can already be found in the literature. In this respect priority undeniably belongs to Andrzej Warminski, who has observed that the relation between Judgment and Being, in Hölderlin's early theoretical note on *Being and Judgment*, can be read as 'more like the relation between the "two" sides of a Möbius band'. Although as Warminski's formulation itself suggests, that is not exactly where the figure is to be found; rather it is found in the more elaborate theory of the alternation of tones.[10] In any case, Warminski's suggestion deserves to be much further developed. Even when read simply as a picture or analogy, it has a surprising degree of explanatory value. And it may be possible to go further. Once Hölderlin's tone tables are fully analyzed, it seems that he can be credited not merely with a more or less obscure

---

7 For these geometrical analogies in Fr. Schlegel, see Menninghaus 1987: 158–67. For Hölderlin and the ellipse see also Honold 2005: 18–73, especially pp. 42–55. Hölderlin's image of the 'eccentric path' is also apt to invoke the hyperbola and the parabola. The use of the same terms in both a geometrical and a rhetorical sense appears to be a coincidence (cf. Hamilton 2014: 10–11).

8 See Friedrich Schlegel, *Literary Notebooks 1797–1801*, ed. by Hans Eichner (London: Athlone Press, 1957), pp. 12–13; and see e.g. fragments 518, 579, 622, 731, and 735. Following the pioneering work of Käte Hamburger, scholarly attention has also been paid to mathematics in Novalis: see now Bomski 2014. And on Heinrich von Kleist and Spherical Geometry see Pourciau 2015.

9 This is the conclusion that can be drawn from the otherwise useful and comprehensive survey in Pickover 2006.

10 See Warminski 1987: 8; also pp. 10, and 20, n. 28 (and see further note 32 below). On *Being and Judgment* — which has been edited under various titles, e.g. 'Seyn, Urtheil, Modalität' (MA, II, 49–50) — see also Chapter 1.2 above.

premonition of the structure that would later be called the Möbius strip, but with something approaching its first exact description.

2. Surfaces and Tone Sequences

The discovery of the one-sided surface was made independently, in 1858, by the mathematicians A. F. Möbius and J. B. Listing.[11] It seems that priority, both of first description and first publication in 1861, in fact belongs to Listing; although the surface is now invariably called the 'Möbius strip' (or 'Möbius band'). Listing is also credited with the invention of the term 'topology' to designate the mathematical discipline in which that discovery has its rightful place.[12] I do not suggest, of course, that Hölderlin made any contribution to the science of topology. Thus it cannot be said that Hölderlin discovered the 'topological space' known as the Möbius strip, for he would have had no clear conception of what a topological space might be.[13] Nonetheless, there is a sense in which the one-sided surface described by Möbius and Listing was anticipated in Hölderlin's poetics. Such an anticipation is perhaps less surprising than it might seem at first sight. The Möbius strip is not in itself a complex structure. The surprising fact may be that, so far as we know, the Möbius strip did not come to anyone's attention earlier.[14]

Such a structure is easily described, and indeed easily created by anyone with access to a rectangular strip of paper. Such a strip clearly has two sides, a 'recto' (which can be defined as the face that is turned towards the viewer of the strip) and a 'verso'. It can be made into a closed loop, by joining the two ends (or shorter edges). The loop then has two surfaces — the outer surface of the loop, formed from the recto side of the strip, and the inside surface formed from the verso side. However, there is an alternative way of forming a closed loop from a rectangular strip. Rather than simply joining the two ends, one can twist one of the edges so that the recto side is joined to the verso, and vice versa. The result is a structure with some remarkable properties. In particular, one can get from one point of the surface to any other point by tracing a continuous line — and this applies even in the case of points which appear initially to be on opposite sides of the surface. When one views any given segment of the strip, it does of course have two sides: a recto face turned towards the viewer, and a verso face turned in the opposite direction. It is only when one considers the strip as a whole that one realizes that those two faces lie on a single side or surface. The strip is two-sided in each of its parts; it is

---

11 See Biggs 1993: 111. One should distinguish between the existence of structures exemplifying the Möbius strip, the description of the strip, and the analysis of its mathematical properties. Pickover, whose researches appear to have been voluminous, could not find a reference to the one-sided surface prior to Möbius and Listing (2006: 29). But more recently a visual depiction of such a strip has been identified in a Roman mosaic (Cartwright and González 2016).
12 Biggs 1993: 110. It has also been known as 'Analysis Situs': the term, but probably not the discipline, is already to be found in Leibniz.
13 For evidence, however, of Hölderlin's appreciation of the science of mathematics see the letter to his brother of 10 January 1797 (MA, II, 644–45) where it is ranked with 'Natural Law' [Naturrecht] as the only other candidate for 'scientific perfection' [wissenschaftlich[e] Vollkommenheit].
14 See Stewart 1993: 159, and similarly Pickover 2006: 29; but see note 11 above.

only when the strip is taken as a whole that the sum of the recto faces can be seen to coincide with the sum of the verso ones.[15]

In what sense, however, can such a spatial model be applied to a poem? To see how it can, I shall recall some further elements of WT. That theory is based on a distinction between the poem as it appears, on the one hand, and the unmanifest basis or ground of the poem. For the first aspect of the poem, Hölderlin uses the term 'Kunstkarakter' [art-character]; for the second, the term 'Grundton' [basic tone] or sometimes 'Grundstimmung' [basic mood]. In the words of Lawrence Ryan (1960: 80):

> [D]er Kunstcharakter ist der scheinbare, der unmittelbar wahrnehmbare und herrschende Ton; der Grundton, als dessen Gegensatz der Kunstcharakter sich konstituiert, schwingt aber im dichterischen Ausdruck mit, so daß sich dieser erst aus seinem Grund hergestellt zu haben scheint.
>
> [The art-character is the apparent, immediately perceptible and dominant tone; but the basic tone, in opposition to which the art-character constitutes itself, also resonates in the poetic expression, so that the latter appears as if first produced from its basis.]

Hölderlin also describes the opposition as between 'Schein' or 'äußer[er] Schein' [outer appearance] and 'Bedeutung' [meaning].[16] Hölderlin's starting point, therefore, is that there is an underlying or inner meaning of the poem, which is articulated to yield an outer expression. But the expression of that inner meaning is not direct, but rather indirect or (as he also says) 'metaphorical'. Thus the outer character of the poem is the displaced expression, or 'metaphor' [Metapher], of its inner meaning.

Hölderlin uses the term 'tone' to analyze both of those sides or aspects of the poem, and conceived of a poem as a double series of such tones, or (to put the same point in a different way) as a series of tone-pairs. Each underlying basic tone ('Grundton', 'Bedeutung') is paired with its corresponding surface expression or art-character ('Kunstkarakter', 'Schein'). To whom does that outer surface of the poem 'appear'? The answer, presumably, is that it appears to the audience or reader of the poem. As a first approximation we can say that, if the poem consists in the communication of a meaning to its audience, the vehicle rather than the content of that communication is the 'art-character' of the poem — the meaning of the poem as it first appears to us, its notional spectators. Thus Hölderlin conceives the poem as an ordered sequence of such art-character tones. In experiencing the poem, its reader traces a path along the surface of its art-character, receiving at each point a communication of a different basic tone or inner meaning. Or to be more exact, the total meaning of the poem results from an interaction between those depth and surface elements, for (in Ryan's words) 'the basic tone [...] resonates in the poetic

---

15 See Barr 1965: 20–22; Barr accordingly prefers the more technical term 'non-orientable' to 'one-sided.' For other examples of non-orientable surfaces (such as the 'Klein bottle') see Pickover 2006: 81–82.

16 MA, II, 102–03; AL, 302–03, trans. modified. On the equivalence of the oppositions 'Bedeutung'/'Schein' and 'Grundton'/'Kunstkarakter', see Ryan 1960: 49, and cf. Louth 1998: 88.

expression.' And as we shall see, there is a sense in which that initial opposition between depth and surface aspects is itself overcome in the poem as a completed whole.

As Nägele has suggested, a central innovative feature of Hölderlin's poetics is to 'confront any aesthetics of expression with a poetics of presentation (*Darstellung*)' (2004: 513). At each point in the poem, the outer expression of the poem conceals, rather than directly reveals, its underlying meaning; although no doubt that meaning will ultimately be expressed by the poem taken as a completed whole. Nägele has suggested also that a poem for Hölderlin is organized along two axes, the 'metaphorical' and the 'metonymic' (1999: 254). Along the horizontal or metonymic axis, the art-character tones follow one another in sequence; but along the vertical axis, each art-character tone corresponds to an underlying basic tone.[17] On that analysis, the basic tone corresponding to a given art-character tone lies beneath it, along the vertical axis of metaphor.

To recapitulate the argument so far: WT analyzes a poem in terms of a surface which presents itself to a notional spectator (the reader or audience of the poem). From that perspective, the poem consists of an immediately visible sequence of art-character tones, together with a series of basic tones hidden beneath them. At each point in the poem, two tones are present, the manifest (or express) art-character tone, and the hidden (or implicit) basic tone. But those two tones are not different in kind: they are the two inseparable elements of poetic expression. Both elements of the tone-pair belong in the end to the horizontal surface of expression; but one belongs to the side of the surface that is turned toward the spectator ('recto'), the other to the side that is turned away ('verso'). Curiously, and presumably coincidentally, the already-mentioned note *Being and Judgment* consists of two closely connected texts, written on the recto and verso of a fly-leaf torn from an unidentified book. The ordering of the texts on each side has given rise to controversy; but the better view, probably, is that neither has priority, being the two inseparable aspects of the same thought — just as recto and verso are united as inseparable sides of a single sheet.[18]

It is important to appreciate that 'Grundton' and 'Kunstkarakter' are not different in kind. As we shall see, Hölderlin does divide tones into three types, which he calls the 'naive', 'heroic' and 'ideal' respectively. But a tone of each type can occupy, successively, the positions of basic tone or art-character; and as noted, the two positions are related as two inseparable aspects of poetic meaning (Ryan

---

17 Here the terminology 'metaphoric' and 'metonymic' belongs to the structural linguistics of Saussure and Roman Jakobson, rather than to the classical doctrine of the rhetorical tropes: cf. Weinrich 1987, and see now Matzner 2016: 266–79.

18 As Friedrich puts it (2007: 70, n. 12), they are 'wörtlich zwei Seiten desselben Blattes'. The different titles under which the note has been edited — 'Urtheil und Seyn'; 'Seyn, Urtheil, ...'; 'Seyn, Urtheil, Modalität' — themselves reflect the ordering problem. As Friedrich acknowledges, a similar view can be found in Warminski (who as we have seen also makes a connection with the two identical 'sides' of the Möbius strip). Note that Strack (2013: 13–17) has identified the unknown fly-leaf as belonging to Schelling's *Philosophische Briefe über Dogmatismus und Kriticismus*. That would suggest a date for the manuscript of December 1795 at the earliest, somewhat later than has previously been suggested (see e.g. Henrich 1993: 3, suggesting April 1795).

1960: 41–42). Hölderlin's rules will show how those two aspects of the poem are connected, and indeed united as the two faces of a single surface. It is now therefore time to look at them in more detail. It must again be emphasized that I am concentrating on the formal features of the theory, in abstraction at times from its wider significance. Such an approach needs no justification, for it was one that Hölderlin himself adopted in his poetological tables. Those formal characteristics of the theory are only one of its aspects; but they repay study in their own right.

3. The Poem as a Two-Sided Surface

From one point of view, Hölderlin's theory is a development, or generalization, of the theory of poetic genres. Hölderlin's starting-point is that there are three fundamental poetic attitudes or effects, which he names after the kinds of poetic work in which they are taken to be dominant. The tragedy (or drama) is the genre in which heroic conflict and opposition predominate: hence the 'heroic' tone. The epic is the genre which narrates and describes the sensible world, giving the 'naive' tone. And the lyric is the genre in which subjective thoughts and feelings are above all expressed, which may often concern the mythical or the unreal: hence the 'ideal' (or 'idealistic') tone.[19] But the decisive complication is this: all three can be expressed in a work of any poetic genre. A lyric poem (say an ode) may contain both tragic and epic elements as well as lyric ones, and the tragic element may actually predominate as compared with other poems of the lyric genre. So one can speak of a 'tragic-lyric' poem, or simply of the 'tragic' ode, it being understood that this is still a poem of the lyric (and hence 'ideal') genre, albeit in this case of the 'tragic' or 'heroic' sub-type.[20] Indeed it is clear from Ryan's analysis that the theory is, above all, the theory of the alternation of tones in a particular kind of lyric poem, namely the ode; although Hölderlin also experimented in applying it to other genres — as can be seen from his labelling of two versions of a tone table as corresponding to the tragedies *Ajax* and *Antigone* respectively (MA, II, 109; AL, 309).

It is in the case, therefore, of the lyric poem that Hölderlin's theory is most consistently exemplified; and more specifically, in the odes which are contemporary with his elaboration of the theory.[21] This is hardly surprising, of course: Hölderlin

---

19 I have preferred to avoid Adler's neologism 'idealic'. Hölderlin also gives those three poetic attitudes a psychological characterization, in terms of 'passion' [Leidenschaft] (corresponding to the tragic or heroic); 'fantasy' or 'imagination' [Phantasie] (corresponding to the lyric or ideal); and 'feeling' or 'sensation' [Empfindung] (corresponding to the epic or naive). See MA, II, 101–02; AL, 299–300.

20 As Ryan puts it (1960: 64) 'der Wechsel der Töne ist das Unterscheidungsprinzip nicht so sehr der Dichtarten an sich, sondern vielmehr erst ihrer Unterarten' [the alternation of tones is the differentiating principle, not of poetic genres as such, but much more of their sub-genres]. On the tragic ode versus the tragic drama, see MA, I, 865–66 (AL, 258–59), and see section 5 below.

21 For a detailed analysis of the extent to which the odes can be analyzed in these terms, see Ryan 1960: 158–229. It will be seen that Ryan's approach does not involve a dogmatic application of Hölderlin's schemata, and is sensitive to the different degrees in which they are exemplified in different cases and categories of case. If a principle of alternation of tones can still be found in Hölderlin's later hymns, the tone sequences may not follow the same rules (Ryan 1960: 5, 316–17).

is a poet in whom theoretical reflection and poetic creation are united to an uncommon degree. But it also means that the odes in question have an exemplary function. Thus the odes of this period are at once a 'lyrical' expression of poetic subjectivity and an exercise in poetic self-reflection. The theory may of course have assisted Hölderlin in any number of his compositions, helping him to find the correct balance between unity and variety of expression in a poem.[22] However, it is clear that the precise sequence that Hölderlin stipulates in his rules goes beyond what would be necessary to achieve such a balance. To the extent that it exemplifies the rules laid down in all their rigour, an ode can itself amount to an alternative exposition of the theory.[23]

Hölderlin's term 'tone' denotes those three basic elements of poetic expression, which can each occur in the two contrasting positions of 'Grundton' and 'Kunstkarakter'. The tone of the art-character is said to be figurative or 'uneigentlich', as if the true or proper meaning resides in the basic tone (which the art-character can express only indirectly). Thus in the case of the 'epic poem' Hölderlin refers to 'Der Gegensaz seiner Grundstimmung mit seinem Kunstkarakter, seines eigentlichen Tons mit seinem uneigentlichen, metaphorischen' [The opposition between its basic mood and its art-character, its actual and its figurative, metaphoric tone]' (MA, II, 103; AL, 303, trans. modified).[24] As to the term 'Ton', the closest analogy is perhaps to musical tones, whether corresponding to individual notes or to keys.[25] And just as a song can be analyzed as a sequence of musical notes or chords, or a symphony as a sequence of keys, a poem can be seen as a sequence of 'tones'. In principle, every poem might be analyzed in terms of such an alternation of tones; but the rules of WT in their fullest sense apply only to Hölderlin's own poetry, and even then only to particular instances of the latter.

As we have seen, tones are divided into three categories: those of the 'heroic', the 'ideal' and the 'naive' respectively. Following Hölderlin's own occasional practice, these can usefully be abbreviated to '**h**', '**i**' and '**n**' (highlighted here in bold typeface). We have also seen that they derive ultimately from an analysis of the dominant features of the Tragic, Lyric and Epic genres respectively. But because a tone can occur in either one of the two positions of 'Grundton' or 'Kunstkarakter', a poem consists not in a single sequence of tones but rather in a double sequence,

---

In the case of the elegies, it seems that only 'Menons Klagen um Diotima' exhibits an alternation of tones comparable to the odes (see Ryan 1960: 241–42; and for an analysis of the tone sequences in that elegy see also Hamlin 1999).
22 See the letter to Neuffer of 12 November 1798 (MA, II, 710–13; AL, 108–10), and cf. Szondi 1978a: 373–76.
23 Thus Hamlin (1999: 311) suggests that the rules of alternation (or, as he prefers, 'modulation') '[impose] upon the reader an obligation to participate in the full cognitive complexity of the poem as performance, like a symphony of reflective thought'.
24 On 'Grundstimmung' as equivalent to 'Grundton' see MA, II, 104; and on the 'Wechsel der Stimmungen' cf. MA, II, 84. For Aristotle's definition of 'metaphor' [μεταφορὰ] as the use of a word 'in uneigentlicher Bedeutung', see Fuhrmann 1982: 66–67; or in Halliwell's version 'the application of a word that belongs to another thing' [ὀνόματος ἀλλοτρίου ἐπιφορὰ]: *Poetics*, ed. and trans. by Stephen Halliwell, in Aristotle, XXIII, LCL 199 (Cambridge, MA: Harvard University Press, 1995; corrected repr. 1999), 1457b (pp. 104–05).
25 Cf. Gaier 1998: 44–45, and 2000: 135–36; and Donelan 2002. See also Chapter 5.2 below.

or a sequence of pairs of tones. It will be recalled that the positions of 'Grundton' and 'Kunstkarakter' correspond to those of 'Bedeutung' and 'Schein' respectively. In any given tone-pair, one element characterizes the poem as it appears to its reader or audience; and the other represents a more hidden meaning, one that (in a sense to be further clarified) forms the underlying basis of the former. The opposition of 'Grundton' and 'Sprache' is sometimes used to denote the same distinction. Accordingly the 'language' of the poem is the medium through which its underlying meaning finds initial expression, as it were the first or most immediate aspect of the poem.[26]

As we have also seen, Hölderlin describes the relationship between two such paired tones as that of 'metaphor'; and a poem accordingly consists of a sequence of such metaphors. Its underlying meaning is expressed indirectly or metaphorically through the tone of its art-character. It is this feature of Hölderlin's theory that allows us to represent the poem as a surface, only one side of which is turned as it were towards the spectator (the reader or audience of the poem). At any given point in the poem, a tone is present which is nonetheless hidden from view, turned away from that spectator. It is as if the sequences of tones in a poem trace a path simultaneously on each side, recto and verso, of a two-sided surface.

Any of the three kinds of tone can appear in one of those two positions: either as a basic tone (hidden from view) or as an art-character tone (presented to the spectator). But because the art-character is a metaphor, rather than a direct expression, of the basic tone, it is clear that the same tone cannot appear in both positions simultaneously. For instance, an 'ideal' basic tone can never be paired with an 'ideal' art-character. Hölderlin sometimes indicates the distinction between the two positions by capitalizing the tone of the art-character. I shall follow him here by writing **H**, **I**, and **N** for tones which occupy the art-character position, but **h**, **i**, and **n** for the tones in the basic-tone position.[27] The sequence of tone-pairs can then be represented schematically as follows, letting T_i be an art-character tone and t_i the corresponding basic tone:

T_1	T_2	T_3	...	...	...
t_1	t_2	t_3	...	...	...

Here the series in the upper row of the table represents the surface of the poem as it appears. The series beneath represents the tones that are hidden from view, because they are expressed only metaphorically.

---

26 See *Die Empfindung spricht* ... (MA, II, 101–02; AL, 299–300), which distinguishes the levels of 'Grundton', 'Sprache' and 'Wirkung' [effect], and where the 'effect' of the poem seems to be equated with its basic tone — as if the underlying meaning is communicated to the reader through the art-character or 'language' of the poem. As Ryan puts it (1960: 45) 'der Grundton geht als Grundton in seinen Ausdruck *ein*, geht aber als *Wirkung* aus diesem Ausdruck wieder *hervor*, indem er *fühlbar* wird'.

27 See MA, II, 109; AL, 309. Note, however, that Hölderlin only capitalizes the initial 'H', 'I' or 'N' when writing out the full names of the tones; when using the abbreviated forms he uses the lower case throughout.

I now set out the algorithms that generate those two series of tones. The first algorithm, which I shall call Algorithm A, governs the relationship between art-character tone and basic tone, and can be divided into three rules:[28]

    A1.   Art-character tone H is paired with basic tone i.
    A2.   Art-character tone I is paired with basic tone n.
    A3.   Art-character tone N is paired with basic tone h.

The second algorithm, Algorithm B, explains how the series of art-character tones is generated. This rule can be deduced from the sequences that Hölderlin sets out in his tables. (As we shall see in section 4, both algorithms undergo an important modification when Hölderlin's full theory is considered, but remain valid as regards the initial part of the tone sequences.) The rule here is that the art-character tone is identical with the basic tone underlying the immediately preceding art-character. Thus if T_i is an art-character tone, and t_i its corresponding basic tone, then $T_{i+1} = t_i$. For instance, if the first art-character in the sequence is the heroic tone, which by Algorithm A will be paired with an ideal basic tone (rule A1), one can predict that the second art-character will itself be an ideal tone. It is as if an initially hidden tone (occurring in the basic-tone position) has now risen to the surface; the same process will then be repeated, yielding the naive tone for the third art-character. One cannot of course use those rules to determine the initial tone-pair in each sequence (since in that case there is no preceding tone). But a sequence must begin with one of the three possible tone-pairs. Depending on the art-character tone with which the poem begins, there are three (and only three) possible sequences, which can be called the 'ideal', the 'heroic' and the 'naive' tone sequences respectively — or as Hölderlin also calls them, the 'Lyric', the 'Tragic' and the 'Epic' (MA, II, 108–09; AL, 308).

Applying Algorithm B, therefore, an occurrence of a heroic art-character tone is followed by that of an ideal tone; an ideal tone is similarly followed by a naive tone; a naive tone is followed by a heroic tone — and the cycle could be repeated indefinitely. Depending upon which tone is taken as the starting-point, one would accordingly get three simple repeating cycles of art-character tones:

    H I N H I N ... I N H I N H ... N H I N H I ...

The relationship between the sequences of art-character and basic tones can again be represented by a table. Thus in the case of a tone sequence of the 'ideal' type which begins with the tone pair I, n:

I	N	H	I	N	H	...
n	h	i	n	h	i	...

28 These correspond to the three fundamental 'metaphors': 'Das lyrische dem Schein nach idealische Gedicht ist in seiner Bedeutung naiv. [...] Das epische dem Schein nach naive Gedicht ist in seiner Bedeutung heroisch. [...] Das tragische, dem Schein nach heroische Gedicht, ist in seiner Bedeutung idealisch.' [The lyric, in appearance ideal poem, is in its meaning naive. [...] The epic, in its appearance naive poem, is in its meaning heroic. [...] The tragic, in appearance heroic poem, is in its meaning ideal.] (MA, II, 102; AL, 302, trans. modified)

And similarly for the 'naive' and the 'heroic' tone sequences, which begin with the tone pairs **N, h** and **H, i** respectively.

Those tone sequences can be represented by means of a physical model. Take a rectangular strip of paper, and divide each of its two sides into three equal segments. In each of the three segments of the recto side, write the first three elements of the art-character sequence (for instance the sequence in the upper row of the table just given: **I, N, H**). Turn the strip over, and on the verso side write the first three corresponding elements in the lower row (**n, h, i**), representing the sequence of basic tones. If the two ends of the strip are joined to form a two-sided loop, the sequence in the upper row of the table above is generated by traversing the outside surface of the loop twice. Similarly the sequence in the lower row is generated by traversing the inside surface. The same loop can also be used to generate the other two possible tables, if one begins instead with the segment marked **N** or the segment marked **H**.

Accordingly, the sequences of art-character tones and basic tones can be represented by the two faces, recto and verso, of a two-sided surface.

4. The Poem as a One-sided Surface

The next step is to observe that Hölderlin introduces an important complication into his tone sequences. And it is this complication which justifies the assertion that his theory invokes the one-sided surface of a Möbius strip, rather than the two-sided surface so far described. To appreciate this step, one has to look more closely at the tables in which Hölderlin set out his most fully developed tone sequences.[29] There one is immediately struck by an apparent anomaly. After the third tone-pair, the sequences seem to depart from the pattern established by Algorithms A and B given in section 3 above. The sequences consist of seven tone-pairs arranged as follows (corresponding to the Lyric, the Tragic and the Epic type respectively):

I	N	H	I	N	H	I
n	h	i	h	i	n	h

H	I	N	H	I	N	H
i	n	h	n	h	i	n

N	H	I	N	H	I	N
h	i	n	i	n	h	i

Rather than a repeating cycle of three tones, here we have sequences of seven tones (or tone pairs). And although the first three pairs obey both of Hölderlin's algorithms, the fourth pair departs from them. So for instance, in the first of the sequences given above, the fourth tone-pair does not obey the rule that an *ideal* art-character tone is the metaphorical expression of a *naive* basic tone. Instead the

---

29   MA, II, 108, ll. 23–30, and 109, ll. 1–13; AL, 308–09.

fourth pair is simply an inversion of the third: in the third, a *heroic* art-character tone is paired (as one would expect) with an *ideal* basic tone; but in the fourth an *ideal* art-character tone is paired with a *heroic* basic tone. And in the remainder of the sequence the rule now seems to be, not that the art-character tone is identical with the basic tone of the preceding tone-pair, but rather that the basic tone is identical with the preceding art-character tone.

Has Hölderlin then violated his own rules for the alternation of tones? Here one has to look more closely at how Hölderlin writes out his tone tables. It is remarkable that in the two most developed versions, the third and fourth pairs are either joined by round brackets (in the version where the tables are set out in vertical columns), or connected by a horizontal dash.[30]

Now could it be that the third and fourth tone-pairs are grouped together in this fashion because they are not in fact two distinct pairs, but rather the same pair? The same pair, that is, but appearing successively in two different configurations: first in the normal configuration (art-character on top of the basic tone in my tables above, or to the right of it in Figure 3.1) and then in an inverted position? That does in fact seem to be the most natural interpretation of Hölderlin's tone sequences. Thus in the first part of the sequences, as one progresses from the first position to the second, and then to the third, it is clear that a different pair of tones is involved in each case. For example, in the case of the Tragic table, which begins with the *heroic* art-character tone, one progresses from the pair **H, i** to the pair **I, n**; and from there to the pair **N, h**. But the next step in the sequence does not amount to a progression to a distinct tone-pair; rather it is a repetition of the same pair in an inverted form, so that **N, h** becomes **H, n** and the forward progress is momentarily suspended.[31]

The reversal of the positions of 'Grundton' and 'Kunstkarakter', when one passes from the third to the fourth position in a tone sequence, has a natural interpretation in terms of the Möbius strip.[32] I have suggested that a tone sequence can be represented by means of a rectangular strip, with each side divided into three equal segments. The first three pairs in Hölderlin's tables then correspond to those three double-sided segments, each consisting of an art-character tone (on the recto side of the strip) and a corresponding basic tone (on the opposite or verso side). With the third tone-pair we would come to the end of the strip; a consequence that can

---

30 For the vertical sequences in the manuscript see Figure 3.1, and for the horizontal sequences FHA, XIV, 332–35.
31 Thus as Ryan observes (1960: 94), 'Mit seiner Umkehrung [...] hört der "Wechsel" auf, in diesem bestimmten Sinne ein Wechsel zu sein'. On the wider significance of this moment of suspension or 'caesura' in Hölderlin's poetics, see also Ryan 1963: 24–25 and 35–38. The question whether this corresponds to the 'caesura' mentioned in Hölderlin's later Sophocles commentary is touched upon in Chapter 5.3 below.
32 Again priority belongs to Warminski, to the extent that he has already suggested that 'the "Möbius band" could be read as a *spatial* and the "chiasmus" [after the third tone-pair] as a *temporal* articulation' of the moment of caesura (1987: 20, n. 28; emphasis in original; see also pp. 33–34, 39). That Hölderlin did indeed at times think in terms of spatial models is shown by the three diagrams drawn at the bottom of the first manuscript page of *Wenn der Dichter ...*: see FHA, XIV, 263. The first of these is the most suggestive in the present context, consisting as it does of two juxtaposed circles, with two diagonal lines meeting and crossing at the point where the circles touch.

The One-Sided Surface and the *Wechsel der Töne*

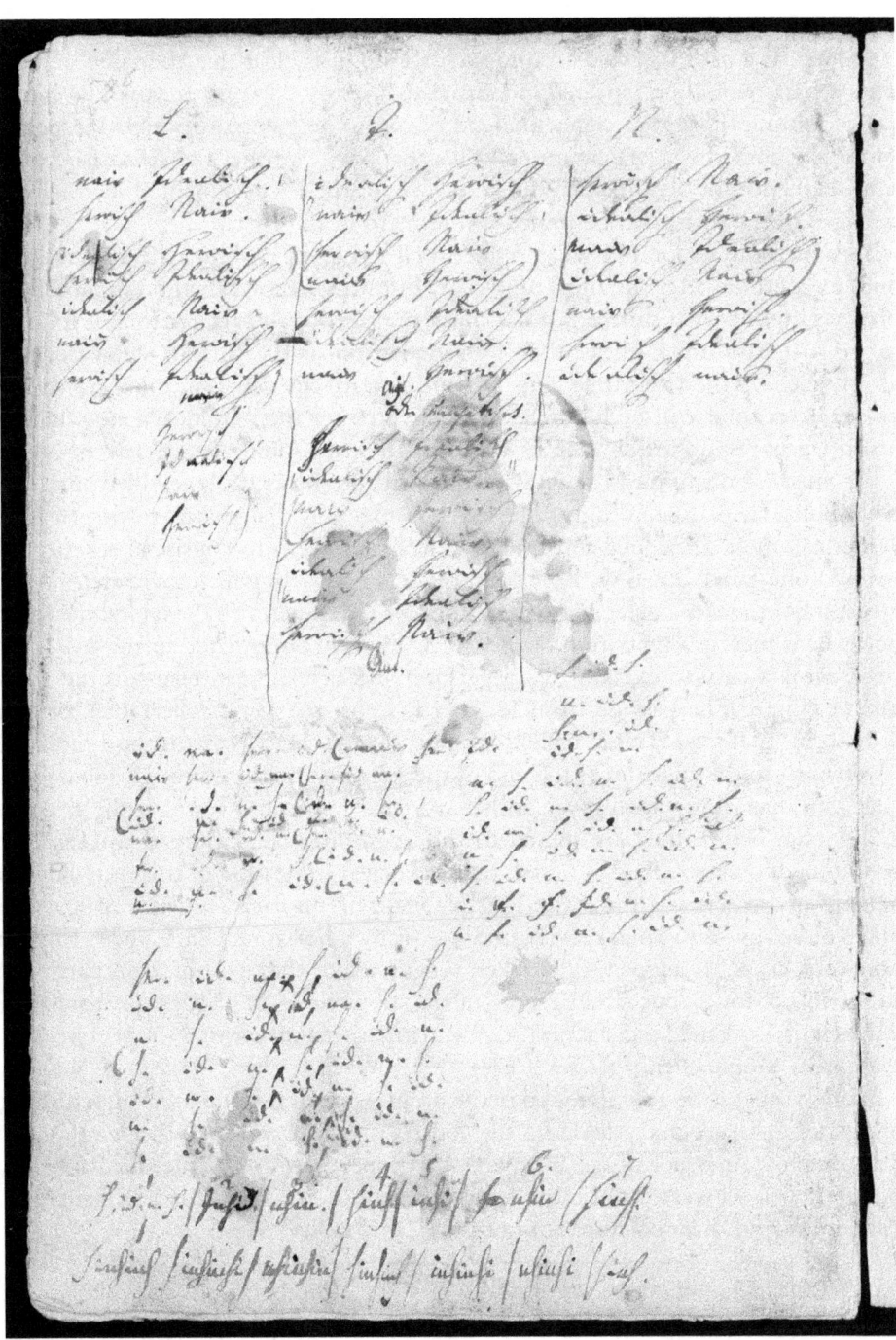

FIG. 3.1. Tone tables in vertical columns, showing a reversal (marked by round brackets) between the third and fourth pairs of tones. In the lower half, algebraic notations.
© Württembergische Landesbibliothek

be averted e.g. by joining the end of the strip to the beginning to make a two-sided loop. If a path is traced around such a loop, it is clear that the same sequence of tone-pairs would be repeated indefinitely. But as we have seen, there is another way of joining those two edges: the end edge can be twisted through 180 degrees before it is joined to the beginning. The result will be that the recto face of the third segment will be joined to the verso face of the first segment; and conversely the verso of the third will be joined to the recto of the first.

Both methods of joining will produce a closed loop, enabling the alternation of tones to continue after the third tone-pair. But if the second method is chosen, the tones will follow in a different order: now the third art-character tone is followed by the first basic tone, rather than by a repetition of the first art-character tone. For instance, in the Lyric tone table beginning with the pair **I**, **n**, the third (heroic) art-character tone will be followed by a naive rather than an ideal tone when the forward progress resumes after its moment of suspension. As we saw in section 2, this method of joining the ends of the strip produces the one-sided surface of the Möbius strip. Accordingly, the latter is precisely the structure described by Hölderlin's most developed tone tables. They may seem to consist of seven rather than six tone-pairs; but as we have seen, there is a sense in which there are in reality only six. For there is an element of repetition or redundancy in the tables: the fourth tone-pair is merely a repetition of the third, albeit in an inverted form.

It is in fact easy to explain that repetition and inversion in terms of the model proposed here. The passage from **H**, **i** to **I**, **h** (in the Lyric tone table), or from **N**, **h** to **H**, **n** (in the Tragic table), or again from **I**, **n** to **N**, **i** (in the Epic table), corresponds to the twisting of the end of the strip, its rotation through 180 degrees. This is an operation which reverses the two faces (recto and verso) at the end edge of the strip, before they are joined to the beginning (verso joined to recto, and recto joined to verso). And as noted, there is a clear indication of this in Hölderlin's manuscripts, where the third and fourth tone-pairs in each sequence of seven are linked either by round brackets (Figure 3.1) or by a horizontal dash, indicating that those tone-pairs are indeed to be taken together. For they do not form part of the alternation of tones, but rather represent the moment of its suspension at what can now literally be called the 'caesura': the 'cutting' that transforms a simple two-sided loop into a Möbius strip.

It follows that if we are interested in the progression of the poem through different tone-pairs, it is necessary to leave the fourth tone-pair out of consideration. For that 'fourth' pair is not in fact a new pair of tones, but simply the third tone-pair appearing in an inverted position. And the result of omitting it is a sequence such as the following, here corresponding to the Lyric table:

I	N	H	N	H	I
n	h	i	i	n	h

The first three tones of the upper series (**I N H**) of course still represent the first three art-character tones in the poem, with the corresponding three basic tones underneath (**n h i**). Using our model of the two-sided strip of paper, **I N H** are the three segments of the recto side of the strip, **n h i** the corresponding three segments of the verso side. But once the art-character face (marked **H**) of the third segment is twisted from the recto to the verso position, enabling it to be joined to the verso side of the first segment, the final three art-character faces of the strip can be seen to coincide with the first three basic-tone faces. At this point, the recto and verso sides of the strip have exchanged positions. If before there were two distinct series of tones, arrayed on the opposite sides of a two-sided surface, there is now a single series which traverses the unique side of a one-sided surface. And if, in the second half of the table, the basic tones **n**, **h**, and **i** are now written in capitals, this is because the perspective of the observing subject has itself undergone a change.

To follow the sequence of tones is to trace the path taken by the reader of the poem, the spectator to whom the segments of the poem (each represented by a single tone-pair) successively 'appear'. And we can now see that this path is traced along the surface of a Möbius strip. It follows that the reader does not only follow a path along a surface, but also experiences a reversal of perspective. As the surface of the strip twists through 180 degrees, the perspective of the spectator follows a similar movement, enabling a circuit to be made which follows first the recto, and then the verso of the original two-sided surface. And after arriving at the sixth tone in the above sequence (corresponding to the face marked **i** of the third segment, which was originally on the verso side of the strip) the reader has returned to the starting-point.

And here we have the final confirmation that Hölderlin is describing the surface of the Möbius strip. For as that model predicts, a tone sequence generated from Hölderlin's algorithms can contain at most seven tone-pairs — or more exactly six, once the repetition of the third pair is taken into account. Thus after the final pair, there will be no further step that can be taken by the alternation of tones. We have seen that, after the reversal in the middle of the Lyric tone sequence, the third art-character tone **H** was joined to the first basic tone **n** (now, by virtue of the reversal in perspective, written in upper case **N**). But conversely, the third basic tone (now written **I**) must correspondingly be joined to the first art-character tone, which was of course itself the ideal tone **I**. It follows that at this point there is no further possibility of alternation: the concluding tone can only be followed by another *ideal* tone, and the sequence of tones must therefore come to an end. And this is indeed the case: in the poems which exemplify Hölderlin's algorithms, the tone sequence consisting of seven pairs is in fact the longest that is envisaged. In his tone tables and in his poetic practice, Hölderlin admits two kinds of tone sequence: a shorter form consisting of three distinct tone-pairs followed by an inversion of the third, making (with that repetition) a table of four pairs in all; and a longer form, consisting of six distinct tone-pairs, again with an inversion of the third pair added, making a table of seven.[33] My analysis explains why this should be so: any continuation of

---

33 As Ryan observes (1960: 109), 'Hölderlin sieht für jede Dichtart eine Verlängerung vor, die sich auf sieben Töne erstreckt — oder vielleicht stellt die viertönige Form, genauer gesagt, eine Verkürzung der längeren Form dar' [for each poetic genre Hölderlin envisages an extended version that runs to seven tones — or more exactly, perhaps, the four-tone form represents a truncation of the longer form].

the sequence would involve a repetition that is at odds with the very principle of alternation.

The observation that Hölderlin's rules describe a one-sided surface may appear, at best, to be a curious discovery, one that lacks any wider significance. As already noted, it can hardly be seen as a contribution to the science of mathematics. In the final section, I shall try to sketch the outlines of a broader context in which it might instead be viewed.

5. Surfaces, Depths, and 'die verkehrte Welt'

As we have seen, the rules for WT define a 'pure' or one-sided surface, one that can be said to lack any dimension of depth: that is to say, a depth that would lie beneath or beyond the 'other' side of the surface (as in the case, say, of the surface of a sphere). I shall accordingly consider in more general terms the relation between surfaces and depths in Hölderlin. I then mention a work of contemporary philosophy — the *Logique du sens* of Gilles Deleuze — in which the notion of a surface has a prominent role in relation to the analysis of language and meaning. And finally, returning to the circle of Hölderlin's immediate contemporaries, I shall consider a closely-related figure found in Hegel, namely 'die verkehrte Welt' [the inverted world].

Surfaces and depths

The relation between 'Grundton' and 'Kunstkarakter' in WT must be considered in the context of the broader distinction between 'Natur' and 'Kunst' found in the Homburg poetics, where 'Kunst' [Art] comprises not only poetry and the fine arts, but all the institutions of human culture. The most important sources here are the ode 'Natur und Kunst oder Saturn und Jupiter', discussed above in Chapters 1.4 and 2, and the essay that provides a basis for his uncompleted drama on the death of Empedokles.[34] It will be recalled that the myth that is central to the ode concerns the banishment by Jupiter (or Zeus) of his father Saturn (or Cronus). Jupiter is the god who rules 'hoch am Tag'' [high up in the day], whereas Saturn was confined to the abyss along with his fellow Titans. In his version of the myth, Hölderlin distinguishes Saturn — as innocent god of harmonious nature — from his savage fellows, the latter being characterised 'die Wilden' [the Wild ones] (l. 8).[35] In his mature thought Hölderlin places ever increased emphasis on this 'Titanic' aspect

---

34 For the ode see MA, I, 285. Hamb, 223–25 translates the longer version of the ode given at KA, I, 297–98; line references below are to the shorter version. The essay, namely *Die tragische Ode* ... (MA, I, 865–78; AL, 258–70), is sometimes named after the title of its longest section ('Grund zum Empedokles'); it is edited by Schmidt under the title 'Über das Tragische' (KA, II, 425–39).

35 On Hölderlin's creative 'correction' of the myth, see Vöhler 1993a. As Vöhler observes, while Hölderlin's early conception of nature was as that of a harmonious whole united by the forces of love, from 1797 onwards a new conception becomes important. Hölderlin finds a new 'Titanic' tendency within it which is associated with the subterranean depths. Vöhler identifies the emergence of this new conception in the poem 'Die Muße' of 1797 (MA, I, 169–71; OE, 11–13) which refers to 'der geheime | Geist der Unruh, der in der Brust der Erd' und der Menschen | Zürnet und gährt' (ll. 28–30). On those two conceptions see further Bennholdt-Thomsen 1998.

of nature, often figured as belonging to the elemental depths; and by the time of the *Sophokles-Anmerkungen*, Zeus becomes defined, conversely, as 'Vater der Erde' [father of the earth] — that is to say as the principle that defines and secures the habitable surface of the globe.[36] The most graphic image of that distinction between habitable surface and elemental depths is found in the *Empedocles* drama itself, which turns on the philosopher's legendary leap into the crater of Etna. The theoretical essay expounds in detail the relation between Nature and Art, as it relates to the argument of the drama (MA, I, 868–71; AL, 261–64). But even more interesting, for our present purposes, is the distinction drawn in the earlier sections between the genres of 'tragic ode' and 'tragic-dramatic poem' (or tragic drama).

Thus the essay begins with an exposition of the sequence of tones in the tragic ode, describing the sequence of art-character tones in its canonical form **HINHINH** (see section 4 above). It explains in particular how the initial heroic tone — corresponding to 'der Zwist' [strife] — arises from the ideal basic tone, characterised as an 'Übermaas der Innigkeit' [excess of intimacy].[37] The second section of the essay then makes clear that the same excessive union is expressed in tragic drama, albeit one that is deeper or more intense; and by means of oppositions or divisions that are correspondingly more extreme (MA, I, 866; AL, 259). The consequence is that the *ode* is a more immediate expression of the poet's own world and experience, whereas the *drama* must disguise that experience in 'ein kühneres fremderes Gleichniß und Beispiel' [a bolder, more alien metaphor and example]. That is to say, the tragic drama is set in a world at one remove from the poet's own. And its form too must exhibit 'mehr den Karakter der Entgegensezung und Trennung' [more the character of opposition and division]. That form differs from the structure of the tragic ode, as defined by the rules of WT. We have seen that the latter define a particular kind space, one which (following Gerhard Kurz) we might call the space of 'lyric subjectivity': that is to say, one that involves 'nicht einfach ein Subjekt, sondern eine Subjektivität, ein Subjekt also, das sich selbst zum Gegenstand macht' [not simply a subject, but a mode of subjectivity, that is a subject that takes itself as object]. The lyric — as opposed to the tragic — subject can find shelter in a space of self-reflection constituted by the cycle of tones, one that (as Ryan puts it) enables the 'self-knowledge' [Selbsterkenntnis] of the poetic subject.[38]

A distinction between a lyric subject who survives, and a tragic hero who perishes, is illustrated by Hölderlin's ode to Empedocles (MA, I, 251; OE, 83). As the ode begins: 'Das Leben suchst du, suchst und es quillt und glänzt | Ein göttlich Feuer tief aus der Erde dir' [You search for life, you search, and a divine fire |

---

36 See Bennholdt-Thomsen 1998: 22, referring to '[die Tendenz] der elementaren Natur, die der Welt der Zivilisation und Kunst entgegensteht. [...] Das Ziel, das Zeus vertritt, ist dagegen die Erde als feste, begrenzte, gestalthafte, gebundene' (and see ibid. p. 34). And in relation to the later elegies and hymns, Tang (2008: 191) has shown the importance of what he calls the 'cultural landscape', defined as a 'visible surface [...] that represents, so to speak, the interface between the natural and the human worlds, vibrating with both natural forces and human activities' (and see ibid. p. 194).
37 For this part of the essay as expounding the canonical sequence of tones in the tragic ode (or 'heroic-lyric' poem), see Ryan 1960: 77–78 and 107–10.
38 See respectively Kurz 2015a: 101, and Ryan 1960: 87.

Gleams and wells from deep within Earth to you]. Here Empedocles' desire is for a union with the inner forces of nature — an excessive union that is incompatible with his personal survival. In the case of the poet, however, the ode concludes: 'Und folgen möcht' ich in die Tiefe, | Hielt die Liebe mich nicht, dem Helden' [And if love no longer held me in its grasp, | I'd gladly follow this hero down into the depths]. The ode to the (legendary) death of the Presocratic philosopher is, in the end, an affirmation of life on the part of the poet — a life sustained by the power of love. This is a love that protects against the heights of Plato's Ideas, as much as from the depths of Empedocles' volcano. Thus in the one-stanza version of the ode 'Lebenslauf' [The Course of Life] (MA, I, 190), the poet's upwards–yearning spirit is brought down 'beautifully' by love: 'aber die Liebe zog | Schön ihn nieder'.[39]

We saw in Chapter 1 how one function of the lyric poem for Hölderlin — more specifically the ode — is to define a space in which the poetic subject finds sustaining refuge ('Asyl' or 'Ruhestätte'). A juxtaposition of Empedocles ode and Empedocles drama demonstrates this in concrete terms, as it were in parallel to the more abstract discussion in the related theoretical essay. We also saw how that theme of 'refuge' or 'sanctuary' belongs to Hölderlin's dialogue with Stoicism, so that the 'Ruhe' in 'Ruhestätte' can be seen as a transformation of Stoic *tranquillitas*. This can be seen also on a larger scale, now in relation to the sphere of 'Kunst' (or human culture) taken as a whole. As already noted, Zeus — the Stoic god — becomes Hölderlin's 'Vater der Erde', where 'earth' connotes the surface of habitable life that supports a landscape of culture. Conversely, to the dimension of depth there correspond the potentially hostile forces of nature, or in the terminology of the *Sophokles-Anmerkungen* 'die Naturmacht' (MA, II, 310, 315; AO [1.14], [3.1]). That is illuminated by a striking image from 'Griechenland' [Greece], a late, uncompleted hymn that probably belongs to the same period as those *Anmerkungen* (cf. TL, 1840). Hölderlin compares the earth to a calf's-hide drum (MA, I, 479, ll. 10–11; Hamb, 699). As Bennholdt-Thomsen and Guzzoni explain, 'die Erde [ist] dünn [...] wie eine Tierhaut. Die Bildung der Erde geht nur ihre Oberfläche an. Im Innere herrschen die (gefangenen bzw. sich losmachen wollenden) Elemente' [the earth is thin like an animal skin. The formation of the earth concerns only its surface. Within rule the elements that are captive or striving to escape] (Analecta 1999: 175, n. 319). And in the late revisions to the elegy 'Brod und Wein' [Bread and Wine], Böschenstein has noted the new emphasis on a 'horizontal' dimension, corresponding to a habitable 'Earth of flowers and woods', in contrast to the 'burning zones' of 'Heaven and the underworld' (1999: 336).

Elsewhere Hölderlin assigns the role of shaping such a surface to the mythological figures of Hercules and Bacchus (or Heracles and Dionysus). Those figures operate precisely on the boundary between the inner, destructive forces of Nature, and the Art that subdues it. For they have an unsettlingly dual character. In the first place,

---

39 Here the adverb 'schön' is captured in neither Hoff's nor Hamburger's versions (OE, 25; Hamb, 81). Note that the poet is also brought down, more forcefully, by suffering ('das Laid beugt ihn gewaltiger'); and in the later, four-stanza version he has to contend with the depths of the underworld, but finding even there 'ein Grades, ein Recht' [a straightness, | A law] (MA, I, 325, l. 8; OE, 95).

they embody civilising forces, as Hercules vanquishes monsters and Bacchus founds the cultivation of the vine. While the attribution to Seneca of the play *Hercules on Oeta* is doubtful, it undoubtedly belongs in the Stoic tradition. There Hercules is 'that glory of the world, its sole defence, whom fate gave to the earth in lieu of Jove' (ll. 749–50); and the concluding chorus still begs the dying Hercules: 'you, great conqueror of beasts and bringer of peace to the world, be with us! Continue to show regard for our earth' (ll. 1989–91).[40] Hercules is the delegate of his father Zeus; or in Hölderlin's words, Hercules is 'Zevs Knecht' [Zeus' servant], or again 'der gerade Mann' [the upright man], where 'gerade' also has the sense of the straightness of law.[41] In *Hercules on Oeta* the hero dies a heroically Stoic death, but the heroism of Hercules' earlier life is more problematic. If he cleanses the earth of its monsters, it is in the course of violent and often questionable adventures.[42] The character of Dionysus embodies a similar paradox, since he is the god of Bacchanalian frenzy as much as of the civilizing cultivation of the earth. In Hölderlin's unfinished hymn 'Der Einzige' [The Only One], the poet worries about the relationship between those ancient bringers of peace and salvation to mortals, and the figure of Christ whom they resemble; for in accomplishing their own works they remain troublingly less spiritual.[43] The surface is a boundary that has constantly to be retraced; and this can be done only by turning against themselves the ambiguous forces of the depths.

The logic of sense

Turning now to Deleuze, we can note how he presents his project as forming a bridge between literature (in the first instance, Lewis Carroll) and philosophy (in the first instance, the Stoics). He also acknowledges the hybrid quality of his own work, which he describes as an attempted 'roman logique et pyschanalytiqe' [logical and psycho-analytical novel], and which is organised in a number of resonating 'series' rather than in a linear sequence of chapters.[44] The eighteenth series contains

---

40   Seneca, *Tragedies*, ed. and trans. by John G. Fitch, II, revised edn, LCL 78 (Cambridge, MA: Harvard University Press, 2018), pp. 405 and 505.
41   For Hercules as 'Zevs Knecht [...] der gerade Mann', see 'Chiron' (MA, I, 439, l. 18; OE, 167), and cf. Schmidt in KA, I, 803–04, and 1978: 52–61; and see further Chapter 6.3 below.
42   On the problematic nature of Hercules' earlier career, see Littlewood 2014: 517 ('Herculean virtue is all too close to vice'). See further the discussion of the *Pindarfragment* 'Das Höchste' in Chapter 6.2 below.
43   MA, I, 387–90; Hamb, 535–41. On Hercules and Dionysus as founders of culture, and 'saviour' (or *sōtēr*) figures comparable in some respects to Christ, see Schmidt 1990: 119–30, and in KA, I, 942–47. The civilizing influence of the vine, as contrasted with the violent drunkenness that can result from the consumption of its fruit, is also at issue in the *Pindarfragment* 'Das Belebende'. See also the notion of a *sōtēr* in the *Pindarfragment* 'Die Asyle'; and for both of these *Pindarfragmente* see Chapter 6.2 below.
44   Deleuze 1969: 7; Deleuze 1990: x (trans. modified). Subsequent page references added in square brackets are to the English translation (a regrettable feature of which is the absence of any punctuation in the series headings after the relevant series number). The emphasis on Lewis Carroll (Charles Lutwidge Dodgson) can be explained by that author's fascination with various paradoxes, as well as his contributions to Logic — both features shared with the Stoics. Carroll's significance for

a portrayal of three 'images' of philosophy, or more exactly of the philosopher, beginning with the Platonist who ascends to the *heights* of the Idea. Then Deleuze pairs Hölderlin with Nietzsche as a discoverer of Empedocles qua philosopher of the *depths*.[45] But as we have seen, Hölderlin can be characterized as much as a poet of the surface as a tragedian of the abyss: the author of the odes and their defining 'alternation of tones', as much as the drama on the death of Empedocles. In that respect he is close to the third kind of philosopher portrayed by Deleuze. For (he says) the Cynics and the Stoics invented a new kind of philosophy, a philosophy of the *surface*:

> C'est la grande découverte stoïcienne, à la fois contre les Présocratiques et contre Platon: l'autonomie de la surface, indépendamment de la hauteur et de la profondeur, contre la hauteur et de la profondeur; la découverte des événements incorporels, sens ou effets, qui sont irréductible aux corps profonds comme aux Idées hautes.
>
> [The autonomy of the surface, independent of and against the depths and the heights; the discovery of incorporeal events, meanings, or effects, which are irreducible as much to 'deep' bodies as to 'lofty' ideas — this is the great Stoic discovery, at once against the pre-Socratics and against Plato.][46]

The Stoic doctrine of the 'incorporeal' was already touched upon in Chapter 2.3. The incorporeal 'events, meanings, or effects' to which Deleuze refers are represented, in the first place, by the Stoic doctrine of the *lekton*. That category of incorporeal corresponds to the meaning of a linguistic expression, and at the same time to the fact or event intended by such an expression. In English it is usually translated as 'sayable'; but it can be rendered approximately as 'sense', or for that matter 'sens' (as in 'logique du sens').[47] As noted in Chapter 2, the Stoic incorporeal comprises a diverse collection of items (time, place, the void, the *lekton*) which none the less seem to be related, even though the nature of that relationship remains controversial.

The *lekton*, in particular, has the important characteristic of what we might term 'acausality': that is to say of being only an effect, never a cause. As Sextus Empiricus observed (LS 55B):

> The Stoics say that every cause is a body [σῶμά] which becomes the cause to a body [σώματι] of something incorporeal [ἀσωμάτου]. For instance, the scalpel,

---

the theory of literature is also explored in the course of Irwin's study of Borges and Poe, the structure of which similarly mirrors the labyrinthine structure of their tales (1994: xxiii, 451–52).

45   Deleuze 1969: 153–54 [146–47]. On Nietzsche's reception of Hölderlin's *Empedocles* drama, see now Castellari 2018: 155–77.

46   Deleuze 1969: 157–58 [150] (trans. modified); and note the characterisation of Hercules as 'le pacificateur et l'arpenteur de la terre' (ibid. 157 [149]). On the anti-Platonism of the Stoics, cf. Brunschwig 2000: 983, 988.

47   As Gourinat puts it (2000: 119), 'quelque chose qui ressemble à ce que nous appelons "sens"'. On the *lekton* see generally LS, I, 195–202, and M. Frede 1994. Frede suggests that the primary meaning of the term is 'a thing to say', and derivatively 'what is signified by the appropriate expressions' (1994: 110–15, 127–28). It seems, in fact, that the *lekton* faces in two directions: one (as it were the subjective) face corresponds to the meaning expressed by the speaker; but the other is turned towards the (equally incorporeal) facts and events that are expressed.

a body, becomes the cause to the flesh, a body, of the incorporeal predicate 'being cut'. And again, the fire, a body, becomes the cause to the wood, a body, of the incorporeal predicate 'being burnt'.

Here 'being cut' and 'being burnt' are *lekta*, events or facts that can be spoken of, but without themselves having the causal efficacy characteristic of bodies. Where then are they located? Not in any Platonic world of Forms: like other incorporeals, the *lekton* does not inhabit a world elevated above corporeal reality; but nor is it to be found in the substance — or depths — of the physical world. Rather, it inhabits what can be described as a 'surface', one where it 'subsists' rather than 'exists', or appears as a surface-effect.[48] As Bréhier put it, the Stoics distinguish 'deux plans d'être: d'une part, l'être profond et réel, la force; d'autre part, le plan des faits, qui se jouent à la surface d'être, et qui constituent une multiplicité [...] d'êtres incorporels' [two levels of being: on the one hand, being that is deep and real, force; on the other hand, the level of facts which play on the surface of being, and make up a multiplicity [...] of incorporeal beings].[49] That is of course only one way of putting the matter, and not one that would commend itself to all scholars of Stoicism. But it is of interest to us here, since it may help to situate Hölderlin's own apparent preoccupation with the figure of the surface, and its relationship to the overwhelming forces of the depths ('die Naturmacht').

More specifically, that 'acausal' character of the Stoic incorporeal may shed light on Hölderlins conception of the 'Grund' or 'Grundton' of a poem. In WT an 'art-character' tone appears initially to be related to its corresponding 'basic tone' as an effect to its cause — as is suggested by the terminology 'Grundton'. But while the art-character of the poem may seem to be the result of an underlying cause which serves as its foundation, it is equally valid to regard the basic tone as an effect of the art-character: after all, the latter is in the end the vehicle by which the meaning of the former receives metaphorical expression (hence the equivalence of 'Grundton' and 'Bedeutung'). It is with the reversal of the tone sequences in their second half that this becomes most evident; for then the positions of basic tone and art-character are themselves reversed. A tone in either of its two possible positions (as 'Grundton' or 'Kunstkarakter') is merely an effect inhering in poetic language, an incorporeal element of poetic meaning rather than a corporeal ground or cause.

This is not the place for a detailed exploration of the relation between Hölderlin's 'poetic logic' and Deleuze's 'logic of sense'. There may be other points of connection between Hölderlin's construction of a double series of 'tones', and Deleuze's account of the serial structures that generate incorporeal 'sense'. The latter can be defined in

---

48 More specifically, it can be said to 'belong' or 'obtain' where presently applicable to the activity of a body as effect to its cause. On the differences between the notions of 'subsist' (*huphestanai*), 'belong' or 'obtain' (*huparkhein*), and 'exist' (*einai*), see Chapter 2.3 above. Thus for the Stoics only corporeal things 'exist' in themselves; incorporeals merely 'subsist', although in certain circumstances they may in addition 'belong' to a corporeal body or process: see M. Frede 1994: 117 (who also brings out the relation between the incorporeal *lekton* and incorporeal time). For Totschnig (2013: 139) the primary notion is that of *huparkhein*, and incorporeals 'subsist' only in circumstances where they are to be regarded as mere objects of thought.
49 Bréhier 1970: 13; cf. Totschnig 2013: 133.

terms of multiple series in which elements are repeated in a displaced configuration — rather as the series of art-character tones is not a mirror image, but a displaced reflection of the corresponding series of basic tones.[50] But we can note, in any event, the centrality to each of the figure of the Möbius strip, the 'pure' or one-sided surface. The surface can be found also in Lewis Carroll, most explicitly in the late work *Sylvie and Bruno Concluded* (1893). There, as Deleuze notes:

> la bourse de Fortunatus, présentée comme anneau de Moebius, est faite de mouchoirs cousus *in the wrong way*, de telle façon que sa surface extérieure est en continuité avec sa surface interne [...]. [C'est] en longeant la surface [...] qu'on passe de l'autre côté [...]. La continuité de l'envers et de l'endroit remplace tous les paliers de profondeur.
>
> [Fortunatus' purse, presented as a Möbius strip, is made of handkerchiefs sewn *in the wrong way*, in such a manner that its outer surface is continuous with its inner surface [...]. It is [...] by skirting the surface [...] that one passes to the other side [...]. The continuity between reverse and right side replaces all the levels of depth.] (Deleuze 1969: 21 [13])

We saw how Hölderlin's algorithms establish such a continuity between at first sight opposing faces — a 'subjective' or recto face turned towards the observing subject, and an 'objective' or verso face turned in the opposite direction. The problem of how the 'Ich' can be at once the subject and object of reflection was already central to Hölderlin's early note on *Being and Judgment*, and in a sense finds its answer in his later theory of tones (cf. Ryan 1960: 87). And as Irwin suggests (1994: 95–101), the theme of spatial orientation and reversal so prominent in Lewis Carroll is itself related to that problem of self-reflection. A fuller analysis might begin with the curiously insistent role played by the image of spatial orientation in Kant: that is to say, the difference between the 'left and the 'right' sides of the human body.[51] But rather than pursuing those connections any further, I now turn to a second aspect of the title 'Logique du sens'. For if that 'logic' is inspired in part by the Stoic theory of the incorporeal, there is also a more immediate source for Deleuze's title — one that, in biographical terms at least, is considerably closer to Hölderlin himself.

---

50 Cf. Deleuze 1969: 54–55, 65–66 [47–48, 60–61]. Thus in terms of Hölderlin's Algorithm B defined in section 3 above, a basic tone t_i is reflected not in its corresponding art-character tone T_i but rather in T_{i+1}. Deleuze's account of a 'paradoxical' or 'nonsensical' element, circulating between the two series and ensuring their communication, might also be compared with Hölderlins account of 'die Begründung und Bedeutung des Gedichts' [the grounding and meaning of the poem]; for the latter is 'das geistigsinnliche, das formalmaterielle, des Gedichts; [...] sie zeichnet sich aus dadurch, daß sie sich selber überall entgegengesetzt ist' [the spiritually sensuous, the formally material quality of the poem; [...] it is characterized by the fact that it is everywhere opposed to itself] (MA, II, 81–82; AL, 281). See also Deleuze 1969: 83–84 [78–79], and cf. Ryan 1960: 41–42.

51 Cf. Tang 2008: 146–47. In Kant, the problem of the orientation of regions in space (sometimes called the problem of 'incongruent counterparts') is first expounded in a 'pre-Critical' essay of 1768, and persists as a central image in the 1786 essay 'Was heißt: Sich im Denken orientiren'. See *Kants gesammelte Schriften*, Akademie-Textausgabe, II, 375–83, and VIII, 131–47 (Berlin: Reimer, 1905 and 1912; repr. De Gruyter, 1968).

Hegel and 'die verkehrte Welt'

Deleuze was a student of the great French Hegel-scholar Jean Hyppolite, and a review of the Hyppolite's second book on Hegel was among Deleuze's earliest publications.[52] As Hyppolite's translator has observed (1997: xiii), the expression 'logique du sens' is in effect taken from that book's discussion of the third part of Hegel's *Wissenschaft der Logik* [*Science of Logic*], characterised as a 'logique du concept ou du sens'. Hyppolite (1991: 228) suggests that Hegel's logic of the 'Begriff' [Concept] embodies an account of the 'genesis of meaning' [genèse du sens] that is already implicit in the earlier parts, the logics respectively of 'Sein' [Being] and 'Wesen' [Essence]. And it is precisely that aspect of Hegel's Logic as a 'logic of sense' which is emphasised in Deleuze's review (2002: 20).

Hegel and Hölderlin were particularly close during the period of the Homburg poetics. Hegel had joined Hölderlin in Frankfurt am Main in January 1797, and they will have kept in close contact after Hölderlin moved to nearby Homburg vor der Höhe in September 1798. Hölderlin then left Homburg in June 1800, and Hegel himself moved to Jena at the beginning of 1801. Hölderlin's mental state deteriorated after he came back from Bordeaux in the summer of 1802, and in 1803 there was some discussion between Schelling and Hegel as to whether he should join the latter in Jena (MA, III, 619–20). In July of the following year, Schelling mentions to Hegel the recently-published Sophocles translations as evidence of Hölderlin's precarious mental condition (MA, III, 631). Shortly afterwards, Hegel began work on the manuscript that would become his first major work, the *Phänomenologie des Geistes* [*Phenomenology of Spirit*] of 1807.[53] In Hegel's analysis of the 'ethical world' of ancient Greece, in Chapter 6 of that work, a prominent role is played by the two tragedies that had recently been translated by Hölderlin.[54]

If Hegel's first book was a work of philosophy, it was philosophy presented in a most unusual way. Rather than simply expounding his philosophical system, Hegel at this stage proposed a new kind of introduction to the system that would study, as it were from the inside, the various 'figures' or 'forms of consciousness' [Gestalten des Bewußtseins] that fell short of the standpoint from which philosophy must ultimately be conducted. The framework is provided by two perspectives, which Hegel calls the 'für es' [for it] and the 'für uns' [for us]. The first perspective is that of the 'Gestalt' under consideration at any particular moment, as it were that 'form of consciousness' considered as a protagonist. The second perspective is that of the

---

52 Hyppolite 1991 (first edition 1952); Deleuze 2002 (originally 1954). There are English translations of both book and review in Hyppolite 1997.
53 I shall refer to the following editions: *Phänomenologie des Geistes*, ed. by Hans-Friedrich Wessels and Heinrich Clairmont; Philosophische Bibliothek, 414 (Hamburg: Meiner, 1988); *Phenomenology of Spirit*, trans. by Michael Inwood (Oxford: Oxford University Press, 2018). These will be abbreviated to 'PhG' and 'Inw' respectively, followed by the relevant page number, and in the case of PhG by a number in square brackets (also given in PhG itself) indicating the page in vol. IX of the North Rhine-Westphalia Academy edition. Hegel's book was essentially completed in October 1806, with a long preface added in January 1807 (see Bonsiepen in PhG, xxiii). But it seems Hegel had begun work on it in 1804–05 (Pöggeler 1993: 207–08).
54 See PhG, 307–13 [253–58], Inw, 186–89; and cf. Billings 2014: 161–77.

philosophical narrator, who is inviting the reader to share in his reconstruction of each protagonist's experience. To simplify somewhat, the various 'Gestalten des Bewußtseins' are arranged in a sequence of increasingly adequate forms of reflection or self-reflection. The end-point is the figure grandiosely described as 'das absolute Wissen' [absolute knowledge], which is the standpoint of philosophy itself. With this figure, the perspective of the protagonist is finally united with the perspective of the author-narrator. For the narration of those earlier experiences turns out to have been an experience all of its own, one in which the original perspective 'für uns' has itself been transformed in an act of self-reflection, and the reader thereby raised to a level adequate for philosophy. A new element is thereby reached, which Hegel calls 'der Begriff' [the Concept] (PhG, 528 [431–32]; Inw, 319).

The structure of narrative reflection that has been described bears a more than passing resemblance to the one we found in Hölderlin's *Hyperion*.[55] This does not mean that Hegel considered that literature (or art generally) provided the proper medium for philosophy. His strategy was to begin with the less adequate medium, with a view to raising it to a more adequate level — that is to say, ultimately to the realm of pure concepts. But it is impossible to overlook his anxiety that conceptual thought, at least in its usual form, was not up to the task. In the preface to PhG he worries that the very nature of a judgment or proposition may be unsuitable for philosophy. And it is striking that in reaching for an analogy, Hegel has recourse to the language of poetics: 'Dieser Konflikt der Form eines Satzes überhaupt, und der sie zerstörenden Einheit des Begriffs ist dem ähnlich, der im Rhythmus zwischen dem Metrum und dem Akzente statt findet' [This conflict between the form of a proposition in general and the unity of the concept which destroys it resembles the conflict that occurs in rhythm between the metre and accent] (PhG, 46 [43]; Inw, 28). Indeed, he had already commended a method of surrender to 'den immanenten Rhythmus der Begriffe' [the immanent rhythm of concepts] (PhG, 44 [42], Inw, 27), as if recalling Hölderlin's own conception of the 'Rhythmus' of tragic representations (MA, II, 310; AO [1.7]–[1.10]).

The transition that Hegel makes between Chapters 3 and 4 of his work is a particularly significant one for our purposes. In the first three chapters, Hegel narrates the experience of a subject that takes as its object a world independent of itself: in his vocabulary, it is one of 'Bewußtsein' [consciousness] rather than of 'Selbstbewußtsein' [self-consciousness]. As he states at the beginning of Chapter 4, 'In den bisherigen Weisen der Gewißheit ist dem Bewußtsein das Wahre etwas anderes als es selbst' [In the previous modes of certainty the true for consciousness is something other than itself]. But with self-consciousness we have 'in das einheimische Reich der Wahrheit eingetreten' [entered the native realm of truth] (PhG, 120 [103]; Inw, 72). How does he get from one to the other? In the final

---

55 See Chapter 1.2 above. PhG is not a work in epistolary form, and there may seem to be no equivalent of the transformation that leads from Hyperion as letter-writing narrator to Hölderlin as the author of the completed novel. But in PhG too author and reader in share a single perspective (the perspective 'für uns'), which does not become 'absolutes Wissen' until the end of the final chapter. And in the act of composing PhG, Hegel (like the letter-writing Hyperion) is in effect the first to engage in the act of self-reflection embodied in the completed work.

figure of Chapter 3, Hegel's protagonist is confronted by something that Hegel calls 'die verkehrte Welt' [the inverted world] (PhG, 111–19 [96–102]; Inw, 67–71). It will become clear that this is a transitional figure, located on the boundary between the forms of 'Consciousness' and those of 'Self-consciousness'.

Hegel reaches the full form of the 'verkehrte Welt' in two stages. In the first, it emerges in the form of a 'supersensible world' [die übersinnliche Welt], contrasted with the world of 'appearance' [die Erscheinung]. The distinction is the one central to Kant's philosophy, but now as re-interpreted by the latest developments in German philosophy and Romantic science. Hegel refers in particular to the relation of polar opposition central to the Romantic philosophy of nature.[56] With his characteristic irony, Hegel plays with the idea that the world beyond sensory experience — the object of both scientific understanding and religious and moral belief — is merely that world of 'appearances', but with its polarities reversed. But Hegel immediately goes on to say that this is a merely approximate view of the matter, and proceeds to define the full notion of the 'inverted world'.[57] This is now a structure whose terms are not related as a something to its opposite — say object to its mirror-image — but in which each term can be said to be the opposite *of itself*:

> Ich stelle wohl das Gegenteil *hieher*, und *dorthin* das andere, wovon es das Gegenteil ist; also das *Gegenteil* auf eine Seite, an und für sich ohne das andere. Ebendarum aber, indem ich hier *das Gegenteil an und für sich* habe, ist es das Gegenteil seiner selbst, oder es hat in der Tat das andere unmittelbar an ihm selbst. —
>
> [Certainly, I put the opposite *here*, and the other of which it is the opposite, *there*, so I put the *opposite* on one side, in and for itself without the other. But just because I have here the *opposite in and for itself*, it is the opposite of itself, or it has in fact the other immediately within itself.] (PhG, 114 [98–99]; Inw, 69, trans. modified)

But how can something be the 'opposite of itself', or have its opposite 'immediately within itself'? Surely, by definition, the opposite is on a different 'side' from its counterpart? How can something be on both sides at once — or is there perhaps only a single side? Hegel continues, after the dash:

> So hat die übersinnliche Welt, welche die verkehrte ist, über die andere zugleich übergriffen, und sie an sich selbst; sie ist für sich die verkehrte, d.h.

---

56 See Wetzels 1973: 37, noting 'ein, wenn nicht das Grundschema des romantisch-naturphilosophischen Denkens: zu jedem Phänomen ein analog gebautes Gegenphänomen zu suchen, das aber die Eigenschaften des ersten [...] umkehrt; zu jeder Welt eine korrespondierende [...] Gegenwelt zu konstruieren'; see also ibid. p. 43 ('die Konstruktion eines Umkehrsystems'), and p. 102.

57 'Oberflächlich angesehen ist diese verkehrte Welt so das Gegenteil der ersten, daß sie dieselbe außer ihr hat, und jene erste als eine verkehrte *Wirklichkeit* von sich abstößt' [Looked at superficially, this inverted world is the contrary of the first in the sense that it has the first world outside of it and repels it from itself as an inverted *actuality*] (PhG, 112 [97]; Inw, 68; emphasis in original). However, on a more exact account, 'solche Gegensätze von Innerem und Äußerem, von Erscheinung und Übersinnlichem, als von zweierlei Wirklichkeiten, sind hier nicht mehr vorhanden' [But such oppositions of inner and outer, of appearance and the supersensible, as of two kinds of actuality, are no longer present] (PhG, 113 [97–98]; Inw, 68).

> die verkehrte ihrer selbst; sie ist sie selbst, und ihre entgegengesetzte in Einer Einheit.
>
> [Thus the supersensible world, which is the inverted world, has at the same time encroached upon the other world and has it within itself; it is for itself the inverted world, i.e. the inversion of itself; it is itself and its opposite in one unity.]

At this point, therefore, Hegel has defined a structure which is 'the inversion of itself', or which coincides with its opposite: 'itself and its opposite in one unity'.

The world as it appears to a subject, and the world as it is in itself (as it were turned away from the subject) may appear to exist on two opposite sides of the same surface: recto and verso. But as it were by a sleight of hand, Hegel has conjured up a surface which — at least when considered in its totality — consists of only one side. For now recto coincides with verso, in an 'inverted world' consisting of 'itself and its opposite'. As Deleuze himself puts it, now in part citing Hegel in Hyppolite's translation: 'C'est à force de glisser qu'on passera de l'autre côté, puisque l'autre côté n'est que le sens inverse. Et s'*il n'y a rien à voir derrière le rideau*, c'est [...] qu'il suffit de suivre assez loin [...] pour inverser l'endroit' [By sliding, one passes to the other side, since the other side is nothing but the opposite direction. And *if there is nothing to see behind the curtain* [...] it is because it suffices to follow it far enough [...] to reverse sides].[58] In both Hegel and in Hölderlin, therefore, there seems to be a connection between the definition of a one-sided surface, and the construction of a space that is adequate to a certain kind of self-reflection: that of a 'lyric' or poetic subjectivity in the case of Hölderlin, or in Hegel's case the transition to a figure of 'Selbstbewußtsein' that will in the end coincide with the absolute standpoint of philosophy.

We do not know, of course, whether this curious structure figured in the two friends' conversations in Frankfurt and Homburg. A few years later, another friend from the Homburg days was much impressed by the style of Hegel's book, in particular the fiery vigour of its exposition. As Isaak von Sinclair said, reading it brought back the memory of those days, and the fellowship of spirit that bound together a circle of friends — a fellowship from which Hölderlin had by now been so cruelly torn.[59]

---

58 Deleuze 1969: 19 [12] (trans. modified). The words I have italicised in that citation come from Hegel's summary of the outcome of his third chapter: see PhG, 118 [102], Inw, 71, and *La Phénoménologie de l'Esprit*, trans. by Jean Hyppolite, 2 vols (Paris: Aubier, 1947), I, 140–41. Note that the same words are cited in Deleuze's review (2002: 20).

59 See the letter from Sinclair to Hegel of 5 February 1812: 'In dem Styl u. der Darstellung habe ich dich m. deinen Eyffer dem ein flammendes Schwerdt zu Gebot steht sehr erkannt, u. an die Zeiten des Bunds unserer Geister gedacht, aus dessen Mitte das Schicksal uns die andern [Hölderlin, and Jacob Zwilling (1776–1809)] entrissen hat' (StA, VII.2, 421). On the circle of those four friends, see Hanke 2015.

CHAPTER 4

Boileau and 'Longinus' in Hölderlin's *Sophokles-Anmerkungen*

> A forward critic often dupes us
> With sham quotations *Peri Hupsous:*
> And if we have not read Longinus,
> Will magisterially outshine us.
> Then, lest with Greek he overrun ye,
> Procure the book for love or money,
> Translated from Boileau's translation,
> And quote quotation on quotation.
> — Jonathan Swift, 'On Poetry' (1733)[1]

> *Camilla.* You have hardly mentioned the French!
> *Andrea.*   That wasn't with any particular intention;
>   I just found no occasion to do so.
> — Friedrich Schlegel, 'Dialogue on Poetry' (1800)[2]

1. The *Moyens* of Poetry

Hölderlin's 'Notes' to his translations of two plays of Sophocles are the most substantial statement of his later poetics. The two sets of those *Anmerkungen* — the 'Anmerkungen zum Oedipus' and 'Anmerkungen zur Antigonä' — follow a similar pattern.[3] Each is divided into three sections: the first section is devoted to a formal analysis of the tragedies concerned; the second to points of translation and interpretation of particular passages; and the third to the more general significance of the form of tragedy.[4] When that pattern is taken into account, the opening four

---

[1] Swift, *Complete Poems*, ed. by Pat Rogers (Harmondsworth: Penguin Books, 1983), p. 529, ll. 271–78.
[2] 'Gespräch über die Poesie', in *Athenaeum*, ed. by August Wilhelm Schlegel and Friedrich Schlegel, 3 vols, 1798–1800 (Berlin; repr. Darmstadt: Wissenschaftliche Buchgesellschaft, 1992), III (1800), 58–128, 169–87 (p. 86): '*Camilla.* Sie haben die Franzosen ja fast gar nicht erwähnt. *Andrea.* Es ist ohne besondre Absicht geschehn; ich fand eben keine Veranlassung.'
[3] MA, II, 309–16, 369–76; unless otherwise indicated, translations of AO and AA are as in Part II below.
[4] On the often-noted three-part structure of the *Anmerkungen*, see e.g. Böschenstein 2002: 247. Note, however, that in the case of the 'Anmerkungen zur Antigonä' the original edition omits any indication of a division between the second and third sections. If this was a printer's error, it is a

paragraphs of the 'Anmerkungen zum Oedipus' can be seen as a kind of preface to both sets of 'Notes', giving an initial indication of Hölderlin's method and purpose.

The reader may be disconcerted by the limited ambition expressed in those opening remarks. Hölderlin declares a goal of giving poetry 'a position in society' [eine bürgerliche Existenz], which is to be achieved by a 'procedure' [Verfahrungsart] that can be 'calculated and taught' [berechnet und gelehrt], and is able 'always to be reliably repeated in practice' [in der Ausübung immer zuverlässig wiederhohlt]. Account must be taken of different 'times and constitutions' [Zeiten und Verfassungen]; but in so far as the Greeks remain a model for Hölderlin, it is again in the 'reliability' [Zuverlässigkeit] of their methods. By contrast, modern poetry is above all lacking 'in schooling and craftsmanship' [an der Schule und am Handwerksmäßigen]. The restraint of those ambitions may appear to sit oddly with the originality and depth of the texts that follow; although at the end of his second paragraph Hölderlin does also hint at additional 'higher reasons' [höher[e] Gründ[e]]. It is true that the notion of a 'school' for poetry is not unfamiliar in the criticism of the time: as Schmidt has observed, similar thoughts were expressed in Friedrich Schlegel's 'Dialogue on Poetry' of 1800; although it seems more in passing than as a programmatic statement.[5]

The relationship between poetry as a craft, and the 'higher reasons' for its prosecution, leads of course to a central enigma in Hölderlin. No poet is more deeply immersed in philosophy, in particular in the post-Kantian German Idealism to which he himself made a significant contribution. But at the same time, few have made so deliberate an attempt to turn away from purely philosophical concerns, towards problems of poetic practice — as if the adequate response to those concerns could only be found in the latter. The result is something like a paradox: if poetry is to be the equal of philosophy, and to address equally lofty concerns, it becomes all the more important for poetic technique to be mobilized. Otherwise it will be all too easy to fall into excessive enthusiasm, on the one hand, or into monotony or bathos on the other. That question of poetic technique — namely how to represent the loftiest ideas and the most sublime emotions — is already present in an untitled series of seven short 'maxims' or 'aphorisms', which are an early document of one of the most important phases of Hölderlin's thought: the 'Homburg poetics' of 1798–1800.[6] As Seifert and Vöhler have separately shown, that text gives evidence of an engagement with one of the most remarkable works of ancient poetics, the treatise *On the Sublime* [Περὶ ὕψους] once attributed to Longinus.[7] In its origins a treatise

---

remarkable one. There were many misprints in the 1804 edition, but only Hölderlin's list of errors in the *Oedipus* translation has survived (see MA, III, 435–36, and Schmidt in KA, II, 1328).

5   'Gespräch über die Poesie', pp. 92–93; see Schmidt in KA, II, 1378–79, noting other terminological similarities between the opening paragraphs of the *Anmerkungen* and that 'Gespräch'.

6   See MA, II, 57–61 (under the title 'Frankfurter Aphorismen'); AL, 240–43 ('Seven Maxims'). The manuscript is a fair copy from 1799; although Hölderlin left Frankfurt for Homburg vor der Höhe in September 1798, the editors of MA speculate that the text is based on earlier drafts composed in Frankfurt (see MA, III, 389). The connection between the vices of excessive enthusiasm, on the one hand, and philosophical abstraction, on the other, is clear in the letter from Schiller of 24 November 1796 (MA, II, 641).

7   [Pseudo-]Longinus, *On the Sublime*, ed. and trans. by W. H. Fyfe, rev. by Donald Russell, in

on rhetoric, it can justifiably be seen as a work of literary criticism, becoming in the seventeenth and eighteenth centuries a key document in poetics and the theory of art.[8]

In those opening paragraphs of the *Anmerkungen*, a reader may also be struck by the unexplained occurrence of a French term. In the second paragraph Hölderlin observes:

> Man hat, unter Menschen, bei jedem Dinge, vor allem darauf zu sehen, daß es Etwas ist, d.h. daß es in dem Mittel (*moyen*) seiner Erscheinung erkennbar ist, daß die Art, wie es bedingt ist, bestimmt und gelehret werden kann.

Note that here the italics indicate the presence of a foreign word rather than an emphasis.[9] The meaning of the first part of this statement (from 'Man hat' to 'erkennbar ist') is not immediately clear. Adler translates the whole sentence as follows:

> Among men, one must above all bear in mind that every thing is *something*, i.e. that it is cognizable in the medium (*moyen*) of its appearance, and that the manner in which it is defined can be determined and taught. (AL, 317)

While translating 'Mittel' as 'medium', in the associated note Adler remarks that *moyen* is 'the French word for "means", here used in the sense of "means of representation"' (AL, 386). However, even that may be to give the statement an unduly philosophical flavour, as if Hölderlin were expounding a Kantian thesis as to the possibility and limits of representation. As we have seen, the context is instead a discussion of the reliability and teachability of poetic methods — indeed one that, at the end of the same paragraph, is expressly distinguished from any 'higher reasons' that may also exist. Furthermore there is no basis in the original for the inclusion of 'and' after 'appearance'; rather than making a separate point, the second part of the statement seems merely to be an elucidation of the first, making the same point in a different way.[10] As in Part II, therefore, I would suggest:

> In human affairs one has above all to make sure, with each thing, that it is Something, i.e. that it is knowable in the means (*moyen*) of its appearance, that the manner in which it is determined can be defined and taught.

Aristotle, XXIII, LCL 199 (Cambridge, MA: Harvard University Press, 1995; corrected repr. 1999), pp. 143–305. See Seifert 1982: 69–79, and Vöhler 1993b; and see also Schmidt 1981: 98–101, and 1983: 185. It is now widely accepted that authorship of the treatise is unknown; both author and treatise will be referred to here as 'Longinus'. References to chapters (abbreviated 'ch.') and their subdivisions correspond to those in the editions of both Fyfe and Schönberger (1988); and unless otherwise specified, page references are to the former.

8   See Fuhrmann 2003: 164–65; Groddeck 2008: 65–67. The emphasis of 'Longinus' on the need to amaze or transport (rather than merely persuade) the audience is one factor in this, as is its focus on literary examples: cf. Till 2006: 89, and 2012: 57–58. On the close relation, none the less, between rhetoric and literary criticism in 'Longinus', see Porter 2016: 57–177, passim, observing the centrality to the treatise of 'the rhetorical construction of the sublime' (p. 83).

9   The original text of the *Anmerkungen* is in fact set mostly in italics, with 'moyen' here put in roman. See the introductory note in Part II below.

10   As Pöggeler observes, '*Das bedeutet*, dass die Art, wie es bedingt ist, bestimmt und gelehrt werden kann' (2004: 90; my emphasis).

Thus an activity or craft, for instance that of poetry, becomes 'Something' precisely when its method can be determined and taught; and this is what Hölderlin means when he refers (somewhat more obscurely) to the *moyen* that enables something to appear or become knowable.[11]

Hölderlin's thought seems to be, therefore, that an art will have a secure status in human society when the rules for its production are sufficiently defined that they can be taught. For instance, a treatise on beauty — giving, say, its supposed philosophical definition, and examples of works of art that are recognized to be beautiful — will provide little insight into the constitution of the beautiful. But knowing how such works came to be the way they are, or by what means they were produced, will provide a more reliable understanding and enable the lesson to be passed on and applied in artistic practice. And if one were seeking a precedent for such a thought, one might do worse than the following:

> D'ailleurs, quand on traite d'un art, il y a deux choses à quoy il se faut toujours étudier. La premiere est, de bien entendre son sujet. *La seconde, que je tiens au fond la principale, consiste à montrer comment et par quels moyens ce que nous enseignons se peut acquérir.* Cecilius s'est fort attaché à l'une de ces deux choses: car il s'efforce de montrer par une infinité de paroles, ce que c'est que le Grand et le Sublime, comme si c'estoit un point fort ignoré: *mais il ne dit rien des moyens qui peuvent porter l'esprit à ce Grand et à ce Sublime.* (my emphasis)

That statement comes from the opening paragraph of 'Longinus', from the first of its two introductory chapters. Here it is cited in the seventeenth-century French translation of Nicolas Boileau (originally 1674).[12] To give the same passage in Fyfe's English version:

> [S]eeing that there are two requisites in every systematic treatise: the author must first define his subject, *and secondly, though this is really more important, he must show us how and by what means* [δι' ὦντινων μεθόδων] *we may reach the goal ourselves.* Caecilius, however, endeavouring by a thousand instances to demonstrate the nature of the sublime, as though we know nothing about it, *apparently thought it unnecessary to deal with the way in which* [δι' ὅτου τρόπου] *we*

---

11 By contrast, Billings suggests that Hölderlin here 'describes a philosophical mode of cognition at the heart of poetic process' (2014: 202). But note how the language corresponds to that of the letter to his mother of 16 November 1799, where he says that 'ich vielleicht billiger geachtet würde *unter den Menschen*, wenn ich durch ein honettes Amt *im bürgerlichen Leben* für sie *erkennbar* wäre' [*people would perhaps respect me more if they could make out that I held a decent office in society*] (MA, II, 841; AL, 166; my emphasis). And later in the same letter he compares his own more problematic vocation with that of his brother: 'Und diß ist der Trost und die Regel meines Lebens, daß kein Mensch in der Wirklichkeit alles seyn kann, daß er *irgend Etwas* [N.B.] *seyn muß*' [And it is the comfort and rule of my life that in the real world no one can be everything and *is forced to become one particular thing*] (MA, II, 842; AL, 167; my emphasis).

12 *Traité du Sublime, ou du merveilleux dans le discours, Traduit du grec de Longin*, in Boileau [Nicolas Boileau-Despréaux], *Œuvres Complètes*, ed. by Françoise Escal (Paris: Gallimard, 1966), pp. 333–440. See also *Les Oeuvres de M. Boileau Despreaux, avec des éclaircissemens historiques. Nouvelle édition revue et corrigée*, 2 vols (Paris, 1735), II, iii–126. These editions will be cited below as OC and OBD respectively, followed by page number. Boileau entitles this chapter the 'Preface to the whole work'. The only edition with a parallel Greek text (but lacking Boileau's own preface) is: *Traité du Sublime, ou du merveilleux dans le discours, Traduit du grec de Longin, Par M. D**** (Paris, 1694).

may be enabled to develop our natures to some degree of grandeur. (ch. 1.1, p. 161; my emphasis, trans. modified)

In his eighth chapter, 'Longinus' offers a fivefold path to the Sublime. The first two of his five sources (the 'power of grand conceptions' and 'the inspiration of vehement emotion') are, he acknowledges, more innate than acquired, but the remainder are a matter of 'art' or 'nobility of language'; all, however rest on 'competence in speaking'. Furthermore we can cultivate the first two qualities in ourselves, not least by letting ourselves be inspired by classical models (chs 9, 13.2). And in any event, Nature cannot be left simply to itself, but requires the guidance and discipline of Art (ch. 2).[13] And if there is no doubt of the importance of 'Longinus' for Hölderlin, it lies more in the technical means for achieving the Sublime than in the cultivation of sublime thoughts and emotions, since for Hölderlin the latter was already a given.[14]

He will have been familiar with the work in the Greek original. On the other hand, it is difficult to exaggerate the significance of Boileau in the dissemination of 'Longinus' in eighteenth-century Europe, in particular England and France. Boileau's first edition of 1674 was followed by numerous further editions both during and after his lifetime.[15] Boileau himself added a 'Preface' to his translation, as well as copious 'Notes' [Remarques]. He was also the author of a series of twelve 'Réflexions critiques' on selected passages, which were eventually all published alongside his translation. The first nine of those 'Critical Reflections' form part of Boileau's contribution to the 'Quarrel of the Ancients and the Moderns', designed to defend Homer and Pindar against the criticisms of Charles Perrault.[16]

Hölderlin's Sophocles translations and associated *Anmerkungen* were completed in the years (1802–04) immediately following his return from Bordeaux. He had spent only a few months there, as a private tutor in a family of German wine merchants. But brief as it was, his period in France left a profound impression on Hölderlin's poetry and thought.[17] The question therefore arises whether Hölderlin

---

13 On these points cf. Groddeck 2008: 69–72. And on the relation between Art and Nature in the production of the Sublime, see further Porter 2016: 60–104, and Fuhrmann 1966: 68–69.
14 See Vöhler 1993b: 159, 171–72, and 1997: 192–93. As Seifert observes, ch. 2 'enthält jenes große Plädoyer für Methode, Regel und besonnene Technik, das selten Erwähnung findet, wenn über die Wirkungsgeschichte Longinus gehandelt wird' (1982: 75). Hölderlin's appreciation of 'Longinus' is already mentioned in a letter from Rudolf Magenau of 10 July 1788 (MA, II, 432), and seems to be reflected in his Master's exercises or *specimina* of 1790 (see n. 33 below). 'Longinus' then becomes central to the development of his poetics, in particular his conception of a poetic 'law' or 'calculus' (see Seifert 1982: 75–77). On his earlier reception of the treatise, see already Montgomery 1923: 171–74.
15 On Boileau's importance for the reception of 'Longinus', see Brody 1958: 12–18; Maurer 1979: 215; Litman 1971: 66–67; Kerslake 2000: 63. But in Porter's disparaging judgment, Boileau was a mere populariser who did more harm than good (2016: 43–51). For the evidence that (at least by 1798) Hölderlin had read 'Longinus' in Greek, see Seifert 1982: 72.
16 For the *Réflexions Critiques* see OC, 493–563; OBD, 129–218. The *Querelle des Anciens et des Modernes* was inaugurated by Perrault in 1687–88; Boileau first replied (in defence of Pindar) in his *Discours sur l'ode* of 1693 (OC, 227–29). See Hamilton 2003: 152–54.
17 See Bennholdt-Thomsen 1997, and on Hölderlin and French culture see Bertheau 2003. Hölderlin may have already begun work on the Sophocles translations in Bordeaux (MA, III, 430; cf. Bertheau 2003: 166, and Castellari 2018: 53, n. 94).

reacquainted himself with 'Longinus' in Bordeaux, in the shape of Boileau's famous translation, and whether in offering *moyen* as the equivalent of '[das] Mittel' he was pointing the reader in that direction. In that case the term would correspond to the Greek *methodos*, for which Schönberger's modern German version does indeed give the translation 'Mittel' (1988: 4–5). It is true that (unlike Schönberger and Boileau) Hölderlin puts both 'Mittel' and 'moyen' in the singular, which may help to explain the tendency to interpret his 'Mittel' as 'medium'.[18] But as we have seen, the context supports the interpretation in terms of poetic rules and methods. True, there are other possible sources for Hölderlin's use of the term in precisely this sense. For instance 'moyens' is used by Marmontel, in the context of a theory of the harmonious relation of the three poetic faculties that has been suggested as an influence on Hölderlin (although here there seems to be little concrete evidence). Indeed Hölderlin could also have heard the term *moyens* from the lips of Goethe.[19] But the particular relevance of Boileau is that the term is used in his translation of the opening methodological remarks of 'Longinus', in a way that parallels its use in Hölderlin's own opening remarks.

Before leaving those introductory paragraphs of the *Anmerkungen*, it is worth considering some further distinctions drawn by Hölderlin. Thus he distinguishes there between: (1) what he calls the 'calculable law', designated by the equivalent expressions '[der] gesezliche Kalkul' and 'das kalkulable Gesez' (AO [1.2]–[1.4]; AA [1.1]); (2) what he calls, more generally, poetic or artistic 'procedure' [Verfahrungsart], of which the calculable law appears to be one aspect; and (3) the 'particular content' [der besondere Innhalt] and 'living sense' [der lebendige Sinn], from which the calculable law is to be distinguished, but with which it must also be brought into relation (AO [1.4]). Returning now to 'Longinus', we may note that the relation between formal poetic rules and living poetic content is precisely the subject of what survives of his second introductory chapter (ch. 2, pp. 164–67).

Thus 'Longinus' asks how a technique or art [τέχνη] of the Sublime can be possible: surely only Nature, in the shape of native genius, can be responsible for poetic heights and profundities, not 'the dry bones of rule and precept [ταῖς τεχνολογίαις]'. He then answers his own question: both are of course required. Left to itself, artistic genius can accomplish nothing; it requires conscious insight to contain it within the right measure, and to choose the most auspicious moment. Nature [φύσις] is the first principle, but one which also requires the constraint of system or method [μέθοδος]. As we have seen, Boileau has previously translated

---

18   The Greek too is in the (genitive) plural. Boileau uses 'moyens' to render both μεθόδων and the genitive singular τρόπου in the passage cited (similarly Fyfe and 'means'), although Schönberger's 'Mittel' corresponds to the first term only. Further on, Boileau uses 'moyen' in the singular to translate ὄργανον [instrument]: OC, 394; OBD, 110; ch. 39.1 (pp. 282–83).

19   On Hölderlin and Jean-François Marmontel (1723–1799), see Stierle 1979: 531; but the doctrine of the faculties was in any event well-established in German eighteenth-century aesthetics (cf. Gaier 1994). As to Goethe, having seen the poems 'Der Wanderer' and 'An den Aether', he writes to Schiller (28 June 1797) that he will withhold his counsel until he has seen whether Hölderlin has '*Moyens* und Talent' in other kinds of verse; Goethe then subsequently had contact with Hölderlin in Frankfurt. See MA, III, 593–98 (p. 594), where the connection with the *Anmerkungen* is also noted by the editor.

the latter as 'moyens', although he now chooses 'méthode' (OC, 342; OBD, 7). Hölderlin's term 'Verfahrungsart' would also be a reasonable translation.[20] For 'Longinus', poetic method does not consist in the dry application of rules; but nor can poetry be left to the blind impulse of natural genius. The true method is to find the just proportion between rule and spontaneity. In the image employed by 'Longinus', genius requires the 'curb' as often as the 'spur' (ch. 2.2, pp. 164–65). In the third of his seven aphorisms Hölderlin employs the same image:[21]

> Da wo die Nüchternheit dich verläßt, da ist die Gränze deiner Begeisterung. Der große Dichter ist niemals von sich selbst verlassen, er mag sich so weit über sich selbst erheben als er will. [...] Das Gefühl ist aber wohl die beste Nüchternheit, und Besinnung des Dichters, wenn es richtig und warm und klar und kräftig ist. Es ist Zügel und Sporn dem Geist.

> [There where sobriety leaves you, there is the limit of your enthusiasm. The great poet is never removed from himself, he may elevate his self as high as he wishes. [...] But feeling is surely the poet's best sobriety and reflection, if it is right and warm and clear and forceful. It is a rein and a spur to the spirit.]
> (MA, II, 58; AL, 240)

Note here the concept of 'enthusiasm' [Begeisterung], so typical for the eighteenth-century discourse on the Sublime, and often associated with Pindar. For as Batteux observed, this was no longer the name simply of a poet but of 'enthusiasm itself', carrying with it the idea of 'transports, leaps, disorder, lyrical digressions'.[22] But for both 'Longinus' and Hölderlin, the relationship between poetic enthusiasm and poetic law is more complex. Both see that poetry achieves its greatest heights not through the disorder of natural genius, but through a Nature educated by Art, and a feeling for the just proportion of the whole.

2. 'Transport'

In the first section I began with a conjecture: namely that in using the French term 'moyen' in the opening paragraphs of the *Anmerkungen*, Hölderlin was in effect citing Boileau's translation of 'Longinus'. I should make it clear that this is intended as a working hypothesis rather than an established fact. Its value will lie in the light it sheds on the argument of his work, and in the connection it suggests between the final phase of Hölderlin's poetics and a text that had long accompanied him in his theoretical reflections. For 'Longinus' was present not only at the beginnings

---

20 Cf. Brody 1958: 44, preferring 'proper procedure' to 'system' (the latter as given e.g. by Fyfe).
21 As noted by Vöhler (1993b: 165–66).
22 L'Abbé [Charles] Batteux, *Principes de la littérature. Nouvelle Edition*, 5 vols (Paris, 1764), III, 31–32: 'Le nom de Pindare n'est guères plus le nom d'un poëte, que celui de l'enthousiasme même. Il porte avec lui l'idée de transports, d'écarts, de désordre, de digressions lyriques.' Pindar had long been associated with 'enthusiasm' (Hamilton 2003: 172), but here Batteux is no doubt echoing Boileau (cf. Dieckmann 1966: 96, 99). Seifert (1982: 69, n. 12) suggests that Hölderlin may have been familiar with Batteux in the translation of Karl Wilhelm Ramler. On the history of Pindar reception before Hölderlin, see also Vöhler 2005; and on Pindar (and Empedocles) in the iconography of the Sublime, see Langdon 2012: 180.

of the Homburg poetics, but also it seems in his Master's exercises (*specimina*) of 1790. And there is further evidence of an encounter with Boileau's translation in the *Anmerkungen* themselves.

Later in that first section of the 'Anmerkungen zum Oedipus', Hölderlin uses another term that can be regarded as French, although this time without expressly giving it as the foreign equivalent of a German expression. This is the term 'der Transport', used in AO [1.6]: 'Der tragische *Transport* ist nemlich eigentlich leer, und der ungebundenste' [For the tragic *transport* is properly speaking empty, and the least constrained] (MA, II, 310). The term is used again in the immediately following paragraph. It is true that, in contrast to the earlier use of 'moyen', Hölderlin does not represent it typographically as a foreign word. But there are other places in the *Anmerkungen* where a foreign word is employed in a similar fashion. And if 'Transport' is also a German word, it was a French import from the seventeenth century.[23] The question, therefore, is whether the term is being used in a sense that is more familiar in a French context — more specifically, that of the French poetics of the seventeenth and eighteenth centuries.

Both 'transport' and the verb 'transporter' have a prominent role in Boileau's version of 'Longinus'. Boileau employs these terms in two places that are particularly significant for our purposes. Leaving aside his own preface to the work, which I shall consider later, the first occurrence is in ch. 1, where — following the methodological remarks already discussed — the author turns to an initial characterisation of elevated or sublime discourse. This is to be distinguished from other forms:

> Car il ne persuade pas proprement, mais *il ravit, il transporte*, et produit en nous une certaine admiration mêlée d'étonnement et de surprise, qui est toute autre chose que de plaire seulement, ou de persuader. (OC, 341; OBD, 5; my emphasis)

> [For its effect] is not to persuade the audience but rather to *transport them out of themselves* [εἰς ἔκστασιν ἄγει]. Invariably what inspires wonder, with its power of amazing us, always prevails over what is merely convincing and pleasing. (ch. 1.4, pp. 162–63; my emphasis)

The central characteristic of the Sublime is the ability to ravish or transport and (as Boileau's version says later in the same paragraph) to 'carry away the soul of the audience' with 'an invincible force' [une force invincible qui enleve l'ame de quiconque nous écoute]. At this point Boileau's 'transport' corresponds to the Greek term *ekstasis*.[24] Or more exactly, since it is used as a verb, it corresponds to the idea of being brought into such a state of rapture or *ekstasis*, or (as in Fyfe's version) being

---

23   See Grimm, s.v. 'Transport', in particular sense 4 ('nur im 17. jh. nach frz. vorbild "gefühlsaufwallung; leidenschaft; taumel"'). For other cases of adoption of a then foreign expression in the *Anmerkungen*, cf. 'Summum' and 'Rapidität', both used in this first section of AO. Böschenstein (2006: 72) has suggested a further example from the 'Anmerkungen zur Antigonä', namely 'sich formalisieren', corresponding to the French 'se formaliser'. On the latter see the commentary to AA [3.6] in Part II below.

24   Noted in a different context by Hamilton 2008: 104. The same passage from 'Longinus' is in fact cited under this rubric in LSJ: '2. *distraction* of mind, from terror, astonishment, anger, etc.'

transported 'out of' oneself. The term is then used again in Boileau's translation, and now as a substantive (although corresponding to a different expression in the original Greek). The passage may be a particularly important one for Hölderlin, since — as Vöhler has suggested — it could be one source of the concept of 'tones' used in the Homburg poetics.[25] Thus 'Longinus' remarks of the tones of a musical instrument (which are in themselves without meaning):

> neanmoins par ces changemens de tons qui s'entrechoquent les uns les autres, et par le mélange de leurs accords, souvent, comme nous voyons, [...] causent à l'ame *un transport et un ravissement admirable*. (OC, 394; OBD, 110–11; my emphasis)

> by the variety of their sounds and by their combination and harmonious blending often exercise, as you know, *a marvellous spell* [θαυμαστὸν θέλγητρον]. (ch. 39.2, pp. 282–85; my emphasis)

Of course, in both of the passages cited above, 'Longinus' is referring to the effect of sublime discourse, the power it exerts on the minds of the audience. It might be thought, therefore, that the concept would be of relatively little interest to Hölderlin in the *Anmerkungen*. For it seems that there Hölderlin is more concerned with what is represented *in* or *by* tragedy, as opposed to its effect on the audience. Indeed, in the second of his opening paragraphs, Hölderlin expressly rejects an aesthetic based merely on the impressions made by works of art; although as we have seen, this is not necessarily to exclude any consideration of the techniques by which such effects are produced.

Furthermore, the same shift in perspective can be found in AO [3.1], in relation to the Aristotelian concept of *katharsis*. There the idea of purification — of 'limitless unification' [das gränzenlose Eineswerden] through 'limitless separation' [gränzenloses Scheiden] — is used to describe the process of tragic 'presentation' [Darstellung des Tragischen], rather than its effect on the emotions of the spectator.[26] But Aristotle cannot in any event be overlooked, for Hölderlin ends the paragraph with a citation from the Greek: not from Aristotle himself, but from a Byzantine lexicon (the *Suda*). The citation in question praises Aristotle as the 'scribe of nature'. That is admittedly an oblique way of invoking the Aristotelian concept; and furthermore it has long been observed that the citation is inaccurate. But note that the error can be traced to a French work that Hölderlin may have been accurately transcribing.[27] It is as if two of the greatest works of ancient poetics

---

25 See Vöhler 1993b: 167–69. On the Homburg doctrine of the 'alternation of tones' see Chapter 3 above.

26 Thus in AO [3.1] 'das gränzenlose Eineswerden [...] sich reinigt'. Cf. Aristotle, *Poetics*, ed. and trans. by Stephen Halliwell, in Aristotle, XXIII, LCL 199 (Cambridge, MA: Harvard University Press, 1995; corrected repr. 1999), 1449b (pp. 46–49).

27 It was Rémi Brague (1994) who first traced this form of the *Suda* citation to the title page of Jean-Baptiste Robinet's *De la nature* (1761–1763); see also Schmidt in KA, II, 1390–91, and Hühn 1997: 172–74; and see the commentary to AO [3.1] in Part II below. The mis-citation is all the more striking, given that the true version is alluded to in the final paragraph of Winckelmann's *Gedanken über die Nachahmung der griechischen Werke in der Malerei und Bildhauerkunst* (1755): see *Winckelmanns Werke in einem Band*, ed. by Helmut Holtzhauer (Berlin: Aufbau Verlag, 1982), p. 36. But given the

— those of Aristotle and 'Longinus' — are present in the *Anmerkungen* in the form of an oblique reference derived from a French source.

In any event, Hölderlin could already have found in Boileau a use of the term 'transport' that corresponds to what is represented *in* tragedy, and not merely to the effect of a sublime work on its audience. For there is another prominent place in which the term is employed, namely in Boileau's own preface. There he observes that the Sublime is to be sought not in an elevated style ('le stile sublime'), but rather in what makes a work 'carry away, ravish and transport' its audience [enleve, ravit, transporte] (OC, 338; OBD, xii). He then goes on to discuss two canonical examples of the achievement of a sublime effect by the most economical of means. The first is one given by 'Longinus' himself, namely the biblical quotation 'Let there be light!' (ch. 9.9, pp. 190–91).[28] The second example ('Qu'il mourût') was added by Boileau in later editions of his work. It is not to be found in 'Longinus', since it is taken from Corneille's tragedy *Horace*:[29]

> [I]l n'y a personne qui ne sente la grandeur heroïque qui est renfermée dans le mot, *Qu'il mourût*, qui est d'autant plus sublime, qu'il est simple et naturel, et que par là on voit que s'est du fond du cœur que parle ce vieux Heros, et dans les transports d'une colere vraiment Romaine. [...] Ce sont là de ces choses que Longin appelle Sublimes. (OC, 340; OBD, xvi–xvii)

> [[N]o-one can fail to sense the heroic grandeur contained in the expression *That he died*, which is all the more sublime for being simple and natural, and that from this one sees that this old Hero speaks from the bottom of his heart, and in the transports of a truly Roman anger. [...] That is the kind of thing that Longinus calls Sublime.]

A tragedy may succeed in representing emotions and scenes that are themselves

---

coincidence in the terms of the mis-citation, it does not seem that Winckelmann is the actual source (contrary to Duarte 2007: 16).

28 For an impressive analysis of this famous 'fiat lux' passage, see Porter 2016: 107–14. However, Porter continues his campaign against Boileau, charging him with ignoring the rhetorical and stylistic dimension altogether (ibid. 45–46). But it is surely hard to object to the example that Boileau actually gives of what must be distinguished from the Sublime, which is achieved not by flowery and pompous language but by skilful composition. Thus '[l]e stile sublime *veut toujours* des grands mots; mais le Sublime *se peut* trouver dans une seule pensée, dans une seule figure, dans un seul tour de paroles' (OC, 338; OBD, xii; my emphasis). Note that Boileau does not say that sublimity is always achieved through simplicity, just that it can be ('se peut'). In this respect the tenth *Reflexion Critique* (cf. Porter 2016: 115–16) is no different: 'rien *quelque-fois* de plus sublime' (OC, 547) and 'ce n'est point [...] les grands mots, qui font *toujours* le Sublime' (OC, 549); my emphasis. More plausibly, if Boileau takes issue with Rhetoric it is with the Roman rhetorical tradition of the *genus sublime*, rather than the Hellenistic tradition that gave rise to 'Longinus': see Till 2012: 57–64, and 2006: 68–87; and see also Brody 1958: 89–90.

29 'JULIE. Que vouliez-vous qu'il fît contre trois? LE VIEIL HORACE. Qu'il mourût' [JULIE. What should one have done against three? OLD HORATIUS. Died, for Rome!]: Corneille, *Œuvres completes*, ed. by Georges Couton, 3 vols (Paris: Gallimard, 1980–87), I (1980, repr. 1996), 878, l. 1021; *Horace*, trans. by Alan Brownjohn (London: Angel Books, 1996), p. 61. The elder Horace is reacting angrily to the news that only two of his three sons had died defending Rome. As Boileau observes: 'Voilà de fort petites paroles' (OC, 340; OBD, xvi). Or as Hölderlin put it in one of his Tübingen *specimina*: 'Kürze ist ein anerkanntes Kennzeichen der Erhabenheit' [Brevity is an acknowledged mark of Sublimity] (MA, II, 34).

sublime, and 'transport' (in Boileau's usage) can describe what is so conveyed — here the emotion of 'anger' or 'wrath' ('une colere vraiment Romaine'). We can say that the hero of Corneille's tragedy is carried away, or transported, by such an emotion because he is dispossessed by it of the normal feelings of paternal love. And it is wrath [Zorn] that is at issue at the beginning of AO [3.1], albeit transposed to a deeper or more abstract level — that of a monstrous or prodigious union of the human and divine spheres: 'wie der Gott und Mensch sich paart, und gränzenlos die Naturmacht und des Menschen Innerstes im Zorn Eins wird' [how god and human being mate, and the power of nature and deepest human inwardness unite limitlessly in wrath] (MA, II, 315). This is more than the anger of a Roman hero: as it were 'une colère vraiment Grecque'. But the sense is still present of a transport or *ekstasis* that carries a human subject beyond their normal bounds.[30]

It is not, of course, a question of reducing Hölderlin's concepts to the corresponding terms of seventeenth or eighteenth-century French criticism. There is no more original thinker than Hölderlin. But it is worth considering the origin of those concepts, the better to assess the direction in which they were developed. Gerhard Kurz has already identified 'Transport' as a term deriving from 'French poetics'.[31] However, Kurz mentions those poetics in general terms only, and for more detail refers to an essay by Herbert Dieckmann. If we consult Dieckmann's informative study, we find that he considers a number of French authors: in particular Boileau, Rémond de Saint-Mard and Batteux. But it seems clear from his analysis (1966: 96) that the seminal texts are Boileau's *Discours sur l'ode*, and the translation of 'Longinus'. In common with some other commentators Kurz then tends to lose sight of those sources, invoking Hölderlin's concept of 'metaphor' as used in the Homburg poetics (Kurz 1988: 99–100). The suggestion seems to be that 'Transport' in the *Anmerkungen* means 'transport' both in the sense current in French poetics (to 'carry away' by extreme feeling or emotion), and in the different sense of 'carry over' (in which case it would be a literal translation of the Greek *metaphora*). And indeed, recent commentators have tended to focus exclusively on the latter interpretation, as if its plausibility were self-evident.[32] This is the question to which I now wish to turn.

---

30 In Hühn's words, '[d]ie Einigung im ekstatischen Zorn' (1997: 217); and see also ibid. pp. 179 and 205. Corßen similarly observes that in AO '"zornig" [...] bedeutet etwa so viel wie "ekstatisch"' (1949: 158, n. 1). In AO [3.1] the union is described as 'das Ungeheure', and in Hölderlin's translation of *Antigone* 'ungeheuer' is used to render the concept of *deinos*: thus πολλὰ τὰ δεινὰ becomes 'Ungeheuer ist viel' (MA, II, 331, l. 349). The Greek term conveys both 'terror' and 'wonder', and their combination can well be related to the idea of the Sublime. See further the commentary to AO [3.1] in Part II below.
31 See Kurz 1988: 99, referring also to his 1975: 286, n. 42. The identification was made as early as 1913 by Hellingrath: see Hell, v, 355.
32 Böschenstein (2006: 72) shares Kurz's view that for Hölderlin 'Transport' has two meanings, one of which is derived from French poetics. But the commentary to '*Transport*' in MA, II, 310 simply cross-refers to the commentary to 'Metapher' in MA, II, 80, as if it could safely be assumed that the two terms, taken from different contexts, mean the same thing: see MA, III, 398 and 438, and similarly AL, 386 (but contrast Schmidt in KA, II, 1389).

3. Metaphor or *ekstasis*?

At this point, it will be useful to examine in more detail the context in which the term 'Transport' occurs in the *Anmerkungen*. We have seen that Hölderlin introduces it early in the first section of the 'Anmerkungen zum Oedipus', after the methodological remarks contained in the opening four paragraphs. Thus in AO [1.5] he turns from a general discussion of poetic law and procedure to the particular case of tragedy, remarking that there the 'law' or 'calculus' is 'mehr Gleichgewicht, als reine Aufeinanderfolge' [more equilibrium than pure succession]. There then follow the two paragraphs in which the concept of 'Transport' is invoked (AO [1.6]–[1.7]):

> Der tragische *Transport* ist nemlich eigentlich leer, und der ungebundenste.
> Dadurch wird in der rhythmischen Aufeinanderfolge der Vorstellungen, worinn der *Transport* sich darstellt, *das, was man im Sylbenmaaße Cäsur heißt*, das reine Wort, die gegenrhythmische Unterbrechung nothwendig, um nemlich dem reißenden Wechsel der Vorstellungen, auf seinem Summum, so zu begegnen, daß alsdann nicht mehr der Wechsel der Vorstellung, sondern die Vorstellung selber erscheint. (MA, II, 310)

> [For the tragic *transport* is properly speaking empty, and the least constrained.
> For that reason, in the rhythmical succession of representations in which the *transport* presents itself, *that which in metrics one calls a caesura*, the pure word, the counter-rhythmical interruption becomes necessary: in order namely to meet the tearing alternation of representations at its highest point, so that it is no longer the alternation of the representation that appears but rather the representation itself.]

Rather than attempting a complete analysis of this difficult passage, I shall focus on those elements that are particularly relevant to the notion of 'Transport'. AO [1.6] provides the reason for the 'law' of tragedy described in AO [1.5]. It is because the 'transport' of a tragedy is 'empty' and 'the least constrained' that the corresponding 'calculable law' is dominated by the element of balance or equilibrium rather than by 'pure succession'. A tragedy still consists in a succession or sequence of representations, and Hölderlin says that the transport 'presents' itself in such a 'rhythmical succession'. But the onward rush — or 'tearing alternation' — of ideas corresponding to the 'transport' requires a counterbalancing element to restore equilibrium. Without enquiring further into how this balance is achieved, the conclusion seems inescapable that 'Transport' refers to an underlying impulse that is manifested in the concision and rapidity of the dramatic action, with a force that threatens to carry things out of equilibrium. It is as if the speed of events is so extreme that a counterpoise is necessary for anything at all to 'appear' to the spectator.[33] Later in this section (AO [1.9]) Hölderlin refers to 'eccentric rapidity'

---

[33] Cf. Kasper 2000: 22; although some take Holderlin to be saying that the effect of the counterpoise is to enable a reflection on the faculty of representation itself (Warminski 1987: 17, 39; Kurz 1988: 100). It is surely significant that in saying that the 'tearing alternation' must be met at its highest point or climax, Hölderlin uses the Latin term 'summum', an expression also used in French (see Littré, s.v. 'summum', with an example from 1813). He had used this term in both of his Tübingen *specimina*,

[exzentrisch[e] Rapidität], as if to emphasize that it is the extreme force of such a movement that removes the tragic subject from their centre, and (in the section's closing words) drags them into the 'eccentric sphere of the dead' [die exzentrische Sphäre der Todten].

Here Hölderlin is discussing not 'transport' in general, but 'tragic transport', as it were an extreme case of the more general phenomenon. That is consistent with the thesis that he is invoking Boileau's concept of 'transport' as an index of the Sublime. For tragedy is only one genre of sublime poetry; and Sophoclean tragedy is only one example of that genre, albeit one which elicits a particularly pure form of 'transport'.[34] But such a tearing alternation of ideas is not sufficient for the expression of the Sublime: the movement must also be arrested by a balancing element, one that is all the more necessary in the case of a tragedy. Here some further light is shed on Hölderlin's meaning by passages in the second section of the 'Anmerkungen zum Oedipus', where he gives examples of Oedipus's 'wrathful curiosity' [zornige Neugier], explained as a knowledge that 'goads itself on to know more than it can grasp or bear' [sich selbst reizt, mehr zu wissen, als es tragen oder fassen kann] (AO [2.2]). And in one scene, Oedipus is as it were impelled by the very force of time itself, with a 'wrathful immoderation that [...] merely follows the tearing rapacity of time' [im zornigen Unmaas [...] das [...] der reißenden Zeit nur folgt] (AO [2.3]). It is as if Time were the true subject of the tragedy of Oedipus, the rapidity of a 'transport' at its purest and most extreme. And that immoderate quest for knowledge, or for the uncovering of the truth, reaches its climax in the latter part of the play — suggesting that it is indeed the 'eccentric rapidity' of the 'transport' in that part that (as Hölderlin explains) calls for a balancing element or 'caesura' that lies more towards the beginning (AO [1.9]).

The discussion of 'transport' in the 'Anmerkungen zum Oedipus' can be usefully compared with the parallel discussion in the 'Anmerkungen zur Antigonä' (MA, II, 369). If, in the former, Hölderlin refers to the tearing succession of ideas (in which the 'transport' is expressed) in terms of its 'eccentric rapidity', at the corresponding place in the latter he refers to the 'rapidity of enthusiasm' [Rapidität der Begeisterung] (AA [1.3]). And similarly, in section 3 of the 'Anmerkungen zur Antigonä' (MA, II, 373), Hölderlin refers to 'infinite enthusiasm' [die unendliche Begeisterung] (AA [3.1]). Such a use of 'Begeisterung' is suggestive in the present context, because it is closely related to 'transport' (in the sense of being 'carried away' by a sublime

---

and in each case it is associated with the idea of the Sublime. So in the one comparing the *Sayings of Solomon* with Hesiod's *Works and Days*, he observes that brevity is a recognised sign of sublimity, and so the biblical formula 'God said: let there be light, and there was light' represents poetry at its highest: 'Kürze ist ein anerkanntes Kennzeichen der Erhabenheit. Die Worte: Gott sprach: es werde Licht, und es ward Licht — gelten für das *summum* der hohen Dichtkunst' (MA, II, 34). This is the famous biblical example that, as we have seen, is cited in ch. 9 of 'Longinus', as well as in Boileau's preface (OC, 338; OBD, xii). In the other *specimen*, on the History of the Fine Arts among the Greeks, Hölderlin remarks that he is almost inclined to call the 'Hymns' of Pindar 'das *Summum* der Dichtkunst', referring again to their compressed brevity of expression: 'in dieser gedrängten Kürze' (MA, II, 24). Pindar is similarly an instance of the Sublime for both 'Longinus' and Boileau.

34   On tragedy, for Boileau also, as supremely equipped to elicit the effects of 'transport' see Brody 1958: 124.

feeling or emotion). In Perrault's dialogue *Paralelle des Anciens et des Modernes*, Pindar is characterised by one party as 'carried off by his enthusiasm'.³⁵ For the party of the Moderns, in their 'Quarrel' with the admirers of the Ancients, Pindar comes under suspicion as a poet who elevates himself above ordinary human reason, pouring out ecstatically ('avec transport') all that furor inspires in him.³⁶ In his *Discours sur l'ode* Boileau replies that those without Greek cannot properly appreciate Pindar, and attempts — admittedly with only limited success — to compose a French ode in the Pindaric manner: that is to say 'pleine de mouvemens et de transports' (OC, 228). Hölderlin himself, at the time of the early hymns of his Tübingen period, wrote in a tradition of 'enthusiastic' poetry initially inspired by Klopstock.³⁷

The notions of eccentricity (the 'eccentric rapidity' of the 'Anmerkungen zum Oedipus') and enthusiasm (the 'rapidity of enthusiasm' of the 'Anmerkungen zur Antigonä') are then combined in Hölderlin's letter of 2 April 1804 to Friedrich Wilmans, the publisher of his Sophocles translations. There, with a perhaps calculated ambiguity, Hölderlin writes that he has written 'gegen die exzentrische Begeisterung' [in the direction of eccentric enthusiasm] (MA, II, 930; AL, 220).³⁸ As in the case of 'Transport', there is of course no doubt that Hölderlin developed the concept of 'Begeisterung' in new directions. But it would surely be unwise to ignore the sources of these concepts in the seventeenth- and eighteenth-century poetics of the Sublime.

As we saw, there has been a tendency to regard 'Transport' instead as a literal translation of the Greek term *metaphora*: 'metaphor' in the sense of a 'transfer' or 'carrying over', as opposed to transport in the sense of *ekstasis* or a 'carrying away'. There can of course be no doubt of the importance of the concept of metaphor for Hölderlin, especially in the Homburg poetics, or of the wide range of meanings that it encompasses (Louth 1998: 90). There is accordingly a natural temptation to regard 'Transport' in the *Anmerkungen* as corresponding to this concept. In some cases the equivalence is assumed without argument.³⁹

---

35   'C'est un Poëte emporté par son enthusiasme [...] qui en cet estat profere avez transport [N.B.] tout ce que sa fureur luy inspire'; see Perrault, *Paralelle des Anciens et des Modernes en ce qui regarde les Arts et les Sciences* [...] (Paris, 1688), p. 29; and cf. Batteux, cited in note 22 above. Note that 'die [...] Begeisterung' in AA [3.1] corresponds to '[der] Zorn' in the parallel section AO [3.1]. An examination of these correspondences reveals the equivalence of 'Transport', 'Zorn' and 'Begeisterung', which all denote an excessive movement in which the human and divine can become momentarily united, leading to a tragic catharsis of division or separation. On that ecstatic meaning of 'Zorn', see note 30 above; and cf. Harrison 1975: 169–70, and Schmidt in KA, I, 821.
36   See the previous note. On Perrault, Boileau, and the *Querelle des Anciens et des Modernes*, see Hamilton 2003: 155–61.
37   See Vöhler 1997: 17, and 2002: 293. Vöhler also observes that the interaction between a 'torrent of words' and a counter-balancing 'caesura' is itself a feature of the odes of Klopstock (1997: 33–35).
38   As Louth points out (AL, 372) 'gegen' can mean 'against' as well as 'towards'; cf. Kocziszky 2009: 112. On the equivalence of Hölderlin's concepts of 'eccentricity' and 'enthusiasm', and their combination in the letter to Wilmans, see Schmidt in KA, II, 1472–73.
39   See the references in note 32 above; and see Hiller 2008: 101–02, as well as various contributors to Jamme and Lemke 2004 — in particular Rudolph Gasché (pp. 422–23), David Farrell Krell (p. 357), and Elizabeth B. Sikes (p. 390). Other writers incline to such an interpretation, while not absolutely excluding the one preferred here: see Nägele 1999: 255, with n. 25 at pp. 462–63; and

Kurz's helpful essay does have the merit of providing such an argument. As we have seen, he identifies the origin of the term 'Transport' in French poetics, but then wishes to say that it also means 'metaphor' (1988: 99). There is no objection in principle to such a strategy. There are other cases where Hölderlin clearly intends a single term to have disparate meanings; as we shall see in Chapter 6.3, this is true of such terms as 'Schiklichkeit' and 'Geschik'. Kurz points to the Homburg essay-fragment in which the 'tragic poem' is said to be 'heroic' only in its outer appearance, such outer appearance being the 'metaphor' for the underlying unity corresponding to an 'intellectual intuition' (MA, II, 102, 104; AL, 302–04). In the same way 'Transport', says Kurz, corresponds to such a 'metaphor': the unbounded, tearing form of tragic representation is the outer, metaphorical form of such an underlying unity. The difficulty, however, is that it may rather be the other way around. In the *Anmerkungen* it is the concepts of 'Transport', 'Zorn' and 'Begeisterung' that seem to correspond to the idea of an excessive unity, in which the limits dividing the human from the divine have been transgressed, and which must be followed by the catharsis of separation. It may also be asked whether the notion of 'metaphor' from the Homburg poetics can truly be applied at this later stage.[40] If the terms of the Homburg poetics were to be applied, it might rather be such features as the dialogic *agōn* ('der immer widerstreitende Dialog'), and the opposition of dialogue and chorus, that corresponded to the level of 'metaphor' (AO [3.2]). That is to say, it would be the furious, unbounded rapidity of tragic 'transport' that required a complementary metaphorical expression, rather than being itself such a metaphor.

4. 'You streets of Palmyra!'

I have suggested that, although Hölderlin had long been familiar with 'Longinus', he may have reacquainted himself with the treatise in Bordeaux in the shape of Boileau's famous translation. We have seen two possible traces of this in the *Anmerkungen*: the term 'moyen', and the term 'Transport'. Admittedly, the evidence is circumstantial and far from conclusive. On the other hand, it is difficult to see any better reason why Hölderlin should invoke terms (as these seem to be) from French poetics. He had no particular reason to be interested by debates in early eighteenth-century French criticism; but he had every reason to be intrigued by a translation of an author who had long accompanied him in his own theoretical reflections. In any event, the question whether Hölderlin actually read Boileau (as opposed to an

---

both Kurz and Böschenstein, cited in notes 31 and 32 above. See also Lacoue-Labarthe 1998: 9, 71; although the latter's position is not entirely clear, since he seems to want 'transport' to correspond both to the tragic 'metaphor' and to the original unity of which it is the metaphorical expression: 'Hölderlin voulait parler aussi de l'intuition intellectuelle comme métaphore, comme transport' (p. 71). See further Taminiaux 1995: 289.

40 On the relation between those two phases of Hölderlin's poetics, however, see also Chapter 5 below, suggesting that the late fragment discussed in that chapter (MA, II, 114) might invoke an extreme or limiting case of metaphorical expression. But it is, I think, less plausible to relate the notion of 'das Zeichen [...] = o' in that fragment to the statement that '[d]er tragische *Transport* ist [...] eigentlich leer' (AO [1.6]).

author influenced by him) is of relatively little interest. The more important point is what is intended by his use of these terms. As we have seen, in the case of the latter term in particular, an appreciation of the tradition inaugurated by Boileau can be crucial to our understanding.

If Hölderlin did come across Boileau's work, he may have appreciated that it was a version of an ancient Greek text that succeeded in making it new for a modern French audience. As a result of Boileau's free and idiomatic translation, 'Longinus' took its place as a seminal text of French (and indeed European) poetics. And as one contemporary observed, the result was a masterpiece 'that has more of the air of an original than a translation'.[41] It would perhaps be fruitless to speculate whether that example had any influence on Hölderlin's own thoughts on the role of translation in the period of the *Anmerkungen*. But in considering Boileau's possible influence, the preface to his work should not be overlooked. This does indeed contain a defence of the relatively free approach taken in his translation. It also contains an initial characterization of sublime emotions and effects, one in which the term 'transport' plays a prominent role. And for the student of Hölderlin, one striking aspect is the biographical sketch it contains of the supposed author of the treatise, Cassius Longinus.

The uncertainty as to the authorship of *On the Sublime* arises in part from an internal inconsistency in the primary manuscript source. The title page attributes authorship to 'Dionysius Longinus', whereas according to the table of contents the treatise is 'by Dionysius or Longinus' [Διονυσίου ἢ Λογγίνου].[42] It seems that the Byzantine scholars who copied the treatise were uncertain as to whether the author was the Augustan historian and critic Dionysius of Halicarnassus, or the third-century scholar and statesman Cassius Longinus. As the editor of the Loeb edition remarks, neither attribution is entirely plausible, but that to Cassius Longinus was for a long time undisputed. In particular, it was appreciated that the tone of the treatise *On the Sublime* was itself sublime, and was accordingly seen as a true reflection of the heroic temperament of its author.[43] Boileau remarks that Cassius Longinus was not only a skilful critic, but also a considerable minister of state, having been so engaged by Zenobia, Queen of Palmyra. He then relates in some detail the story of the siege of Palmyra by the Roman emperor Aurelian, and his execution of Cassius Longinus after the fall of the city (OC, 334–36; OBD, v–vii).

Among Hölderlin's works from the period of the *Anmerkungen* is a cycle of nine poems, probably those he describes in a letter to Wilmans as 'Nachtgesänge', that is to say 'Night Poems' or 'Nightsongs'.[44] From that letter it is clear that the poems were being finalized after the completion of the Sophocles translations (since Wilmans had already sent him a sample of the print). The eighth poem in the

---

41 René Rapin, cited by Brody (1958: 23): 'Le chef-d'œuvre de l'auteur, et qui a plus d'air d'original que de traduction'; see also Maurer 1979: 215–26, 257.
42 The title page and table of contents are reproduced in Porter 2016: 2–3.
43 See Russell in *On the Sublime* at pp. 145–46; Fuhrmann 2003: 163; and indeed Boileau's preface (OC, 333–34; OBD, viii). On the treatise as exemplifying the principles and techniques it expounds, see further Hösle 2009: 71–74; Groddeck 2008: 74; and Porter 2016: 147–51.
44 MA, I, 439–46; OE, 165–83. See the second letter to Wilmans of December 1803 (MA, II, 926–27; AL, 217–18). On the *Nachtgesänge* see further Chapter 6.3 below.

cycle, 'Lebensalter' [Ages of Life], begins as a meditation on the ruins of Palmyra: 'Ihr Städte des Euphrats! | Ihr Gassen von Palmyra!'.[45] As Wolfram Groddeck has argued, the imagery of that poem (and in particular its emphasis on the 'forests of columns' left in the ruins) may echo the account in a famous work by Constantin-François de Volney: *Les ruines, ou méditation sur les révolutions des empires* (1791), a work also well-known in the early German translation by Georg Forster (1792). In this respect, the scene depicted in the frontispiece of the French edition is of particular interest. Other contemporary accounts and engravings of Palmyra have been put forward as possible influences, although the connection with Cassius Longinus has tended to be overlooked by commentators (a notable exception being Hans Gerhard Steimer).[46]

It is true that the fate of Cassius Longinus at Palmyra is mentioned in other available sources (Steimer 2004: 195, n. 4). But it is interesting, to say the least, that the story should figure so prominently in the preface to Boileau's translation, thereby providing another link with Hölderlin's writings in the period following Bordeaux. Scholars have noted the influence of 'Longinus' in certain other poems of the cycle, specifically 'Hälfte des Lebens' [Half of Life] and 'Vulkan' [Vulcan], although there the relevant theme may also be present in drafts preceding his Bordeaux period.[47] However, that is not the case in the fifth, and therefore central, poem of the cycle. In the ode 'Blödigkeit' [Timidity], the poet reflects on the nature of his calling and offers himself encouragement. In contrast to the earlier versions of the poem (MA, I, 275–76, 284–85; OE, 232, 113), the concluding stanza is remarkable for its emphasis on craft and on the need to be useful for 'something.' It therefore echoes the language of the introductory paragraphs of the 'Anmerkungen zum Oedipus'; and by the same token, I would argue, the opening chapter of 'Longinus'.[48] Or in other words, it is a tribute to the *moyens* of poetry:

> Gut auch sind und geschikt einem zu *etwas* wir,
>   Wenn wir kommen, mit Kunst, und von den Himmlischen
>   Einen bringen. Doch selber
>   Bringen *schikliche Hände* wir.

45 'You cities of the Euphrates! | You streets of Palmyra!' (MA, I, 446; OE, 181).
46 See Groddeck 1996: 153–56, and Reitani in TL, 1497–98. (The frontispiece is reproduced at Groddeck 1996: 155; for a much better reproduction see Groddeck 1995: 76.) In preference to de Volney, Kocziszky (2009: 37–40) cites Robert Wood's *The Ruins of Palmyra* (1753) and *The Ruins of Balbec* (1757). In a detailed study of the visual sources, Steimer (2004: 207–11) suggests that in France Hölderlin may have seen the impressive recent engravings of Palmyra by Louis-François Cassas. For a general account of the literary treatment of Palmyra in this period, see Tausch 2016 (also mentioning the connection with Cassius Longinus at p. 277).
47 On 'Hälfte des Lebens' and the doctrine of 'sobria ebrietas' in ch. 16.4 of the treatise (pp. 228–29), see Schmidt 1983, and in KA, I, 837–39; and on 'Vulkan' and the contrast between domestic and volcanic fire in ch. 35.4 (pp. 274–76), see Bennholdt-Thomsen 2002: 339, and Analecta 2004: 30 (although there the connection is perhaps more debatable). Tausch himself identifies in 'Lebensalter' the theme of a failed aspiration to the Sublime (2016: 282); and that poem does post-date Bordeaux.
48 The connection between 'Blödigkeit' and opening paragraphs of the 'Anmerkungen zum Oedipus' is noted by Indlekofer 2007: 220. On 'Blödigkeit' see also Chapter 1.4 above, and Chapter 6.3 below.

[We too are good, sent to serve someone, and useful
For *something* when we bring forth one of the gods
With our art. Yet we ourselves
Bring our *skillful and suitable hand*s.]
(MA, I, 444; OE, 177; my emphasis)

CHAPTER 5

Hölderlin on Tragedy and Paradox

1. The Meaning of Tragedies

Hölderlin's theoretical writings command attention as the reflections by a great poet on the nature and significance of his craft. However, they also give rise to formidable problems of interpretation. There are a number of reasons for those difficulties, often varying according to the text in question. In several cases the essays are fragmentary or unfinished, and appear sometimes to be rapid drafts in which the poet's thoughts are caught on the wing.[1] In other cases the texts are carefully composed, but seem to have a hermetic or riddling quality, as in the annotations to Pindar (or *Pindarfragmente*).[2] In many cases, a theoretical text has to be considered in the context of a poetic work for which it may provide a commentary or a programme.[3] In others, its status as a commentary may be explicit, but that form developed in novel or surprising ways. The only theoretical texts that Hölderlin himself saw into print were his 'Anmerkungen' [Notes] to two plays of Sophocles. Like the *Pindarfragmente*, those *Sophokles-Anmerkungen* are presented as commentaries to Hölderlin's unorthodox translations of the respective Greek works, while transcending the limits normally assigned to philological commentary. And the *Pindarfragmente* themselves defy any easy categorization as poetry, translation, or theoretical reflection.[4]

Even where a full understanding cannot yet be achieved, it may still be possible to characterize the context and shape of Hölderlin's argument, while guarding against over-simplifications that may not do justice to the difficulty of the texts. It is in that spirit that I propose to consider one of the shortest, but in some ways

---

[1] Ryan rightly points to 'the constant reformulation of thoughts that often do not find their final expression' (1990: 558). Cf. Hiller 2008: 125 ('eine Selbstvergewisserung im Schreiben').
[2] MA, II, 379–85; AL, 334–39. On these pieces, each of which consists of a translated fragment of Pindar followed by a commentary, see further Chapter 6 below.
[3] The essay *Die tragische Ode ...* (MA, I, 865–78; AL, 258–70) is clearly intended as a basis for Hölderlin's unfinished drama on the death of Empedocles, and is often referred to under the title of its third section, 'Grund zum Empedokles'. Arguably the essay *Das untergehende Vaterland ...* (MA, II, 72–77; AL, 271–76) is similarly so to be understood (see Mögel 1994: 58–74).
[4] On those *Anmerkungen* see also Chapter 4 above, and the translation and commentary in Part II.

most representative, of his theoretical writings. This consists of a single paragraph beginning with the arresting statement that 'Die Bedeutung der Tragödien ist am leichtesten aus dem Paradoxon zu begreifen' [The meaning of tragedies is most easily understood by means of paradox] (MA, II, 114). I shall refer to this untitled text as 'BT'. It consists of only five sentences:

> [1] Die Bedeutung der Tragödien ist am leichtesten aus dem Paradoxon zu begreifen. [2] Denn alles Ursprüngliche, weil alles Vermögen gerecht und gleich getheilt ist, erscheint zwar nicht in ursprünglicher Stärke nicht wirklich sondern eigentlich nur in seiner Schwäche, so daß rechteigentlich das Lebenslicht und die Erscheinung der Schwäche jedes Ganzen angehört. [3] Im Tragischen nun ist das Zeichen an sich selbst unbedeutend, wirkungslos, aber das Ursprüngliche ist gerade heraus. [4] Eigentlich nemlich kann das Ursprüngliche nur in seiner Schwäche erscheinen, insofern aber das Zeichen an sich selbst als unbedeutend = 0 gesezt wird, kann auch das Ursprüngliche, der verborgene Grund jeder Natur sich darstellen. [5] Stellt die Natur in ihrer schwächsten Gaabe sich eigentlich dar, so ist das Zeichen wenn sie sich in ihrer stärksten Gaabe darstellt = 0.

In what follows a single number in square brackets designates the corresponding sentence in the above text, the whole of which is translated in Part II below.

The difficulties involved in interpreting BT should already be apparent. It begins by referring to 'paradox': but is this a reference to a specific paradox, or to 'paradox' in the sense of a more general category of paradoxical utterance? The manuscript shows that he did indeed begin by referring to the specific paradox 'daß alles Ursprüngliche [...] nur in seiner Schwäche erscheint' [that everything elemental [...] appears only in its weakness], before separating the thought into two sentences (FHA, XIV, 382). In that revision, does the initial 'Denn' of the second sentence preserve the initial meaning, or mark the first step in a more complex argument? Furthermore, in this theoretical fragment — turning as it does on the distinction between 'the hidden ground' [der verborgene Grund] connected with 'the elemental' [das Ursprüngliche], on the one hand, and 'appearance' [die Erscheinung] on the other — what is the significance of the distinctly more poetic term 'das Lebenslicht' [the light of life]? Most mysteriously of all, perhaps: what is the null sign ('das Zeichen [...] = 0'), and how does it relate to the concept of 'weakness' [Schwäche]? When the meaning of a sign is set at zero, how does that enable the 'hidden ground' to display itself? Or is that sign not so much without meaning, as 'insignificant' in the sense of being powerless (cf. 'unbedeutend, wirkungslos'). Another difficulty centres on the concept of 'presentation': what is the relation between the notions of 'erscheinen' and 'sich darstellen'? And how does each relate to the idea that, in tragedy, the elemental reveals itself directly, is 'straight out' [gerade heraus]?

Although editors formerly assigned BT to the period of Hölderlin's first stay in Homburg vor der Höhe (1798–1800), the scholarly consensus now places it in the final phase of his poetics that followed his return from Bordeaux in 1802. It has been suggested, in fact, that it belongs with the *Sophokles-Anmerkungen* published in 1804. For in addition to those 'Notes' to his translations of *Oedipus Tyrannnus* and

Antigone, Hölderlin had promised his publisher an 'introduction' to the tragedies, and it is possible that the text is the only surviving remnant of the latter.[5] That would suggest that BT is a fragment of a larger whole. On the other hand, despite the difficulty of the thought expressed the argument appears to be self-contained, comprising a series of deductive steps leading to a definite conclusion. While I shall follow some other commentators in referring to the text as a 'fragment', that qualification should be borne in mind. In support of the later dating, Hölderlin's more recent editors cite lexical and other similarities with manuscripts of that period, in particular the use of the term 'das Lebenslicht' in the letter to Casimir Ulrich Böhlendorff of November 1802 (MA, II, 920–22; AL, 213–15) as well as in a manuscript of the elegy 'Brod und Wein'. The expression also figures in other poetic manuscripts of the period.[6] But part of the fascination of the fragment is the bridge it provides between those two phases of Hölderlin's poetics: between the 'Homburg poetics' of the first Homburg period, and the final phase of his thought that followed his return from Bordeaux.[7]

One commentator, Ernst Mögel, continues to attribute the fragment to the first Homburg period, linking it in particular to Hölderlin's reflections on the basis for his tragedy on the death of Empedocles. That might give us pause, since Mögel also offers what is perhaps the single most convincing interpretation of one aspect of the text.[8] On the other hand, he does not address all the arguments for the later dating, including paper-type and handwriting; and nor are his considerations based on the usage of the term 'das Lebenslicht' wholly convincing.[9] Again, the very possibility of this debate illustrates the centrality of the fragment, seeming as it does to connect the thought world of the Homburg poetics with that of the Sophocles translations.

If BT has the form of a deductive argument, one way of reading it would be to focus on its conclusion, interpreting the text in the light of the final sentence. This appears to turn on the contrast between two modes of 'presentation', each involving a different aspect of 'Nature': '[5] If Nature presents itself properly in its weakest endowment, then the sign when it presents itself in its strongest endowment = 0'. Here 'Nature' is to be taken as an all-encompassing whole, rather than the individual natural things referred to in the immediately preceding sentence ('[4] the hidden ground of every nature'). For that reason I shall where appropriate capitalize the term in what follows. Nature is being considered in two distinct aspects, that of its greatest strength (or 'strongest endowment') and that of its greatest weakness (or 'weakest endowment'). Hölderlin can be read as saying that a distinct kind of presentation corresponds to each: in its aspect of weakness Nature can present itself

---

5   See the letters to Wilmans from September and December 1803 (MA, II, 924–27; AL, 215–17).
6   See MA, III, 402, citing MA, II [actually I], 413; MA, II, 921; and MA, III, 213; and see also MA, III, 254. The editors also point to a passage of Herder, cited by Jacobi, and containing the slightly different expression 'des Lebens Licht'. See further Schmidt in KA, II, 1252–53, and Groddeck 2012: 268, 316.
7   Cf. Lemke 2002: 60, n. 4.
8   Mögel 1994: 78–81, discussed further below.
9   On those additional arguments for the later dating see FHA, XIV, 379, and on 'das Lebenslicht' see further below.

'truly' or 'properly' [eigentlich]; in its aspect of strength a more oblique kind of presentation seems to be required, since use must be made of what Hölderlin calls 'das Zeichen [...] = o', the zero or null sign. And the latter case is precisely that of the presentation involved in tragedy, since '[3] in the tragic the sign is in itself insignificant'.

However, that is by no means the most familiar reading of the fragment. It is more usual to see 'das Zeichen [...] = o' as an instance of the 'weakest endowment' referred to in the first half of sentence [5]. The 'so' in 'so ist das Zeichen' would then have the sense of 'so similarly' rather than 'so conversely'. For the moment, I will merely observe that such a reading is hard to reconcile with the wording of the immediately preceding sentence, which seems to imply that the presentation that is achieved by means of the null sign is distinct from the mode in which Nature, or 'the elemental', appears in its 'weakness'. As Mögel puts it (1994: 79), Hölderlin's argument seems to have the form '[eines] Umkehrschlusses' [of an argument *a contrario*]. And that contrast is confirmed by the distinct terms: 'erscheinen' [appear], and 'sich darstellen' [presents itself]. The latter seems to be more general concept, since in [5] it covers the 'strongest' and 'weakest' aspects of Nature, whereas 'erscheinen' in [2] and [4] seems to relate specifically to the aspect of weakness.

One must also consider how the notions of 'erscheinen' and 'sich darstellen' are related to the idea that, in tragedy, '[3] das Ursprüngliche ist gerade heraus' [the elemental is straight out]. On the one hand, 'gerade heraus' seems to convey the idea of something manifesting itself directly, without the mediation of an 'appearance' or a meaningful 'sign'. That is the interpretation given by Schmidt (KA, II, 1253).[10] But on the other hand, Hölderlin does refers to a 'sign', one which presumably has a role in the presentation of 'das Ursprüngliche'. Unless of course 'das Zeichen [...] = o' is less a particular sign than a marker for the absence of any sign: as it were, the abolition of language.

In the most general terms, the fragment is concerned with how the 'elemental' [das Ursprüngliche] — original or primal Nature — can manifest itself: whether directly; or in the form of an appearance; or by means of a 'sign'.[11] The relation between the natural realm, on the one hand, and the human sphere of culture on the other (that is to say the relation between Nature and Art) is a central theme in Hölderlin: see for example the programmatic ode 'Natur und Kunst oder Saturn und Jupiter' discussed in Chapter 2 above. That relation is central also to his thought about tragedy, which is little interested in the moral problem posed by the fate of the tragic hero. Rather than being founded on the idea of moral fault, or of the

---

10   Note that in the manuscript Hölderlin originally wrote 'Nun erscheint zwar in Tragödien das Ursprüngliche gerade heraus', but then amended the text to read '[...] das Ursprüngliche ist gerade heraus' (FHA, XIV, 382). This may be because the notion of 'appearance' implies a consciousness to which something appears, whereas the emergence of the hidden ground is an event that is liable to eclipse consciousness, at least when considered from the point of view of the tragic protagonist: cf. 'in Gegensäzen, im Bewußtseyn, welches das Bewußtseyn aufhebt' (AA [3.1]; MA, II, 373).

11   As we have seen, Hölderlin seems to distinguish the special case of 'appearance' from the more general concept of 'presentation'; the idea of a 'sign' belongs with the latter, so that 'die Erscheinung' might be regarded as a special case of 'das Zeichen' — as may be suggested by the way in which the latter is introduced in [3].

clash between different ethical principles, its essence lies for Hölderlin in the idea of an excessive union with the ground of Nature. That idea already seems present in the essay *Die tragische Ode* ..., written between the second and third drafts of his *Empedocles* drama. The essay begins with an analysis of a lyric genre, namely the tragic ode, before turning to the general problem of tragic drama (the section entitled 'Allgemeiner Grund'), and finally to the basis for Hölderlin's own tragedy (the section entitled 'Grund zum Empedokles'). In order to frame a comparison of lyric and tragic-dramatic genres, Hölderlin invokes the concept of 'die Innigkeit' (connoting intimacy, or intensity of feeling). This can be expressed to different degrees in the two genres:

> Es ist die tiefste Innigkeit, die sich im tragischdramatischen Gedichte ausdrükt. Die tragische Ode stellt das Innige auch in den positivsten Unterscheidungen dar [...]. Das tragische Gedicht verhüllt die Innigkeit in der Darstellung noch mehr [...] weil es eine tiefere Innigkeit, ein unendlicheres Göttliches ausdrükt.
>
> [It is the deepest intimacy that expresses itself in a tragic-dramatic poem. The tragic ode, too, presents the intimate in the most positive differentiations [...]. The tragic [i.e. tragic-dramatic] poem conceals the intimacy in the presentation even more [...] because it expresses a deeper intimacy, a more infinite divinity.] (MA, I, 866; AL, 259, trans. modified)

If such 'Innigkeit' is interpreted in terms of a union with elemental Nature, a comparison with BT lies to hand.

However, another match may be found in the discussion of tragic presentation in the third section of the 'Anmerkungen zum Oedipus' (AO [3.1]). There '[d]ie Darstellung des Tragischen' is said to involve a prodigious or monstrous unity of divine and human spheres: 'das Ungeheure, wie der Gott und Mensch sich paart'. That encounter is characterized as a limitless union of 'die Naturmacht' [the power of nature] with 'des Menschen Innerstes' [deepest human inwardness]. As Hühn has suggested (1997: 215), this may be the sense in which '[3] das Ursprüngliche ist gerade heraus', as contrasted with the 'normal case' [Normalfall] described in [2] in which Nature appears, conversely, 'in seiner Schwäche'. An aspect of Nature that is normally hidden, and indeed unbearable when encountered directly, is revealed in the action of a tragedy.

The idea of Nature as an elemental, and potentially destructive, force is undoubtedly the context in which Hölderlin's fragment is to be read. Having stated that in tragedy, '[3] das Ursprüngliche ist gerade heraus', he then glosses 'das Ursprüngliche' as '[4] der verborgene Grund jeder Natur' [the hidden ground of every nature]. This is the aspect of Nature that is normally hidden from view, but that in tragedy is 'straight out'. However, Hölderlin's use of the term 'das Ursprüngliche' can also give rise to confusion. Evidently its primary meaning is that of an originating principle or force, and as such is identified with that 'verborgen[er] Grund'. However, he begins in [2] by distinguishing between two aspects of 'das Ursprüngliche': one of 'original strength' and one of 'weakness'. And in [4] he similarly distinguishes 'das Ursprüngliche [...] in seiner Schwäche' from 'das Ursprüngliche, der verborgene Grund'. This may be why, in the final sentence of the fragment, he prefers the more general term 'die Natur', while again distinguishing two separate aspects: Nature in its 'strongest' and its 'weakest' endowments respectively. While 'das Ursprüngliche' more readily connotes a primal (and normally hidden) ground of things, it is easier to see 'die Natur' as containing two distinct but complementary aspects, as it were a tranquil surface and fiery depths. From that point of view Nature 'in its weakest endowment' is not a deficient form, as the term 'weakest' might otherwise seem to imply. Rather it is the aspect that has the virtue of being able to appear, of being bathed in the light of appearance: '[2] das Lebenslicht und die Erscheinung'. This then would be a compensating virtue of Nature considered in its aspect of 'weakness', or in its mild or tender aspect: '[2] weil alles Vermögen gerecht und gleich getheilt ist' [because all capacity is justly and equally apportioned]. Hölderlin's fragment seems to be interested in both of those aspects, each with its distinct virtue, just as it is interested in the distinct mode of presentation that corresponds to each. Because 'die Erscheinung' attaches above all to the aspect of weakness, it is in this aspect that Nature can present itself 'actually' or 'properly' [eigentlich]. Conversely in tragedy the aspect of overwhelming strength emerges into the open, while the sign that allows it to present itself becomes as it were a paradoxical signifier, connoting precisely the opposite of what is presented: '[5] so ist das Zeichen wenn sie sich in ihrer stärksten Gaabe darstellt = 0' [then the sign when it presents itself in its strongest endowment = 0].

The analysis above has focused on what seems to be Hölderlin's argument in his two concluding sentences. However, commentators have often taken a different approach, reading them more in the light of the preceding ones. The fragment is read as a development of a single 'paradox', namely the paradox that 'original strength' can appear only in the form of 'weakness'. The sign that is without intrinsic meaning or effect, introduced in [3], would then merely be an extreme form of such weakness. That might indeed have been Hölderlin's starting point when he began to compose the fragment. As we have seen, he initially referred not to '[das] Paradoxon' in general, but rather to the more specific paradox that 'everything elemental' appears 'only in its weakness'.[12] And support for such a reading can also be found in the concept of metaphorical presentation that is central to the Homburg poetics. Thus rather than considering two distinct modes of presentation, one exemplified by 'erscheinen' or 'sich eigentlich [darstellen]' and another by 'das Zeichen [...] = 0', the fragment is interpreted in terms of a single concept of metaphorical presentation: here the presentation of 'strength' by means of 'weakness'. The limiting case of 'das Zeichen [...] = 0' could then be seen, either

---

12   Thus the first version of the text, as constituted in FHA ('Konstituierter Text I'), reads: 'Die eigentliche Bedeutung aller Tragödien erklärt sich aus dem Paradoxon, daß alles Ursprüngliche, weil alles Gut gerecht und gleich getheilt ist, nicht wirklich sondern eigentlich nur in seiner Schwäche erscheint' [The true meaning of all tragedies is explained by the paradox that everything elemental, because every good is divided justly and equally, does not appear really but actually only in its weakness] (FHA, XIV, 382). See also the letter to his brother of 4 June 1799 ('das Paradoxon [...] daß der Kunst- und Bildungstrieb [...] ein eigentlicher Dienst sei, den die Menschen der Natur erweisen' (MA, II, 769–70; AL, 136).

as one in which metaphor as it were falls away, leaving 'das Ursprüngliche' to manifest itself directly ('gerade heraus'); or alternatively as a similar (but extreme) case of metaphorical expression of strength by weakness.

In his interpretation of the fragment, Lawrence Ryan accordingly refers expressly to that concept of metaphor:

> Es handelt sich im Grunde genommen um eine weitere Anwendung des bekannten Prinzips, wonach ein jeweiliger Grund(ton) sich in seinem direkten Gegensatz äußert; hieraus wird gefolgert, daß 'alles Ursprüngliche ... zwar nicht in ursprünglicher Stärke, sondern eigentlich nur in seiner Schwäche' erscheint.
>
> [It is basically a matter of a further application of the familiar principle, by which any basic tone expresses itself in its direct opposite; from which it is concluded that 'everything elemental ... appears to be sure not in original strength, but properly only in its weakness'.][13]

It is true that, as we saw in Chapter 3, the Homburg poetics of the *Wechsel der Töne* analyses a poem in terms of the opposed aspects of 'Grundton' [basic tone] or 'Grundstimmung' [basic mood], and 'Kunstkarakter' [art-character] — where the latter corresponds to the poem as it most immediately appears, the former to an underlying meaning that is expressed only indirectly. And that notion of indirect expression is described in terms of an extended concept of 'metaphor'. Thus the 'basic tone' can only be expressed figuratively by the 'art-character' tone, which presents that underlying meaning in metaphorical form. It follows that the meaning corresponding to the basic tone can be described as 'eigentlich' (the 'actual' or 'proper' meaning), whereas the one corresponding to the 'art-character' tone is 'uneigentlich' or 'metaphorisch'.[14] The interest of this is that the term 'eigentlich' occurs repeatedly, almost obsessively, in BT itself: [2] 'eigentlich nur in seiner Schwäche', 'rechteigentlich'; '[4] Eigentlich nemlich'; '[5] Stellt die Natur [...] sich eigentlich dar'. And it is always used to convey the idea of Nature appearing 'actually' or 'properly' — quite the reverse of the notion of a mediated, figurative or metaphorical representation.[15] Thus by the time he reaches his concluding sentence, Hölderlin is willing to say that 'die Natur in ihrer schwächsten Gaabe [stellt] sich eigentlich dar' [Nature presents itself properly in its weakest endowment]. It seems that the 'weakness' of Nature cannot be regarded as a metaphor for its strength.

One problem in interpreting the fragment is that, up to this point 'das Ursprüngliche' has been used confusingly in two different senses: namely as including, and as not including, the aspect of 'weakness'. The use of the broader

---

13 Ryan 1960: 331 (ellipsis in original; note also the omission of the words 'nicht wirklich', common to all versions of the text prior to FHA). See similarly Bachmaier 1979: 133; and cf. Louth 1998: 77, and the classic account in Szondi 1978d: 161–63.
14 'Der Gegensaz seiner Grundstimmung mit seinem Kunstkarakter, seines eigentlichen Tons mit seinem uneigentlichen, metaphorischen' [The opposition between its basic mood and its art-character, its actual and its figurative, metaphoric tone] (MA, II, 103; AL, 303, trans. modified). On Hölderlin's extended concept of 'metaphor', see also Ryan 1963: 29–31.
15 Szondi appears to appreciate this, observing that the fragment establishes the necessity of a sign in which 'die Natur [erscheint] nicht mehr *eigentlich*' (1978d: 162).

term 'die Natur' seems to resolve that ambiguity; and the way now appears to be open to read 'eigentlich' — as in the Homburg poetics — in terms of a non-figurative rather than a metaphorical mode of presentation. Thus in the case of Nature in its 'weakest' aspect, there is no longer any distinction separating the thing itself from its means of expression. Conversely, when it is considered in its 'strongest' aspect, the distinction could not be more extreme: for here its means of expression has reached, as it were, degree zero: 'das Zeichen [...] = 0'.

As already observed, that capacity for non-figurative presentation — the capacity to simply 'appear' — might be regarded as the compensating virtue of Nature in its weakness. It is a capacity that 'belongs to' (or is characteristic of) the weakness of every whole. Conversely, it would be characteristic of the strength of the elemental ground, or Nature at its most inwardly intense, that its sign '= 0'. If that null sign can be taken to be a metaphor, it is a metaphor of the most extreme kind, since greatest strength is presented here by a zero quantity. But again, such nullity is not to be confused with '[5] Nature [...] in its weakest endowment'. For the latter enjoys a purely non-figurative mode of expression. If the presentation of Nature in its 'weakest endowment' is seen as an expression without metaphor, a non-figurative appearance, the presentation of Nature in its 'strongest endowment' would be at the opposite extreme: a non-congruence between sign and meaning. And by the time the fragment reaches its final sentence, Hölderlin is indeed speaking of extremes: 'in ihrer schwächsten [...] in ihrer stärksten'.

Among previous commentators, it is Mögel who seems to come closest to the approach suggested here (1994: 79–80). He suggests that the fragment describes two contrasting situations, only one of which belongs to the realm of the 'tragic': 'Das Argument dieses Umkehrschlusses beruht darauf, daß Hölderlin zwei einander entgegengesetzte Lebenszustände annimmt: auf der einen Seite einen Zustand des an sich selbst "bedeutenden" [...] "Zeichens" oder "Lebenslichts", auf der andern Seite den Zustand des Tragischen' [This argument *a contrario* depends on Hölderlin assuming that there are two opposed conditions of life: on the one hand a condition of the 'sign' that is 'significant' in itself or of the 'light of life', on the other hand the condition of the tragic]. The first of Mögel's cases stands in direct contrast to the 'presentation' involved in tragedy:

> Bei dem ersten haben wir offenbar an einen Zustand der relativen Ruhe zu denken, in welchem die einzelnen Zeichen und Erscheinungen des verborgenen Grundes [...] mehr oder weniger in sich selber ruhen und gleichsam in ihrem je eigenen 'Lebenslicht' erstrahlen.
>
> [In the first we are evidently to think of a condition of relative tranquillity, in which the individual signs and appearances of the hidden ground [...] repose more or less in themselves, and as it were shine each in their own 'light of life.'][16]

---

16 As Mögel also observes, presentation in the second case can be seen as involving a particularly pure form of the sign, as it were uncontaminated by the content of experience: 'Indem das Zeichen "an sich selbst als unbedeutend = 0 gesetzt wird", *erfüllt* es also seinen Charakter als Zeichen gerade erst in völliger Reinheit!' (1994: 80, n. 48).

We have already seen that the use of the term 'das Lebenslicht' is relevant to the dating of the fragment. But as Mögel suggests, the term may also be a clue to its proper interpretation, indicating that the fragment is not only concerned with the case of tragedy, or presentation by the 'sign = 0', but also with a converse case: a state of relative tranquillity in which life stands illuminated by its own light. Indeed, given the use of the superlative in [5], it may be appropriate to speak of 'absolute tranquillity'. As we shall see below, that converse case arguably corresponds to an important strand in Hölderlin's poetics.

As regards the term 'das Lebenslicht' itself, it must be admitted that the parallel usages in Hölderlin are sparse and themselves call for interpretation. It should not perhaps be assumed that the meaning is identical on each occasion. The most striking parallel is in the second letter to Böhlendorff, where he describes his impression of southern France at the time of the revolutionary upheavals (MA, II, 920–21; AL, 213–14). He mentions first the tranquillity of those who live contentedly in the natural world, as compared with the violence of elemental nature: '[d]as gewaltige Element, das Feuer des Himmels' [the violent element, the fire of the sky] as opposed to 'die Stille der Menschen, ihr Leben in der Natur' [the quiet of the people, their life in the open]. But he then turns to the warlike region bordering the Vendée, which had witnessed a counter-revolutionary uprising. There, he says, he was interested by 'das wilde kriegerische [...], das rein männliche, dem das Lebenslicht unmittelbar wird in den Augen und Gliedern' [the wild, warlike quality [...], the purely male, where the life-light is immediate in the eyes and limbs]. For Mögel, such a use of the term sheds no light on the later dating of the fragment, as it does not seem to correspond to the idea of tranquil appearance that is there associated with its use (1994: 79, n. 44). Schmidt seems to draw a different conclusion: because the term is used in both places, 'Lebenslicht' in BT also has tragic connotations. But in this letter Hölderlin may merely be saying that, in exposing himself to the risk of death, the warrior has a heightened and more immediate sense of life, at least as compared with the peaceful shepherds described earlier.[17]

The term is found again in drafts for a hymn sometimes edited under the title 'An die Madonna' [To the Virgin Mary] (MA, I, 408–13; Hamb, 617–27). It occurs in the following context: 'denn es hasset die Rede, wer | Das Lebenslicht das herzernährende sparet' [for he hates speech | Who husbands the light of life that nourishes the heart].[18] The apposition with 'das herzernährende' suggests that 'das Lebenslicht' is something that gives sustenance to the heart, at once illuminating and vivifying. Hölderlin seems to be concerned with the relation between words and feelings, and in particular with the possibility of speaking or singing in the presence

---

17 See KA, II, 1253. Although the term 'das Lebenslicht' itself appears to be peculiar to the later period, as Mögel notes (1994: 80, n. 46) the similar expression 'das Flämchen des Lebens' is used in the first stanza of 'Die Muße' (MA, I, 169–70, l. 6), a poem in hexameters from early 1797. And it is used there in a context that clearly connotes an idyllic state of harmony with nature (cf. Schmidt in KA, I, 608: 'Die Wahl des Hexameters entspricht der episch-idyllischen Darstellung'). But the later occurrence of the distinctive form 'das Lebenslicht' remains relevant for dating purposes.
18 MA, I, 413, ll. 149–50; Hamb, 627. The relevant page of the manuscript is transcribed at FHA, Suppl. III, 124. On this hymn see generally Analecta 2007: 179–215.

(or absence) of 'das Lebenslicht'; however, the precise interpretation is difficult to resolve.[19] The wider context is also susceptible of different interpretations; but on one approach at least, one can associate 'das Lebenslicht' with the 'light of love' invoked in the elegy 'Menons Klagen um Diotima' [Menon's Lament for Diotima], and hence with Hölderlin's own love for Susette Gontard.[20] Thus the third stanza of the elegy begins with the apostrophe 'Licht der Liebe!', and both this and the following stanza evoke scenes that are bathed in that light. Of particular interest is the scene depicted in the fourth stanza: that of two loving swans looking down at the surface of the water in which the blue of the sky is reflected, as is the silver of the clouds. For the scene is also apt to evoke the fragility of the lovers' bliss. The swans are looking not at a reality but at a glittering image of the heavens, and also no doubt at their own reflections. Does the light of love attach only to transient appearances, to the captivating illusions of a reflecting surface?

In a well-known article, Karl Eibl has drawn the consequences of such a thought for the interpretation of Hölderlin's poem 'Hälfte des Lebens' [Half of Life].[21] That short lyric is one of the series of nine published poems (the so-called 'Nachtgesänge') that are contemporary with the *Sophokles-Anmerkungen*, and hence probably with BT itself.[22] The first of its two stanzas depicts an idyllic scene in which a landscape is reflected in water. This is opposed to the second stanza, as a scene of plenitude and beauty is opposed to one of anguish and absence of meaning. But the movement between the two can be interpreted as the breaking of a narcissistic illusion, as the inebriated swans in the poem break the surface of the water (ll. 5–7):

> Und trunken von Küssen
> Tunkt ihr das Haupt
> Ins heilignüchterne Wasser.
>
> [And drunk with kisses
> You dip your heads
> In the holy, sober water.]

For our present purposes, 'Hälfte des Lebens' could stand for the thought that the world can be considered as a world of beautiful appearances, bathed as it were in its own light; but the plenitude of the world of appearances has an intrinsic weakness or vulnerability: it is in danger of tipping into narcissistic captivation and disillusion. That might provide an initial gloss on the statement that '[2] das Lebenslicht und die

---

19 For instance, both Hamburger and Reitani (TL, 1043) assume that 'sparen' here has the meaning of 'husband' or 'conserve'; a congenial interpretation in the present context, but queried in Analecta 2007: 204, n. 485 (pointing to Grimm, s.v. sparen, 4.) In the manuscript the cited words replace: 'und es hätte die Schwermut | Mir von den Lippen | Den Gesang genommen'.
20 MA, I, 291–95, l. 29 (p. 292); Hamb, 293–301 (p. 295). On this connection see Analecta 2007: 203–04. That interpretation may be supported by reminiscences, elsewhere in the hymn, of the lovers' journey to Bad Driburg with Wilhelm Heinse: see Schmidt in KA, I, 1064–65; and on Heinse see further below.
21 MA, I, 445; OE, 181. See Eibl 1983, and see further Louth 2004
22 See the letters to Wilmans of December 1803: MA, II, 926–27; AL, 216–17 (note that they were not published under that title). On the *Nachtgesänge*, and in particular 'Hälfte des Lebens', see further Chapter 6.3 below.

Erscheinung der Schwäche jedes Ganzen angehört'. But we should at the same time guard against the thought that such 'weakness' has only negative connotations. The world of appearances is after all the only one that we can experience, and is also the world in which aesthetic beauty can be said to reside. And conversely, as BT itself suggests, an encounter with the hidden ground of Nature is the stuff of tragedy.

In a recent study of 'Hälfte des Lebens', Winfried Menninghaus has identified an important strand of Hölderlin's poetics that is distinct from the poetics of the Tragic and the Sublime with which he is more often associated. Beginning with an analysis of the poem's metrical signature (the Sapphic *adoneus*), Menninghaus proceeds to demonstrate the significance of the underlying myths of Narcissus and of Adonis:

> Die rituelle Klage um Adonis, in welcher die historische Sappho-Rezeption zugleich die metrische Struktur der sapphischen Strophen-Klausel wiedererkannt hat, ist [...] eine Grundfigur der sapphischen Dichtung selbst: der Jüngling [...] konnotiert unwiderstehliche Schönheit, aber zugleich Schwäche [...] und frühzeitigen Tod.
>
> [The ritual lament for Adonis, in which Sappho-reception has historically also recognized the metrical structure of the Sapphic stanza, is [...] a basic figure of Sapphic poetry itself: the youth [...] connotes irresistible beauty, but also weakness [...] and untimely death.]²³

As Menninghaus observes, if the myth of Adonis is evoked by the poem's metrical signature, that of Narcissus is implied by the image of the drunken swans (2005: 48, 55–56). The fate of an Adonis or Narcissus is to be distinguished from that of a tragic hero. It reflects a vulnerability that is intrinsic to beauty, or to any perfection belonging to the sensuous world of appearances. And as he also observes, the figure of Diotima in *Hyperion* can be seen in this context. Thus the myth of Adonis is expressly evoked in Hölderlin's novel, with Hyperion assuming the position of Aphrodite, Diotima 'diejenige des sprachlosen Adonis' [that of the speechless Adonis] (2005: 42). And in Hyperion's captivation by Diotima's beauty, the structure of the Narcissus myth is also present (2005: 66–67).

Here we should recall that Diotima's silent and inward quality is one of her most important characteristics in the novel, and her beauty can itself provoke speechlessness (although in both cases this is a silence that can speak volumes).²⁴ From the point of view of Hyperion at least, it is as if Diotima inhabits a realm of

---

23 Menninghaus 2005: 35; see also pp. 39–47 and 62–68, and in particular p. 56: 'Die Geste des Ins-Wasser-Hängens schreibt so bereits der Imago vollendeter Schönheit die Tendenz auf einen tödlichen Ausgang ein.' For a sceptical response see Bagordo 2012: 284–95; but Bagordo's perspective is perhaps too narrow, as he fails even to discern a Narcissus reference in the poem (contrast Eibl 1983: 228–29, and Louth 2004: 174).

24 'Sie schien immer so wenig zu sagen, und sagte so viel' (MA, I, 662); 'Ich kann nur hie und da ein Wörtchen von ihr sprechen. Ich muß vergessen, was sie ganz ist, wenn ich von ihr sprechen soll' (MA, I, 664); 'Sprechen? o ich bin ein Laie in der Freude, ich will sprechen! Wohnt doch die Stille im Lande der Seeligen, und über den Sternen vergißt das Herz seine Noth und seine Sprache' (MA, I, 655). See similarly MA, I, 656, 666, and 676; and in Diotima's own final letter: 'Stille war mein Leben; mein Tod ist beredt' (MA, I, 748). Note also the ode 'Diotima', which in all three versions begins: 'Du schweigst und duldest' (MA, I, 189, 256, and 327).

immediate expression, a realm of pure 'tones' [Töne] rather than linguistic signs.[25] The musical connotations are obvious, although 'tone' here means music of a particular kind, as it were an immediate expression of natural harmony.

For Hölderlin, poetry itself participates in this realm of musical expression; and it is significant that the elements of the poetic calculus described in the Homburg poetics are themselves described as 'tones'. But poetry nonetheless inhabits the realm of language, not of pure music; and the tones of the Homburg poetics do not simply sound forth in their immediacy, but are rather subject to the rules of 'alternation' or 'modulation' (the *Wechsel der Töne*). As we have seen, those rules themselves involve a relationship described as 'metaphor', in which an underlying 'basic tone' achieves indirect or figurative expression in the corresponding surface or 'art-character' tone. In Hölderlin's conception, therefore, poetry partakes of both realms: the non-figurative realm of music and the figurative realm of language.

2. Of the Dolphin

I have suggested that, if the structure of metaphor is present in BT, it is in the shape of its two opposite and limiting extremes. On the one hand '[5] Nature presents itself properly in its weakest endowment': as it were the extreme of non-figurative representation. And on other hand 'the sign when it presents itself in its strongest endowment = o': that is to say a sign that could not be more different from what is presented, as it were an extreme of poetic figuration. The first extreme corresponds to the idea of a pure 'tone' rather than a linguistic sign. And it is a case that is described most eloquently in a short piece belonging to the latest phase of Hölderlin's poetics.

That piece is the *Pindarfragment* 'Vom Delphin' [Of the Dolphin] (MA, II, 381; AL, 336). There Hölderlin refers to circumstances in which the 'song of nature' manifests itself: 'Der Gesang der Natur, in der Witterung der Musen [...]. Um diese Zeit giebt jedes Wesen seinen Ton an, seine Treue, die Art, wie eines in sich selbst zusammenhängt' [The song of nature, in the weather of the Muses [...]. At this time every creature gives its tone, its faithfulness, the way it hangs together in itself] (trans. modified). That identification of the concepts of 'Ton' and 'Treue' calls to mind the opposite extreme treated in section 3 of the 'Anmerkungen zum Oedipus'. Thus in AO [3.3] tragedy is described as a process that turns on a moment of 'Untreue' [unfaithfulness]. The pure musicality of a 'tone', and the trueness to self connoted by the idea of 'loyalty' or 'faithfulness', stand at the opposite pole to tragedy. Indeed, as I shall argue in Chapter 6, the *Pindarfragmente* as a whole can be viewed as a kind of anti-tragic counterpart to the *Sophokles-Anmerkungen*, as can be gathered from some of their titles: 'Von der Wahrheit' [Of Truth]; 'Von der Ruhe' [Of Rest]; 'Die Asyle' [The Sanctuaries]. And if the term 'Untreue' also figures in

---

25 'Wir sprachen sehr wenig zusammen. Man schämt sich seiner Sprache. Zum Tone möchte man werden und sich vereinen in Einen Himmelsgesang' (MA, I, 658); 'seelig vereint, wie ein Chor von tausend unzertrennlichen Tönen' (MA, I, 678; see also 672–73). See further Siekmann 1980, in particular pp. 55–56, and Albert 1998: 169–72.

the title of what is usually regarded as the first of the sequence, this is surely in a sense opposed to the tragic 'unfaithfulness' of the *Sophokles-Anmerkungen*: for the full title is 'Untreue der Weisheit' [Unfaithfulness of Wisdom], and the commentary describes in effect how wisdom is revealed in adaptability to circumstances.

The commentary in 'Vom Delphin' expounds a concept of purely musical or non-linguistic expression. It describes a scene in which 'die Trennung' [division] is virtually absent: the only divisions in evidence are those that arise naturally as differences between the natural species, which are contrasted with those imposed by (human) language. Even 'need' is said to be absent, as the equivalent in the natural world of the separations created by language (and Hölderlin accordingly refers to the 'accent' of need). Instead, everything participates in the pure voice of song: 'Nur der Unterschied der Arten macht dann die Trennung in der Natur, daß also alles mehr Gesang und reine Stimme ist, als Accent des Bedürfnisses oder auf der anderen Seite Sprache' [Then only the difference between species makes a division in nature, so that everything is therefore more song and pure voice than accent of need or on the other hand language].[26] The scene depicted in Hölderlin's commentary, and also expressed in its melodious language, is one of softness, melting and sympathetic echoing: 'wenn über Blüthen die Wolken, wie Floken, hängen, und über dem Schmelz von goldenen Blumen' [when the clouds hang like flakes over blossoms, and over the lustre of golden flowers] (trans. modified). As Bartel observes — and Adler actually translates — 'Schmelz' connotes a 'melting' quality, as well as the lustre of the golden flowers themselves (2000: 110). And as Fink points out (1982: 57), this is a setting in which language (as opposed to song) is notably absent:

> Bleibt die 'Sprache' so aus der Harmonie einer Natur, die bei sich selber ist, ausgeschlossen, nimmt der Gesang gerade die Möglichkeit wahr, sich selber darzustellen, d.h. in die Erscheinung zu treten. [...] 'Sprache' meint eine unsinnliche Aussageweise, in der ein Wesen sich selber nicht begreift, während 'Gesang' erscheinend sich selber ausspricht.
>
> [If 'language' thus remains excluded from the harmony of a self-sufficient Nature, song takes the opportunity to present itself, i.e. to come into appearance. [...] Here 'language' means a non-sensuous mode of expression, in which a being does not grasp its own self, while 'song' pronounces itself in appearing.][27]

Fink's commentary might also serve as an explication of BT. On the one hand, we have the 'harmony' of a Nature that can present itself by appearing *as* itself; and on the other, 'eine unsinnliche Aussageweise', which at the extreme is so 'unsinnlich' as to be void or null, an empty signifier ('das Zeichen [...] = 0'). Nature, in 'song', is able to achieve unmediated expression, as opposed to an expression in

---

26 On language and need, cf. *Hyperion*: 'und über den Sternen vergißt das Herz seine Noth und seine Sprache' (MA, I, 655); and conversely on 'tönen' and 'treu' cf. MA, I, 621.
27 See also the reference in Hölderlin's commentary to 'das Echo des Wachstums'. For 'echo' in Hölderlin as corresponding to a non-linguistic mode of expression, a musical dimension of poetic language that amounts to a 'eine Phase der Sprachlosigkeit', see Frey 1990: 77–88 (p. 84).

the inevitably figurative medium of language. In the idyllic scene evoked in the *Pindarfragment* a creature can remain faithful to itself, for its self-expression is merely the singing forth of its own nature: 'seine Treue, die Art, wie eines in sich selbst zusammenhängt.' And this idea of loyalty or faithfulness corresponds to a Nature conceived as a living and harmonious whole. In the words of *Hyperion*'s Diotima in her valedictory letter: 'im Bunde der Natur ist Treue kein Traum. Wir trennen uns nur, um inniger einig zu seyn' [in the union of nature, loyalty is no dream. We part only to be more intimately at one] (MA, I, 749; RB, 199). Not that this is the novel's final word regarding Nature, which (as we saw in Chapter 1) must in its fullest sense embrace suffering and division.

The connection between Diotima and the idea of a purely musical means of expression has already been noted. The figure is of course of some biographical significance, recalling as she does Susette Gontard (the object of Hölderlin's love, and the wife of his employer in Frankfurt). It would no doubt be incorrect simply to identify Susette with the character in the novel. The correspondences are nonetheless striking, and even uncanny to the extent that Susette came to occupy a place already marked out for her in the novel's early drafts (Laplanche 1969: 61). The remainder of this section traces a further connection, both biographical and textual, between Diotima and the figure of the dolphin.

The 'dolphin' in the *Pindarfragment* is the sea creature so famously benevolent to mariners, and perhaps also a figure representing the poet Pindar himself (or more generally the poet as singer).[28] But the image also occurs in another context, this time belonging to the period of the composition of *Hyperion*. If that context also provides a connection between the dolphin and Diotima, the mediating figure here is the writer and art-critic Wilhelm Heinse. Thus Gaier has shown the importance of Heinse's novel *Hildegard von Hohenthal* both for the composition of *Hyperion* and the development of the poetics of the *Wechsel der Töne*.[29] Heinse was close to Susette Gontard, and his friend Sömmerring was the family doctor of the Gontards in Frankfurt (as well as a leading anatomist). Heinse admired Susette for her beauty and cultivation, and gave encouragement to Hölderlin.[30] In May 1796 Heinse gave Susette a copy of the second volume of his novel; both she and Hölderlin will no doubt have read the first, while Hölderlin had already been impressed by Heinse's earlier novel *Ardinghello*.[31] In 1796 an invasion of French forces seemed to threaten the safety of the Gontard household, and this provided a rare opportunity for the two lovers to travel together. In the course of their flight to Kassel and Bad Driburg, they met up with Heinse. The latter was not only a witness of the love between the

28 See Bartel 2000: 107–09. Note that a dolphin also surfaces in the idyllic opening scene of 'Der Archipelagus' (MA, I, 295, ll. 3–4; SP, 103).
29 Gaier 1998: 43–48; see also Gaier 2000, and 2002b: 88–89.
30 See Hölderlin's letter to his brother of 2 November 1797: 'Heinze [sic], der Verf. des Ardinghello, hat bei *Dr.* Sömmering [sic] sich sehr aufmunternd über Hyperion geäußert' (MA, II, 670). Hölderlin (MA, I, 188) wrote two epigrams on Sömmerring's treatise *Über das Organ der Seele* (Königsberg: 1796). For his part, Sömmerring contributed anatomical drawings of the organs of hearing to *Hildegard von Hohenthal*.
31 *Ardinghello und die glückseligen Inseln* [1787], ed. by Max L. Baeumer, 2nd edn (Stuttgart: Reclam, 1998; repr. 2004). See Hock 1995: 79–80 and 98, and Baeumer 1966: 71–76.

two; he also embodied some of the same simplicity and sympathy with the natural world that Hölderlin found in Susette.³²

Hildegard von Hohenthal opens with a scene (p. 10) that may have helped to justify the author's somewhat scandalous reputation, but is at the same time an evocation of primal innocence. In this scene the musician Lockmann, on a hot day towards the end of May, takes up a telescope, and in gazing at the surrounding landscape discovers a woman — Hildegard — swimming naked 'like a dolphin':

> Unvermerkt drangen seine Blicke unter die Schatten des Lindengewölbes in einem Garten [...] wo ein Frauenzimmer sein Morgengewand ablegte, nackend, göttlich schön wie eine Venus, da stand, die Arme frey und muthig in die Luft ausschlug, und [...] sich in eine große Wasservertiefung stürzte, darin verschwand [...]; dann die ganze zauberische Mädchengestalt wie ein Delphin sich wieder empor warf, und Wasserstrahlen und Schaum von sich schleuderte.

> [Absent-mindedly his gaze pierced the shadows cast by the lime-tree in a garden [...] where a woman took off her morning garment, stood there naked, as divinely beautiful as a Venus, swinging her arms freely and bravely in the air, and [...] dived into a big watery hollow in which she disappeared from view [...]; then the whole captivating figure of the girl flung herself up again like a dolphin, and shook off foaming streams of water.]

Once she has dried herself 'auf dem grünen Schmelze' [on the lustrous sward] (p. 11), Hildegard puts her clothes back on and disappears. We are not far removed from the setting of the *Pindarfragment*, which is, as Bartel observes, that of a spring day (but also of a scene which is somehow timeless) in which water and vegetation are blended together in a lustrous melting softness ('[der] Schmelz').³³

A few pages later, we are introduced to Lockmann's ideas on the performance of Allegri's *Miserere* (p. 14). They echo his previous vision of Hildegard: at the end of the piece 'die Töne schmelzen in einander' [the notes melt into one another]; furthermore, in it 'Die Stimmen haben gar keine Begleitung von Instrumenten, nicht einmal der Orgel. Die bloße Vocalmusik ist eigentlich, was in den bildenden Künsten das Nackende ist' [The voices have absolutely no instrumental accompaniment, not even the organ. Pure vocal music is in truth what nakedness is in the fine arts].³⁴ Such music is characterized by simplicity of harmony, and an almost complete absence of rhythm: such as there is arises naturally from words that are sung, and the result is one of immediate impression in which those words themselves disappear (p. 15). Accordingly, to the nakedness of Hildegard in the opening scene there corresponds a species of 'naked' music that appears denuded of metre, or even of the words that give it shape. This is a music of pure tones, corresponding to a world of prelapsarian harmony and beauty (p. 15): 'Das Zusammenschmelzen und

---

32   In Hock's words, 'Einfalt, Kindersinn, Heiterkeit' (1995: 96). In the remainder of this section, page references in the text are to the edition of the novel included in *Hildegard von Hohenthal* [1795–96]. *Musikalische Dialogen* [op. posth. 1805], ed. by Werner Keil (Hildesheim: Olms, 2002).
33   Bartel 2000: 110; Bartel also makes a connection with the idyllic scene evoked in the first stanza of 'Hälfte des Lebens'.
34   On the parallel between these two scenes, see Keil 1998: 151–52, and see further von Arburg 2009: 149–54.

Verfließen der reinen Töne offenbart das innre Gefühl eines himmlischen Wesens, welches sich mit der ursprünglichen Schönheit wieder vereinigen möchte, von der es Schulden trennen' [The melting and running together of the pure tones reveals the inner feeling of a divine being, one that would like to reunite with the original beauty from which it is separated by guilt]. Here we have a purely musical means of expression, at the furthest remove from the divisions instituted by language; and as such, it can be related to the dolphin in the *Pindarfragment* as much as to the 'dolphin' in the earlier vision of the naked Hildegard. Indeed, the significance of the latter becomes clear once we learn that Hildegard is a singer. And as we have seen, Diotima herself participates in this realm of musical expression, in which the plenitude of appearance is opposed to the mediation of the linguistic sign. Hölderlin dedicated two of his greatest poems to Heinse: not only 'Brod und Wein' [Bread and Wine], but also (originally) 'Der Rhein' [The Rhine], where Heinse is directly addressed in the earlier version of the final stanza. There his cheerfulness of soul is contrasted with the poet's more agitated dream of 'des Meergrunds köstlicher Perle' [the ocean bed's precious pearl] (MA, I, 341, l. 8; Hamb, 801). If the reference to Susette Gontard is unmistakable in that dream, those submarine depths may also be the ones evoked in 'Vom Delphin'.[35]

3. The Sign '= o'

I have been concerned to emphasize Hölderlin's concept of non-figurative presentation — 'das Lebenslicht' as the immediate light of appearance — because it is an aspect of his poetics that is sometimes overlooked in the interpretation of this fragment. The question remains, however, whether we are now in any better position to understand the enigmatic concept of 'das Zeichen [...] = o'? I have argued that, if the pure music of nature occupies one pole of Hölderlin's poetics, the empty or 'meaningless' sign might be said to occupy its opposite pole. The former corresponds to an expression that is faithful to the thing expressed, and full of its presence. But the latter corresponds to a limiting extreme of metaphor or indirect expression, one in which any correspondence between literal and figurative meaning has been broken. Or, to use the term that is central to Hölderlin's interpretation of Sophocles, the signifier is now absolutely 'unfaithful' [untreu] to its signified. At the same time, as many have insisted, there may be a more concrete interpretation of Hölderlin's concept of the null sign as it relates to tragedy. In the cases that interest him, the tragic hero is a figure who is sacrificed or brought low in the course of the play; and on the traditional account, the crux of a tragedy consists in such an unfortunate reversal.[36] More recently, the plot of *Oedipus Tyrannus* has been said to turn on a reversal of the 'superhuman' — the Oedipus who rivals the gods — into a 'subhuman' Oedipus who becomes a beast and a scapegoat, combining in

---

35   See Böschenstein 1989c: 101, and Hamburger's note at Hamb, 802.
36   For the classic account of tragedy as founded on a reversal of fortune into misfortune that arouses the pity and fear of the spectator, see Aristotle, *Poetics*, ed. and trans. by Stephen Halliwell, in Aristotle, XXIII, LCL 199 (Cambridge, MA: Harvard University Press, 1995; corrected repr. 1999), 1453a (pp. 70–71).

his person 'one who is both the equal of the gods and the equal of nothing at all' (Vernant 1988: 139, 136). An interpretation of Hölderlin's 'Zeichen [...] = 0' should not perhaps neglect such elements, at least as components of a final analysis. But what must be excluded, at least on the basis of the arguments presented above, is any account based on the tragic hero as simply an embodiment of 'weakness'.[37]

Are there any further contexts that might help to explain this notion of a null sign? Here it is difficult to resist citing the famous lines from a draft of the late hymn 'Mnemosyne' (a draft sometimes edited as 'die Nymphe'):

> Ein Zeichen sind wir, deutungslos
> Schmerzlos sind wir und haben fast
> Die Sprache in der Fremde verloren.
>
> [A sign we are, without meaning
> Without pain we are and have nearly
> Lost our language in foreign lands.]
> (MA, I, 436; TL, 1106; HF, 117)

As a matter of first impression, the language echoes that of our fragment: compare '[3] das Zeichen [ist] an sich selbst unbedeutend, wirkungslos' with 'Ein Zeichen sind wir, deutungslos'. But the appearance is perhaps deceptive. In the first place, 'deutungslos' more literally translates as 'without explanation' or 'without interpretation'.[38] It is true that this is equivalent to the idea of having no graspable meaning — as well as being free from an ambiguity that afflicts 'unbedeutend', which (like 'insignificant' in English) can mean either 'without meaning' or 'without importance'.[39] But more importantly, BT presumably expounds a theory of ancient Greek tragedy, whereas by the time of 'Mnemosyne' (and presumably BT itself) Hölderlin had begun to develop a distinct account of modern tragedy. The heroes of Greek tragedy are consumed by a too-immediate encounter with the divine forces of Nature: in the words of the first letter to Böhlendorff, 'in Flammen verzehrt die Flamme büßen, die [sie] nicht zu bändigen vermochten' [pay for the flames [they] have been unable to control by being consumed by fire] (MA, II, 913; AL, 208). By contrast, a tragedy of the modern condition would be one of the absence of meaning — as it were too little fate rather than too much.[40] That seems to be the condition evoked in those lines from 'Mnemosyne'. A similar point can be made about the emptiness of the world described in the second stanza of 'Hälfte

---

37 As in Hamacher's statement that 'Das Zeichen [...] läßt [...] die Sache auch nur geschwächt zur Erscheinung kommen. Wenn aber die Schwäche ins Extrem getrieben und die Erscheinung annulliert wird, kann die Sache [...] in ihrer ganzen Gewalt sich darstellen' (2006: 109). For the tragic hero as the 'sign [...] = 0', see e.g. Rosenfield 2003: 163; Lönker 1989: 294, n. 11; Louth 1998: 227. I would also distinguish the present notion of 'Schwäche' from the one in AA [3.2]; for the latter relates to an aspect of (Greek or modern) culture, rather than to an aspect of nature.
38 It is Sieburth's translation that is cited above. But cf. Constantine (SP, 172): 'with no interpretation'; Reitani (TL, 1107): 'senza spiegazione'. Hamburger's version relentlessly pursues that alternative: 'A cipher we are, no key decodes it' (Hamb, 593).
39 The fact that BT is referring specifically to the effect (or lack of effect) of a sign suggests that the reference is to a lack of semantic content rather than to the property of being trivial or small.
40 On modern tragedy as a symptom of 'das Schiksaallose', see Chapter 6.3 and the commentary to AA [3.2] in Part II below.

des Lebens', which stands in contrast to the plenitude evoked in the first stanza. The empty signs of the flags (or more probably weather-vanes) that clatter in the wind, and the walls that stand '[s]prachlos und kalt' [speechless and cold], do not evoke a hidden ground whose presence is now revealed. Rather, they correspond to a state in which language and feeling have departed.[41]

To shed further light on 'das Zeichen [...] = 0', therefore, it may be preferable to turn to the *Sophokles-Anmerkungen*. Here several commentators have focused on the notion of 'caesura', described in both sets of *Anmerkungen* as a constitutive feature of the tragedy concerned (see AO [1.7]–[1.10] and AA [1.3]–[1.4]). Thus Hölderlin assigns a particular function to a pause or discontinuity within each piece, which he describes as 'die gegenrhythmische Unterbrechung' [the counter-rhythmical interruption] and assigns to the scenes with the prophet Tiresias (MA, II, 310). He compares the speeches of the latter with the 'caesura' in Greek metrics, that is to say the break that divides the rhythm of a line of verse, and also refers to this 'Cäsur' as 'das reine Wort' [the pure word]. It occurs either towards the beginning of the piece (*Oedipus*), or towards the end (*Antigone*). In effect the caesura determines the 'calculable law' of each tragedy.[42] If that formal feature is described in the first section of each set, Hölderlin returns to the question of form at the beginning of their third sections. And here we can note a correspondence between his accounts of the form and the content of the tragedy. This is particularly clear in the 'Anmerkungen zum Oedipus'. In AO [3.1] the action of a tragedy is described as a process of purification, in which a too-close encounter between the god (or the power of nature) on the one hand, and the human individual on the other, is purged by an equally extreme (or 'limitless') separation [gränzenloses Scheiden] (MA, II, 315). But in the following paragraph this is immediately taken as the basis for formal features of the tragedies concerned: the disputatious dialogic exchanges, the opposition of dialogue and chorus, and the articulation of the larger parts of the tragedy. The formula he uses to sum up these features is particularly interesting for our present purposes: 'Alles ist Rede gegen Rede, die sich gegenseitig aufhebt' [Everything is speech against speech, cancelling each other out].

This self-cancelling effect of the form of the tragedy can perhaps be compared to the notion of 'das Zeichen [...] = 0'. Indeed there appears to be a connection between the notion of pure form, as a constituent element of a poetic work, and that of such a cancellation. For if the content of what is said is cancelled out, it is precisely the form of the saying that is thrown into relief. And if one interprets 'caesura' in its broadest sense, as meaning any hiatus that signifies by virtue of its pure form, the concept is prominent elsewhere in Hölderlin's poetics. As Ryan has noted, just as the *Sophokles-Anmerkungen* borrow the notion of 'caesura' from the poetics of metre, Hölderlin had previously borrowed the notion of tragic 'catastrophe' for

---

41   Cf. Groddeck 2007: 171–72, also making the connection with 'Mnemosyne'.
42   See AO [1.11]–[1.12], and AA [1.1]. Thus Kasper suggests that 'Die Zäsur ist offensichtlich das Zeichen, das "= 0" ist und das der Natur "in ihrer stärksten Gaabe" zur Darstellung verhilft' (2000: 28, n. 10). See similarly Lemke 2002: 61, 68–69; Hiller 2008: 108–09. On the original metrical concept of 'caesura' cf. D'Angour 2006: 493; and for a modern account of the dramatic function of the Tiresias scenes see Ugolini 1995.

the purposes of his doctrine of the *Wechsel der Töne*.[43] As we saw in Chapter 3, the 'tones' of the Homburg poetics can be regarded as the constituent elements of poetic meaning, and the rule-governed sequence of tones in a poem corresponds to the progressive development of that meaning. But on Hölderlin's account of those sequences, the development is punctuated by a paradoxical moment. At this point, what makes itself felt in the poem is not a particular tone, but rather a reversal in the rule-governed sequence of tones. This runs counter to the normal rules that generate the sequences, and as a result gives rise to a momentary suspension in the poem's forward progress. As Ryan points out, it is by virtue of this reversal that a higher totality is expressed, rather than by any of the particular tones that have been sounded so far in the poem.[44] In the absence of any tone giving a determinate meaning, the element of pure form can emerge; and such a moment of paradoxical reversal might be regarded as an example of 'das Zeichen [...] = 0'.

As already noted, many commentators construe 'das Zeichen [...] = 0' instead in terms of the fate of the tragic hero: the hero is as it were annulled by that fate. And this may be one element of an eventual interpretation, if such a tragic reversal is not equated with the notion of 'weakness', that is to say '[5] die Natur in ihrer schwächsten Gaabe'. As I have tried to argue, the latter is rather to be read in terms of a notion of non-figurative presentation. Nature in its 'weakest endowment' can appear directly, reflected in its own light; but then it is also afflicted with the fragility intrinsic to pure appearance. Here the governing myths would be those of Adonis and Narcissus, rather than the tales of the tragic heroes. Conversely, although the tragic sign is said to be '[3] an sich selbst unbedeutend, wirkungslos', it is not weak. Although it is void of intrinsic meaning or effect, 'das Zeichen [...] = 0' could be said to embody the highest power of language, the power of pure form. That is not to say, however, that the relation between the form and content of tragedy can be ignored: for Hölderlin himself points to a correspondence between the two.

I began this chapter by commenting on the difficulties facing the commentator of Hölderlin's theoretical works. Many of the same factors are present, of course, in BT. Thus we have been trying to understand a text that is (probably) a fragment, taken from a context that is itself unknown (presumably an interpretation of Sophoclean tragedy). There is also evidence that Hölderlin's thoughts developed

---

43 Ryan 1963: 27; see *Löst sich nicht ...* (MA, II, 108; AL, 307). However, although this text allows one to link the reversal characteristic of the *Wechsel der Töne* with the concept of 'Katastrophe', other details of the text seem to be provisional thoughts that are superseded by the full versions of the tables that follow (see Ryan 1960: 121–24). Furthermore is not clear how far this analogy can be pressed in the case of the Tiresias scenes themselves, which do not necessarily coincide with a moment of tragic reversal. See, on the other hand, Lemke 2002: 69, 74, n. 49, and 80; and Ryan 1960: 125–26.

44 Thus Ryan observes that 'in dem Tonschema, das den Verlauf des Gedichts wiedergibt, erhält sie [die Unendlichkeit] keinen eigenen Ton, sondern kann nur als genaue Umkehrung der Zuordnung der Töne fühlbar gemacht werden' (1963: 38); note that for Ryan 'die Unendlichkeit' corresponds to 'das Ursprüngliche' in BT (1963: 25, 32–33). And in language reminiscent of BT, Hölderlin speaks of a 'poëtische Individualität' that allows 'die Vergegenwärtigung des Unendlichen', and 'kann [...] gar nicht erscheinen, oder nur im Karakter eines positiven Nichts, eines unendlichen Stillstands' (MA, II, 87–88; AL, 286–87).

as he was writing them down. For we have noted a shift, in the course of the fragment, from the use of the term 'das Ursprüngliche' to the use of the broader (and possibly more adequate) term 'die Natur', as well as noting revisions in the manuscript that may reflect the progressive elaboration of his thought. And if a riddling quality is characteristic of some of Hölderlin's later theoretical texts, we can note that the fragment itself has something of the quality of a riddle, in that it expounds the meaning of tragedies in terms of an absence of meaning.

CHAPTER 6

The Tragic and the Anti-tragic: *Pindarfragmente* and *Nachtgesänge*

Ein Scherz des Weisen, und das Räthsel sollte fast nicht gelöst werden.
— Hölderlin, 'Das Unendliche'[1]

1. Introduction

Along with poems published in literary yearbooks and periodicals, Hölderlin published only two books: his novel *Hyperion*, and the Sophocles translations and commentary.[2] While the latter was being printed, he was also preparing for publication a sequence of nine poems, probably those that he described to his publisher as 'Nachtgesänge' [Nightsongs] (MA, I, 439–46; OE, 165–83). He also prepared, in a form that was suitable for publication, a sequence of nine commentaries to translated fragments of Pindar (MA, II, 379–85; AL, 334–39).[3] The date of that manuscript is uncertain, but current scholarly consensus places it in the period of the Sophocles commentary and 'Nachtgesänge', or shortly thereafter.

All three projects — referred to here as the *Anmerkungen*, *Nachtgesänge* and *Pindarfragmente* — are of capital importance for Hölderlin's poetics. The presence of these texts in the period 1803–05 invites the question of how they are related. From the point of view of form alone, the correspondences are remarkable: on the one hand, nine (mostly short) pieces consisting of Pindar text and commentary;

---

[1] 'A jest of the sage, and the riddle is almost not to be solved' (MA, II, 383): see section 4 below.
[2] The first collected edition of Hölderlin's poetry was published in 1826, by Ludwig Uhland and Gustav Schwab — hence in the poet's lifetime, but without his participation.
[3] For the term 'Nachtgesänge' see the letter to Wilmans of December 1803 (MA, II, 927). Those 'Nightsongs', or 'Night Poems' (AL, 217), were duly published in autumn 1804 in Wilman's *Taschenbuch für das Jahr 1805*, but without any collective title; it is not known whether Hölderlin worked on any other poems that he would have described in those terms (cf. Groddeck 1995: 67, n. 20). One plausible candidate is 'Die Dioskuren', a fragmentary revision of 'An Eduard' that probably dates from the same period: see MA, III, 161, and cf. FHA, V, 662; note that it is included in Hamb, 226–27 in preference to the earlier version. Similarly no collective title attaches to the nine Pindar translations with commentary, which may well be the 'something' of 'particular value' promised to Wilmans in the letter of 2 April 1804 (MA, II, 930; AL, 220; see Fink 1982: 129, n. 7). In addition to AL, there are English translations of that sequence in Hamb, 703–23, and SP, 240–46; in the translations given below I have drawn on both Adler's and Hamburger's versions, sometimes with silent modifications. I shall refer to them (according to the order given in all more recent editions) as PF 1, PF 2, etc. The most thorough commentary to any individual one (PF 8) is in Seifert 1998.

on the other, nine (mostly short) lyric poems. On the one hand, a set of Pindar commentaries seamlessly integrated with a translation from the Greek; on the other, a pair of Sophocles commentaries attached to a corresponding translation. From the point of view of content, there are parallels as well as eloquent contrasts. The largely sombre mood of the *Nachtgesänge* might be said to have a tragic quality; but if so, this is tragedy in a different register to Sophocles — a difference that may correspond to a contrast, drawn in the *Anmerkungen*, between ancient and modern poetic forms. Thematic links between *Pindarfragmente* and *Nachtgesänge* have long been observed, in particular the recurring figure of the Centaur.[4] But there is a striking difference between the optimism of the *Pindarfragmente*, and the darker worlds of the *Anmerkungen* and *Nachtgesänge*. Thus the Pindar commentaries seem designed to be cheering and consoling, rather than tragic or sombre. As an initial hypothesis, we might say that the *Pindarfragmente* are united in their opposition to the darkness of those other texts, forming a kind of treatise on the anti-tragic.[5]

Why fragments of Pindar, as opposed to selections from the corpus of Pindar's well-preserved victory odes? The latter were of course well-known to Hölderlin; indeed, he engaged in an intensive study of them, taking the form of translations made, it seems, for his own instruction.[6] But numerous fragments of Pindar have also been preserved, often in the form of quotations by other authors. The choice of such fragments as the basis for commentary is itself worthy of reflection. An obvious feature of a fragment is that it invites an act of restoration or completion. Hölderlin's commentaries can be taken in this spirit: as forming, along with the relevant fragment, a newly integral whole. And while the fragmentary nature of Pindar's originals is a source of their obscurity, each of Hölderlin's interpretations seems to have a calculatedly enigmatic character, calling for an interpreter to complete it with a commentary of their own. In that sense, the *Pindarfragmente* can themselves be regarded as fragments.[7]

---

4   See Bartel 2000: 32. Bartel also notes the resemblance between the idyllic setting of the *Pindarfragment* 'Vom Delphin' and the first stanza of the *Nachtgesang* 'Hälfte des Lebens' (2000: 110). As Franz points out (1988: 140, and 2002: 256–57), nine is the number of the Muses according to Hesiod; but this observation seems in practice to have limited explanatory value.
5   Contrasts with the *Anmerkungen* are noted by Schmidt in relation to PF 1 and 4 (KA, II, 1293–94), PF 5 (KA, II, 1303–04) and PF 8 (KA, II, 1309–10). Adler and Louth comment that the *Pindarfragmente* 'can be thought of as post-tragic' (AL, liii); and see similarly Seifert 1988: 177 (referring to a 'Jenseits der Tragödie'). By contrast Theunissen, somewhat idiosyncratically, sees their tendency as at best 'antiutopische' and at worst 'utopiefeindliche' (2000: 972). On Pindar's victory songs as themselves the 'antitype to tragedy', defusing or resolving the conflicts and tensions dramatized by the latter, see Kurke 2013: 6.
6   MA, II, 187–246; see Louth 1998: 103–49, Bremer 2001, and Christen 2007. Hölderlin translated all or part of seventeen victory odes. PF 1 ('Untreue der Weisheit') is the only *Pindarfragment* that includes an extract from one, namely the Fourth Pythian (which also happens to be the longest).
7   Cf. Fleming 2002: 273–74; also Constantine 1986: 395–97. On the *Pindarfragmente* as exemplifying a kind of 'poetic archaeology', see Adler and Louth in AL, lii. Fink's nine finely-composed interpretations can themselves be taken in the spirit suggested above.

2. Pindarfragmente

There are, at least in principle, two possible orderings of the *Pindarfragmente*, since they are found on two distinct sheets of manuscript (consisting of single and double leaves respectively). All more recent editors concur on a sequence that begins with 'Untreue der Weisheit' [Unfaithfulness of Wisdom] and ends with 'Das Belebende' [The Life-Giving].[8] A striking feature of such a sequence is that it begins and ends with the theme of the Centaur: the wise centaur Chiron, in PF 1; and in PF 9, the unruly mob who disturbed the wedding of Peirithous and Hippodameia (Graves 1958: 360–61). Chiron is also present by name in PF 9, his tutelage of Achilles being remembered in its final words, which would then be the final words of the entire sequence. Note further that 'Chiron' is the title (and Chiron himself the subject) of the first and longest of the *Nachtgesänge*.[9]

'Das Belebende' is a particularly striking example of what Böschenstein has called 'le renversement du texte'. That is to say, Hölderlin does not so much offer an unorthodox or debatable interpretation of the translated fragment as deliberately invert its sense. He thereby transforms an episode of anarchic drunkenness into an allegory of cultural foundation. Böschenstein rightly draws attention to the phenomenon, and explains the connection between Hölderlin's interpretation of the Centaur (as 'spirit of a river') and other myths and themes, both ancient and contemporary. But he does not directly address the question why Hölderlin should engage in such a project of 'reversal'.[10] It seems that the answer must be sought in the project of the *Pindarfragmente* taken as a whole. The technique is not peculiar to 'Das Belebende', and cannot be attributed merely to the fact that it is 'impossible for wine to have negative connotations for Hölderlin'.[11]

---

8   Prior to StA an alternative sequence was sometimes assumed, beginning with 'Die Asyle' and 'Das Belebende' (PF 8 and PF 9) rather than with 'Untreue der Weisheit'. But this was no doubt influenced by the fact that PF 8 and PF 9 were the first to be discovered, in a transcription by the poet Eduard Mörike. The remaining pieces only came to light later, so that in Hellingrath's edition they had originally to be included as a supplement to the volume already devoted to translations: see Hell, v (1913), 271–73, and vi (1923), 6–10. The second edition of volume v (1923) then included them all, but in a sequence beginning with PF 8 and PF 9.

9   PF 9 is also the longest of the *Pindarfragmente*. In addition to the references PF 1, PF 2 etc., I shall refer to the relevant fragments of Pindar in the standard modern numbering, preceded by 'Fr.': see Pindar, ed. and trans. by William H. Race, 2 vols, LCL 56 and 485 (Cambridge, MA: Harvard University Press, 1997; revised repr. 2012), ii, 225–431; this edition cited below as 'Race'. Thus the basis for Hölderlin's translation in PF 9 is Fr. 166 (Race, ii, 398–99). Hölderlin himself used Estienne's handy pocket-size edition, which included a facing Latin translation: Pindar, *Olympia, Pythia, Nemea, Isthmia* etc., ed. by Henr. Stephanus [Henri II Estienne], 2 vols ([Geneva] 1560), cited below as 'Stephanus'. However, he had used the more recent Heyne edition of 1798 in his translation of the victory odes. In his edition Courtine helpfully includes both the modern and (where different) Stephanus versions of the Greek fragments: Hölderlin, *Fragments de poétique et autres textes*, ed. and trans. by Jean-François Courtine (Paris: Imprimerie nationale Éditions, 2006), pp. 441–69. The Stephanus versions, along with an interlinear German translation, can also be found in FHA, xv, and Bartel 2000. Although the sequence of fragments in Stephanus differs from either of the possible orderings of the *Pindarfragmente*, those that figure in PF 5, PF 6 and PF 7 occur in that order on a single page (Stephanus, ii, 350), as do PF 2 and PF 3 (Stephanus, ii, 360).

10 Böschenstein 1995c: 56–60. See also Bartel 2000: 164–73; Killy 1961: 42–43; and Louth 1998: 251–52, commenting that 'really the sense of the whole fragment is inverted' (p. 251).

11 Böschenstein 1995a: 62 ('daß es Hölderlin schlechterdings unmöglich ist, den Wein negativ

The same technique can be observed in 'Das Höchste' [The Highest], which is the fifth — and therefore presumably central — member of Hölderlin's sequence. PF 5 is based on a Pindar fragment (part of Fr. 169a) that is cited in Plato's *Gorgias*. In his commentary Hölderlin concludes that if, in the opening words of the fragment, 'The law' [Das Gesez] is 'King of all' [Von allen der König], this is in the sense of being 'the sign for the highest ground of knowledge, not for the highest power' [das Zeichen [...] für den höchsten Erkentnißgrund, nicht für die höchste Macht]. And in his translation he renders the βιαίως of Stephanus as 'gewaltig', rather than the 'gewalttätig' of the FHA interlinear version: that is to say as 'powerfully' or 'mightily' rather than 'violently'. But as he will have been aware, the fragment refers to an episode from the deeds of Heracles, namely the Tenth Labour, which consisted precisely in an act of force, even violence (Graves 1958: 494–95). It is true that the reference is omitted from Stephanus. But it is not omitted in the *Gorgias* itself, which that edition cites clearly as its source. Hence although the precise relationship between violence and law in Fr. 169a is open to interpretation, and depends in part upon the correct constitution of the text, the overall context is clear enough.[12] Like several of Heracles' exploits, the Tenth Labour involves an element of violence, even injustice: for the task was to rob Geryon of his famously beautiful cattle. That is why it figures in Plato's discussion of the relationship between 'might' and 'right'.[13] Hölderlin's interpretation of PF 5 expressly controverts the element of force, just as his interpretation of PF 9 draws a veil over the drunken orgy of the Centaurs. It is true that Pindar's own intention has long been debated, and cannot be equated with that of Plato's Callicles.[14] But it seems clear that Hölderlin deliberately avoids the underlying difficulty: namely the extent to which violence can be sanctified by law.

In what way does this relate to the theme of the anti-tragic? It is true that the Heracles of Fr. 169a is not a tragic hero in the usual mould, for all that he figures in certain tragedies — just as the drunken Centaurs in PF 9 are themselves hardly

---

zu konnotieren'); and Böschenstein 1995c: 57 ('pour lui le vin est toujours sacré'). It is true that, in recommending the Frankfurt wine-merchant Gogel to his friend Hegel as a potential employer, Hölderlin does not omit to mention that he will be served 'sehr guten Rheinwein oder französischen Wein' (MA, II, 631; AL, 78).

12 See Stephanus, II, 350 (ἐν τῷ Γοργίᾳ). The significance of the constitution of Pindar's text and Plato's citation of it is discussed in Baum 1965: 66–68; see also Dodds 1959: 270–72. In Stephanus, as in *Gorgias*, the superlative (δικαιότατον) attaches to the idea of justice, whereas it should probably attach to the idea of violence (βιαιότατον). Note that Hölderlin possessed a twelve-volume edition of Plato's works: see StA, VII.3, 388.

13 Plato's own citation continues 'in proof I take the deeds of Heracles, for unpurchased', at which point his character Callicles breaks off, saying 'the words are something like that [...] but it tells how he drove off the cows as neither a purchase nor a gift from Geryones; taking it as a natural right that cows or any other possessions of the inferior and weaker should all belong to the superior and stronger': see *Gorgias*, ed. and trans. by W. R. M. Lamb, in Plato, III, LCL 166 (Cambridge, MA: Harvard University Press, 1925), 484b–c (pp. 386–87).

14 Dodds' interpretation is closest in some respects to Hölderlin's: 'It is a likelier guess that his [Pindar's] νόμος [rather than meaning "custom"] is the law of Fate, which for him is identical with the will of Zeus' (1959: 270). But contrast Ostwald's view that Pindar is accepting (rather than endorsing) the fact that Heracles' deeds are sanctified by the common opinion of 'all mortals and immortals' (2009: 123–24).

tragic figures. But Hölderlin's interpretation of tragedy is based on the encounter of the human sphere with the overwhelming force of nature: what in the *Anmerkungen* is called 'die Naturmacht'. Tragedy consists in the transgression of a primordial boundary between divine Nature and human Culture, and the tragic hero comes to grief in consequence of such a transgression. The same boundary can be said to be at issue in the case of Dionysus or Heracles; but with the difference that they are gods or demigods, rather than fragile mortals. They can accordingly operate on both sides of the boundary, cleansing the surface of the habitable earth, or instituting the culture of the vine. The violence involved in the former activity, or the ecstatic frenzy that can result from the latter, are not things to which they themselves fall victim, but rather means to the creation of order (or a new order). They represent both 'die Naturmacht', and its limitation or conquest, turning the unbounded power of nature against itself in an act of cultural foundation.[15] In PF 5, on the other hand, Hölderlin concerns himself with the law as so established, rather than its origin, and with its role in separating the divine and human spheres. As a result, it can become a figure of the anti-tragic.

That dimension becomes clearer still when the language of PF 5 is compared with that of the *Anmerkungen*. AA [3.1], echoing and elaborating on AO [3.1], speaks of 'der unmittelbare Gott' as 'ganz Eines mit dem Menschen' [the immediate god, wholly one with the human being]. That immediate union is the starting point of tragedy. But in PF 5, 'immediacy' is declared to be 'strictly speaking [...] impossible' [streng genommen [...] unmöglich]. Instead, there is a requirement of 'strict' or 'rigorous mediacy' [strenge Mittelbarkeit], identified in turn with 'das Gesez'. According to AO [3.1], an excessive intimacy of human and divine — as it were a transgressive immediacy — is purged in a catharsis of extreme separation. Or as Hölderlin had put it a few years earlier, in tragedy the necessary separation of human and divine spheres is demonstrated *per contrarium*.[16] The *Pindarfragmente* speak instead in terms of a meeting or a recognition of the two spheres, rather than their fusion: an encounter that is made possible by the law that codifies their separation.[17] But the law that is purged of its associations with the questionable deeds of the demigod, is also the law that is demonstrated *per contrarium* in the sufferings of the tragic hero.

'Untreue der Weisheit' (PF 1) can also be seen in terms of a 'reversal' of the original text, although here the anti-tragic consequences are more oblique. Hölderlin departs from the likely meaning of Fr. 43, turning the image of an octopus craftily taking on the colour of its surroundings into that of the wise Centaur.

---

15 On the status of Dionysus and Heracles as respectively god or demigod, see Analecta 2004: 135–41; and on each as representing 'eine Stifterfigur', cf. Honold 2002: 192, and Schmidt 1990: 126. See also Oudemans and Lardinois 1987: 92.
16 See the draft letter to Mehmel, probably end of 1800 (MA, II, 851; AL, 184); and on this letter see further section 3 below. In AO [3.1] the tragic fusion of the two spheres is described as 'das Ungeheure', which Hühn (surely correctly) relates to 'die Verletzung der "strengen" Mittelbarkeit' (1997: 212).
17 'Die Zucht, so fern sie die Gestalt ist, worinn der Mensch sich und der Gott begegnet' (PF 5); 'der Gott und der Mensch sich wiedererkennt' (PF 8). On PF 8 see further below.

As a result, an opportunistic adaptation to circumstances can become a kind of 'intelligence' [Klugheit], one informed by the wisdom learned in Chiron's grotto. It is true that Pindar's image is closer to Hölderlin's version than might first be supposed. The octopus (like the fox) is an exemplar of the Greek notion of *mētis*, a form of devious practical intelligence that is itself informed by wisdom. The active cunning of an octopus is to be contrasted with the passive adaptation of a chameleon, and embodies a virtue that was admired highly by the Greeks. In this case it may be difficult to decide to what degree the transformation of Pindar's original meaning is deliberate.[18] PF 2, on the other hand, seems a clear example of such a 'renversement'. In Hölderlin's commentary, the danger posed by falsehood — the ostensible subject of Pindar's prayer to 'Queen Truth' in Fr. 205 — becomes a fear of the truth itself, as an object too lofty for the mind or sense. The stage is thereby set for an exposition of the anti-tragic. In AO [2.2] the tragic error of Oedipus is described as the pursuit of an ultimately unbearable truth: knowledge goads itself 'mehr zu wissen, als es tragen oder fassen kann' [to know more than it can grasp or bear] (MA, II, 312). But in PF 2, it is Truth herself who is implored to save us from such a fate. To that end, Hölderlin's commentary makes Pindar's 'rough falsehood' (*trakhus pseudos*) — captured well enough by his translation 'rauhe Lüge' — into the blinding effect of Truth herself. But not all the *Pindarfragmente* need to apply such a technique of reversal. If Hölderlin's object was to compose a treatise on the anti-tragic, some of the available fragments already provided suitable material. This seems to be the position in the case of PF 3 ('Von der Ruhe'), PF 4 ('Vom Delphin'), PF 6 ('Das Alter') and PF 8 ('Die Asyle'). There the original fragment is already suitable for Hölderlin's purpose, as if he need only unfold a latent meaning. And here he is of course assisted by the fragmentary character of Pindar's texts.[19]

If it is indeed the opening member of the sequence, PF 1 might be expected to provide additional clues as to how the *Pindarfragmente* are to be interpreted. And it is here that Fink introduces a theme that is common to his various interpretations: the theme of self-reflection. That is to say, in reflecting upon a fragment of Pindar, each discovers a principle that is applicable to itself and its own process of interpretation.[20]

18 On the octopus as exemplifying the 'cunning intelligence' of *mētis*, see Detienne and Vernant 1974: 45–47 (referring to Fr. 43 at 46, n. 79); and on *mētis* see further section 4 below, and cf. Bartel 2000: 60–67 (similarly citing Detienne and Vernant, and finding both octopus and Centaur in PF 1). Hölderlin's (mis)interpretation of Fr. 43 is defended by Theunissen (2000: 983–84). But Theunissen fails to appreciate the parallel for προσφέρων — in the sense of 'becoming like' rather than 'clinging to' — in the first stanza of Pindar's Sixth Nemean Ode: see Brill, s.v. προσφέρω, 1.F, and LSJ, s.v. προσφέρω, A.III; and contrast Theunissen's own account of that stanza (2000: 227–34). Hölderlin would have been aware of the parallel, and in effect cites the beginning of the stanza in his hymn 'Kolomb': 'Eines der Götter eines wäre | Der Menschen Geschlecht' (MA, I, 426–27, ll. 32–33); cf. Analecta 2007: 72–73. Note that the same hymn refers to 'Chirons | Schüler' (MA, I, 426, ll. 17–18).
19 The important remaining instance, PF 7 ('Das Unendliche'), is discussed in section 4 below.
20 For self-reflection in the *Pindarfragmente* see Fink 1982: 27–28 (PF 1); 34–35 (PF2); 47–48 (PF 3); 57–59 (PF 4); 77–78 (PF 5); 85–86 (PF 6); 93–95 (PF 7); 108–10 (PF 8); 122 (PF 9). Kreuzer similarly observes that '[die] Koinzidenz von Reflexionsform und Reflexionsgegenstand zeichnet [...] alle neun Stücke aus': see Hölderlin, *Theoretische Schriften*, ed. by Johann Kreuzer; Philosophische

Thus Hölderlin's commentary to Fr. 43 begins with the observation: 'Fähigkeit der einsamen Schule für die Welt' [Capacity of the solitary school for the world]. As Fink suggests, one could regard Hölderlin's previous exercise in Pindar translation — the wilfully faithful studies of the victory odes — as just such a 'solitary school'. There he clung to Pindar's text, rather as the child (in Hölderlin's idiosyncratic translation) clings to the Centaur's pelt.[21] His lonely communion with Pindar can be compared to those of Chiron's famous pupils with their master.[22] According to Hölderlin's inventive commentary, the knowledge or wisdom so acquired is applied when a pupil ventures out again into the wider world, remaining 'faithful' [getreu] even 'in different circumstances' [unter verschiedenen Umständen]. In Hölderlin's case that wider world comprises the world of poetry, including the *Pindarfragmente* themselves. It was the earlier Pindar studies that now enabled the poet to 'think otherwise in another age' [anderes denk in anderer Zeit]: for instance, in the interpretation of Fr. 43 itself. Remaining true to that solitary school has also given Hölderlin the wisdom to be 'unfaithful' (as in 'Untreue der Weisheit'). The commentary closes with a citation from Pindar's Fourth Pythian Ode, depicting the scene where Jason returns from his studies with Chiron to claim his throne back from a usurper. The point of that second citation would then be to demonstrate (with some justice) a continuity of succession between Pindar as father poet, and Hölderlin as rightful heir.

In what then does the 'anti-tragic' character PF 1 consist? The connection is to be found in the notion of 'Untreue' [unfaithfulness]. The latter has an important place in the *Anmerkungen*, and is associated with a moment of discontinuity or radical forgetting (AO [3.3]–[3.5]). Here, by contrast, it founds a continuity of ancient and modern eras. The self-reflexive character of the *Pindarfragmente* provides the basis for such a continuity, for they can speak at the same time of ancient fragment and modern interpretation. Thus in PF 1 the notions of 'Treue' [faithfulness] and 'Untreue' stand in a complex relation. In PF 4, by contrast the notion of 'Treue' receives a peculiarly direct expression. As we saw in Chapter 5.2, the musical character of its commentary directly echoes that of the translated text, combining the notions of 'Ton' and 'Treue' and exemplifying a particularly pure form of the anti-tragic.

We have also already seen the importance of the notions 'Ruhe' ['repose' or 'tranquillity'], 'Ruhestätte' [places of rest] and 'Asyl' [sanctuary] in the period of the Homburg poetics (see Chapter 1.4). But those notions also lie at the centre of at least

---

Bibliothek, 509 (Hamburg: Meiner, 1998), Einleitung, p. 1. On poetological self-reflection in the earlier translation of the victory odes, see Christen 2007: 61–75.

21 As already noted, Fr. 43 is better taken as referring to the octopus whose skin imitates its surroundings, than a Centaur to whom a grateful pupil is attached; and the injunction is to 'become like' the former, rather than to 'cling to' the latter. For a nuanced view of the earlier translation-project, see Vöhler 2005: 118–19 and Bremer 2001: 170

22 Louth observes that, in the earlier Pindar translation, 'Hölderlin deliberately narrowed the focus to an intensely personal, unmediated encounter with Pindar' (1998: 110). Böschenstein distinguishes three phases in Hölderlin's translation practice, characterized in the case of the earlier Pindar-translation as 'abhäng[ig]' and with '[d]as äußerste Maß an Selbstverleugnung', whereas the translation of the *Pindarfragmente* is 'reflektierend ausgleiche[nd]' (1995a: 48).

two of the *Pindarfragmente*, namely PF 3 and PF 8. Note again how the language of PF 3 responds to that of the *Anmerkungen*, with the recurrence of such terms as 'reißend' ['tearing' or 'rapacious'], 'Schiksaal' [fate] and 'Vaterland' [nation] — and with 'stetigere' [more steady] as a contrasting alternative to 'reißendere' [more rapacious].[23] The commentary also establishes a connection between 'Ruhe' and 'Gesez': indeed 'die Geseze' are defined, in words taken from the Pindar translation, as 'der großmännlichen Ruhe heiliges Licht' [holy light of lordly repose]. And in speaking of the 'law', it seems that Hölderlin is also speaking of the way in which poetry can grasp the conditions of its age, and hence of successive epochs of poetic law-giving.[24] Here it might also be promising to explore the resonances with Rousseau's *Du contract social*. For in treating of the conditions of passage from a state of nature to a civil order governed by laws, Rousseau too refers to a 'prince ou législateur' (cf. in PF 3 'ein Gesezgeber oder ein Fürst'), and distinguishes a mere 'bourgeois' from a true 'Citoyen' (cf. '[der] eigentlicher[e] Bürger').[25]

The idea of 'law' is as central to PF 8 ('Die Asyle') as it is to PF 3 and PF 5.[26] And again there is a connection with the concept of 'Ruhe', since the 'sanctuaries' mentioned in its title are defined as 'die stillen Ruhestätten' [the still places of rest]. In treating of the origin of those sanctuaries, here too the commentary seems to respond to the account of tragedy in the *Anmerkungen*. Thus while AO [3.4] speaks of a forgetting of god and human being ('der Mensch [vergißt] sich und den Gott'), here the reference is to their renewed recognition ('der Gott und der Mensch sich wiedererkennt').[27] PF 8 describes a happier time in which human beings can 'hold' themselves, rather than being abandoned to the tragic process of forgetting: '[der Mensch ist froh] da, *wo er sich halten kann*'. But that new encounter takes place 'an den Spuren der alten Zucht' [on the traces of ancient discipline], a phrase that seems to point back to the earlier encounter represented in tragedy.

That phrase also provides an important clue to the meaning of 'Treue' and 'Untreue' in the *Pindarfragmente*. Those concepts figure expressly in PF 4 and PF 1;

---

23   Thus compare 'reißendere[s] oder stetigere[s] Schiksaal eines Vaterlandes' (PF 3) with 'de[r] reißend[e] Wechsel der Vorstellungen' (AO [1.7]), 'd[ie] reißend[e] Zeit' (AO [2.3]), and 'de[r] reißend[e] Zeitgeist' (AA [2.2]); and with 'Schiksaal seiner Zeit und Form seines Vaterlandes' (AA [3.9]). Compare also 'die Mittel, jenes Schiksaal [...] festzuhalten' (PF 3, said of 'die Geseze'), with 'den Geist der Zeit [....] festzuhalten' (AA [3.9]), said of '[d]ie vaterländischen Formen unserer Dichter'.

24   Cf. the contrast drawn between 'griechisch[e] Natursöhn[e]' and 'Menschen von Erziehung', discussed at Fink 1982: 47–48. But Fink may go too far in suggesting a correspondence with the two contrasting tragic 'caesurae' treated in the *Anmerkungen* (1982: 48–50). On PF 3, as well as Bartel 2000: 92–104, see Seifert 1998: 95–98, and Franz 2002: 260–61.

25   See Jean-Jacques Rousseau, *Du contrat social*, in *Œuvres complètes*, ed. by Bernard Gagnebin and Marcel Raymond, 5 vols (Paris: Gallimard, 1959–95), III (1964), 347–470 (pp. 351, 361–62, and 364).

26   The place of the concept of 'law' in PF 8 is demonstrated conclusively by Seifert 1998. For this theme in PF 3, PF 5 and PF 8, see also Fleming 2002: 275–76 (reaching to some extent different conclusions from those found here, but also emphasizing the anti-tragic).

27   On the problems raised by such formulae, see Fink 1982: 74, n. 2, and 104; Fleming 2002: 284–85; and the commentary to AO [3.5] in Part II below. Thus there is a (perhaps deliberate) uncertainty as to whether god and human encounter (respectively forget) each other, or themselves, or indeed both.

but 'faithfulness' can also be said to figure in PF 8, as can its connection with the notion of 'law'. Thus PF 8 is the only *Pindarfragment* for which an additional manuscript source has survived, on a page of the bundle known as the *Homburger Folioheft*.[28] The phrase 'die Spuren der alten Zucht' is found there, together with a citation from the beginning of Pindar's Thirteenth Olympic Ode. This relates to the theme treated in PF 8, namely the progeny of the goddess Themis.[29] Most striking, however, is the title that Hölderlin provides for the Pindar extract, with its curious mixture of German and French: 'Ursprung der Loyoté [sic]'. As Seifert points out, if the last word is a version of 'loyauté' — which would now be translated as 'faithfulness' or 'loyalty' — it also contains the French term for 'law': 'loi' (or in its older spelling 'loy'). Seifert resists the idea that 'loyauté' might connote the virtue of honesty or faithfulness as well as the attribute of lawfulness (1998: 50–52). But might it not mean both? Seifert is surely correct in saying that Hölderlin's 'loyoté' corresponds to the Greek *eunomia*, meaning 'legality' or 'good order' and found in the Pindar extract as the name of one of three daughters of Themis (the Horae).[30] And it is true that the distinction between the French terms 'loyal' and 'légal' only became firmly established at the end of the eighteenth century. But Hölderlin could well be playing precisely on an ambiguity of 'loyal', which might then connote both 'faithful' and 'legal'.[31] And 'loyoté' would then also correspond to the German 'Treue', the opposite of the 'Untreue' found at the centre of tragedy. If the fusion of divine and human spheres breaches the law of 'strenge Mittelbarkeit' (PF 5), and requires a tragic catharsis of forgetting ('in der allvergessenden Form der Untreue', AO [3.3]), now it is 'law' (or 'loy') that makes possible a relation of faithfulness (or 'loy-alty').

I would again follow Fink in discerning here the element of poetic self-reflection.[32] The poet too is a law-giver, and the poem accordingly a sanctuary

---

28 See FHA, Suppl. III, 108 (307/82); MA, I, 430. The *Homburger Folioheft* is named for the library that owns it, rather than the place necessarily of composition; hence one cannot infer that the *Pindarfragmente* were written during Hölderlin's second Homburg period of June 1804–September 1806.
29 The source of the citation appears to be the edition used for the *Pindarfragmente*, rather than the later edition used for the translations of the victory odes (see Stephanus, I, 140; although Hölderlin omits the verb ναίει [dwells]). See now Race, I, 192, ll. 6–8.
30 The Horae, daughters of Themis by Zeus, are named in the extract as 'Order' [Εὐνομία], 'Justice' [Δίκα], and 'Peace' [Εἰρήνα], already demonstrating a connection with both 'Gesez' and 'Ruhe' (Race, I, 192–93, ll. 6–7). Hölderlin's translation of her progeny in Fr. 30 as 'die Ruhestätten' must be seen in relation both to the Stephanus Greek text, which gives σωτῆρας [saviours], and the emendation accepted in modern editions and mentioned in Stephanus, namely Ὥρας [Horae] (Stephanus, II, 375; Race, II, 236); see Seifert 1998: 52, and Bartel 2000: 154–56. Note that l. 5 of Fr. 30 already describes Zeus as 'saviour' [σωτῆρος].
31 See *Dictionnaire historique de la langue française*, ed. by Alain Rey and others, 2nd edn (Paris: Robert, 2010), s.vv. légal, loyal; and Littré, s.v. légal. See also the translations offered in MA, III, 253 ('Rechtschaffenheit'), and TL, 1093 ('lealtà').
32 By now the theme has become so evident for Fink that he leaves the details almost as an exercise for the reader (1982: 108–09). But he notes, in particular, the characterisation of 'der Mensch' in Hölderlin's commentary as 'ein Sohn der Themis'. If the human law-giver follows in the footsteps of Themis, and establishes the sheltering sanctuary of a legal order, the poet-commentator follows in the footsteps of Pindar: 'Die Sprache, der Text würde damit zum Asyl' (1982: 109), citing also the ode 'Mein Eigentum' (ibid. n. 16).

or place of repose. In PF 5, Hölderlin is careful to distinguish the laws treated there from any we may find in the realm of the arts: for they are said to operate 'strenger, als die Kunst' [more rigorously than art], that is to say when 'sie halten [...] die lebendigen Verhältnisse fest' [they hold fast the living relations]. The quasi-deductive form of PF 5 is itself an expression of that distinction: a simulacrum, within Hölderlin's commentary, of the rigorous domain of the non-poetic. But the comparative ('strenger') itself concedes the analogy between poetic and non-poetic law-giving.[33] And PF 8 sheds further light on the idea of the poem as a 'sanctuary'. The essence of the 'Ruhestätten' lies in their concentration of recollected time: 'an ihnen das Wirken und das Leben der Natur sich konzentrirte, und ein Ahnendes um sie, wie erinnernd, dasselbe erfähret, das sie vormals erfuhren' [in them the working and life of nature concentrated itself, and one around them who divines, as if remembering, experiences the same as what they experienced formerly]. This may be again be contrasted with the tragic process of 'forgetting'.[34] To concern oneself with these 'Asyle' is to experience a concentration of the past within the interval of a present. And as a reader of the *Pindarfragmente* attempts to divine their interpretation, those texts themselves become a sanctuary of recollection.

3. *Nachtgesänge*

It is difficult to establish a one-to-one correspondence between the nine *Nachtgesänge* on the one hand, and the nine *Pindarfragmente* on the other. But it is equally difficult to deny a connection between the sequences taken as a whole. As already observed, the formal and thematic similarities are striking even where their differences in mood are taken into account.[35]

Schmidt's thesis — that the *Nachtgesänge* are evidence of a late 'recantation' [Widerruf] — also seems to have a limited explanatory value.[36] It is true that both *Nachtgesänge* and *Pindarfragmente* must be seen in the context of Hölderlin's renewed emphasis on law, boundaries and limits. Those themes are equally present in the late hymn-fragments, and prominent in some late revisions to the elegies. But it seems

---

33 Seifert similarly notes '[die] neben der graduellen Differenzierung ausgedrückte prinzipielle Vergleichbarkeit von Dichter und Gesetzgeber, Kunstwerk und Gesetz' (1998: 106).
34 For an earlier use of the verb 'konzentrieren' in connection with a notion of lyric subjectivity ('von den conzentrirenden Theilen') see MA, II, 107, and cf. Ryan 1988: 113. And see also the two arguably Stoic conceptions of time discussed in Chapter 2.3 (*aiōn* and *khronos*), which might on this basis be described as 'tragic' and 'anti-tragic' respectively.
35 Sattler's arguments for such a correspondence (1996a and 1996b) are not always convincing, even where they are intelligible (although he makes the obvious connection between 'Chiron' and 'Untreue der Weisheit'). He also speculates that the *Pindarfragmente* were a rejoinder to the hostile review of the *Nachtgesänge* in the *Jenaische Allgemeine Literatur-Zeitung* of 2 May 1805: see FHA, XV, 331. That would of course imply a date of summer 1805, at the earliest, for the composition of the *Pindarfragmente*. But the arguments for the end of 1803 or beginning of 1804 may be stronger: see Seifert 1998: 14–16, 119–23.
36 See the title to Schmidt 1978, and for 'Blödigkeit' as a 'recantation' of its precursor ode 'Dichtermuth' see 1978: 132. But Schmidt's thesis may ultimately be more nuanced, as he speaks subsequently in terms of a 'bis zum Widerruf reichende Gegenbewegung' or 'eine entschiedene Gegenwehr' (p. 177).

excessive to characterize this as a 'recantation', especially given the continuities with works of an earlier period. Furthermore, an argument based on the *Nachtgesänge* must allow the possibility that they have a more specific function, one corresponding to that generic title or description. True, their composition involved the substantial revision of several earlier odes; but that may merely reflect the unsuitability of the latter for the subsequent programme.[37] As we saw in the last section, only some of the *Pindarfragmente* required Böschenstein's 'renversement du texte'. In a similar way, if the composition of the *Nachtgesänge* required some extensive rewriting of earlier poems, others required fewer changes — or were indeed composed specifically for that purpose.[38] As regards the continuities with Hölderlin's earlier work, we have seen the role played by such concepts as 'Gesez', 'Asyl' and 'Ruhestätte' in the first Homburg period. There the idea of the poem as a 'sanctuary' or 'place of repose' is already important, just as the notion of a poetic 'law' is strikingly exemplified by the poetics of the *Wechsel der Töne*. The association of 'law' and 'calculus', so prominent in the *Anmerkungen*, is clearly present in the earlier poetological 'tables' or 'schemata'.[39] If such ideas receive particular attention in the later period, this is an amplification of earlier tendencies rather than a new departure.

Of all the *Nachtgesänge*, it is the ode 'Chiron' that has the most obvious thematic links with the *Pindarfragmente*.[40] As already noted, the latter begin and end with the figure of Chiron, the wise and benevolent Centaur. Furthermore the figure of Heracles is also central to the ode, since Chiron's wounding by his poisoned arrow forms part of its mythological background. We saw how Heracles was also present by implication in PF 5, in the shape of his Tenth Labour — a theft of cattle that is nonetheless sanctified by law. But we saw too how the elision of any express reference to Heracles focused attention on the result of his endeavours: 'das Gesez' as a boundary between divine Nature and human Culture. Before that 'law' is definitively established, we are in the ambivalent realm of the heroes: heroes of cultural foundation who trace that boundary, or heroes of tragedy who come to grief as a result of its transgression.

In the ode, Heracles is described as 'Zevs Knecht [...], der gerade Mann' (l. 18). If Heracles is 'upright' and a 'servant of Zeus', this is because he implements the latter's supreme law.[41] Nonetheless, Heracles has a more specific function in the ode, with results that are tragic after their own fashion. In the background myth,

---

37 For a table setting out the relationship between earlier and later versions, see TL, 1473. On whether the rewritten odes are to be regarded as replacing their earlier versions, cf. Frey 1990: 88–106.

38 An interesting case is the transformation of a personal lament of the poet Sappho, in 'Sapphos Schwanengesang', to the more universal one reflected in the new title 'Thränen' (see Groddeck 2006: 637–38).

39 See above, respectively Chapter 1, sections 3–4, and Chapter 3, sections 3–4.

40 On this ode see especially Schmidt 1978: 33–99, and in KA, I, 795–818; and Indlekofer 2007: 119–68. Here the earlier version is 'Der blinde Sänger' [The Blind Singer] (MA, I, 281–83; OE, 117–19).

41 On the figure of Heracles in 'Chiron', and the connotations of 'gerade', see Schmidt 1978: 52–61 (in particular p. 54, n. 44). The implications of the latter epithet are explored further in section 4 below. On Heracles see also Chapter 3.5 above.

immortal Chiron suffers as a result of his wounding by a poisoned arrow, and must await Heracles' return with its promised deliverance of death (Graves 1958: 475). But as Schmidt suggests (KA, I, 804–05), it seems that Heracles is responsible also for a different kind of poison, one that disenchants the natural world for which Chiron previously had a more instinctive sympathy:

> Nun siz' ich still allein, von einer
> Stunde zur anderen, und Gestalten
>
> Aus frischer Erd' und Wolken der Liebe schafft,
> Weil Gift ist zwischen uns, mein Gedanke nun.
>
> [Now I sit alone in silence from one
> Hour to the next, and my thoughts
>
> Spin shapes from the virgin soil and clouds
> Of love, since poison is between us.]
> (MA, I, 439, ll. 19–22; OE, 167)

It is difficult in a translation to do justice to Hölderlin's syntax, where the position of the words 'Gift ist zwischen uns' at least momentarily identifies the interpolated 'poison' with the speaker's own shape-spinning thought. We might conclude that thought itself is the poison, at least until the larger syntactical unit is taken into account. And once the spectre has been raised, the idea somehow persists that the poison which Heracles has brought is that of disenchanted reflection itself.

Schmidt has noted how Hölderlin's revision of the precursor ode systematically replaces ecstatic feeling by thought, and instinctive sympathy by reflection — a process that is narrated in the ode itself. But it is also enacted by a poetic language that exalts the signifier, and its labyrinthine tropes, at the expense of any transparent meaning. This is a 'thought' that, at the limit, is so alienated from itself that its referent is lost.[42] But Schmidt is less convincing when he argues that this subordination of feeling to reflection — and hence of poetry to science, or philosophy — corresponds to Hölderlin's own position. It corresponds, rather, to the tragedy of Chiron's situation. After all, it is in this period that Hölderlin articulates the difference between 'poetic logic' and the logic of philosophy; and there is no suggestion that poetry is intended to be disparaged by such a comparison.[43]

Such devices are typical of the *Nachtgesänge*, or at least of those that are rewritten versions of earlier odes. The rewriting process seems to generate a concentration upon the workings of language, to the extent that meaning threatens temporarily to be lost or incompatible meanings proliferate. In relation to the ode 'Ganymed', Louth observes how 'the opaque quality of individual words means that we are less disposed to look through them at what they signify, but remain under their actual spell' (1998: 197). We might say that the language of the poem takes on a life of its

---

42 As Degner observes (2008: 205), the poison can also be said to fall between word and meaning, disrupting an ideal harmony of sense.

43 On 'poetic' versus philosophical 'logic' see AA [1.2]. For Schmidt, Hölderlin in 'Chiron' embraces the role of philosopher rather than poet, and his position is assimilated to that of Hegel (1978: 97–98; KA, I, 796–98).

own, alienated at times from an extra-linguistic realm of meaning, in a manner that almost anticipates the method of Mallarmé.[44] Again, consider the disconcerting opening lines of 'Chiron': 'Wo bist du, Nachdenkliches! das immer muß | Zur Seiten gehn, zu Zeiten, wo bist du, Licht?' [Where are you, pensive one, who must always | Move aside at times, where are you, light?].[45] It seems that 'Seiten' and 'Zeiten' are used to evoke the periodic absence and return of daylight, where the precursor ode refers simply to the speaker being woken by the morning light ('das immer mich | Zur Stunde wekt des Morgens'). The revision appears to have been inspired by the phonetic play on 'S' and 'Z', rather than the other way around: a play that paradoxically generates an obscurity around the return of the light. There is no denying the strange beauty of these lines, and of similar passages elsewhere in the *Nachtgesänge*. But rather than being simply the affirmation of a novel poetic form (modern, or 'Hesperian', as opposed to 'Greek'), such techniques seem to be taken to a deliberately uncomfortable extreme.[46]

To put the matter in Hölderlin's own vocabulary: with such devices he attains an extreme of poetic 'sobriety' [Nüchternheit] by means of an ostentatious deployment of poetic 'skill' ['Geschik' or 'Schiklichkeit']. Here 'Nüchternheit' is to be contrasted with 'Begeisterung' [enthusiasm]. We saw in Chapter 4 how Hölderlin's use of those concepts responded to the ancient treatise *On the Sublime*; and I argued that the category of the Sublime remained relevant to his reflections on Greek tragedy. But what if the *Nachtgesänge* were intended to embody a different kind of tragedy — if they were not so much anti-tragic, in the manner of the *Pindarfragmente*, as anti-sublime?[47] If the Greek tragic hero perishes through a transport of enthusiasm, a

---

44 See for example Malcolm Bowie's comments on the syntax of the 'Prose pour des Esseintes' (1978: 42–49), and in particular its 'suspensions of sense' (pp. 43–44).

45 I have modified Hoff's translation of 'Nachdenkliches' (cf. SP, 73: 'thoughtful'; TL, 285: 'pensierosa'), but his solution ('thought-provoking') is equally valid, and shows how the language here has taken on a new indeterminacy; see also Hamb, 249 ('thought-infusing'). Following Groddeck, Indlekofer identifies here the rhetorical figure of 'hypallage', with a resulting 'syntaktische Verwirrung' (2007: 127; cf. Groddeck 2008: 198–99). By contrast, in the precursor ode the morning light is unambiguously addressed as 'Jugendliches' [youthful one] (MA, I, 281, l. 1; OE, 117).

46 Similarly, in 'Ganymed', Degner notes the 'Lautwanderungen zwischen semantisch unzusammenhängenden Bereichen', e.g. 'shief'/'schlief', 'schauend'/'schaudernd', 'Kluft'/'Lüfte' (2008: 246); and see also Reitani 1999: 107. On radical lexical ambiguity in 'Chiron' see Indlekofer 2007: 151–52; and, in 'Ganymed', ibid. 169–70. In relation to 'Vulkan', Christen (2018) notes how the poem ends with a curiously self-referential figura etymologica ('doch liebt die Liebe'), which is itself almost an anagram of a formula in the earlier draft 'Der Winter' (MA, III, 267: 'doch bleibt die Liebe'); it is as if the figure is designed to withdraw any consolation offered by its precursor. For such techniques as exemplifying a specifically 'hesperian' poetic language ('die Wende hin zur "hesperischen" Sprache'), see Indlekofer 2007: 150; and on the term 'Hesperian' see further below.

47 For Bennholdt-Thomsen (2002: 339), the inclusion of the 'Vulkan' in the *Nachtgesänge* can be related to ch. 35 of the treatise, which contrasts the 'little fire we kindle for ourselves' with the 'fires of Heaven' or 'craters of Etna'. It is true that the title seems to refer to a friendly fire-god rather than to the geological phenomenon (cf. Schmidt 1978: 7–8); but see also Analecta 2004: 30, pointing to the connection between the parallel Greek god Hephaestus and Etna, found e.g. in Pindar's First Pythian Ode. See *On the Sublime*, ed. and trans. by W. H. Fyfe, rev. by Donald Russell, in Aristotle XXIII, LCL 199 (Cambridge, MA: Harvard University Press, 1995, corrected repr. 1999), pp. 143–305 (pp. 274–75).

too-close identification with the divine, or by being engulfed by an overwhelming fate, might a modern one perish through an excess of sobriety — or what the *Anmerkungen* (AA [3.2]) refer to as 'das Schiksaallose' [fatelessness]?

The relation between 'Nüchternheit' and 'Begeisterung' lies at the centre of the most famous *Nachtgesang*, 'Hälfte des Lebens' — indeed literally so, being found at the end of its first (of two) stanzas. The first stanza describes an idyll, but one that tips into the desolation of the second when swans cool their inebriated heads in the water:

> Und trunken von Küssen
> Tunkt ihr das Haupt
> Ins heilignüchterne Wasser.
>
> [And drunk with kisses
> You dip your heads
> In the holy, sober water.]
> (MA, I, 445; OE, 181)

We might say that the water is not so much 'holy, sober' — or even, as in Hamburger's version, 'holy-and-sober' — as 'holy-sober'. Thus 'heilig' qualifies the sobriety itself, rather than merely adding to it. Here it implies the opposite of excess, a sobriety that balances the intoxication of the swans.[48] But then, with the transition to the second stanza, that equilibrium is lost. The poem now portrays a desolate world in which meaning has departed, described as a world of wintry desolation. It seems that an excess of sobriety (the 'all-too sober') is a specifically modern tragic condition — as it were the converse of Greek tragic excess.[49]

The apparent simplicity of 'Hälfte des Lebens' is far removed from the involved syntax of a poem such as 'Chiron'. But Hölderlin seems to be striving for the same effect, albeit with different means: the evocation of a world of desolate sobriety. The point is that there is a parallel between an extreme of poetic craft or 'Schiklichkeit', on the one hand, and the loss of meaning in extreme 'Nüchternheit' on the other. Here the last stanza of 'Blödigkeit' is helpful. We already saw in Chapter 1 how it plays, with a kind of self-reflexive virtuosic awkwardness, on phonetic, etymological and semantic connections between the terms 'Geschik', 'geschikt', and 'schiklich'.[50] By an adroit manoeuvre, an extremity of poetic 'Nüchternheit' has been turned

---

48 It has long been observed that for Hölderlin 'heilig' can connote wholeness and balance (Zuberbühler 1969: 73–74). See also Groddeck 2012: 73, on 'das Heiligtrunkene' in the second stanza of the elegy 'Brod und Wein', and cf. the notion of 'heilige Schiklichkeit' in the draft letter to Mehmel discussed below. On the significance of the term 'heilignüchtern' see further Schmidt 1983, and Reitani in TL, 1495; although for Reitani 'nüchtern' qualifies 'heilig' (as in 'sobriamente sacra') rather than the other way around.

49 As Strauß observes, '[d]as Nüchterne schlägt ins Allzunüchterne um' (1963: 489), also pointing (p. 487) to the parallels in the poem 'Elegie': 'im allzunüchternen Reich' (MA, I, 289, l. 69); and in a draft of 'Lebenslauf', l. 7: 'im nüchternen Orkus' (MA, III, 180). See also, in 'Menons Klagen um Diotima' (a later version of 'Elegie'), 'das nüchterne Lied' (MA, I, 291, l. 20); and, in the letter to his sister of 11 December 1800, 'so kalt und allzunüchtern' (MA, II, 880; AL, 185).

50 See Chapter 1.4, where a similar constellation of terms was noted in a letter to his publisher, indeed in the one that first promised the poems later described as 'Nachtgesänge': see MA, II, 926 ('in schiklicher Zeit zuschiken', 'nicht unschiklich', 'glüklich Geschik').

against itself, becoming the affirmation of a poetic vocation. But the very terms employed point unmistakably to a corresponding passage in the *Anmerkungen*. That is to say, they point to the discussion in AA [3.2] of the distinction between the 'Geschik' of the Greeks and the 'Schiklichkeit' of the moderns.

It will be useful, therefore, to look more closely at this passage of the *Anmerkungen*, together with letters that provide an indispensable theoretical context: the letters (especially the first) to Böhlendorff; and the somewhat earlier letter that was probably intended for Mehmel.[51] The letters shed light on Hölderlin's conception of the specific characteristics of Greek art, including Tragedy. Similarly, in AA [3.2] and [3.3], he interpolates a long and difficult discussion of the distinction between ancient Greek, and modern or 'Hesperian' poetic representation. In B1 the emphasis is on the respective strengths of those different epochs of culture, while AA [3.2] dwells on the aspect of tragic 'weakness' [Schwäche]. In the words of the latter, for the Greeks the 'main tendency' [Haupttendenz] of their culture is 'to be able to grasp oneself' [sich fassen zu können], because it is in this that they were originally deficient. This corresponds in B1 to the development of a 'faculty of exposition' [Darstellungsgaabe] beginning with Homer, for 'dieser außerordentliche Mensch seelenvoll genug war, um die abendländische *Junonische Nüchternheit* für sein Apollonsreich zu erbeuten, und so wahrhaft das fremde sich anzueignen' [this extraordinary man had the feeling necessary to capture the *Junonian sobriety* of the occident for his Apollonian realm, and so truly to appropriate the foreign]. There is something extraordinary too about this statement, which identifies an essential quality of Homer as something that was 'foreign' to the Greeks. It is no wonder that Hölderlin was attracted to the myth related by Pindar in his Third Olympian Ode, according to which olive trees for the Games were brought back by Heracles from the banks of the Danube, providing both shade and Olympic crowns — as if the olive tree were not native to Greece.[52] For Hölderlin it is no doubt significant that it is Heracles, the hero of cultural foundation, who is responsible for contributing a cooling sobriety to a fiery Apollonian endowment. Heracles and Zeus, as opposed to Apollo, already correspond to 'Hesperian' principles developed by the Greeks; which is presumably why, in AA [3.2], Hölderlin can describe Zeus as being for us more 'proper' or 'authentic'.[53] And that is no doubt why Hölderlin can use a Greek

---

51 See respectively MA, II, 912–14 (AL, 207–09); MA, II, 920–22 (AL, 213–15); and MA, II, 850–51 (AL, 183–85). I shall refer to these letters as 'B1', 'B2' and the 'Mehmel letter' respectively. The latter is preserved only as an incomplete draft, dating probably from November or December 1800. Gottlieb Ernst August Mehmel was the editor of the Erlangen 'Litteratur-Zeitung [sic]', and Hölderlin was writing to set out the principles he would apply as prospective contributor. On the dating and intended recipient of the letter see Härtl 2000.
52 See Race, I, 80–81, ll. 13–15 (also MA, II, 193, ll. 24–27); and see the draft hymn known as 'Der Ister': 'Da der, sich Schatten zu suchen | Vom heißen Isthmos kam' (MA, I, 476, ll. 30–31), with Christen 2013: 217–41.
53 MA, II, 373: 'da wir unter dem eigentlicheren Zevs stehen'. As Warminski observes (1999: 210), the peculiarity of Hölderlin's conception lies in his threefold classification (the Oriental, the Greek, and the Hesperian), which treats the properly Greek as an originally Oriental inheritance, and the originally Greek cultural achievement as something that is properly our own; see further Kocziszky 2009: 107–17.

expression (from *hespera*, meaning 'evening' or 'west') to designate the character of the Modern.[54] The Hesperian is our endowment, as developed by the Greeks, but which takes on a different character in its modern context. Within Greek culture itself there can be said to be a tension, dramatized in tragedy — in *Ajax* for instance — between the heroic values of the aristocracy and the new democratic values of Periclean Athens (see Segal 1981: 109–10, and cf. AA [2.13]). And that may explain, conversely, why Hölderlin introduces titles based on ancient mythological figures in the final versions of certain *Nachtgesänge* ('Chiron', 'Ganymed', 'Vulkan'). For it is at our own tragic, 'all-too sober' extreme that this Hesperian inheritance is reduced to the tokens of Greek or Roman myth.[55]

The first Böhlendorff letter describes the Greek native endowment in terms of a 'sacred pathos' [heilige[s] Pathos] or 'heavenly fire' [Feuer vom Himmel], in relation to which Greeks paradoxically attained relatively less mastery. But while the letter dwells, conversely, on their conquest of a faculty for sober presentation, the tragic hero in the *Anmerkungen* tests the limits of that achievement. Such figures confront circumstances so tremendous that a latent vulnerability is exposed: as it were a pathos that is now unholy, or a fire that is all-consuming. AA [3.2] then contrasts the case of modern poetic forms. The situation of own time is described as being the converse of the Greeks'. The 'main tendency' [Haupttendenz] of modern culture is to be able to 'encounter something' [etwas treffen zu können], to 'have a fate' [Geschik zu haben]. In the case of a Hesperian tragedy, therefore, a corresponding weakness would be exposed: not resembling 'fate' in the Greek tragic mode, but the converse misfortune of 'fatelessness' [das Schiksaallose].[56] In the more positive language of B1, the Hesperian native endowment is precisely 'clarity of exposition' [Klarheit der Darstellung], and the complementary cultural achievement is the conquest of 'fine passion' [schön[e] Leidenschaft]. But to that native endowment too there corresponds a tragic weakness in which the balance between sobriety and enthusiasm is lost.

By the end of AA [3.2], Hölderlin speaks a language that resonates with the final stanza of 'Blödigkeit': 'Deswegen hat der Grieche auch mehr *Geschik* und Athletentugend [...]. Bei uns ist diß mehr der *Schiklichkeit* subordinirt' [For this reason a Greek also has more *dexterity* and athletic virtue [...]. With us this is subordinated more to the *proper and fitting*] (my emphasis). But the language not only echoes 'Blödigkeit';

---

54 The term 'hesperischer', as indicating a contrast between Greek and modern forms of representation, is found in AA [3.4], the concept having been already used in a poetic context (e.g. 'Frucht von Hesperien', MA, I, 381, l. 150). It evidently corresponds to the adjective 'abendländische' in B1. On the concept see also Analecta 2007: 7–8. Although the term 'Hesperian' has long existed in English, it does not seem that it was current in German. See also AA [2.5].

55 As regards those titles see also 'Die Dioskuren', a fragmentary revision of 'An Eduard' that (as suggested above) may belong in the same category as the published *Nachtgesänge*. Conversely, in AA [2.10] Hölderlin justifies the replacement of Greek names for the gods with descriptions of their functions: e.g. 'Vater der Zeit' or 'Vater der Erde' for Zeus (MA, II, 372; and see MA, II, 341, l. 626), 'Geist der Liebe' or 'Friedensgeist' for Eros (MA, II, 347, ll. 811–12), and 'Schlachtgeist' for Ares (MA, II, 353–54, ll. 990 and 1009). For here he aims to bring out the spirit (rather than repeat the letter) of the original.

56 On this term, and Hölderlin's (at first sight surprising) explanation of it in terms of the Greek *dusmoron*, see the commentary to AA [3.2] in Part II below.

it is haunted by the same ambiguities. It will be recalled that, immediately before the words just cited, Hölderlin has suggested that the tendency of modern poetry is towards having a 'destiny' or 'fate' [Geschik zu haben]; here 'Geschik' must indeed mean 'fate', since it is immediately contrasted with 'das Schiksaallose'. Most, if not all, translators then understand the subsequent occurrence of the term differently: essentially as meaning 'skill' rather than 'fate'. But it is also clear that Hölderlin contrasts such Greek 'skill' with modern 'Schiklichkeit', that is to say a skilfulness dominated by propriety.[57] Some of the same ambiguity afflicts the use of 'Geschik' in B1. After comparing the respective strengths of ancient and modern poetry, Hölderlin concludes with the declaration: 'Ich [...] weiß nun daß außer dem, was bei den Griechen und uns das höchste seyn muß, nemlich dem lebendigen Verhältniß und Geschik, wir nicht wohl etwas *gleich* mit ihnen haben dürfen' [I [...] know now that apart from what must be the supreme thing with the Greeks and with us, that is, living craft and proportion, we cannot properly have anything *in common* with them] (MA, II, 912–13; AL, 207). The interpretation of 'Geschik' here as poetic craft or skill goes back at least to Szondi's seminal interpretation of the letter. But there are dissenters: Ryan considers it impossible for Hölderlin to have used 'Geschik' in any sense other than 'fate'; and, in his own translation of the letter, Pfau renders these words as 'living relationship and destiny' — and this despite having opted for 'skill' for both instances in AA [3.2].[58] There is perhaps only one rational explanation for these difficulties, and it is one that emerges from the last stanza of 'Blödigkeit' itself. Not only can 'Geschik' mean both 'destiny' and 'skill', and 'geschikt' both 'sent' (by destiny) and 'skilful' or 'adroit'; in Hölderlin it can mean both at the same time. And 'Schiklichkeit' too can mean both cunning 'skill' and (at its worst) mere rule-bound 'propriety'.[59]

It is interesting to observe, therefore, that similar terms already occur in the Mehmel letter, which speaks of the 'heilige Schiklichkeit' [sacred propriety]

---

57   Thus it is clear that, while for Hölderlin 'schiklich' can connote 'skill' as well as rule-bound 'propriety', the former sense may be dominated to a greater or lesser extent by the latter. Conversely, in its second occurrence in AA [3.2] 'Geschik' seems to be coloured by its proximity to 'Athletentugend', taking on the sense of corporeal daring and dexterity (on 'Tugend' as etymologically related to 'Tapferkeit' as well as 'Tüchtigkeit', see also Zuberbühler 1969: 18–19). B2 also seems relevant here, insofar as it establishes a connection between the 'athletic' [[d]as Athletische] character of southern peoples, and the need for a 'rule' [Regel] that protects against the elemental power of nature, and refers to the 'heroic body' [heroisch[er] Körper] of the Greeks. The connection between Greek heroic virtue and athletic contest is evident in the Pindaric victory ode (cf. Kurke 2013: 97–102).
58   See respectively Szondi 1978c: 366 ('Das *Geschik*, von dem das Werk sowohl des hesperischen wie des griechischen Künstlers zu zeugen hat, wäre das Geschick seiner Hände, seine Fähigkeit, die Töne zu ordnen und so dem Gedicht ein *lebendiges Verhältniß* zu geben'); Ryan 2006: 263, n. 7; Friedrich Hölderlin, *Essays and Letters on Theory*, trans. by Thomas Pfau (Albany: State University of New York Press, 1988), p. 150, contrasting p. 114, and cf. Schmidt in KA, I, 820. For a corresponding divergence among Italian translators ('destino' versus 'abilità'), see Castellari 2016: 136.
59   For an analogous disagreement regarding the term 'geschiklich' in the first stanza of 'Thränen': 'o ihr geschiklichen, | Ihr feur'gen' (MA, I, 441, ll. 2–3), see Schmidt in KA, I, 820 (suggesting the equivalent 'von einem Geschick betroffen'); and contrast Groddeck 2006: 632–33 (suggesting that the meaning is unambiguously 'geschickt, kunstfertig').

fundamental to Greek poetic art (MA, II, 851; AL, 184). This is contrasted, on the one hand with the mischaracterisation of Greek art as a 'wohlberechnetes Vergnügen' [nicely calculated amusement], and on the other with the fate of the Greek tragic hero. Thus a 'holy' or 'sacred' propriety is one that preserves the proper distance of human and divine spheres. And this is demonstrated in Greek tragedy '*per contrarium*' (ibid.): for there the separation of those spheres is violated, and accordingly the balance between proximity and distance disturbed.

If the term 'heilig' can connote an element of harmonious balance, as observed above in the case of 'heilignüchtern', the Mehmel letter gives another description of that balance which is of particular interest in the present context: 'So stellten sie das Göttliche menschlich dar, doch immer mit Vermeidung des eigentlichen Menschenmaaßes, natürlicher Weise, weil die Dichtkunst, die in ihrem ganzen Wesen, *in ihrem Enthusiasmus, wie in ihrer Bescheidenheit und Nüchternheit* ein heiterer Gottesdienst ist [...]' [So they presented the gods in human form, but always avoiding actual human proportions; quite naturally, because poetry, which in its whole nature, *in its inspiration as in its modesty and sobriety*, is a joyous service rendered unto the gods [...]] (ibid.; my emphasis). There 'inspiration' translates 'Enthusiasmus', which also corresponds to the 'Begeisterung' referred to in AA [3.1].[60] This is a balance that the tragic hero fails to maintain, being driven by 'Zorn' [wrath] (AO [3.1]) or 'Begeisterung' (AA [3.1]) into a too-close identification with the divine. But conversely, an excess of 'Schiklichkeit' or 'Nüchternheit' (or indeed of a modest 'timidity') would correspond to a peculiarly modern weakness, and this too might be the subject of a tragic demonstration *per contrarium*.

Accordingly, the ode 'Blödigkeit' might be said to reflect upon the conditions of a peculiarly modern tragedy, and in that sense provide a programme for the *Nachtgesänge* as a whole. But if the ode exhibits some of the involved syntax (and ingenuity in the use of tropes) of 'Chiron' or 'Ganymed', such effects are kept at a distance by the element of self-reflexive jocularity. While other *Nachtgesänge* speak from a sense of tragic desolation, here the poet affirms himself in his craft, making 'Blödigkeit' a worthy successor to 'Dichtermuth'. But taken together, the *Nachtgesänge* might correspond to the *Pindarfragmente* as the tragic to the anti-tragic — albeit that the tragedy here is in a modern key, a tragedy of 'Schiklichkeit' rather than of 'Geschik'. There is no 'philosophy of the tragic' in Hölderlin, if by that is meant the analysis of tragedy as a timeless essence distinct from a poetics of tragic representation. For him it is instead a mode in which a culture explores its own limits. Greek and Hesperian cultures are tragic each in their own way; but there may also be a genre in which they are happily united. That would be the fusion of poetic creation and reflective interpretation that is found in the *Pindarfragmente*. But it remains to consider the seventh (and in some ways most enigmatic) member of that sequence.

---

60   See also the earlier set of 'aphorisms' or 'maxims' influenced by the treatise *On the Sublime*, discussed in Chapter 4 above. As Hölderlin's third aphorism observes: 'Da wo die Nüchternheit dich verläßt, da ist die Gränze deiner Begeisterung' [There where sobriety leaves you, there is the limit of your enthusiasm] (MA, II, 58; AL, 240).

4. 'Das Unendliche'

The subject of PF 7 is Pindar's Fr. 213, which in turn concerns a problem of being 'in two minds'. As with other *Pindarfragmente*, translation and commentary are intimately united, here with phrases from the former recurring in the latter. The latter is also the case, most notably, in PF 9; but here the commentary contains a citation that is expressly marked as such, and takes the form of a distinct sentence. The words stand at the centre of the commentary, enclosed (in effect) within quotation marks:

'Ich habe zweideutig ein Gemüth genau es zu sagen.'[61]

In modern editions this corresponds to a single line of Greek verse, and indeed to the last line of the fragment, which Race translates as 'my mind is divided in telling precisely'.[62] This is close enough to Hölderlin's version, one might think; but one difference can immediately be noted. Rather than rendering δίχα simply as 'divided' (as in 'I am in two minds'), Hölderlin chooses 'zweideutig': that is to say 'ambiguous' or 'equivocal' — a term that applies above all to a statement or an utterance.[63] In his original translation the fragment ends: 'Hab ich zweideutig ein | Gemüth, genau es zu sagen' [I have an equivocal | Mind, to say it exactly]. Note here the comma between 'Gemüth' and 'genau', one that is lacking in the subsequent citation, and which introduces a degree of ambiguity as compared with Race's version. Am I, the speaker, ambivalent as to which option precisely to choose? Or am I making an exact statement as to the extent of my indecision?

In Pindar's formulation, the dilemma involves the choice between 'justice' (*dikē*) and 'crooked deceit' (*skolia apatē*). Hölderlin renders it, accurately enough, as that between '[das] Recht[ ]' and '[die] krumm[e] Täuschung'; but then in his commentary it becomes one between justice (again) and 'intelligence' [Klugheit]. We have already encountered the latter term in PF 1. And again following Bartel's illuminating suggestion, one can say that here too 'Klugheit' corresponds to the Greek concept of *mētis*.[64] That transformation of 'deceit' into 'intelligence' seems to correspond to the strategy of reversal we noted, for example, in PF 5. For we

---

61 In the manuscript the sentence straddles the fourth and fifth of the commentary's eight lines, and includes an opening quotation mark (see FHA, xv, 336 and 341–42). The closing quotation mark is added by the editors, but the end-point of the quotation is clear when it is compared with the corresponding words in the translation. Some of those words are repeated again at the end of the commentary, in the form 'darum hab' ich ein zweideutig Gemüth'. In PF 5, only the single word 'König' (rather than a complete sentence) is placed within quotation marks.

62 δίχα μοι νόος ἀτρέκειαν εἰπεῖν (Race, II, 420–21). In Stephanus (II, 350) this occupies slightly more than one line; but otherwise (and in contrast to the remainder of Fr. 213) there is no divergence between it and modern editions.

63 On the significance of this choice, cf. Bartel 2000: 146. Note that the Stephanus Latin translation (II, 351) gives 'in ambiguo mihi mens'.

64 See Bartel 2000: 142, referring again to Detienne and Vernant 1974. For 'Klugheit' as *mētis* in PF 1, see section 2 above and Bartel 2000: 60–63. Cf. Kant, *Grundlegung zur Metaphysik der Sitten*, in *Kants gesammelte Schriften*, Akademie-Textausgabe, IV, (Berlin: Reimer, 1903 and 1911; repr. De Gruyter, 1968), distinguishing '*Regeln* der Geschicklichkeit', '*Rathschläge* der Klugheit' and '*Gebote* (*Gesetze*) der Sittlichkeit' (p. 416).

saw there how Hölderlin's commentary glossed over the fact that the 'law' in question sanctified the misdeeds of Heracles. In the same way, to characterize 'crooked deceit' as a mode of intelligence is to rescue it from the accusation of mere wickedness. And in both cases, the darker meaning belongs to a context in which the fragment is cited by Plato: in the *Gorgias* in the case of the PF 5 and Fr. 169a, or the *Republic* in the case of PF 7 and Fr. 213.[65]

Mētis, for the Greeks, was also a goddess. Indeed, according to Hesiod she was the first wife of Zeus, being immediately swallowed by him so that her wisdom might (literally) be contained.[66] The concept of *mētis* certainly includes a dimension of deceit; but viewed more positively it is the essence of practical ingenuity, which may frequently need to pursue the more devious path. Accordingly, if PF 5 celebrates a justice expressed as the law of theoretical reason, or 'ground of knowledge' [höchste[r] Erkentnißgrund], PF 7 is concerned with a more cunningly practical form of intelligence. The Zeus of Hesiod's mythology can be said to combine both powers. By contrast, as we saw in Chapter 2, the addressee of the Stoic 'Hymn to Zeus' rules according to 'law' (*nomos*) and 'justice' (*dikē*); he makes 'crooked things straight'.[67] But PF 7 does not merely oppose *mētis* to *dikē*. If its object is 'Das Schwanken und das Streiten zwischen Recht und Klugheit' [the wavering and the conflict between right and intelligence], it also aims to discover a relation between the two.

We saw how in PF 5 certain laws are said to operate 'more rigorously' than art: 'sie halten strenger, als die Kunst, die lebendigen Verhältnisse fest.' In that sense 'die Kunst' can be related to the domain of *mētis*, being as much practical as theoretical, less rigorous than 'der Kirche und des Staats Gesez und anererbte Satzungen [the law of church and state and inherited statutes] (PF 5) and correspondingly more cunning. That would certainly apply to the subtle craft of poetry, with its devices and tropes, even while a poem may be governed by its own peculiar 'law'.[68] How then might a conflict between right (or justice) and intelligence — between *dikē* and *mētis* — be resolved?

---

65   Citing the first part of Fr. 213, Plato's character Adeimantus explains the dilemma as follows: there may be no advantage to justice unless one also appears to be just; but by mere appearance one can obtain the benefits without any of the drawbacks. It is true that he then goes on to refer to the cunning fox, who along with the octopus is a canonical figure of *mētis*. See Plato, *Republic*, 1: Books 1–5, ed. and trans. by Chris Emlyn-Jones and William Preddy, LCL 237 (Cambridge, MA: Harvard University Press, 2013), 365a–c (pp. 146–47).
66   See *Theogony*, ll. 886–900, in Hesiod, I, ed. and trans. by Glenn W. Most, 2nd edn, LCL 57 (Cambridge, MA: Harvard University Press, 2018), pp. 72–75; and see Detienne and Vernant 1974: 61–62. By contrast, in Pindar's Fr. 30 it is Themis, not Metis, who is the 'primordial' [*arkhaia*] wife of Zeus.
67   See LS 54I (LS, II, 326), l. 18: τὰ περισσὰ [...] ἄρτια; literally, he makes 'the odd even'. See also Wilamowitz-Moellendorff 1925: 326 ('aus unpar | par zu machen'), and Steinmetz 1994: 577 ('das Krumme gerade zu machen'), recalling that 'straightness' can be a synonym for 'law' in Hölderlin, as in 'ein Grades, ein Recht' (MA, I, 325, l. 8). For the Zeus of Hesiod as incorporating, by contrast, the wisdom of both Themis and Metis, see Detienne and Vernant 1974: 104–06, 292–93.
68   Note that the *mēkhanē* invoked in AO [1.1], in connection with the 'calculable law' of poetry, can also be applied to *mētis* (see Detienne and Vernant 1974: 18, n. 3, and 48–50). More precisely, *mēkhanē* would correspond to the combination of 'calculable law' and 'other kind of procedure' (AO [1.2]).

A further way of expressing the dilemma is in terms of the choice between exactness and ambiguity. We have already seen how Hölderlin describes the speaker as 'zweideutig': as having an 'ambiguous' or 'equivocal', rather than simply a 'divided', mind. The term can describe a text as much as a mind; indeed it can describe Hölderlin's own text, and we are by now alert to such an element of self-reflection. We saw how ambiguity is already present in Hölderlin's translation of Fr. 213, where he includes a comma missing from the subsequent citation: 'Hab ich zweideutig ein | Gemüth, genau es zu sagen'. This raises an issue that is central to the commentary, namely the relation between speaking exactly and speaking ambiguously. Fink (and others following him) have noted how Hölderlin's commentary itself suffers — or more precisely benefits — from ambiguity. From one point of view, this is merely a further illustration of the self-reflection that is endemic to all nine *Pindarfragmente*. Again a comparison with PF 5 lies nearest to hand, for this presents itself as a deductive demonstration of the concluding words of its translated text: 'Deswegen aber führt es gewaltig das gerechteste Recht mit allerhöchster Hand' [And for this reason it powerfully maintains the most correct justice with the very highest hand]. The commentary in PF 7 similarly concludes with words taken from the end of the translation ('hab' ich ein zweideutig Gemüth'). But that assertion of an equivocal mind comes at the end of a sentence that is itself equivocal — just as in PF 5, conversely, the concluding affirmation of supreme 'justice' was clothed in the trappings of logical rigour. The text, as Fink suggests (1982: 91):

> erinnert an ein Vexierbild, das in dem einen Bild, welches es darstellt, noch ein anderes versteckt. Die Zweideutigkeit wird nicht einfach gedeutet, sie ist auch Kennzeichen des Textes, der sie zu deuten unternimmt. Die Deutung selber ist nicht weniger das, als was sie ihren Gegenstand bezeichnet: Scherz und Rätsel — kein einfaches Rätsel immerhin und ein 'Scherz des Weisen'.

> [recalls a puzzle-picture that, in one image that it presents, conceals another. Ambiguity is not simply interpreted, it is also a feature of the text that undertakes its interpretation. The interpretation itself, no less than how it describes its object, is: jest and riddle — all the same not a simple riddle, and a 'jest of the sage'.]

For Fink the principal ambiguity consists in whether the speaker is in two minds *in order to* unite 'Recht' and 'Klugheit' exactly, or as to *whether* they can be so united. And here he draws attention to the replacement of the 'darüber' of the translation, with the more equivocal 'darum' at the end of the commentary (1982: 92, 94).

As Fink also notes, the sentence that Hölderlin places in quotation marks is affected by a similar ambiguity. For convenience I shall call it sentence 'Σ'. Given its presentation, Hölderlin seems to attach a particular importance to this sentence, as if it best embodied the sagacious jest referred to at the beginning of his commentary.[69] It will be recalled that it reads as follows (I include the quotation marks):

'Ich habe zweideutig ein Gemüth genau es zu sagen.'

---

69 See epigraph and n. 1 above. On the identification of this 'jest', see also Indlekofer 2007: 154, n. 303.

We already have noted that (in contrast to the preceding translation of the fragment) there is no comma between 'Gemüth' and 'genau'. If such a comma is silently understood, this would be an exact statement of my equivocal mind:

> 'I am in two minds[,] to say it [that I am in two minds] exactly.'

But if no such comma is understood, Σ might express a different uncertainty; for example:

> 'I am in two minds [whether to] say it [this sentence Σ] exactly'; or indeed

> 'I am in two minds [in order to] say it [this sentence Σ] exactly.'[70]

In those examples, and especially the last two, I have treated Σ as if it were a self-reflexive statement. The justification for doing so is that — in contrast to the corresponding wording at the end of his translation — Hölderlin has separated the proposition from its context in the translated fragment. In the latter case we know what dilemma may be designated by 'es': namely Pindar's choice between justice and deception. But what if the dilemma is now a purely semantic one, namely the choice between exactness and ambiguity? In that case we need look no further than sentence Σ itself. As already observed, being 'in two minds' here means having an 'ambiguous' mind, one that may well be expressed in an ambiguous utterance. And there may be no contradiction in a sentence that affirms of itself that it is ambiguous; for it may do so truly, and in that sense speak the exact truth. But to remain true, it must nonetheless have more than one meaning, as indeed seems to be the case here. Hölderlin may accordingly have wished to construct a sentence that says of itself (truly or exactly) that it is ambiguous, but which can be true (or exact) only by virtue of its own ambiguity.[71]

While Hölderlin's statement may not involve a contradiction, it seems nonetheless to embody a paradox of a kind, combining as it does the attributes of ambiguity and truth. And if it is taken in this way as a self-referential utterance, it also has an obvious precedent: namely the Liar Paradox. Known to the early Stoics as the 'Lying Argument', Hölderlin will have been familiar with Cicero's account of its formulation by Chrysippus: 'If you say that you are lying and speak the truth, you are lying'. It was of great concern to the Stoics, for it seemed to contradict a fundamental thesis of their logic, namely that every proposition must be either true or false.[72] Furthermore, as Diogenes Laertius reports, Chrysippus was similarly

---

70 These latter alternatives also correspond to Fink's account of the final sentence of the commentary; thus he reads the 'daß ... darum' construction in that sentence as meaning both 'damit ... deswegen' [so that ... for that reason], and 'ob ... darüber' [whether ... about that] (1982: 92).

71 Cf. Bartel's formulation (2000: 148–49): 'Hölderlin stellt hier eine Beziehung zwischen Zweideutigkeit und Genauigkeit her, in der das eine das andere nicht ausschließt, sondern umfaßt. [...] Das Unendliche ist ein Text, der mit Präzision Zweideutigkeiten einführt.'

72 Cf. Gourinat 2000: 198–202, and see Cicero, *Academica* 2.95–96, in Cicero, XIX, ed. and trans. by H. Rackham, LCL 268 (Cambridge, MA: Harvard University Press, 1933; repr. 1972), pp. 588–91 (p. 589); also in LS 37H. Strictly speaking the 'Lying Argument' may be the paradox in the form: 'If you say that you are lying and you say so falsely, you are telling the truth'; whereas in the form cited above it would be the 'Truth-telling Argument': see LS, II, 223–24 (editors' comment on LS 37C). For a recent modern account of the Liar Paradox, see Jago 2018: 279–319.

exercised by the problem of ambiguity.[73] He might therefore have had reason to be alarmed by Hölderlin's own paradoxically self-referential statement.

If Hölderlin's statement is a 'Scherz des Weisen', it would not therefore be a jest of the Stoic sage, who follows the exactness of *dikē* rather than the equivocations of *mētis*. And its jocular spirit is also opposed to the sombre ambiguities of the *Nachtgesänge*, represented above all by the divided figure of Chiron. But it can stand for an ideal of Hölderlin's poetics, which is to unite the exactness of thought and the willed ambiguity of poetic utterance. If philosophy must distinguish the true from the false, the just from the unjust in accordance with the law of Zeus, poetry can follow a more devious path, the path of Metis. But not resting there, it must also invent the forms in which precision and ambiguity are truly combined. Nothing less can be required of a 'poetic logic', or indeed a law of poetry.

---

73   See Diogenes Laertius, *Lives of eminent philosophers*, ii, ed. and trans. by R. D. Hicks, LCL 185 (Cambridge, MA: Harvard University Press, 1925; repr. 1979), 7.193–96 (pp. 304–09); also in LS 37B. Diogenes lists numerous treatises, not only on the 'Lying Argument' (Περὶ τοῦ ψευδομένου), but also on 'ambiguities' (Περὶ ἀμφιβολιῶν).

PART II

Translations

The *Sophokles-Anmerkungen*

Die Sprache in der Antigonä schien mir nicht lebendig genug. Die Anmerkungen drükten meine Überzeugung von griechischer Kunst auch den Sinn der Stüke nicht hinlänglich aus. Indessen thun sie mir noch nicht genug.

[The language in the *Antigone* did not seem lively enough. The notes did not express sufficiently my convictions about Greek art or the meaning of the plays. Even now I am still not satisfied with them.]

— to Wilmans, 8 December 1803

Introduction

As suggested by their titles, these 'Anmerkungen' are to be read in the first instance as annotations to the Sophocles translations to which they are attached (*Oedipus der Tyrann* and *Antigonä*).[1] None the less, the third section of each set of 'Notes' contains a broader account of the nature of tragedy, just as the first sections include reflections on poetic form and poetic method generally. Given his dissatisfaction with them, Hölderlin intended to add a more general 'introduction to the tragedies of Sophocles' that is mentioned repeatedly in letters to his publisher.[2] It seems also that Hölderlin planned to publish further volumes of Sophocles translations, and translations of parts of *Ajax* and *Oedipus at Colonus* have survived. It should also be remembered that Hölderlin intended his translations to be used for performance, and some of his remarks can even be interpreted as stage directions or director's notes.[3]

There have been a number of previous translations. I have gratefully consulted three English versions (by Thomas Pfau, David Constantine, and Jeremy Adler), and two French ones (by François Fédier, and Jean-François Courtine), and in some cases Ruschi's Italian version.[4] The aim has been to provide a translation that serves as a basis for commentary, and which accordingly tends towards the literal.

---

1 *Die Trauerspiele des Sophokles*, trans. by Friedrich Hölderlin, 2 vols (Frankfurt a.M.: Wilmans, 1804), I, 97–108, and II, 89–103. See MA, II, 309–16 and 369–76; and KA, II, 849–57 and 913–21.
2 See the letters from December 1803 (MA, II, 925–27; AL, 216–17), as well as that of 28 September 1803 (MA, II, 925; AL, 215).
3 For an admirably comprehensive treatment of Hölderlin's Sophocles (and *Empedocles*) projects, and especially their subsequent reception and performance history, see Castellari 2018.
4 See respectively: (1) *Essays and Letters on Theory*, trans. by Thomas Pfau (Albany: State University of New York Press, 1988), pp. 101–16; (2) SP, 312–17 and 367–73; (3) AL, 317–32; (4) *Œuvres* (Paris: Gallimard, 1967), pp. 951–66; (5) *Fragments de poétique et autres textes*, ed. and trans. by Jean-François Courtine (Paris: Imprimerie nationale Éditions, 2006), pp. 383–440; and (6) *Scritti di estetica*, trans. by Riccardo Ruschi, 2nd edition; Testi e documenti, 144 (Milan: SE, 2004), pp. 135–48. Note that SP also contains a translation of the entire text of Hölderlin's Sophocles translations, and Courtine's version includes an extensive commentary.

I have striven to preserve gender neutrality, by translating Hölderlin's 'Mensch' as 'human being' (or occasionally 'person') rather than 'man' (or indeed 'Man'), and with correspondingly neutral pronouns.

The commentary addresses difficulties in translation as well as some more detailed questions of interpretation. It also occasionally attempts to compare Hölderlin's at first sight idiosyncratic account of Greek tragedy with some of the conclusions of more recent classical scholarship. This is less to show how his account may anticipate that of modern scholars, than to provide an additional framework within which his often enigmatic pronouncements may be understood. Many difficulties of course remain, and my aim has been to measure the extent of our knowledge rather than to provide a definitive solution. Hölderlin will have been particularly dissatisfied with the final form of the 'Notes on *Antigone*', which in its last section shows evidence of last-minute interpolations.

Conventions and abbreviations

I have followed both the original and MA in putting the main body of the text (including titles) in italics, with text cited from the translations of the plays in roman type. However, the names of speakers are given in roman capitals (as in MA and Hölderlin's actual translations) rather than the original spaced italic. Emphases are indicated by underlining rather than by the spacing used in the original, and have been checked against the latter.[5] In the second section of the 'Anmerkungen zur Antigonä', certain words and phrases are in roman type in the original. That may indicate an additional level of emphasis, and is accordingly followed here (as it is in MA).[6] To assist the reader I have not always followed Hölderlin's punctuation. Where parts of the text are cited in the commentary, any ellipses are my own (without being indicated by square brackets).

As in Part I above, 'AO' abbreviates the 'Anmerkungen zum Oedipus', and 'AA' the 'Anmerkungen zur Antigonä', followed by the paragraph numbers inserted below. In cross-references, the prefix 'AA' or 'AO' is added only where necessary to avoid ambiguity. References to the line numbers in Hölderlin's translations are as in MA (note that in the case of *Oedipus* they differ slightly in KA), and are followed by the corresponding line numbers of current Sophocles editions. My modern reference texts for the two plays are those edited by Dawe and by Griffith for the series Cambridge Greek and Latin Classics.[7] Comparisons in the commentary with

---

5   In some cases it can be difficult to decide whether spacing has been used, with a resulting divergence between MA and KA: see e.g. 'gefaßt' in AA [3.4] and [3.9], where one can be misled on account of the occurrence of the letters 'f' and 'ß'.

6   See MA, II, 370, 372. This may correspond to a double underlining in the lost manuscript (cf. FHA, XVI, 312). In two other cases in AO, however, roman type is used to indicate a foreign expression. Note also that Greek citations and expressions are in spaced format in the original; I have not used any equivalent here.

7   *Oedipus Rex*, ed. by R. D. Dawe (Cambridge: Cambridge University Press, 1982; repr. 1986); *Antigone*, ed. by Mark Griffith (Cambridge: Cambridge University Press, 1999). See also the two-volume Sophocles edition and translation by Hugh Lloyd-Jones, LCL 20 and 21 (Cambridge, MA: Harvard University Press 1994; repr. 1997–98); and *Antigone*, trans. by Elizabeth Wyckoff, in *Greek*

modern interpretations of Sophocles are placed at the end of a note, and preceded by an em dash (—).

In the commentary, 'H.' stands for Hölderlin, 'Oed.' for Oedipus, 'Ant.' for Antigone, and 'Haem.' for Haemon. I also use the following abbreviations:
In relation to the previous translations of Hölderlin referred to above and in n. 4:

A.	Adler
C.	Constantine
Court.	Courtine
F.	Fédier
P.	Pfau
R.	Ruschi.

In relation to the Sophocles editions and translations referred to in n. 7 (and followed by the relevant page number):

Dawe	Dawe's commentary in *Oedipus Rex*
Griff	Griffith's commentary in *Antigone*
Loeb	Lloyd-Jones' edition and translation in the LCL
Wyck	Wyckoff's translation of *Antigone*.

The relation between the two plays

As already observed, Hölderlin will have intended to follow the published Sophocles translations with further instalments.[8] The choice of *Oedipus Tyrannus* and *Antigone* for the first two volumes has given rise to a certain amount of speculation. It is clear that there is a new emphasis in AA on the difference between ancient and modern forms of poetic representation. But in addition, it has been suggested that *Antigone* represents for Hölderlin a more modern — in his terminology more 'Hesperian' — mode of tragedy, as compared with the more originally 'Greek' *Oedipus*. Others by contrast have seen *Oedipus* as the more Hesperian tragedy in Hölderlin's account, *Antigone* as the more originally Greek. And to add to the confusion, some have seen his altered translation practice in *Antigone* as evidence of an intention to make a more Greek play more Hesperian; or alternatively, to make a more Hesperian play even more so; or indeed, for one commentator, apparently to make a more Greek play still more Greek.

The idea that *Oedipus* is, for Hölderlin, the more modern of the two tragedies seems to have its source in the influential essay by Jean Beaufret, which originally served as an introduction to the Fédier translation. Beaufret reaches his conclusion, in part, by minimizing the difference between the two Oedipus plays.[9] But Hölderlin

Tragedies, ed. by David Grene and Richmond Lattimore, 3rd edn by Mark Griffith and Glenn W. Most, 3 vols (Chicago: University of Chicago Press, 2013), I, 187–239. The Greek text that probably served as Hölderlin's own main basis, at least for *Antigone*, can be found (with an interlinear German translation) in FHA, XVI. But on the latter see Schmidt's reservations in KA, II, 1325–26.

8   See Castellari 2018: 47–49. Note that the *Anmerkungen* themselves make occasional reference to *Ajax* and *Oedipus at Colonus*.

9   See Beaufret 1983; originally in *Remarques sur Œdipe. Remarques sur Antigone*, trans. by François Fédier (Paris: Union Générale d'Éditions, collection 10/18, 1965), but cited here in the Kindle electronic version. Thus Beaufret suggests that 'Œdipe, au lieu d'être foudroyé par les dieux, est au

himself is clear: it is in *Oedipus at Colonus* that Sophocles comes closest to a modern, or Hesperian, mode of tragedy (AA [3.3]). *Oedipus Tyrannus* is not mentioned in that connection. The converse case — *Antigone* as the more Hesperian — has been argued with some cogency by Ryan.[10] But the lack of consensus in the literature should give us pause. If a case can be made for either alternative, that may be because neither is correct. On the one hand, Hölderlin proposes the same analytical framework for *Oedipus Tyrannus* and *Antigone*, a parallel that that is recalled expressly at the beginning of AA [3.1], and illustrated at the end of AO. And on the other, Greek and Hesperian elements can be found in his interpretation of both tragedies, which (I would argue in both cases) he sees as representing a passage between the two.[11] And if Ryan makes out a case for Antigone as a more Hesperian figure, Hölderlin also attaches importance to the play's other tragic protagonists (Creon and Haemon). Indeed, at one point he suggests that the best perspective on the play is one of 'purest generality' [reinste Allgemeinheit], and of 'highest impartiality' [höchste Unpartheilichkeit] as between the characters of Antigone and Creon (AA [2.11]–[2.12]). His view can be compared with that of modern commentators, such as Jean-Pierre Vernant, who have found in Greek tragedy a conflict between two sets of values: one more archaic, the other contemporary to the performance of the plays. In Goldhill's words (1997b: 334), tragedy for Vernant takes place 'at a crucial moment of conflict between the archaic religious system, with its view of human action, and the democratic legal and political system, with its very different sense of behaviour, authority and causation'. In Hölderlin's terms that would be the conflict between the originally Greek or 'oriental', and a more 'Hesperian' set of values to which we ourselves are heirs. Both will be present, in *Oedipus Tyrannus* as well as in *Antigone*. If his interpretation of *Antigone* resonates with the events of the French Revolution (Billings 2014: 219–20), one may equally say that his Oedipus is a precursor of the Enlightenment — as he puts it, 'Freigeist gegen getreue Einfalt' [free thinker against faithful simplicity] (AA [2.13]). And his account in the third section of AO, with its almost Kantian reference to the pure conditions of 'space' and 'time', seems to describe not only a process within the temporal continuum, but also a transition to a new form of temporality characteristic of the modern age.[12] It is true that it is in his 'Notes on *Antigone*' that Hölderlin is most exercised by these

---

contraire voué à la solitude d'une longue déambulation terrestre qui aboutira à une seconde tragédie *dont la première n'est que le prélude*' (location 155; my emphasis). He is able to conclude that *Antigone* 'apparut à Hölderlin, sans qu'il ait jamais expressément dit, comme une tragédie plus typiquement grecque' (location 473). Here Beaufret is followed e.g. by Dastur (2013: 22, 57–58), Koppenfels (1996: 367), and Lacoue-Labarthe (1989: 220), as well as by Courtine in his commentary (p. 440, n. 24). Taking Beaufret's assimilation of the two Oedipus plays a step further, Lacoue-Labarthe (erroneously) states that Hölderlin 'propose[d] *Oedipus the King* in his later work as the model for a modern tragedy' (1989: 217).

10 Ryan 1988; and see also Böschenstein 1995b.

11 As he puts it in AA [2.5]: 'how a character categorically follows categorical Time, and how the Greek goes towards the Hesperian' [wie ein Karakter der kategorischen Zeit kategorisch folget, und wie es vom griechischen zum hesperischen gehet] (the first half of that statement echoing AO [3.5]).

12 Again one can compare this with the observations of some modern commentators: see n. 21 to AO [3.4] below. And on Kant in AO, cf. Beaufret 1983 (locations 224–27).

issues, and by their implications for modern poetic practice. But it is equally clear that his thoughts were not worked out even there to his own final satisfaction.

A further level of complexity is added by the new translation practice that is evident in *Antigone*, and which is itself the subject of commentary in section 2 of the corresponding 'Notes'. It has been seen by some as revealing the latently Hesperian character of the play, and even as 'making the work a depiction of the birth of modern theology out of ancient polytheism' (Billings 2014: 212). Alternatively, in Lacoue-Labarthe's view, the translation has to be more Hesperian precisely because Hölderlin's starting point is a text that is more Greek.[13] Any interpretation must begin with the letters to Wilmans in which Hölderlin speaks of the need to make his translation more 'lebendig' [lively] and to bring out, in comparison with the original, 'das Orientalische, das sie verläugnet hat' [the oriental element that it has denied] (MA, II, 925; AL, 215–16). A striking example is the rendering of *deinos* (in the first stasimon of *Antigone*) as 'ungeheuer' rather than, as previously, 'gewaltig': the sense of the monstrous, even the uncanny, is added to the idea of the powerful. But note that the same term becomes central to the analysis of the tragic in AO [3.1], surely confounding any attempt to distinguish the two plays on that basis. One has also to consider how the various elements of the new translation practice relate. Another striking feature of the *Antigone* translation is its tendency to avoid the names of the Greek gods, preferring either a descriptive elaboration (e.g. 'Father of Time' for 'Zeus') or a monotheistic reinterpretation ('the name of God' for 'the honour of the gods').[14] Despite appearances, here too the purpose may be to make the play more vivid or comprehensible to the modern audience, rather than to make it into a more modern or Hesperian tragedy. But the position is further complicated by his interpretation of the figure of Zeus, who (as a principle of order and limits) takes on a peculiarly Hesperian character.[15] As we saw in Chapter 6.3, he employs a converse procedure in the *Nachtgesänge* — that is to say in a sequence of poems that was completed at the same time as the Sophocles translations. Thus in some of their final versions he adds titles drawn from Greek or Roman mythology: 'Chiron', 'Ganymed', 'Vulkan'. It is as if these are intended as hollow tokens of a vanished world, making the poems if anything more Hesperian. In any event, as we have seen, neither *Antigone* nor *Oedipus Tyrannus* is Hölderlin's cited model for a Hesperian tragedy: that is rather *Oedipus at Colonus*. And as suggested in Chapter 6, his most fitting tribute to it may be found in the unexpected context of the *Nachtgesänge* rather than in any work for the stage.

13 '*Antigone* is [...] consequently transformed by the translation [...] in order to "bring it closer to our mode of representation" [...] and make it correspond to this "Hesperian" age which defines our historical situation' (Lacoue-Labarthe 1989: 220; the citation is from AA [2.10]). But Koppenfels appears to take the opposite view: the translation makes 'die "griechischste" der Tragödien' even more Greek (1996: 367).
14 'Vater der Zeit' (MA, II, 353, l. 987); 'Gottes Nahmen' (MA, II, 346, l. 774). And see Holderlin's own commentary at AA [2.4]–[2.5] and [2.10].
15 See the statement in AA [3.2] that we 'stand under the more authentic Zeus' [unter dem eigentlicheren Zevs stehen]. Note that, as well as 'Vater der Zeit', Hölderlin also proposes the translation 'Vater der Erde' [Father of the Earth]; and as Rosenfield observes (2003: 36), each may be related to the conditions of 'space' and 'time' mentioned in AO [3.4].

Notes on 'Oedipus'[1]

1.

[1.1] It will be good, to secure for our poets too a position in society,[2] if poetry for us too is raised to the μηχανη[3] of the Ancients, taking into account the difference in the times and constitutions.[4]

[1.2] Other works of art too are lacking in reliability, as compared with the Greek ones; at least they have until now been judged more according to the impressions they make than according to their calculable law[5] and other kind of procedure[6] whereby beauty is brought forth. Modern poetry is, however, particularly lacking in schooling and craftsmanship, that is to say in its procedure being calculated and taught, and once learned always able to be reliably repeated in practice.[7] In human affairs, one has above all to make sure, with

---

1   on 'Oedipus' [zum Oedipus]: i.e. the play known variously as *Oedipus Rex*, *Oedipus Tyrannus* (in Greek *Oidipous Turannos*), or in English now more usually *Oedipus the King*. In his translation of the play H. renders the title as 'Oedipus der Tyrann' [Oedipus the Tyrant] rather than 'König Oedipus'. — The correct translation of the term τύραννος remains controversial. Knox (1998: 53–66) suggests that a *turannos* (as opposed to a king or *basileus*) is characterized by the status of usurper or intruder rather than one who has derived his power by normal constitutional means. See similarly Vernant 1988: 127; and on the meaning of the term see also Budelmann 2000: 214–19. For Schmidt (KA, II, 1336), H.'s translation is an error, and here at least *turannos* means simply a king. But the matter is not quite so clear, and note that H. is followed by Laks and Most (EGP, II, 127).
2   *position in society* [bürgerliche Existenz]: cf. the letter to his mother of 16 November 1799 (MA, II, 841–42; AL, 166–67), and see Chapter 4.1 above (in particular n. 11).
3   μηχανη: in Greek in the original, without diacritical marks. *Mēkhanē* can mean 'plot', 'device' or 'apparatus'; also 'expedient', 'contrivance' or 'means' (Brill, s.v. μηχάνή); on the concept of poetic 'means' in the *Anmerkungen*, see the commentary to 'moyen' in [1.2]. Note that in e.g. [1.9] and [1.10] the poetic structure of the two plays is described in expressly mechanical terms (cf. Nägele 2005: 136–40). The Greek term was also used for the machine used to hoist actors to an elevated position on the stage, including those representing gods (Billings 2014: 202), although it is doubtful that this is H.'s primary meaning.
4   *constitutions* [Verfassungen]: cf. 'conditions' (A.); 'institutions' (P.); 'political systems' (C.). See also the reference in **AA [3.2]** to our different 'time and mode of representation' [Zeit und Vorstellungsart]. — H.'s sense is not to be taken as narrowly political; but on the close relation of Greek tragedy to the Athenian *polis* see Cartledge 1997.
5   *calculable law* [gesezliche[r] Kalkul]: H. refers apparently without distinction to '[der] gesezliche Kalkul' (literally 'lawlike' or 'lawful calculus'), and in [1.4] and AA [1.1] to 'das kalkulable Gesez'. Following C. and A., I have translated in accordance with the latter formula throughout. The equivalence is also suggested by **AO [1.5]**, which begins 'Das Gesez, der Kalkul'.
6   *other kind of procedure* [sonstig[e] Verfahrungsart]: or 'other procedures' (C. and A.). Hence the concept of 'procedure' extends further than that of 'calculable law'. See also [1.4], and cf. the essay *Wenn der Dichter* ..., which has been edited under the title 'Über die Verfahrungsweise des poëtischen Geistes' (KA, II, 527) on account of its references to such a 'procedure' or 'mode of procedure' [Verfahrungsweise]: see MA, II, 80–81, 84; AL, 280–81, 284.
7   Cf. the letter to Neuffer of 4 December 1799, pointing to 'the sure, thoroughly purposeful

each thing, that[8] *it is Something,*[9] *i.e. that it is knowable in the means* (moyen) *of its appearance,*[10] *that the manner in which it is determined*[11] *can be defined and taught. For this and for higher reasons poetry requires particularly certain and characteristic principles and limits.*

[1.3] *Among them is just such a calculable law.*

[1.4] *Then one has to see how the content is differentiated from it, through what procedure,*[12] *and how in the infinite but thoroughly determined*[13] *connection the particular content relates to the general calculus, and the onward movement and what has to be fixed,*[14] *the living sense that cannot be calculated, is brought into relation to the calculable law.*

[1.5] *The law, the calculus, the manner in which a sensibility, the whole person,*[15] *develops*

---

and considered progression of ancient works of art' [den sichern, durch und durch bestimmten und überdachten Gang der alten Kunstwerke], and recommending the 'true recognition of poetic forms' [die wahre Erkenntniß der poëtischen Formen] (MA, II, 849; AL, 171).

8   *to make sure ... that* [darauf zu sehen, daß]: following P. Others read this in the sense of 'see that' (C.) or 'bear in mind that' (A.); similarly Court. and F. The immediate context, namely the remarks about the deficiencies of modern poetry, suggests a need to make sure (or 'see to it') that something is the case.

9   *Something* [Etwas]: the primary sense appears to be that, if poetry is to have a proper role in society, it must benefit from the discipline of a craft. See further the discussion of this passage in Chapter 4.1 above.

10 *in the means* (moyen) *of its appearance* [in dem Mittel (*moyen*) seiner Erscheinung]: 'moyen' is in roman in the original, no doubt to indicate that it is a foreign expression. See Chapter 4.1 above, arguing that here 'Mittel' or 'moyen' corresponds to the Greek *methodos*. And see further Nägele (2005: 137), noting 'moyen' as a possible French translation of *mēkhanē* in [1.1]; and Binder (1992: 82), suggesting that 'Verfahrungsart' in the present paragraph itself corresponds to *methodos*.

11 *the manner in which it is determined* [die Art, wie es bedingt ist]: or 'the conditions of its existence' (C.).

12 *procedure* [Verfahrungsart]: see [1.2] and note 6 above.

13 *in the infinite but thoroughly determined connection* [im unendlichen aber durchgängig bestimmten Zusammenhange]. The terminology recalls the earlier fragment on religion (1799/1800?): cf. 'durchgängig[er] Zusammenhang', 'eine unendlichere, durchgängigere Befriedigung', 'jener unendlichere mehr als nothdürftige Zusammenhang' (MA, II, 53–54; AL, 235–36). Note also that such a 'more thorough' or 'more infinite connection' is distinguished there from a purely 'mechanical' one ('Maschinengang', 'mechanisch[er] Zusammenhang[ ]'), and from what H. describes as 'die [...] allgültigen [...] Geseze des Lebens', the latter being contrasted in turn with the 'ungeschriebene göttliche Geseze' invoked by Ant. (MA, II, 51, 53–54; AL, 234–36). On the dating of that fragment, and its relation to H.'s earlier involvement with Sophocles, see Louth 2015: 130–32.

14 *what has to be fixed* [das Vestzusetzende]: cf. 'the things it has to bring into shape' (C.); 'ce qu'il faut fixer' (Court.). Perhaps not 'the intended statement' (A.), although Binder suggests that the 'living sense' in question may correspond to the meaning of the piece as grasped by an interpreter (1992: 86).

15 *the whole person* [der ganze Mensch]: cf. the statement in **AA** [1.2] that poetry, as distinct from philosophy, engages all the human faculties, not just a single one (such as the faculty of cognition). On the notion in its historical context see Gaier 1994.

as under the influence of the element,[16] *and representation and feeling and reasoning*[17] *emerge one after the other in different sequences, but always according to a sure rule, is in the case of tragedy more equilibrium*[18] *than pure succession.*[19]

[1.6] *For the tragic* <u>transport</u>[20] *is properly speaking*[21] *empty, and the least constrained.*[22]

[1.7] *For that reason,*[23] *in the rhythmical succession*[24] *of representations in which the* <u>transport</u> *presents itself,* <u>that which in metrics is called a caesura</u>, *the pure word,*[25] *the*

---

16 *as under the influence of the element* [als unter dem Einflusse des Elements]: 'als' — 'as', or 'as if' (P.) — seems important here, suggesting that H. is drawing an analogy between the poetic work and the development of a person under natural influences ('the element'). H. may not yet be referring specifically to the elemental power of the tragic 'Naturmacht' mentioned in [1.14], although contrast Schmidt in KA, II, 1379–80.

17 *representation and feeling and reasoning* [Vorstellung und Empfindung und Räsonnement]: see similarly AA [1.2]. See also a corresponding classification of the human faculties in the earlier treatment of the tragic ode: 'das Bewußtseyn, das Nachdenken, oder die physische Sinnlichkeit' [consciousness, reflection or physical sensuality] (MA, I, 865; AL, 258); where 'consciousness' might correspond to 'representation', and 'reflection' to 'reasoning'. Schmidt relates the three to the traditional classification 'imagination', 'feeling' and 'understanding' (KA, II, 1489). There is a slightly different classification of the faculties in *Wenn der Dichter …* (MA, II, 80; AL, 279–80), and in *Die Empfindung spricht …* (MA, II, 101; AL, 299). Here, and in the following reference to 'sequences', H. seems also to be recalling his earlier doctrine of the alternation of the three poetic tones (on which see Chapter 3 above).

18 *equilibrium* [Gleichgewicht]: see [1.8]–[1.10].

19 *pure succession* [reine Aufeinanderfolge]. The contrast drawn in this paragraph is essentially between the epic and tragic genres (cf. Binder 1992: 87). — Csapo and Miller (1998: 112) point to the 'agglomerative' nature of the epic, as opposed to tragedy which 'observes narrow temporal and causal constraints' and where 'temporal concentration is replicated by the logical development of the plot'.

20 *transport* [Transport]: the interpretation of this term is controversial. In Chapter 4.2–4.3 above, I argue that it is to be read in the sense of the French poetics of the Sublime, hence as the equivalent of the Greek *ekstasis* rather than *metaphora* (a 'carrying away' rather than a 'carrying over'). For a similar view, see Courtine's commentary (p. 413, n. 9); Schmidt in KA, II, 1389; and already Hell, V, 355. Here and in the next paragraph the word is in spaced format, possibly as a way of indicating a term with a foreign origin. As Hühn observes (1997: 198), 'transport' can be taken to refer to both the content of the tragedy and the form of its presentation.

21 *properly speaking* [eigentlich]: cf. 'of itself' (C.); 'essentially' (A.); 'proprement' (Court.). What H. means here by 'empty' [leer] can be debated, although it is difficult to follow Billings' explanation that 'Tragic *transport* is "actually empty" because it is only a superficial expression of the law of the genre' (2014: 203).

22 *the least constrained* [der ungebundenste]: cf. [2.3] 'im zornigen Unmaas', where such 'wrathful immoderation' is connected with a self-destructive urge to be swept along by 'the tearing rapacity of time'.

23 *For that reason* [Dadurch]: since, according to [1.6], 'tragic transport' is 'the least constrained', it seems that a balancing element is necessary to establish the 'equilibrium' mentioned in [1.5] and further discussed in [1.8]–[1.10].

24 *rhythmical succession* [rhythmisch[e] Aufeinanderfolge]: on the 'calculable law' as 'rhythm' cf. [1.8] and AA [1.2]. A conception of 'rhythm' as a specifically poetic vehicle of sublime pathos can already be found in Klopstock; see Menninghaus 1991: 133, referring to '[die] Steigerung des Rhythmus […] zu einer Art autonomer Evokation der πάθη', and his 'Theorie und Praxis metrisch-rhythmischer Wortbewegung'. And as Castellari observes, the emphasis on 'rhythm' also highlights H.'s interest in the dimension of performance (2018: 57).

25 *caesura, the pure word* [Cäsur … das reine Wort]: in Greek metrics, a caesura is the break in the

counter-rhythmical interruption becomes necessary: in order namely to meet the tearing alternation of representations[26] *at its highest point,*[27] *so that it is no longer the alternation of the representation that appears but rather the representation itself.*[28]

[1.8] *The calculable succession,*[29] *and the rhythm,*[30] *is thereby divided, and so relates to itself in its two halves, one to the other, that they appear as having equal weight.*[31]

[1.9] *Now if the rhythm of the representations is so constituted that, in eccentric rapidity,*[32] *the <u>earlier</u> are more carried away*[33] *by the <u>succeeding</u> ones, the caesura or the counter-rhythmical interruption must lie <u>in front</u>, so that the first half is as it were*

rhythm at (or near) the centre of a line of verse (D'Angour 2006: 493). As a break rather than a signifying expression, it might therefore be called a 'pure' word. But at [1.13] H. will identify this caesura with the intervention of Tiresias. Accordingly 'das reine Wort' may also be a reference to the words of the prophet, as opposed to the action of the plot, and therefore to be contrasted with the word that H. describes as 'factisch', that is to say as 'active' or 'effective' (AA [3.2] to [3.4]). Benn suggests that the Tiresias scene 'reveals in words, discursively, what the action of the play reveals in dramatic terms — the will of the gods' (1959: 162); see similarly Corßen 1949: 145, and cf. Binder 1992: 90.

26   *tearing alternation of representations* [reißende[r] Wechsel der Vorstellungen]: cf. 'the pull of the succession of scenes' (C.); 'the speeding alternation of ideas' (A.). In his letter to Neuffer of 3 July 1799, H. already refers to the 'hinreißende[r] Fortgang' [irresistible progress] and 'schnell[e] Kürze' [rapid concision] characteristic of tragedy (MA, II, 782; AL, 146); see also [1.14] and [2.3]. — Knox similarly notes rapidity as a characteristic feature in Sophocles, referring to the 'swiftness of the exposition' in *Ajax*, 'headlong forward movement' in *Philoctetes*, and 'frantic speed of the final revelation in the *Oedipus Tyrannus*' (1964: 7).

27   *highest point* [Summum]: as noted in Chapter 4.3 above, this Latin (and also French) expression is used in both of H.'s Master's exercises (*specimina*) in Tübingen. It appears from [1.9] that the point is 'met' in the sense that the caesura matches it in weight or dramaturgical significance.

28   *alternation of the representation ... the representation itself* [Wechsel der Vorstellung ... die Vorstellung selber]: here 'Vorstellung' is now in the singular. It is not entirely clear what distinction is being drawn. The argument is possibly that succession of events in the play (in which the tragic 'transport' is embodied or expressed) is so rapid that a counter-balancing element is needed to prevent it from appearing merely 'empty' (cf. [1.6], and Kasper 2000: 22). Alternatively, Warminski has suggested that the distinction is between the play, as consisting in a sequence of representations, and the faculty of representation itself; so that 'the caesura is the place where the tragedy explicitly turns upon itself, where, in short, representation represents itself *as* representation' (1987: 17).

29   *calculable succession* [Aufeinanderfolge des Kalkuls]: or more literally 'succession of the calculation' (A.); cf. 'calculated sequence' (C.). See the distinction made in [1.5] between a poetic 'law' or 'calculus' consisting purely in 'succession' (as in the case of the epic), and that of tragedy characterised by a certain 'equilibrium'. In his earlier poetics, discussed above in Chapter 3, H. analysed a poem as a calculable sequence of 'tones'.

30   *rhythm* [Rhythmus]: see [1.7], where the 'caesura' has been described as a 'counter-rhythmical interruption' of the 'rhythmical succession of representations'; and on the 'calculable law' as 'rhythm, in the higher sense', see AA [1.2].

31   *appear as having equal weight* [als gleichwiegend, erscheinen]: or possibly 'as having equal weight, appear', as in 'de telle sorte [...] que les deux parties, à égalité de poids, font apparition' (F.); corresponding perhaps to the thought that the caesura allows there to be a 'representation' at all rather than a headlong succession of representations. It is clear from what follows that these two 'halves' are not parts of equal length.

32   *in eccentric rapidity* [in exzentrischer Rapidität]: on the parallel expression in AA [1.3] ('Rapidität der Begeisterung'), see Chapter 4.3 above. 'Rapidität' appears to be another example of an adopted French expression (cf. Link 1999: 28).

33   *carried away* [hingerissen]: cf. [1.7] 'tearing alternation of representations', with commentary.

*protected*³⁴ *against the second; and the equilibrium*³⁵ — *precisely because the second half is originally more rapid, and appears to weigh more heavily — will incline more from the back towards the beginning, on account of the counterbalancing caesura.*³⁶

[1.10] *If the rhythm of the representations is so constituted that the <u>succeeding</u> are more pressed upon by the <u>beginning</u> ones, the caesura will lie more towards the end, because it is the end that must as it were be protected against the beginning; and the equilibrium will consequently incline more towards the end, because the first half extends further, the equilibrium consequently comes later. So much for the calculable law.*

[1.11] <u>*Now the first of the tragic laws indicated here is that of 'Oedipus'.*</u>

[1.12] *'Antigone' follows the second touched upon here.*

[1.13] *In both plays the speeches of Tiresias*³⁷ *constitute the caesura.*

[1.14] *He enters the course of fate,*³⁸ *as guardian over the power of nature*³⁹ *which, tragically, removes a human being from their life-sphere,*⁴⁰ *the centre of their inner life, into another world, and drags them into the eccentric*⁴¹ *sphere of the dead.*

34 *protected* [geschüzt]: presumably because without the counter-balancing weight of the caesura it would be eclipsed by the hurtling rapidity of the second half.
35 *equilibrium* [Gleichgewicht]. It seems that the 'caesura' is supposed to provide a counterpoise to the weight of dramatic events in the opposite half of the play, and that H. assumes that the point at which the resulting 'equilibrium' occurs is a consequence of where that counterbalancing element is to be found (which is perhaps questionable from the point of view of a strictly physical mechanics). See similarly [1.10], and AA [1.1], [1.3] and [1.4] (where the image of an equilibrium 'inclining' in a particular direction is given diagrammatic representation).
36 *counterbalancing caesura* [entgegenwirkend[e] Cäsur]: according to [1.13] that balancing element is provided by the speeches of the Tiresias. As Benn suggests (1959: 162–63), the thought seems to be of 'a balance of prophetic interest and dramatic interest. If the dramatic interest is concentrated on the end [the case of *Oedipus*], the Teiresias scene must be placed near the beginning [and conversely in the case of *Antigone*]. [...] Sophocles uses prophecy contrapuntally to plot'.
37 *speeches of Tiresias* [Reden des Tiresias]: for these scenes see respectively MA, II, 261–67, ll. 304–468 [300–462], and MA, II, 354–58, ll. 1025–1136 [988–1090]. — The function of the Tiresias scenes in Sophocles and Euripides has been analysed more recently by Ugolini. Although his results differ from those suggested here, he acknowledges H.'s pioneering attempt to uncover a structural role for the scenes (1995: 21–24). It seems that, for Ugolini, Tiresias has the role of accelerating tragic catastrophe rather than of restoring equilibrium.
38 *course of fate* [Gang des Schiksaals]: cf. AA [3.4], 'fatefully' [schiksaalsweise]. The contrast seems to be between the fateful concatenation of the unfolding plot, and a higher prophetic perspective (see also n. 25 above).
39 *power of nature* [Naturmacht]: rather than 'natural order' (C.). The reference is to an unbounded and elemental natural power, to which H. returns in [3.1]. On this concept see Analecta 2017: 220–45.
40 *life-sphere* [Lebenssphäre]: following P. Cf. 'zone of life' (C.); 'orbit of life' (A.), with n. 41 below. The concept of a 'Sphäre' also figures prominently in the already-mentioned fragment on religion (n. 13 above).
41 *eccentric* [exzentrische]: cf. [1.9] ('eccentric rapidity'), and the discussion in Chapter 4.3 above. On the difference between this notion and the 'eccentric path' [exzentrische Bahn] of human destiny invoked in the earlier prefaces to *Hyperion* (MA, I, 489, 558), cf. Bay 2002: 600. Thus in the present case there would no longer be an analogy with the lawlike regularity of a planetary orbit.

2.

[2.1] *The <u>intelligibility</u> of the whole depends principally upon examining the scene where Oedipus <u>interprets</u> the oracle's message <u>too infinitely</u>,[1] is tempted <u>into the</u> nefas.[2]*

[2.2] *For the oracle's message is:*

> Phoebus, the King, has clearly commanded us:
> The country's shame that has been nourished on this ground
> Must be hunted down, the incurable must not be nurtured.[3]

That could mean: Uphold, generally, a pure and rigorous justice; maintain good civic order.[4] Oedipus, however, immediately goes on to speak in a priestly fashion:

> Through what purification, etc.[5]

And descends to the <u>particular</u>,[6]

> And for which man does he indicate this fate?[7]

And <u>thus</u> brings Creon's <u>thoughts</u> to the fearful word:

---

1   *too infinitely* [zu unendlich]: H. interprets tragic error in Greek tragedy in terms of an excessive union of the human and divine spheres, one characterized in [3.1] as 'gränzenlos', or in AA [3.1] as 'unendlich'. Here it is manifested by an excessive desire to uncover the truth: see the commentary to AO [2.2] below. — Modern interpreters too have noted how the play 'is permeated with the language of finding, exposing, throwing light, revealing. The plot is driven by Oedipus' quest to unveil knowledge' (Taplin 2015: 5). See also Knox 1998: 127–28, 183–84.

2   *nefas*: Latin for a deed that is contrary to (divine) law. The word is also used in *Die tragische Ode ...*: 'je unendlicher, je unaussprechlicher, je näher dem *nefas*' [the more infinite [...], the more inexpressible, the more near to the *nefas*] (MA, I, 866; AL, 259). Constantine (1996: 43) suggests that, here too, 'nefas' is related to 'nefandus' i.e. 'unspeakable' or 'unutterable'. The term is used again later in this paragraph, where it is linked more specifically to the death of Laius; but the point may be that the sin is less parricide than the 'compulsion to bring the whole truth into the daylight' (1996: 54–55). See also Constantine 1988: 294–95, pointing to H.'s 'compulsive repetition of words of learning, seeing, disclosing, and interpreting'. But modern interpreters have found the same in Sophocles himself (see n. 1 above), and such an emphasis can no longer be regarded as 'odd' (ibid.) or 'idiosyncratic' (SP, 252).

3   As reported by Creon at MA, II, 254, ll. 95–97 [96–98].

4   Hardly a plausible reading, but one made possible by H.'s translation of μίασμα in l. 96 [97] as 'shame' [Schmach] rather than 'pollution'. This in turn enables H. to emphasise that the plot is driven by Oed.'s quest for knowledge. See Lönker 1989: 287–91; although it is hard to agree with Lönker's conclusion (p. 303) that the emphasis is based solely on that mistranslation. — Note also Segal's observation: '"Drive out the miasma," Apollo's oracle commanded [...], saying nothing of Laius or his killer. Yet both Creon and Oed. assume that Laius' killer is meant' (1981: 234).

5   MA, II, 254, ll. 98 [99]; or as Constantine translates the complete line: 'Through what cleansing? What ill thing is it?' (SP, 262).

6   Creon has already reported the need to banish, or to avenge a murder (ll. 99–100 [100–01]). But it is true that Oed.'s following question seems to assume it is a particular murderer that has to be banished, an assumption upon which H. also comments below.

7   MA, II, 254, l. 101 [102]: i.e. who is it who should suffer death or banishment? Rather than the man 'who had this fate' (C.).

> Laius, O King, was formerly our lord
> Here in this land, before you led the city.[8]

In this way the oracle's message is brought together with the story of the death of Laius, which does not necessarily belong with it. But in the immediately following scene[9] Oedipus' spirit, knowing everything, with angry premonition actually pronounces the nefas, by suspiciously giving a particular meaning to the general command,[10] and applies it to a murderer[11] of Laius, and then also takes the sin to be an infinite one:

> Who among you, the son of Labdacus,
> Laius, knew by whom he died,
> I say to him: tell all of it to me etc.[12]

>   Regarding this man
> I curse, whoever he may be, here in this land
> Of which I command the power and the thrones,
> Let no-one invite or speak to him;
> Not to holy oaths and not to sacrifices
> Take him.[13]

> This the divine oracle,
> The Pythian, shows me clearly, etc.[14]

Hence, in the subsequent dialogue with Tiresias,[15] the wondrous wrathful curiosity,[16] because knowledge — when it has broken through its limits, as if intoxicated in its splendid

---

8 MA, II, 254, ll. 102–03 [103–04].
9 *scene* [Scene]: in the play as translated, 'acts' are subdivided into 'scenes'; here the first scene of Act 2, beginning at MA, II, 258, l. 220 [216].
10 *command* [Gebot]: i.e that, as Creon has explained, the murderers (in the plural) be punished (l. 106 [107]).
11 *to a murderer* [auf einen Mörder]: i.e. to a single murderer. It is already clear that the god's command relates to the punishment of the crime of murder. The sense in which the command is 'general' relates, it seems, to the number of perpetrators. In spite of the plural in l. 106 [107], and Creon's subsequent reference to several robbers (ll. 121–22 [122–23]), Oed. refers to a single robber at l. 124 [124], and again at l. 229 [225]. — H. certainly has a point, although it may be more accurate to say that Oed. repeatedly blurs the distinction between the 'one' and the 'many': see Dawe, 9, and Segal 1981: 214–15. The distinction subsequently becomes a crucial test for his guilt: see MA, II, 282, ll. 865–70 [842–47].
12 MA, II, 258–59, ll. 228–30 [224–26]. H. follows the syntax of the Greek, with a resulting estranging effect in the translation. The question relates to who knew the killer of Laius, not who knew Laius himself, i.e. 'at whose hands Laius, son of Labdacus, perished' (Loeb, I, 347).
13 MA, II, 259, ll. 240–45 [236–40]; H. modifies his own text very slightly.
14 MA, II, 259, ll. 247–48 [242–43].
15 Namely at MA, II, 261–67, ll. 304–468 [300–462].
16 *wrathful curiosity* [zornige Neugier]: 'anger' or 'wrath' is a key concept in AO; see [3.1] and commentary. Note the earlier reference in this paragraph to Oed.'s 'angry premonition' [zornig[e] Ahnung], and in [2.3] to 'wrathful immoderation'. Rather than merely a psychological state, this 'Zorn' involves a state of ecstatic union with the divine, here expressed in the hero's frantic quest for knowledge: see Chapter 4.3 above.

harmonious form, that can still at first[17] *remain — goads itself on to know more than it can grasp or bear.*

[2.3] *Hence the suspicion, in the scene afterwards with Creon,*[18] *because unbridled thought, burdened with sorrowful secrets, becomes uncertain, and the faithful sure spirit suffers in the wrathful immoderation*[19] *that, joyful in destruction,*[20] *merely follows the tearing rapacity of time.*[21]

[2.4] *Hence, in the middle of the play,*[22] *in the speeches with Jocasta, the sorrowful calm,*[23] *the fearfulness,*[24] *the pitiably naive error of this powerful man — where he tells Jocasta of his supposed birthplace and of Polybus, whom he fears that he will kill because he is his*[25] *father, and of Merope, whom he wishes to flee so as not to marry her because she is his mother — given the words of Tiresias;*[26] *for the latter after all told him*[27] *that he was the murderer of Laius who was his father. For Tiresias says, in the already-mentioned dispute between Oedipus and himself:*

17   at first [vorerst]: it seems that for H., Oed. begins to lose his mental balance in the later scene with Creon (see [2.3]), with subsequent vain attempts to recover his 'consciousness' ([2.4] 'das närrischwilde Nachsuchen nach einem Bewußtseyn'; [2.5] 'das geisteskranke Fragen nach einem Bewußtseyn').
18   See MA, II, 270–74, ll. 539–641 [532–630].
19   in the wrathful immoderation [im zornigen Unmaas]: see 'wrathful curiosity' in [2.2], and cf. AA [2.2] and commentary at n. 6.
20   joyful in destruction [zerstörungsfroh]: Oed.'s desire for knowledge becomes an identification with the force that will destroy him, namely the annihilating power of time itself. On the tragic hero's relation to the pure forms of 'space' and 'time' see further [3.4]–[3.5] and commentary.
21   tearing rapacity of time [reißend[e] Zeit]: following A. While 'rapids of the times' (C.) may miss the sense of time as a personified force, it chimes with a possible source for the image of time as an annihilating power. See Marcus Aurelius, *Meditations*, trans. by Martin Hammond (London: Penguin Books, 2006), 4.43: 'There is a river of creation, and time is a violent stream. As soon as one thing comes into sight, it is swept past' (p. 31); and similarly ibid. at 5.23, 6.15 and 7.19. See also Chapters 1.4 and 2.3 above, and the further references at nn. 46 & 47 to Chapter 2. And see n. 24 to [3.5].
22   middle of the play [Mitte des Stüks]: identified here as MA, II, 277–83, ll. 717–885 [697–862]. Cf. [3.6].
23   sorrowful calm [traurige Ruhe]. H. seems to be describing successive traits of Oed. in this scene: at first calmed down by Jocasta after his argument with Creon; then taking fright when she tells him the circumstances of Laius' death; then self-deludedly clinging to the notion that Laius was not his father.
24   the fearfulness [das Blöde]: assuming that the word is being used in the older sense of being 'timid' or 'fearful'. See Grimm, s.v. blöde, 6; and cf. the ode 'Blödigkeit' [Timidity] (MA, I, 443–44; OE 177) which is contemporary with these *Anmerkungen*. Cf. 'simplicity' (A.); 'foolishness' (C.); 'le trouble' (Court.); 'l'abêtissement' (F.).
25   his [sein]: in MA (corrected in later printings) and FHA incorrectly given as 'der'.
26   given the words of Tiresias [den Worten des Tiresias nach]: preferring 'after the words of Teiresias' (C.) to 'according to Teiresias' words' (A.). The point presumably is that it can already be gathered from those words that Oed. may be a parricide, so that in reporting the prophecy that made him flee Corinth he is being pitifully naive or wilfully blind.
27   after all told him [doch ihm sagte]: Tiresias accused him of being the murderer at MA, II, 263, l. 366 [362], and in effect of being Laius and Jocasta's son at MA, II, 267, ll. 463–66 [457–60], cited by H. below. — As Taplin suggests, Tiresias speaks there in the form of a riddle that Oed. is unwilling to decipher (2015: 295–96).

> The man that you have long
> Been seeking, threatening and proclaiming <u>the murder</u>
> <u>Of Laius</u>, he is here; as stranger, it is said,
> He lives among us, but soon as native Theban
> He'll be shown and not be glad
> At that mischance.[28]
>
> He will be shown to be living with his children
> As brother and as father, and of the woman who
> Bore him, son and husband, <u>in one bed with</u>
> <u>The father and his murderer.</u>[29]

Hence then, at the beginning of the second half, in the scene with the Corinthian messenger,[30] where he is tempted back to life, the despairing struggle to come to his senses,[31] the demeaning, almost shameless attempt to master himself, the foolishly savage search for consciousness.

> JOCASTA
> For upwards Oedipus bends his spirit
> In manifold torment, not like a thoughtful man
> Does he interpret new things from old.[32]
>
> OEDIPUS
> O dearest, you, my wife Jocasta's head!
> Why did you call me here out from the houses?[33]
>
> OEDIPUS
> The old man withered, it seems, from sickness.
> MESSENGER
> And being measured enough by long time.[34]

---

28 MA, II, 267, ll. 455–60 [449–54]: emphasis added in H.'s citation.
29 MA, II, 267, ll. 463–66 [457–60], word omitted and emphasis added in H.'s citation.
30 See MA, II, 286–92, ll. 972–1109 [950–1085].
31 *come to his senses* [zu sich selbst zu kommen]: or more literally 'to come to himself' (C.); cf. 'to find himself' (A. and P.).
32 MA, II, 284–85, ll. 935–37 [914–16]. These lines of Sophocles have two possible interpretations. The usual one is that Oedipus 'does not gauge new thoughts by past experience, as should a thinking man' (Taplin 2015: 48). Alternatively, it is not that Oedipus fails to judge the present from the past, but rather that he fails to do so 'like a man of sense' (Dawe, 188). The latter seems closer to H., and is also reflected in C.
33 MA, II, 286, ll. 972–73 [950–51]; with a slight variation of wording and punctuation in H.'s citation. Here and elsewhere, most famously in the first line of *Antigone* (MA, II, 319), H. gives a literal translation of the Greek mode of address κάρα [head]. This can be seen as an example of his technique of reproducing, in German, the foreignness of the original; although such a rendering of the '"dead" metonym' was by no means unusual in the period (Matzner 2016: 191; and cf. Billings 2014: 198). Similarly H. translates literally the plural form 'houses' [δωμάτων] for what is properly speaking a single 'house' (Loeb, I, 420–21).
34 MA, II, 286–87, ll. 984–85 [962–63].

[2.5] *It should be noted how Oedipus' spirit is lifted here by the fine saying;*[35] *so that the following speeches can appear to arise from a nobler motive.*[36] *By no means bearing things now on Herculean shoulders, here at the height of weakness, to master himself he casts his kingly cares away:*[37]

> Well then! Who now, O wife, once more
> Would question the prophesying hearth, or
> The birds screaming from above? according to which
> I would kill my father, who slumbers
> Dead beneath the earth; but here
> I am and my lance is clean, unless otherwise
> He perished in dreaming of me; in that way
> He may have died from me; at the same time
> He took the present prophecies with him, and lies now
> In Hades, Polybus does, no longer valid.[38]

In the end the speeches are dominated by a sick mind's questing after consciousness.[39]

> MESSENGER
> Well you show, child, that you know not what you are doing.
> OEDIPUS
> How, for god's sake, old one, <u>say something</u>![40]

> OEDIPUS
> What are you saying? Polybus did not plant me?
> MESSENGER
> About as much as one of us.
> OEDIPUS
> How so? A father who is equal to a nobody?
> MESSENGER
> A father, exactly. Not Polybus; not I.

---

35 *by the fine saying* [an dem guten Spruche]: i.e. the messenger's l. 985 [963]. — Dawe similarly draws attention to this line (p. 194), while singling out for praise the messenger's preceding l. 983 [961].
36 *from a nobler motive* [aus edlerem Motiv]: presumably as compared with the 'almost shameless attempt to master himself' mentioned in [2.4].
37 Following the news of Polybus' death, Oedipus is temporarily relieved of his fear of parricide (see the following citation).
38 MA, I, 287, ll. 986–95 [964–72]. In the last line it is evidently the prophecies, rather than Polybus, that are 'no longer valid'. H. will have been misled by an edition having in that line the singular ἄξιος οὐδενός, rather than the ἄξι' οὐδενός of modern editions.
39 *sick mind's questing after consciousness* [das geisteskranke Fragen nach einem Bewußtseyn]: following C.
40 MA, II, 288, ll. 1032–33 [1008–09]. Emphasis added in H.'s citation. A more natural translation of δίδασκέ με would be 'tell me what you mean' (Taplin 2015: 52).

OEDIPUS
Why then does he call me child?⁴¹

MESSENGER
I free you, because your toes are stitched.

OEDIPUS
Out of my swaddling clothes I brought a mighty disgrace.

MESSENGER
So that you are named after this thing.

OEDIPUS
That, O gods! that, by mother, father, speak.⁴²

JOCASTA
By the gods, no! If you have any care for life,
Then do not search. I have sickened enough.

OEDIPUS
Be of good courage. If I came from three mothers
Threefold a slave, it would not make you worse.⁴³

OEDIPUS
Break out what must! My lineage, I want,
However humble, I want to know it.
She is rightly, for women have big ideas,
Ashamed of my lowly birth.
But I, taking myself as child of fortune,
Of the rich in gifts, will not be dishonoured.
For that is my mother. And small and great
The moons of my birth surrounded me,
And so engendered I will not leave off,
Not until I've found out completely what I am.⁴⁴

[2.6] *It is also precisely because of this searching for everything, interpreting of everything, that his spirit succumbs in the end to the rough and simple language of his servants.*⁴⁵

---

41 MA, II, 289, ll. 1041–45 [1017–21]. Note the strangeness of this translation: 'plant' for engender in l. 1041 (does H. momentarily confuse the verbs *ekphuō* and *phuteuō*? cf. the metaphorical use of the latter, rendered literally by H. in l. 896 [873]). Note also the rendering of the thought (ll. 1043–44) that Polybus was as little the father of Oedipus as the nobody who is the messenger. — Dawe (p. 198) remarks on the 'parataxis' in Sophocles' l. 1020, which H. here takes to extremes.
42 MA, II, 290, ll. 1058–61 [1034–37]. H. reproduces the historical present in l. 1058 [1034]. The last line should be a question: was it his mother or his father who pierced his feet? — Not, evidently, which of them named him (Loeb, I, 433).
43 MA, II, 291, ll. 1084–87 [1060–63].
44 MA, II, 292, ll. 1100–09 [1076–85]; but the last line of the citation has 'was ich bin' instead of 'weß ich bin' [whose I am] (SP, 296).
45 *of his servants* [seiner Diener]: in the plural, but the reference seems to be specifically to the dialogue with the Theban herdsman, the old servant of Laius, who is brought in by Oedipus' own servants and becomes 'der Diener' in H.'s translation; see MA, II, 293–97, ll. 1131–1211 [1110–85].

[2.7] *Because such people stand in violent circumstances, their language too — almost in the manner of the Furies — speaks in a more violent connection.*

Thus in the end, Oedipus is driven to learn his true identity from a shepherd (l. 1207 [1183]).

3.

[3.1] *The presentation of the tragic[1] rests principally upon this, that the prodigious[2] — how the god and human being mate,[3] and the power of nature and deepest human inwardness unite limitlessly in wrath[4] — comprehends itself[5] by limitless unification purifying itself[6]*

1   *The presentation of the tragic* [Die Darstellung des Tragischen]: see the parallel discussion of '[d]ie tragische Darstellung' in AA [3.1]. Both AO and AA appear to distinguish between 'Darstellung' and 'Vorstellung', rendered here as 'presentation' and 'representation': cf. [1.5], [1.7], and AA [1.2]. On the concept of 'Darstellung' in post-Kantian philosophy and poetics, cf. Menninghaus 1994.
2   *the prodigious* [das Ungeheure]: or 'fearful enormity' (A.), 'monstrousness' (C.), 'the tremendous' (P.). Corresponding evidently to the Greek *deinos*, signifying a combination of wondrous and fearful, as in his final version of the first stasimon of *Antigone* (MA, II, 331, ll. 349–50 [332–33]). An earlier version (MA, II, 186) renders *deinos* as 'gewaltig', i.e. 'powerful' or 'mighty' (SP, 233); on the two versions see Louth 1998: 159–67. That revision does not extend to *Oedipus* even where such an intensification might seem to be called for, as at MA, II, 302, l. 1359 [1327]; cf. Loeb, I, 464 ('dreadful deeds'). But this may indicate only that a revision of the *Oedipus* translation was not a priority in the limited time H. had available. An element of 'monstrosity' might also be said to be conveyed by H.'s subsequent reference in this paragraph to the 'coupling' or 'mating' of divine and human spheres. — Griffith notes (p. 185) that in the first stasimon of *Antigone* 'it soon becomes obvious that the epithet has been chosen precisely because of its multivalence ("terrible", "awe-inspiring", "wonderful", "strange", "clever", "extraordinary")'. Thus H. foreshadows more recent accounts of Greek tragedy, such as that of Vernant: 'What is this being that tragedy describes as a *deinos*, an incomprehensible and baffling monster [...], whose industrious mind can dominate the whole of nature yet who is incapable of governing himself?' (Vernant and Vidal-Naquet 1988: 32). See similarly ibid. p. 91, and Knox 1964: 23–24; and cf. Oudemans and Lardinois 1987: 87, 125–29.
3   *how god and human being mate* [wie der Gott und Mensch sich paart]: following P.; cf. 'pairing' (C.), 'uniting' (A.). F. captures the singular form of the verb: 'comment le Dieu-et-homme s'accouple' (on this kind of construction in H. see further n. 17 below). It is difficult to avoid associating this monstrous union with one result of Oed.'s enquiries, namely the uncovering of his incest with Jocasta. — Knox observes how Oed. claims for himself 'attributes of divinity', namely 'knowledge, certainty, and justice' (1964: 147). On the transgression of boundaries between human and divine, on the one hand, and human and beast on the other, cf. Vernant 1988: 136–38, and also Irwin 1994: 220–23.
4   *unite ... in wrath* [im Zorn Eins wird]: here 'Zorn' corresponds to 'Begeisterung' [enthusiasm] in AA [3.1], which similarly speaks of god and human 'uniting wholly' [ganz Eines]. See also 'angry premonition', 'wrathful curiosity' and 'wrathful immoderation' in AO [2.2] and [2.3]. On the connection between the concepts 'Zorn' and 'Begeisterung', and their connection with 'Transport' (in AO [1.6] and [1.7]), see Chapter 4.2 and 4.3 above.
5   *comprehends itself* [sich begreift]: note that the subject of this process is the impersonal force designated by 'das Ungeheure'. Such a description of the tragic process is prefigured to an extent in *Die tragische Ode ...*, in relation to H.'s tragedy *Empedocles*. For there it is said that, in order for 'pure life' [reine[s] Leben] to be 'knowable' [erkennbar], it must 'present itself' by 'dividing itself' in a process beginning with an excess of unity or 'intimacy' [dadurch sich darstellen, daß es im Übermaaße der Innigkeit [...] sich trennt] (MA, I, 868; AL, 261, trans. modified).
6   *purifying itself* [sich reinigt]: not exactly in the sense of an Aristotelian *katharsis*; cf. Aristotle, *Poetics*, ed. and trans. by Stephen Halliwell, in Aristotle, XXIII, LCL 199 (Cambridge, MA: Harvard University Press, 1995; corrected repr. 1999), 1449b (pp. 46–49). H. comes closer to the latter in a letter probably to Mehmel from the end of 1800: 'Der Gott und Mensch scheint Eins, darauf ein Schiksaal, das [...] am Ende [...] ein gereinigtes Gemüth als Menscheneigentum zurükläßt' [God and man appear one, then comes a fate that [...] in the end leaves behind as human property [...] a purified soul] (MA, II, 851; AL, 184–85). On that letter see also Chapter 6.3 above. — The purification invoked here is closer to the *katharsis* required by a pollution or transgression than it is to Aristotle; cf. Segal 1981: 234 (purification as 'the major ritual of the play').

through limitless separation. Της φυσεως γραμματευς ην τον καλαμον αποβρεχων ευνουν.[7]

[3.2] *Hence the always disputatious dialogue, hence the chorus in opposition to it.*[8] *Hence the all-too chaste, all-too mechanical and artfully ending*[9] *interlocking of the different parts, in the dialogue, and between chorus and dialogue, and the large passages or dramas*[10] *consisting of chorus and dialogue. Everything is speech against speech, cancelling each other out.*

[3.3] *So in the choruses of 'Oedipus'*[11] *the lamenting, the peaceful and the religious, the*

---

7   In Greek in the original, without diacritical marks, and meaning: 'The scribe of nature dipping the well-minded pen'. A slightly inaccurate quotation of a description of Aristotle given in a Byzantine lexicon (the *Suda*) which should actually read 'dipping the pen in thought [εἰς νοῦν]'. It seems that H. was relying on a French source, namely Jean-Baptiste Robinet's *De la nature* (1761), in which the same version is given on the title-page: see Schmidt in KA, II, 1390–91, following Brague 1994. Schmidt postulates a corrupt source that would also be responsible for a similar miscitation by J. G. Hamann; but note that the Hamann citation is simply a reproduction of Robinet's title page in his review of the work. For Taminiaux (1995: 287) the more correct sense is one actually intended; and Duarte (2007: 16) notes that a paraphrase of the correct citation can be found in Winckelmann (see further Chapter 4.2 above). H.'s thought may be that the divisions characteristic of tragic presentation (see [3.2]) are comparable to an act of inscription.

8   *in opposition to it* [als Gegensaz gegen diesen]. On the role of the chorus in AO and AA, cf. Billings 2013a: 323–28. — As Goldhill explains: 'One basic articulation of tragedy is the difference between scenes and choral odes. The scenes are conventionally divided into *rhēseis* and stichomythia. A *rhēsis* [...] is a set speech of varying length [...]. Stichomythia is the rapid exchange of mostly single lines between one or more characters. Often the formal exchange of *rhēseis* breaks down into violent argument in stichomythia, and such a scene is known as an *agōn* [...], "contest". [...] The choral odes [...] are strikingly different. [...] The language of the choral odes is not merely dense, heightened lyric poetry, but also is largely in a version [...] of Doric dialect' (1997a: 127–28). On the opposition between chorus and tragic hero, in which 'tragedy pitted the realm of mythic heroes against the civic community', see Kurke 2013: 6; and cf. Vernant and Vidal-Naquet 1988: 24, and on the latter Goldhill 1997b: 334–35.

9   *artfully ending* [factisch endigende]. The translation of the term 'factisch' gives rise to a number of difficulties. It appears to be H.'s own coinage, and is used in a corresponding pair of neologisms in AA [3.2]–[3.3], and again in AA [3.4]. It is possible, but not certain, that it has the same meaning there. I have supposed that in the present context it is version of the French *factice* (cf. Littré, s.v. factice, 1), whereas in AA it is to be understood more in the sense of 'active' or 'effective' (cf. Schmidt in KA, II, 1391). As Binder points out, here it is associated with idea of a mechanism and the parts of a drama being articulated with the precision of a machine (1992: 101); the latter may also be an allusion to stichomythia (see n. 8 above, and Corßen 1949: 147). But other solutions have of course been proposed: 'factually ending' (A.); 'correctly closing' (P.); 'ending in facts' (C.). P., C. and Court. all give different translations here as compared with in AA; conversely Fédier's 'se terminant par une fin brutale' looks forward to his translation in AA, but sits uneasily in this context. See further the commentary below to AA [3.2].

10   *large passages or dramas* [groß[e] Parthien oder Dramaten]: following C. In H.'s translation the play is divided into 'Acts', consisting of both dialogue and choral song, and this may be the intended meaning (cf. Corßen 1949: 146).

11   As noted by Schmidt in KA, II, 1391–92, and Corßen (1949: 147, n. 1), the descriptions apply to each of the five choral songs taken in turn: (1) MA, II, 256–58, ll. 150–219 [151–215]; (2) MA, II, 267–69, ll. 469–519 [463–511]; (3) MA, II, 283–84, ll. 886–931 [863–910]; (4) MA, II, 292–93, ll. 1110–30 [1086–1109]; and (5) MA, II, 297–98, ll. 1212–30 [1186–1222].

pious lie (if I am a prophet, etc.[12]), *and the pity to the point of total exhaustion in the face of a dialogue that in its angry sensitivity would rend the soul of precisely this audience;*[13] *the terrifyingly ceremonial forms in the scenes,*[14] *drama like a trial for heresy, as language for a world where, amidst plague, confusion of sense and a generally enflamed spirit of prophecy,*[15] *in an idle time,*[16] *god and human being <u>communicate</u>*[17] <u>*in the all-forgetting form of unfaithfulness*</u>, *so that the course of the world has no gaps and* <u>*the memory of the heavenly ones does not perish*</u>, *for divine unfaithfulness can best be retained.*

[3.4] *In such a moment*[18] *the human being forgets themselves and the god,*[19] *and turns round, to be sure in a holy fashion, like a traitor.*[20] — *For at the outermost limit of suffering nothing more remains than the conditions of time or of space.*[21]

---

12   This is the beginning of the fourth choral song (or third stasimon): 'Wenn ich Wahrsager bin' (l. 1110 [1086]). — Cf. 'baseless optimism' (Dawe, 205); 'false celebration' (Taplin 2015: 300).
13   *of precisely this audience* [eben dieser Hörer]: i.e. the chorus.
14   *scenes* [Auftritten]: presumably in the sense of *epeisodion*, or dialogic scenes as opposed to choruses (Binder 1992: 23). But Court. limits the meaning to 'les entrées en scène'.
15   *plague ... spirit of prophecy* [Pest ... Wahrsagergeist]. — Macintosh (2009: 7) observes that the 'misery and desperation of the Thebans in the opening scene of the play are paralleled in contemporary accounts of the plague at Athens, and the criticism of seers and oracles that runs throughout the text was also symptomatic of the prevailing sense of despair'.
16   *in an idle time* [in müßiger Zeit]: following C. and P. The meaning appears to be: a time grown neglectful of the gods (cf. Corßen 1949: 150–52). See also **AA** [3.4] ('in der furchtbaren Muße[?]'), with commentary.
17   *god and human being communicate* [der Gott und der Mensch ... sich mittheilt]: in H. such a construction (with a plural subject but a verb in the singular) is not unusual. See [3.1] ('sich paart'), and indeed in the early note on *Being and Judgment*: 'Wo Subject und Object [...] vereiniget ist' (MA, II, 49); as well as in the *Pindarfragmente* 'Das Höchste' and 'Die Asyle' (MA, II, 382–83). See Fleming 2002: 284–85, and Benn 1962: 15, n. 18.
18   *In such a moment* [In solchem Momente]: i.e. in that of the turn from union to separation referred to in [3.1], at the point described as the 'middle' [Mitte] of the play in [3.6].
19   *forgets themselves and the god* [vergißt ... sich und den Gott]: although this formula is it seems explained further in [3.5], there is an apparent inconsistency between the two passages (see n. 23 below). On the theme of 'forgetting' in H. see Analecta 2017: 61–80 (here pp. 73–80).
20   *in a holy fashion, like a traitor* [heiliger Weise, wie ein Verräther]. — On the Sophoclean hero as combining an identification with, and a betrayal of (or abandonment by) the gods, cf. Knox 1964: 33, 43–44, 66, 108–09.
21   *conditions of time or of space* [Bedingungen der Zeit oder des Raums]. The language recalls that of Kant, where the 'pure intuitions' of space and time serve as a priori 'conditions' of sensory experience. See *Kritik der reinen Vernunft*, ed. by Ingeborg Heidemann (Stuttgart: Reclam, 1966; repr. 1980): 'unter den dem Subjekt ursprünglich anhängenden Bedingungen, von Raum und Zeit' (B60; p. 107); 'reine Anschauungen a priori, Raum und Zeit' (B 73; p. 118). As explained further in [3.5], the 'forgetting' of (or by) the god seems to consist in the replacement of the latter by these pure forms; and it is in relation to that pure continuum of past and future time that the tragic hero appears to be 'wholly in the moment' [ganz im Moment]. — This can be compared to modern accounts in which Greek tragedy sees the emergence of a new form of temporality, defined by the consequences of acting in the critical moment. Thus for Csapo and Miller it involves the emergence of a democratic and Classical conception of 'linear' or 'historical' time, focused on the problem of taking a deliberative decision in the opportune moment (*kairos*), as opposed to an aristocratic and Archaic temporality privileging the distant past and a timeless present (1998: 98–111; cf. D'Angour 2011: 17–18, and Segal 1995: 25). Here the notion of *kairos* 'captures the act of decision in the intensity

[3.5] There[22] *the human being forgets themselves, because they are wholly in the moment; the god,*[23] *because he is nothing but Time;*[24] *and both are unfaithful, Time, because in such a moment it turns round categorically,*[25] *and in it beginning and end absolutely cannot be made to rhyme; the human being, because in this moment they must follow the categorical reversal, and so in the following are absolutely unable to remain equal to the beginning.*

[3.6] *Thus stands Haemon*[26] *in 'Antigone'. Thus Oedipus himself in the middle*[27] *of the tragedy of Oedipus.*

of the briefest possible moment' (1998: 103). Or as Knox also observes, 'The Sophoclean [as opposed to Aeschylean] hero acts in a terrifying vacuum, a present which has no future to comfort and no past to guide, an isolation in time and space which imposes on the hero the full responsibility for his own action and its consequences' (1964: 5).

22   *There* [In dieser]: i.e. at the 'outermost limit [Gränze] of suffering' referred to in [3.4].
23   *the god* [der Gott]: is 'the god' a subject of this act of forgetting or only its object, as suggested in [3.4.] by the use of the accusative 'den Gott'? Here the nominative suggests that the god is indeed a subject. But there is a question whether one or the other paragraphs should be emended. Lüders (1968: 57, n. 58) proposed that 'den Gott' in [3.4] should read 'der Gott'; although that does not sit very easily with the syntax of the sentence. Conversely, Bröcker (1959: 23) suggested that here 'der Gott' should read 'den Gott'. It is true that consistency would thereby be restored; but the use in this paragraph of the notion of 'unfaithfulness', with its characterisation as 'all-forgetting' in [3.3], may indicate that H. now intends a more inclusive statement based the idea of a mutual (as well as a self-) forgetting of god and human. Bröcker's hypothesis is rejected by Hühn (1997: 241). As already noted in Chapter 6.2, a similar issue is raised by analogous constructions in the fifth and eighth *Pindarfragmente* (cf. Fink 1982: 74, n. 2, and 104). The parallel is all the more striking, given that there the notions of 'encounter' and 'recognition' are as it were anti-tragic counterparts to the present notions of 'unfaithfulness' and 'forgetting'.
24   *nothing but Time* [nichts als Zeit]: see also n. 21 to [2.3]. — Knox observes that 'all-powerful Time' is the 'real adversary' of the Sophoclean hero (1964: 27). Similarly, for de Romilly, time in Sophocles assumes the status of an 'intermediate power', taking the place of the gods that are still directly present in Aeschylus (1968: 56), and in a manner comparable to Heraclitus (1968: 97). As in H., therefore, on this account the gods withdraw in favour of time as an autonomous principle of devastating change. See further n. 21 to [3.4].
25   *categorically* [kategorisch]: cf. Kant's notion of a 'categorical', as opposed to 'hypothetical', imperative ('you must do X' as opposed to 'you must do X if you want to obtain Y'). Most relevant here perhaps is Kant's explanation of its force as the principle of morality, namely its dependence on the pure form of the moral law. Analogously, a 'categorical' reversal for H. would be one that pertains to the pure form of Time. See Kant, *Grundlegung zur Metaphysik der Sitten*, in *Gesammelte Schriften*, Akademie-Textausgabe, IV (Berlin: Reimer, 1911; repr. De Gruyter, 1968), pp. 414–16, 421.
26   *Thus stands Haemon* [So stehet Hämon]: i.e. in the central scene with Creon, described as the 'middle' of the play in AA [2.4] and [2.5]. It is in relation to that scene that AA [2.5] invokes again the idea of following the 'categorical' turning of Time ('wie ein Karakter der kategorischen Zeit kategorisch folget'), further underlining the parallel.
27   *middle* [Mitte]: according to AO [2.4] this corresponds to the scene with Jocasta at MA, II, 277–83, ll. 717–885 [697–862].

Notes on 'Antigone'

1.

[1.1] *The rule, the calculable law of 'Antigone' is related to that of 'Oedipus' as* ⌐ *to* ⌐ ,[1] *so that the equilibrium[2] inclines more from the beginning towards the end than from the end towards the beginning.*

[1.2] *It[3] is one of the various sequences in which representation and feeling and reasoning develop[4] in accordance with poetic logic.[5] For just as philosophy always treats of only one faculty of the soul, so that the presentation of this single faculty constitutes a whole, and the mere interrelation <u>of the members</u> of this single faculty is called logic; so poetry treats of the various human faculties, so that the presentation of these various faculties constitutes a whole, and the interrelation <u>of the more self-contained parts</u> of the various faculties can be called rhythm, in the higher sense,[6] or the calculable law.*

[1.3] *But if this rhythm of representations[7] is so constituted that, in the rapidity of enthusiasm,[8] the <u>earlier</u> are more carried away by the <u>succeeding</u> ones, the caesura a) or the <u>counter-rhythmical interruption</u> must then lie <u>in front</u>, so that the first half is as it were protected against the second; and the equilibrium — precisely because the second half is originally more rapid and appears to weigh more heavily — inclines more from the back b) towards the beginning c), on account of the counterbalancing caesura.[9]* $\;_c{}^a\!\diagdown_b$

---

1 See [1.4] and [1.3] respectively, corresponding to AO [1.10] and [1.9]. The diagrams appear to indicate that a notional point of equilibrium is shifted from the centre, in one or other of the two directions mentioned.
2 *equilibrium* [Gleichgewicht]: declared to be a characteristic of the law of tragedy in AO [1.5].
3 *It* [Sie]: i.e. the 'rule' or 'calculable law'. On this paragraph, see Schmidt in KA, II, 1489–90, and the commentary above to AO [1.5].
4 *develop* [sich ... entwickelt]: note the singular form of the verb, brought out by F. ('l'un des divers modes de succession dans lesquels ce qui est représentation et sentiment et raisonnement se développe'). On such constructions, see n. 17 to AO [3.3] above.
5 *poetic logic* [poëtisch[e] Logik]: now adding a further characterisation of the 'calculable law', and bringing out the distinction between poetics and philosophy.
6 *rhythm, in the higher sense* [Rhythmus, im höhern Sinne]: yet another characterisation of poetic law; cf. AO [1.8].
7 *representations* [Vorstellungen]: the term is apparently being used in a wider sense than in the preceding paragraph, which distinguished between the faculties of 'Vorstellung', 'Empfindung' and 'Räsonnement'. See Schmidt in KA, II, 1490–91.
8 *rapidity of enthusiasm* [Rapidität der Begeisterung]: corresponding to 'exzentrisch[e] Rapidität' in the parallel discussion of AO [1.9]. On that parallelism see further Chapter 4.3 above.
9 The wording of this paragraph is mostly identical to AO [1.9], with the addition of a diagram and corresponding references to the points a), b) and c).

[1.4] *If the rhythm of the representations is, however, so constituted that* the succeeding *are more pressed upon by* the beginning *ones, the caesura a) will lie more towards the end, because it is the end that must as it were be protected against the beginning; and the equilibrium will consequently incline more towards the end b), because the first half c) extends further, while the equilibrium comes later.*[10]   c ⎯⎯ᵃ⎯⎯ b

---

[10] The wording of this paragraph is again very similar to **AO** [1.10], with a diagram and corresponding references.

2.

[2.1] "How dared you break such a law?"[1]

"Because my Zeus did not pronounce it to me,
Nor in this house the justice of the gods of death etc."[2]

The boldest moment in the course of a day or a work of art is where the spirit of time and nature, the heavenly that seizes a human being, and the object of the latter's interest,[3] stand most savagely opposed to one another; because the object of the senses extends only to the first half, <u>but the spirit most powerfully awakes where the second half[4] begins</u>. In this moment a person must <u>most keep a secure hold</u> on themselves; and, for that reason, it is there too that their character stands most exposed.

[2.2] *The tragically-moderate lassitude of the age,[5] whose object is after all of no real interest to the heart, follows the tearing spirit of time most immoderately;[6] and this then*

---

1 MA, II, 334, l. 466 [449]: Creon is referring to his decree that Polynices is to be neither buried nor mourned (MA, II, 320, ll. 28–34 [26–32]). This exchange between Creon and Ant. is in inverted commas in the original.
2 Ant.'s reply, beginning MA, II, 334, ll. 467–68 [450–51]. Although the possessive 'mein Zevs' is not found in the Sophocles text (οὐ γάρ τί μοι Ζεὺς ἦν), it serves to emphasize that Ant. does not regard Zeus as having commanded *her* to follow Creon's decree. Cf. 'For me it was not Zeus' (Wyck, 207); 'announced to me' (Griff, 200). See Corßen 1949: 170; but for a suggestion that 'mein Zevs' is a specific reference to the god of the underworld ('der unterirdische Zeus [...] der Herrscher des Totenreichs'), see Analecta 2017: 261–63 (p. 262).
3 *object of the latter's interest* [Gegenstand, für welchen er sich interessirt]. This object might be the unburied corpse of Polynices (Binder 1992: 149; Böschenstein 2015a: 10–11; also Hell, v, 360), or more generally the dispute concerning his burial (Corßen 1949: 174). On that view, H. contrasts the ostensible conflict between Ant. and Creon with a deeper one regarding the interpretation of the divine command.
4 *second half* [zweite Hälfte]: roman type in the original, as with the preceding word 'spirit' [Geist] and probably for additional emphasis (see also [2.10]). Contrary to Böschenstein (2015a: 11), this would not seem to be a reference to what H. later calls the 'middle' [Mitte] of the play, i.e. the dialogue between Creon and Haem. (see [2.4]–[2.5], and cf. AO [3.6]). It seems rather to be a different division of the play into two parts or halves, occurring at this 'boldest moment' itself (Corßen 1949: 174). As Binder notes, 'Hälfte' for H. does not necessarily refer to an arithmetical half; and there are a number of different points of such division in the plays (cf. [1.3]–[1.4] and AO [1.8]–[1.10]). Binder sees this 'moment' as the one dividing the part concerned with a quarrel concerning rites of burial, and a remainder dominated by Ant.'s claim to implement the will of Zeus (1992: 149–50). See also n. 13 below.
5 *tragically-moderate lassitude of the age* [tragischmäßige Zeitmatte]: the neologism 'tragischmäßige' is distinct from, but no doubt related to, the idea of 'müßig[e] Zeit' [idle time] in AO [3.3]; although the latter still seems present in the coinage 'Zeitmatte'. On the interpretation of the latter, cf. Analecta 2007: 125, n. 299 ('Mangel an Lebhaftigkeit, an Lebendigkeit'). For Binder (1992: 152), such 'Zeitmatte' is exemplified by Creon's fixation on political calculation and reasons of State.
6 *most immoderately* [am unmäßigsten]: the parallel with 'tragischmäßige' above seems to confirm that the latter is not a misprint for 'tragischmüßige' (contrast Corßen 1949: 174–75). Binder again links this to the position of Creon, driven beyond measure by his encounter with Ant. (1992: 152). Creon would then be in the same position as Oed. in AO [2.3], namely of following 'the tearing rapacity of time' [der reißenden Zeit] (here 'dem reißenden Zeitgeist'), there in a state of 'wrathful immoderation' [im zornigen Unmaas].

appears wild, not sparing human beings like a daytime spirit, but unsparing, as spirit of the eternally living unwritten wilderness[7] *and the world of the dead.*

[2.3]   CREON
But the bad are not to be taken as equal to the good.
        ANTIGONE
Who knows, for below there may be a different custom.[8]

The amiable, the sensible in misfortune. Dreamily ingenuous. True language of Sophocles, whereas Aeschylus and Euripides know better how to depict[9] *suffering and anger, but less human understanding moving among the unthinkable.*

[2.4]   CREON
If I remain true to my origin, do I lie?[10]
        HAEMON
That you are not, hold <u>you not sacred the name of God</u>.[11]

instead of: trample on the honour of the gods. It was necessary, to be sure, to alter the sacred expression[12] *here, given its significance in the middle*[13] *as serious*[14] *and self-standing word, around which everything else takes shape and is illuminated.*[15]

[2.5] *To be sure, the manner in which Time turns around in the middle*[16] *cannot well be*

---

7 unwritten wilderness [ungeschrieben[e] Wildniß]: cf. Ant.'s appeal, in the cited passage, to the unwritten ordinances of the gods (MA, II, 335, ll. 471–72 [454–55]).
8 MA, II, 337, ll. 541–42 [520–21].
9 depict [objectiviren]: following P.; literally 'objectify' (A. and C.).
10 Here the Greek *arkhē* suggests 'authority' (Griff, 249) or 'office' (Loeb, Wyck), but H. finds the alternative (and older) meaning of 'origin' (Brill, s.v. ἀρχή, A). His rendering of ἁμαρτάνω as 'lie' [lüg' ich] (rather than 'do wrong') may simply be a mistake.
11 MA, II, 345–46, ll. 773–74 [744–45]; emphasis in citation only.
12 *sacred expression* [heilige[r] Ausdruck]: cf. [2.5] ('sacred name'). H. in effect gives a monotheistic reinterpretation of Sophocles' reference to 'the gods'; as Böschenstein puts it, this amounts to 'eine Hesperisierung des antiken Wortlauts' (1995b: 230). The purpose, at least in the first instance, seems to be to make it more vivid for a modern audience (cf. Binder 1992: 155). But for Billings (2014: 209) it is also a sign that Haem. and Creon are 'on different sides of a theological divide', so that the process of transformative translation corresponds to a movement within the tragedy itself. Böschenstein (1995b: 230–38) suggests also that the difference between the standpoint of Creon and the (more Hesperian) standpoint of Ant. is reflected in the two choral songs on either side of this central episode, namely the second and third stasima.
13 *in the middle* [in der Mitte]: this dispute between father and son (MA, II, 342–46, ll. 655–794 [631–765]) is a crucial turning-point of the play, and literally in the 'middle' (cf. AO [3.6]). But note also the 'halves' divided by Ant.'s appeal to 'my Zeus' (AA [2.1]), or by the intervention of Tiresias (see n. 4 above). — Seidensticker too describes the scene with Creon and Haem. as the 'tragic turning-point of the play' (2005: 301).
14 *as serious* [als Ernst]: or 'in its seriousness' (C.); possibly in the sense of a point of general significance for the play. On this term see also [2.10] and n. 34 below.
15 *takes shape and is illuminated* [sich ... objektiviret und verklärt]: cf. 'objectified and made clear' (C.); 'objectified and transfigured' (A.).
16 *in the middle* [in der Mitte]: see [2.4] and commentary; and on the 'turning' of Time at the central moment of a tragedy cf. AO [3.5]–[3.6].

altered, nor how a character categorically follows categorical Time,[17] and how the Greek goes towards the Hesperian;[18] but it is otherwise with the sacred name under which the highest is felt or occurs. The speech refers to Creon's oath.[19]

[2.6]   You will not brood much longer
        In the jealous sun.[20]

On the earth, among human beings, the sun, as it becomes relative in a physical sense, can actually become relative in the moral sphere.[21]

[2.7]   I have heard, become like the desert etc.[22]

Surely Antigone's highest trait. The sublime mockery — in so far as holy madness[23] is

---

17 *categorically follows categorical Time* [der kategorischen Zeit kategorisch folget]: AO [3.5] similarly refers to how the tragic protagonist follows the 'categorical' turning of Time.
18 *how the Greek goes towards the Hesperian* [wie es vom griechischen zum hesperischen gehet]: this seems to amount to a further explanation of the 'categorical' turning or reversal referred to in AO [3.5]. In that case both plays would be concerned with a transition from the original 'Greek' towards the more 'Hesperian', that is to say to forms that anticipate and provide the foundation for modern culture. While Ryan concedes this, he suggests that the transition is nonetheless to be considered more 'Greek' in the case of *Oedipus Tyrannus*, more 'Hesperian' in the case of *Antigone* (1988: 105). See also the introductory note above to these *Sophokles-Anmerkungen*.
19 *Creon's oath* [Schwur des Kreon]: as Corßen suggests (1949: 168), the reference may be to Creon's earlier oath by Zeus (or, in H.'s translation, 'der Erde Herr'), requiring delivery of the as yet unknown perpetrator (MA, II, 329, ll. 319–21 [304–05]). Creon appeals to the highest god as the foundation of his authority, while Haem. interprets his command as a dishonour to the gods. The reference does not (as assumed in Court.) appear to be a reference to the immediately following citation of Tiresias. — On Creon's 'solemn oath' at ll. 304–05 see Griff, 175–76, observing that the clash between Creon and Ant. is 'not simply between "human" and "divine" law', but between principles 'both of which can lay legitimate claim to divine sanction' (p. 176).
20 MA, II, 357, ll. 1106–07 [1064–65]: actually 'you will not complete many more racing circuits [τρόχους ἀμιλλητῆρας] of the sun' (Griff, 306). Tiresias is warning that it will not be long before Creon has to surrender the body of Haem. in exchange for those of Polynices and Ant. Note that the citation is out of step with the otherwise linear sequence running from ll. 466–68 cited in [2.1], to ll. 987–88 in [2.10].
21 It is difficult to explain why H., with this citation, jumps forward to the Tiresias scene, unless it is intended as a further illustration of the transformative translation practice already mentioned (and justified) in [2.4]–[2.5]. Note also that in the original, but not MA, these lines and their commentary are treated as part of the preceding paragraph. If the original Greek involves an analogy between the sun and an athletic competitor ('relative in a physical sense'), H. seems again to be giving a contemporary equivalent with an analogy drawn from the domain of human emotion ('relative in the moral sphere'). But Schmidt offers a different explanation, in terms of the sun as an 'elemental power' [Elementargewalt] (KA, II, 1476).
22 Ant.'s reply to the chorus, beginning MA, II, 348, l. 852 [823]. As she confronts the prospect of entombment in a rocky cavern Ant. invokes the myth of Niobe who, after her children were slain in punishment by the gods, was turned in her grief into a weeping rock (Graves 1958: 258–59). On H.'s interpretation of this passage, cf. Bennholdt-Thomsen 2005: 184–87; Böschenstein 2015a: 12–16, and 2015b: 113–16; Harrison 1975: 177–80.
23 *sublime mockery ... holy madness* [erhabene Spott ... heiliger Wahnsinn]: note the insistent references to the 'highest', the 'sublime', the 'superlative' in this paragraph. As Böschenstein suggests (2015b: 123), Ant.'s 'Wahnsinn' corresponds to the 'Zorn' [wrath] of Oedipus (cf. AO [2.2]–[2.3] and [3.1]), a term that recurs here too in H.'s translation (MA, II, 350, ll. 887, 906). But what is

the highest human manifestation, and here more soul than speech — surpasses all her other utterances; and it is necessary too to speak of beauty thus in the superlative, given that the attitude rests among other things on the superlative of human spirit and heroic virtuosity.[24]

[2.8] *It is a great resource of the soul, in its secret workings, that at the highest point of consciousness it evades consciousness,*[25] *and before actually being seized by the god that is present, it meets the latter with a bold — often even blasphemous*[26] *— word, and so maintains the holy living possibility of the spirit.*

[2.9] *At the height of consciousness the soul then compares itself always with objects that lack consciousness, but in their fate assume the form of consciousness.*[27] *Such a one is a land that has become desert, that in its originally luxuriant fertility too greatly increases the effects of the sunlight, and thereby becomes arid. Fate of the Phrygian Niobe;*[28] *as everywhere fate of innocent nature, which everywhere passes in its virtuosity*[29] *into the all-too organic, to just the same degree as the human being approaches the aorgic,*[30] *in more heroic circumstances and emotions. And Niobe too is then quite properly the image of early genius.*

[2.10] She counted for the Father of Time
 The strokes of the hours, the golden ones.[31]

---

the 'mockery' referred to here? In Sophocles such a reference comes later, in Ant.'s retort to the chorus: 'Weh! Närrisch machen sie mich [γελῶμαι]' (MA, II, 349, l. 867 [839]). But Binder sees Ant.'s comparison of herself with Niobe as itself a mockery of the 'god of death' (1992: 157; cf. Corßen 1949: 178); see n. 26 below. Niobe's own behaviour might be regarded as involving a blasphemous mockery of the goddess Leto (cf. Griff, 269).
24 *heroic virtuosity* [heroisch[e] Virtuosität]. The latter term is also used in the second letter to Böhlendorff: 'das wilde kriegerische [...] das im Todesgefühle sich wie in einer Virtuosität fühlt' (MA, II, 921; AL, 213), where, as Bertheau suggests (2003: 153), it will have the sense of heroic virtue, as in the Italian 'virtù'; thus here 'virtù eroica' (R.).
25 *evades consciousness* [dem Bewußtseyn ausweicht]: apparently in the sense that, at her highest point of anguish, Ant. has recourse to a comparison that saves her from madness (cf. Bennholdt-Thomsen 2005: 185).
26 *blasphemous* [blasphemische[s]]. For Binder (1992: 157), Ant. upholds her spirit by words that mock specifically the god of death, this being the god that is 'present' to her at this stage; thus he reads this passage with the statement at the end of **[3.1]** (ibid. p. 160).
27 *assume the form of consciousness* [des Bewußtseyns Form annehmen]: as presumably the rock in the legend, which has the form of the weeping Niobe. H. seems to interpret the legend in reverse: it is not the living creature who becomes a rock, but rather a desert landscape that assumes human form. Then later in this paragraph he is reminded of his earlier analysis of the interchange between 'aorgic' character of Nature and 'organic' character of human culture or Art (see n. 30).
28 *Niobe*: who in the myth was punished for boasting of her fruitfulness. But the idea of a land becoming a desert by virtue of its own luxuriance is H.'s own addition, and seems to be an attempt to give a naturalistic explanation of the myth.
29 *virtuosity* [Virtuosität]: cf. **[2.7]** and n. 24 above.
30 *all-too organic* [...] *aorgic* [Allzuorganische ... Aorgisch[e]]: H. here employs categories previously used in his discussion of the basis for his *Empedocles* drama (see MA, I, 868–70; AL, 261–63).
31 MA, II, 353, ll. 987–88 [950]. The chorus is speaking, and offering in this fourth stasimon a

instead of: administered for Zeus the golden stream of becoming.[32] *In order to bring it closer to our mode of representation. With more, or less, exactness*[33] *one has no doubt to say Zeus.* <u>*With full seriousness*</u>[34] *it is better to say: Father of Time, or: Father of the Earth,*[35] *because his character is — against the eternal tendency — to turn* <u>the striving out of this world to the other, into a striving out of another world to this one</u>.[36] *For we must everywhere present the myth* <u>more demonstrably</u>. *The golden stream of becoming no doubt means the rays of light, which also belong to Zeus*[37] *in so far as the time that is indicated is more easily calculated by such rays. But so is it always when time is measured in suffering,*

mythic parallel to Ant.'s suffering. H. immediately goes on to explain his unorthodox translation. — On this (relatively speaking) straightforward comparison of Ant. to Danae, cf. Sourvinou-Inwood 1989: 143–47, and n. 32 below. The comparisons in the remainder of the stasimon pose particularly difficult questions of interpretation (see Griff, 283–85, 291–95).

32   *golden stream of becoming* [das goldenströmende Werden]: in Griffith's translation of the original l. 950, 'she was treasurer for Zeus's golden-flowing seed' (Griff, 288). According to the myth, Danae was imprisoned by her father Akrisius so that she would not bear a son, but was nonetheless impregnated by the golden seed or rain of Zeus. In H. the theme of natural (or supernatural) generation is transformed into a peculiarly modern image of temporality, the tolling of the hours. The first step in this process is his interpretation of 'Zeus' as 'Father of Time', followed by that of his golden seed as the rays of the sun, and finally by the anachronistic metaphor of the tolling of bells (on the latter see Bennholdt-Thomsen 2005: 191). — Sourvinou-Inwood (1989: 146) observes that the immediately following ll. 989–92 [951–54] can be taken to refer to Akrisius' unsuccessful attempt to evade his fate (one similar to that of Laius) by imprisoning his daughter.

33   *With more, or less, exactness* [Im Bestimmteren oder Unbestimmteren]: cf. 'To be more definite, or indeed less definite' (C.); 'In more particular or vaguer contexts' (A.). Cf. the letter to Ebel of 3 July 1799, where (in relation to his journal project in Homburg) H. refers to 'was man bisher bestimmter und unbestimmter, unter Humanität verstanden hat' (FHA, XIX, 392). That is to say, a particular term (here 'humanism') may not necessarily convey an exact meaning; and cf. the reference in the parallel letter to Schelling, to 'den Gesichtspunct sogenannten Humanität' (FHA, XIX, 390; MA, II, 792; AL, 152). As Binder suggests (1992: 141), the point seems to be that for us the Greek name has ceased to convey its original meaning, and accordingly benefits from being explained as 'Father of Time' etc.

34   *With full seriousness* [Im Ernste]: following C. ('for the full seriousness'); cf. A. ('In serious contexts'). See also [2.4] ('als Ernst'), and [3.5] ('ernstliche Bemerkungen'). 'Ernst' can carry the meaning of scientific or theoretical generality: see again the letters referred to in n. 33 above, suggesting an equivalence between 'vom ernsten Nachdenken' and 'von der Wissenschaft'. There is also perhaps a reminiscence of Aristotle: 'poetry is more philosophical and more elevated [σπουδαιότερον] than history, since poetry relates more of the universal, while history relates particulars'; see *Poetics*, ed. and trans. by Stephen Halliwell, in Aristotle, XXIII, LCL 199 (Cambridge, MA: Harvard University Press, 1995; corrected repr. 1999), 1451b (pp. 58–59). That Greek term can be translated as 'Ernsthafteres' (Fuhrmann 1982: 28–29).

35   *Father of the Earth* [Vater der Erde]: for this translation, see MA, II, 341, l. 626 [604], and similarly MA, II, 319, l. 2 [2] ('der Erde Vater').

36   In roman type in the original, as in the cases noted in [2.1] (although here spacing is also used for emphasis). See the parallel passage in [3.2], saying that the 'more authentic Zeus' is one who 'forces the course of nature that is eternally hostile to humanity, on its way into the other world, more decidedly down to earth'. The equivalents 'Father of Time' or 'Father of the Earth' seem intended not only to be more informative for a modern audience, but in this case to be a revelation of the god's more essential character. See also the commentary to [3.2], and Bennholdt-Thomsen 1998: 22–23.

37   *also belong to Zeus* [auch dem Zevs gehören]: one would normally associate the sun's rays with Apollo, but here they are treated as a way of measuring time, and Zeus has been described as 'Father of Time' [Vater der Zeit] (cf. Bennholdt-Thomsen 2005: 192).

for then the soul follows time's course much more with its feeling, thereby grasping the simple passage of the hours, without the intellect inferring the future from the present.

[2.11] *But because this most steadfast endurance before changing time,[38] this heroic hermit's existence actually is the highest consciousness,[39] the subsequent chorus[40] is thereby justified as purest generality and truest perspective for the comprehension of the whole.*

[2.12] *For this contains, as a contrast to the all-too great sympathy[41] of this preceding passage,[42] the highest impartiality between the two opposing characters that give rise to the actions of the different persons of the drama.*

[2.13] *In the first place, that which characterizes the antitheos, where someone acts in God's sense[43] as if <u>contrary to</u> God, and knows the spirit of the Highest One in a lawless fashion.[44] Then the pious fear in the face of destiny, and with it the honouring of God*

---

38   *before changing time* [vor der wandelnden Zeit]: MA has the misprint 'von' for 'vor'. For Zeus as a god of 'wandelnde' or 'wechselnde Zeit', see the ode 'Natur und Kunst oder Saturn und Jupiter' discussed in Chapters 1.4 and 2 above.
39   *highest consciousness* [das höchste Bewußtseyn]: cf. [2.8] and [2.9], there in relation to the comparison with Niobe. Böschenstein (2006b: 68) suggests that H.'s intention is to confront two contrary forms of 'highest consciousness': one that finds itself in Danae's 'heroic hermit's existence', the other in Niobe's blasphemous 'mockery' (cf. nn. 23 & 26 above).
40   *subsequent chorus* [der folgende Chor]: i.e. the fourth stasimon, but only it seems the remainder of the chorus from which H. has just cited, i.e. MA, II, 353–54, ll. 989–1024 [951–87]. See Schmidt in KA, II, 1492; and cf. F. ('la suite du chœur'). The first four of those lines still belong to the Danae myth, probably relating to the fate of Akrisius (see n. 32 above). Note that, if those lines are included, the passage both begins and ends with a reference to 'das Schiksaal' (see also n. 45 below). On H.'s interpretation of the fourth stasimon see generally Böschenstein 2006b.
41   *all-too great sympathy* [das Allzuinnige]: cf. 'excessive passion' (C.); 'over-intimate quality' (A.); 'l'excès de sympathie' (F.). The fourth stasimon offers three mythic parallels to the fates of Ant. and Creon; H. may be saying that only the first comparison expresses unequivocal sympathy for Ant. (see the next note).
42   *of this preceding passage* [dieser vorhergegangenen Stelle]: i.e. presumably the comparison of Ant. to Danae (ll. 981–88 [944–50]). That is followed (ll. 993–1003 [955–65]) by a description of the fate of Lycurgus, who attempted to oppose the entry of Dionysus into Thrace (Griff, 289–91); and then (ll. 1004–24 [966–87]) one of Cleopatra, the daughter of Boreas, and her sons (Griff, 291–92). The question arises whether each myth corresponds to the character-type of Ant. and Creon respectively, or the correspondences are more equivocal. In either case, H. would perhaps be justified in saying that the chorus demonstrates an 'impartiality' between the two. — On the difficulty of interpreting the comparisons in this stasimon, see Griff, 283–85; and cf. Sourvinou-Inwood, who reaches the conclusion that Lycurgus corresponds to Creon, Cleopatra to Ant., while stressing the ambivalence of the chorus regarding the latter (1989: 151–53, 159–61). Cairns stresses the difficulty of making unequivocal comparisons between Ant. or Creon and the relevant mythological figure (2016: 33–34).
43   *in God's sense* [in Gottes Sinne]: cf. 'after God's own mind' (C.), 'according to God's intent' (A.). For Böschenstein (2015a: 15–17) the paradoxical formula 'in God's sense as if contrary to God' is to be understood in terms of the encounter of Lycurgus and Dionysus (see n. 42 above); see also Harrison 1975: 181–83. The difficulty is that Lycurgus might be thought to more resemble Creon, whereas H. assigns to Ant. this alternative of the 'antitheos'.
44   Böschenstein (2015a: 17) points to H.'s translation of the stasimon at ll. 998–99 [960–61]: 'Und kennen lernt' er, | Im Wahnsinn tastend, den Gott mit schimpfender Zunge'.

as of something established.⁴⁵ *This is the spirit of the opposites set out impartially in the chorus. Antigone acting more in the first sense. Creon in the second.⁴⁶ Both, in so far as they are opposed, not in the manner of national and anti-national, hence cultivated, like Ajax and Ulysses;⁴⁷ nor in the manner of Oedipus against the Greek country people and ancient original nature, as free-thinker against faithful simplicity; but rather weighed equally against each other and differing only in temporal position, so that the one loses principally <u>because it begins</u>, the other <u>wins because it follows</u>.⁴⁸ In that way, precisely the strange chorus that is under discussion fits most skilfully into the whole, and its cold impartiality is warmth just because it is so peculiarly apt.⁴⁹*

---

45   *established* [gesezten]: or (bringing out the contrast with 'lawless') 'set in law' (C.), 'lawfully given' (A.). The preceding reference to 'destiny' [Schiksaal] echoes the similar references in l. 989 [951] and l. 1024 [987].
46   On the balance between the positions described in this paragraph, cf. Corßen 1949: 170–72. — Modern commentators too resist the idea that one or other of Ant. or Creon represents a position that is endorsed by the play: see Cairns 2016: 29–57, and Holt 1999 (see also n. 48 below).
47   *Ajax and Ulysses* [Ajax und Ulyss]: i.e. Ajax (or Aias) and Odysseus in Sophocles' *Ajax*. The contrast between the 'national', and the 'anti-national' or 'cultivated', is to be read in the sense of the first letter to Böhlendorff : 'das eigentliche nationelle wird im Fortschritt der Bildung immer der geringere Vorzug werden' (MA, II, 912; AL, 207); cf. Schmidt in KA, II, 1493, and Harrison 1975: 208–09. For other comparisons between these three plays see [3.6] and [3.7]. — On Odysseus as looking forward to the values of a new democratic society (in H.'s terms the 'Hesperian' aspect of Greek culture), as opposed to the 'older and fiercer set of heroic values' or 'unbending epic heroism' represented by Ajax, see Segal 1981: 109–10, and also 1995: 17, 23–25. For Odysseus as providing 'another model of subjectivity' relevant to the 'new and different world in which the play was first presented — and for our own' see Burian 2012: 81, in effect finding H.'s concept of the 'Hesperian'.
48   Cf. the comparison in [3.7] of *Antigone* to a running competition. — One can say indeed that Creon, who begins in the dominant position as upholder of the law, has by the end had to acknowledge his defeat, whereas Ant. is vindicated despite her violation of the norms of the polis. Or as Holt puts it 'The premise of the *Antigone* is skewed almost as heavily in Kreon's favor as its conclusion is skewed in Antigone's' (1999: 687).
49   *most skilfully ... apt* [aufs geschikteste ... schiklich]: cf. 'most apt ... fitting' (C.); 'most appropriately ... appropriate' (A.). But H.'s characteristic word-play on these and related terms must always be borne in mind: see [3.2] with the commentary at nn. 21 & 22.

3.¹

[3.1] *As indicated in the Notes on 'Oedipus', the tragic presentation rests on this: that the immediate god,² wholly one³ with the human being (for the god of an Apostle is more mediate,⁴ is highest understanding in highest spirit), that <u>infinite</u> enthusiasm grasps itself⁵ <u>infinitely</u>, that is to say in oppositions,⁶ in a consciousness that abolishes consciousness, dividing itself in a holy fashion, and the god is present in the form of death.⁷*

[3.2] *Hence, as already touched upon⁸ in the Notes on 'Oedipus', the dialogic form and the chorus in opposition to it. Hence the perilous form in the scenes,⁹ which, in a more Greek fashion,¹⁰ necessarily end effectively in the sense that the <u>word</u> becomes <u>more mediately effective</u>,¹¹ in that it seizes the more sensuous body; according to our time and*

1   The section numbering and division are omitted in the original, presumably as a result of an error (of the printer if not of H. himself). But what follows clearly corresponds to the third section of AO.
2   *the immediate god* [der unmittelbare Gott]: despite the close parallel between this paragraph and AO [3.1], the contrast drawn between the 'immediate' and the 'more mediate' [mittelbarer] is new. The former corresponds to the 'mating' or 'coupling' of human and divine in AO [3.1] ('sich paart'). On the latter see n. 4 below, and cf. the concept of 'strict mediacy' [strenge Mittelbarkeit] in the fifth *Pindarfragment* (MA, II, 381; AL, 336), discussed in Chapter 6.2 above.
3   *wholly one* [ganz Eines]: cf. AO [3.1] ('im Zorn Eins wird') and commentary.
4   *more mediate* [mittelbarer]. Cf. a later version of the hymn 'Der Einzige' [The Only One]: 'mit Gewalt | Des Tages oder | Mit Stimmen erscheinet Gott als | Natur von außen. Mittelbar | In heiligen Schriften.' [with the daylight's |Violence or | With voices God appears as | Nature from without. Mediated | In holy writ] (MA, III, 286; SP, 153). But it seems that a more fundamental distinction is not that between pagan and Christian religion ('the god of an Apostle'), but rather between an immediate (and fateful) contact with the divine and one that is mediated by a text, whether the Old Testament, the Gospels, or indeed Greek tragedy itself (cf. Schmidt 1978: 3, n. 4).
5   *grasps itself* [sich faßt]: corresponding to 'comprehends itself' [sich begreift] in AO [3.1]. Note also the parallel between 'infinite enthusiasm' [unendliche Begeisterung] as the impersonal subject of this process, and the wrathful unity of 'the prodigious' [das Ungeheure] in AO [3.1].
6   *infinitely, that is to say in oppositions* [unendlich, das heißt in Gegensäzen]: corresponding to 'limitless separation' [gränzenloses Scheiden] in AO [3.1]. It is as if the structure of self-consciousness analysed in the early note on *Being and Judgment* is taken to a self-cancelling extreme: cf. 'daß ich mich mir selbst entgegenseze, mich von mir selbst trenne' (MA, II, 49; AL, 231).
7   *in the form of death* [in der Gestalt des Todes]. Binder interprets this as meaning that the god can be taken as an object by assuming the form of death: 'Der gegenwärtige Gott steht ihr [Ant.] in der Gestalt des Todes entgegen' (1992: 160). See also n. 26 to [2.8].
8   *touched upon* [berührt]: i.e. in AO [3.2]. H. here similarly passes from the content of tragedy to the question of its form, and initially in quite similar terms. But the parallel points made here are then developed in considerably more detail.
9   *the perilous form in the scenes* [die gefährliche Form, in den Auftritten]: see AO [3.3], with commentary at n. 14, which similarly refers to 'the terrifyingly ceremonial forms' [die schröklichfeierlichen Formen].
10 *in a more Greek fashion* [nach griechischerer Art]. H. now introduces a new theme, in what is in effect a long digression extending to the end of [3.3], namely the distinction between ancient Greek and modern forms of representation. The latter are here called 'national' [vaterländisch] forms, or in [3.4] 'Hesperian' (on which see already [2.5]). The awkwardness and complexity of the discussion may arise from it being a last-minute addition: see the letter to Wilmans of 8 December 1803, apologising for a 'delay in sending the manuscripts' (MA, II, 925; AL, 216).
11 *more mediately effective* [mittelbarer factisch]: on the term 'factisch', here translated as 'effective'

mode of representation more immediately so, in that it seizes the more spiritual body. The Greek tragic word is mortally-effective,[12] *because the body that it seizes actually kills. For us, because we stand under the more authentic Zeus,*[13] *who not only holds himself*[14] *between this earth and the savage world of the dead, but also forces the course of nature that is eternally hostile to humanity, on its way into the other world,*[15] *more decidedly down to earth* — *and because this greatly alters the essential and national*[16] *representations, and our poetic art must be national, so that its material is selected according to our view of the world, and its representations national* — *the Greek representations change*[17] *in so far as their main tendency is to be able to grasp oneself, this being where their weakness lay.*[18] *Whereas, on the other hand, the main tendency in the modes of representation of*

rather than 'factive' (C.) or 'factual' (A. and P.), see also AO [3.2] (with commentary at n. 9). I have translated it differently here as compared with AO, taking the emphasis now to be on the agency of the tragic 'word' rather than on its artfulness or artificiality.

12 *mortally-effective* [tödtlichfactisch]: various ways have been proposed for translating this awkward neologism, including 'lethally factive' (C.); 'deadly-factual' (A. and P.); 'efficacement meurtrière' (Court.); 'brutalement meurtrière' (F.); 'fattiva in modo mortale' or 'mortalmente effettiva' (R.). The sense seems to be: resulting in actual death as a result of the agency of the body, hence 'more mediately'. See further [3.3], which introduces the contrasting (and equally unlovely) term 'tödtendfactisch'.

13 *under the more authentic Zeus* [unter dem eigentlicheren Zevs]: probably in the sense that Zeus reveals his true character when seen as a Hesperian god of limits and division. Thus 'un Zeus plus authentique' (Court.); 'Zeus ... plus proprement lui-même' (F.); 'the more essential Zeus' (A.); but alternatively, 'a Zeus more our own' (C.). Binder suggests that Zeus 'bends us back' in the direction of our earth-bound origin: 'uns ins Eigene, in Richtung auf unseren Ursprung zurückbiegt' (1992: 171). Or one might say that it is in relation to we moderns that the god reveals his true nature: 'Zeus [muß] bei den Abendländern größere Mühe aufwenden, daher seinen "Karakter" in einem höheren Grade zeigen' (Analecta 2017: 226). It follows that the true character of the god is better revealed by his role as 'Father of Time' or 'Father of the Earth': see [2.10] and commentary at nn. 35 & 36.

14 *holds himself* [inne hält]: cf. 'stays' (P.); 'pauses' (C. and A.); 'si mantiene' (R.). The sense seems to be that Zeus (for the Greeks) maintains the limits that separate the habitable nature that sustains life, from nature in its ferocious aspect. Hence, elaborating slightly, 'tient à distance' (Court.); 'érige une limite' (F.).

15 *on its way into the other world* [auf seinem Wege in die andre Welt]. A. takes the pronoun to refer to Zeus, rather than to the course of nature; the reading is implausible, especially in view of the parallel passage at [2.10], but consistent with rendering 'innehält' as 'pauses' (see n. 14 above). See also the reference to 'another world' and 'the eccentric sphere of the dead' in AO [1.14].

16 *national* [vaterländischen]: following C. and A., although this is not to be seen as a reference necessarily to a nation state. But cf. 'patriotic' (P.), 'patriotiques' (Court.); and Stierle 1989: 483, n. 4 (suggesting H.'s 'vaterländische Gesänge' as the equivalent of the revolutionary 'chant patriotique'). Here 'vaterländisch' seems to refer to the general character of a culture, which may transcend the limits of a particular nation. In letters to his publisher H. refers apparently without distinction to 'vaterländisch[e] Gesänge' and poems that directly concern 'das Vaterland [...] oder die Zeit' [our country or the times] (MA, II, 926–27; AL, 216, trans. modified), so that Louth can justifiably translate the former as 'poems on our times' (AL, 217); see similarly Pöggeler 1988: 35, and generally Gaier 1987. But 'Vaterland' and 'vaterländisch' may have a more specific meaning in [3.5], from which it is also clear that the ancient forms themselves relate to a (Greek) 'Vaterland'.

17 *change* [verändern sich]: apparently in the sense that, as one passes from the Greek to the modern age, the underlying forms of representation alter. Thus in Court. 'les représentations grecques sont différentes des nôtres'.

18 *their weakness lay* [ihre Schwäche lag]. This passage must be read in the light of the paradox

our own time is to be able to encounter something,[19] *to have a fate, since fatelessness, the* δυσμορον,[20] *is our own weakness. For this reason a Greek also has more dexterity and athletic virtue,*[21] *and however paradoxical the heroes of the Iliad may appear to us, must have this as true <u>excellence</u> and serious virtue. With us this is more subordinated to the proper and fitting.*[22] *And so too the Greek modes of representation and poetic forms are more subordinated*[23] *to the national ones.*

[3.3] *And so <u>the mortally-effective, the actual killing</u>*[24] *<u>through words</u>, is doubtless <u>to be considered more as a peculiarly Greek art-form, and as subordinated to one that is more national</u>. As may well be demonstrated, a national one may be more a deathly-effective*[25] *than a mortally-effective word; not truly ending with murder or death,*[26] *because this is*

expounded in the first letter to Böhlendorff ('Es klingt paradox'), namely that as a result of the process of cultural development ('im Fortschritt der Bildung') an original deficiency is replaced by an advantage (MA, II, 912; AL, 207). Conversely, as discussed in Ch. 6.3 above, it seems that it is above all that original cultural weakness that is exposed in tragedy.

19 *to be able to encounter something* [etwas treffen zu können]: cf. 'to hit upon something' (C.), 'atteindre quelque chose' (Court.). As the context suggests, the sense is that of meeting one's destiny [Geschik]; cf. 'auf solch Schiksaal zu treffen' [τοῦδε τοῦ μόρου τυχεῖν] (MA, II, 335, l. 482 [465]). But see also Analecta 2017: 226, n. 424, suggesting the equivalent 'etwas zu wagen'.

20 δυσμορον: the Greek term connotes a fate that is unhappy rather than absent, and may therefore seem surprising as a gloss on 'fatelessness' [das Schiksaallose]. The term marks a difference from H.'s earlier use of 'schiksaallos' in *Hyperion*, where it describes the blessed state of the gods (MA, I, 745; RB, 192). As Billings points out (2013b: 119–20), *dusmoros* is used repeatedly in *Oedipus at Colonus*: see in particular l. 1109, δυσμόρου γε δύσμορα [sad staves of a sad man], where it is applied to Oed. and the two daughters who support him in his final wanderings; l. 224, where Oed. similarly describes himself as δύσμορος; and ll. 557–59 (respectively Loeb, II, 534–35, 438–39, and 478–79). In [3.3] that second *Oedipus* play is cited as a Greek precursor of modern tragedy. Here, therefore, 'das Schiksaallose' would correspond to the misfortune of the old Oed. in his long wanderings, in contrast to the younger hero who was all-too ready to confront his destiny. See further Chapter 6.3 above.

21 *dexterity and athletic virtue* [Geschik und Athletentugend]: cf. 'skill and greater virtue as athletes' (C.), 'd'adresse et de vertu athlétique' (Court.). On the problem of translating 'Geschik' in this passage see Chapter 6.3 above. It does not seem that it can have the same meaning as in its preceding occurrence; but there is no doubt that in this period H. enjoys exploiting the connections and resonances between 'Geschik', 'Schiksaal', and 'schiklich'. — Note the heroic and Homeric connotations of the athletic victories celebrated in Pindar's *epinikia*, as mentioned in Kurke 2013: 77, 99–102.

22 *the proper and fitting* [Schiklichkeit]: cf. 'propriety' (C.), 'that which is fitting' (A.). See again the discussion in Chapter 6.3.

23 *subordinated* [subordinirt]: apparently in the sense that a modern tragedy would follow instead principles more in accord with our own forms of representation. Cf. [3.3] ('subordinirte Kunstform'), and [3.9] ('der Unterordnung nach').

24 *killing* [Mord]: literally 'murder'; but the subsequent reference to 'murder or death' suggests that a broader meaning is intended.

25 *deathly-effective* [tödtendfactisches]: now putting a name to the contrast already made in [3.2], albeit obscurely, between a violence relating to the body and one that relates more to the spirit or to 'the more spiritual body' [den geistigeren Körper]. Other solutions: 'killing-factual' (A.); 'works killingly' (C.); 'effectivement meurtrissante' (F. and Court.).

26 *not truly ending with murder or death* [nicht eigentlich mit Mord oder Tod endigen]. Cf. 'factisch endigende' in AO [3.2] (although it is not clear that the meaning is the same).

where the tragic must be understood,[27] but more in the manner of 'Oedipus at Colonus',[28] so that *the word* from an inspired mouth is terrible, and kills, but not in a graspable Greek way,[29] in an athletic and plastic spirit[30] where the word seizes the body so that this kills.

[3.4] *Thus the tragic presentation, whether more Greek or more Hesperian,[31] rests upon a more violent or more inexorable dialogue, and choruses[32] — supporting or interpreting the dialogue — which give to the infinite quarrel direction or force, as* suffering organs *of the divinely contending body, which cannot indeed be dispensed with, for even in a tragically-infinite form the god cannot communicate itself to the body absolutely immediately, but must rather be grasped in thought or appropriated in a living fashion. Most of all, however, the tragic presentation consists in the effective word[33] that, more interrelation than something*

---

27 *must be understood* [muß gefaßt werden]. Cf. Aristotle's analysis of the tragic plot or *muthos*: 'These, then, are two components of the plot [τοῦ μύθου] — reversal and recognition. A third is suffering [which is] a destructive or painful action, such as public deaths, physical agony, woundings, etc.'; see *Poetics*, ed. and trans. by Stephen Halliwell, in Aristotle, XXIII, LCL 199 (Cambridge, MA: Harvard University Press, 1995; corrected repr. 1999), 1452b (pp. 66–67). This can also be compared with H.'s conception of the tragic 'word', the latter being a primary meaning of the term *muthos* (Brill, s.v. μῦθος, A); see also n. 34 below.

28 *Oedipus at Colonus* [Oedipus auf Kolonos]: see n. 20 above. The allusion that follows to 'the word from an inspired mouth' [das Wort aus begeistertem Munde] has been taken to be a reference to Oedipus' curse of Polynices (Loeb, II, 558–59, ll. 1383–96): see Böschenstein 2000: 165; Billings 2013b: 120–21, and 2014: 217. But as Billings himself observes 'Polyneices and Eteocles will go into battle and kill one another', so that the curse is 'violent through mediation' (2013b: 121). That might be thought to correspond to the 'more mediately effective' tragic word mentioned in [3.2]. Alternatively the reference could be to the mysterious and terrible voice that summons Oedipus to his death, a death that does not seem to have any physical cause (Loeb, II, 580–85, ll. 1627–28, 1656–65).

29 *graspable Greek way* [griechisch faßlich]: following C.; cf. 'Greek, palpable way' (A.). Contrast 'selon la conception grecque' (F.); 'compréhensible pour les Grecs' (Court.).

30 *in an athletic and plastic spirit* [in athletischem und plastischem Geiste]. The language here can be compared with the second letter to Böhlendorff, where H. speaks of 'Das Athletische der südlichen Menschen' [The athleticism of people in the south] (MA, II, 921; AL, 213). See also the reference to 'athletic virtue' in [3.2].

31 *more Hesperian* [hesperischer]: signifying the 'modern' as opposed to the originally 'Greek'; the term has already been used in [2.5]. It seems that the opposition between the Greek and the Hesperian (or 'more Hesperian') may be found within Greek tragedy itself, as well as corresponding to a broader difference between the ancient and the modern age. On the concept of the Hesperian see further Chapter 6.3 above. — As already noted in relation to the parallel passage in AO [3.2], according to some commentators the contrast between heroic protagonist and chorus reflects one between an archaic Greek past and the contemporary Athenian polis. Thus 'tragedy pitted the realm of mythic heroes against the civic community (in the form of protagonists and chorus)' (Kurke 2013: 6, following Vernant and Vidal-Naquet 1988: 24).

32 *choruses* [Chören]: I have assumed that the remainder of the text (up to the full stop, or semicolon in the original) relates to chorus rather than dialogue (following C., P. and Court., rather than A. or F.). Schmidt (KA, II, 1482–83) observes that the present paragraph has both a retrospective and a prospective function: it recapitulates or elaborates upon points that have already been made, or looks forward to those that are later addressed in more detail.

33 *in the effective word* [in dem factischen Worte]: associated in [3.2] with the dialogic scenes as opposed to the choruses. As Corßen puts it, 'in dem "faktischen Wort", das heißt, in dem gesamten Schicksalszusammenhang des Dramas, der dem Dialog [...] zu Grunde lieg' (1949: 148). This 'Wort'

*expressed,*³⁴ *runs fatefully from beginning to end; in the nature of the action;*³⁵ *in the grouping of the characters*³⁶ *against one another; and in the form of reason*³⁷ *that takes shape amid the fearful idleness*³⁸ *of a tragic age, which, as it presented itself in oppositions in its savage origin, afterwards, in a humane age, stands as secure opinion born of divine fate.*

[3.5] *The nature of the action in 'Antigone' is that of an uprising,*³⁹ *which — insofar as it is a national matter — depends on everyone, being seized as by an infinite reversal, and shaken, feeling themselves in the infinite form in which they are shaken. For a national reversal is the reversal of all modes of representation and forms.*⁴⁰ *However, a total reversal in these is, like any total reversal with no restraint, forbidden to a person as a knowing being. And in a national reversal, where the whole shape of things changes, and nature and necessity (which always remain) incline to another shape, going over into wilderness or a new shape — in such a change everything merely necessary is a partisan of change, so that in the possibility of such a change the neutral also*⁴¹ *(not only those who are* <u>opposed</u> *to the national form, being seized by a spiritual power of the age*⁴²*) can be compelled*

is also, it seems, to be contrasted with the 'das reine Wort' (see AO [1.7] and commentary at n. 25), and with 'das Wort aus begeistertem Munde' (AA [3.3]).
34   *more interrelation than something expressed* [mehr Zusammenhang, als ausgesprochen]: cf. 'more a context than an utterance' (C.); 'par sa cohérence plutôt que par son expression' (Court.). H. seems to be referring to the plot of the tragedy operating as machine of fate, Corßen's 'Schicksalszusammenhang des Dramas' (n. 33 above), comparable to the Aristotelian *muthos* (n. 27 above, and cf. Koppenfels 1996: 361).
35   *nature of the action* [Art des Hergangs]: following A.; cf. C. ('how the plot proceeds'). This looks forward to [3.5].
36   *grouping of the characters* [Gruppirung der Personen]: see [3.6] and [3.7].
37   *form of reason* [Vernunftform]: see [3.8].
38   *amid the fearful idleness* [in der furchtbaren Muße]: following the emended text in KA, II, 919, rather than MA, II, 375 (which like the original has 'Muse', as in Melpomene the Muse of tragedy). The emendation can be justified by a comparison with AO [3.3] ('in müßiger Zeit'), and see the commentary there at n. 16. Beißner also gives an orthographical argument (1961: 61–62).
39   *uprising* [Aufruhr]: as Cairns notes (2016: 124), H.'s translation similarly describes Ant.'s action against the city as an 'Aufstand' (MA, II, 321, l. 81 [79], and 351, l. 942 [907]), corresponding to βίαι πολιτῶν [in defiance of the citizens] (Griff, 279).
40   *modes of representation and forms* [Vorstellungsarten und Formen]: cf. the letter to Ebel of 10 January 1797, speaking of 'eine künftige Revolution der Gesinnungen und Vorstellungsarten' [a future revolution of attitudes and ways of seeing things] (MA, II, 643; AL, 84). On the one hand the notion of a 'national reversal' [vaterländische Umkehr] may seem to have a more specific, even political flavour here than the reference to 'national' poetic forms in [3.2]; but on the other, here too the 'reversal' extends to the modes of representation themselves (and indeed to the 'religious, political and moral').
41   *the neutral also* [auch der Neutrale]: apparently a reference to the position of Haem., who has loyalties to both of the opposing figures of Ant. and Creon (Harrison 1975: 189); or even, Böschenstein suggests, to the Swiss Confederation (see n. 43 below).
42   *by a spiritual power of the age* [von einer Geistesgewalt der Zeit]: the original has a semicolon after 'Zeit', so that this phrase may be intended to apply only to those who are actively 'opposed', and not to the more 'neutral'. That solution is tentatively adopted here, as it is by P. and R. (but not by others). Schmidt offers the same interpretation, but notes that the semicolon may be a printer's error (KA, II, 1495). The latter hypothesis might indeed be the more plausible one, i.e. that it is only the spirit of the age that can compel an otherwise 'neutral' figure to take sides.

to be patriotic, present, in infinite form, the religious, political and moral form of their native land. (προφανηθι θεος).[43] And such serious observations[44] are necessary for the understanding of Greek, or any authentic, works of art. The proper kind of procedure[45] in the case of an uprising (which admittedly is only one kind of national reversal, and has a still more defined character) has just been indicated.[46]

[3.6] *If such a phenomenon is tragic, it proceeds by reaction, and the formless takes fire at the all-too formal.*[47] *What is characteristic here, therefore, is that those subsumed by* <u>such</u> *a fate do not, as in 'Oedipus', stand in the form of ideas, as quarrelling over the truth, and like someone who defends their intellect; nor as one who defends their life, property or honour, like the characters in 'Ajax'; but rather that they stand against one another as persons in the narrower sense, as persons of a certain rank,*[48] *that they take sides against one another.*[49]

[3.7] *The grouping of such persons is, as in 'Antigone', to be compared to a running competition, where the loser is the one who first runs out of breath and jostles their opponent, while the struggle in 'Oedipus' can be compared to a boxing match, that in 'Ajax' to a fencing bout.*[50]

43   προφανηθι θεος: i.e. 'be manifest, god!'. The deity in question is the Dionysus of the fifth stasimon (MA, II, 360–61, ll. 1198–99 [1149]: 'Zevs Geburt! | Werd' offenbar!'), here invoked as the god of revolutionary transformation. See Böschenstein 1989d: 12–16, also finding references to the French Revolutionary wars, and even to the Swiss Confederation ('der Neutrale'). Note how, in accordance with his interpretative translation practice, H. renders Bacchus as 'Freudengott' at l. 1169 [1121].
44   *serious observations* [ernstliche Bemerkungen]: apparently in the sense of those aspiring to theoretical generality (see n. 34 to [2.10]).
45   *kind of procedure* [Verfahrungsart]: i.e. perhaps its specific method of poetic presentation (cf. AO [1.2]).
46   *just been indicated* [eben angedeutet]: although it does not seem that H. has explained the more specific character of an 'uprising', as opposed to a 'national reversal' generally.
47   *the formless ... at the all too formal* [das unförmliche ... an allzuförmlichem]: in the sense perhaps that Creon relies on his formal authority as ruler of Thebes (MA, II, 345, ll. 765–73 [736–44]), Ant. on the unwritten laws of the gods (MA, II, 335, ll. 470–72 [453–55]). See also [3.8].
48   *persons of a certain rank* [Standespersonen]: see also n. 49 below. Note that there are further comparisons between the three plays in both [2.13] and [3.7]. For H., the first Oedipus play, *Oedipus Tyrannus*, turns above all on the hero's quest for the truth (see AO [2.2]). In *Ajax* the hero has been driven mad following a slight to his honour (the award of Achilles' arms to Odysseus). Here, by contrast, what is at stake is Creon's position as ruler of Thebes, and Ant. as disobedient subject from an illustrious if ill-fated family.
49   *take sides against one another* [sich formalisiren]: cf. Littré, s.v. (se) formaliser, and Grimm, s.v. formalisieren. Böschenstein (2006b: 71–72) finds the meanings here both of standing opposed (including as one meaning of 'Standespersonen') and of balancing out, with an allusion also to the terms 'förmlich' etc. found in this paragraph and in [3.8]. It does seem that H. is again engaging in some characteristic word-play.
50   These comparisons might be regarded as directions for performance (see Castellari 2018: 59–60).

[3.8] *The form of reason that here tragically takes shape is political, and indeed republican, because the balance is held too equally between Creon and Antigone, the formal and the anti-formal.[51] That shows itself particularly at the end, where Creon is almost mistreated by his servants.[52]*

[3.9] *Sophocles is right. This is the fate of his times and form of his native land. One can no doubt idealize, e.g. choose the best moment; but the national modes of representation — at least with respect to their subordination[53] — may not be altered by the poet, who presents the world on a reduced scale.[54] For us such a form is precisely of use,[55] because the infinite — such as the spirit of nation states and the world — can in any event be grasped only from a skew perspective.[56] But the national forms of our poets, where they exist, are nonetheless to be preferred, because they are not merely there to learn to understand the spirit of the times, but to hold it fast and to feel it[57] once it has been comprehended and learned.*

51   *between ... the formal and the anti-formal* [zwischen ... förmlichem und gegenförmlichem]: cf. [3.6] with n. 47.
52   *mistreated by his servants* [von seinen Knechten ... gemißhandelt]: or 'manhandled' (C.). The reference may be to MA, II, 367, ll. 1375–76, 1390 [1320–21, 1339], where Creon orders (or begs?) his 'servants' [Diener] to lead him away 'step by step' [Schritt vor Schritt] (SP, 365–66). Thus H.'s commentary might again be taken as a stage direction, indicating how the scene is to be played. Billings' reference to ll. 1388–89 [1337–38] is surely less plausible (2014: 220). It is true that H.'s edition attributes those lines to the messenger rather than, as in Griff or Loeb, the chorus; but in any event that would be a single messenger rather than a plurality of servants, and the sense of being roughly treated is lost.
53   *with respect to their subordination* [der Unterordnung nach]: following A.; cf. 'in their hierarchy' (C.). The thought seems to be the same as at the end of [3.2] and beginning of [3.3] (which employ the term 'subordinirt'). Thus poetic forms are products of a particular time and place with its governing modes of representation, and in that sense are 'subordinated' to those forms. See similarly Kurz 1998: 187.
54   *on a reduced scale* [im verringerten Maasstab]. Cf. the formula in *Wenn der Dichter* ...: 'als eigene Welt der Form nach, als Welt in der Welt' [as an own world according to its form, as a world in the world] (MA, II, 86; AL, 285); and see generally Kurz 1998: 182–89.
55   *precisely of use* [gerade tauglich]: cf. 'justement précieuse' (Court.); rather than 'may still just about be used' (C.), or 'is just usable' (A.). Thus the ancient forms are without doubt useful (or 'suitable') in understanding matters that are difficult to grasp by more direct means (see below).
56   *from a skew perspective* [aus linkischem Gesichtspunct]: cf. 'from an askew perspective' (P.); 'from some off-centre point of view' (C.). The apparently more literal 'from a clumsy standpoint' (A.), or 'd'un point de vue maladroit' (Court. and F.), do not give the right sense. Thus it seems that 'linkisch' is used here in accordance with one of the senses of the French 'gauche', namely that of 'skew' or 'oblique' (Littré, s.v. gauche, 1). Cf. Kurz 1998: 187–88, relating this image of an oblique perspective to the thought that poets represent the world on a 'reduced scale'; although like Billings (2014: 221) Kurz still discerns an element of awkwardness ('schief, unbeholfen, beschränkt'). It seems, in any event, that H. is using the term in a different sense from his translation of ἀμήχανος (MA, II, 321, l. 81 [79]), or in the *Nachtgesang* 'Ganymed' (MA, I, 444, l. 13).
57   *to hold it fast and to feel it* [ihn festzuhalten und zu fühlen]. Cf. the opening lines of *Wenn der Dichter* ...: 'Wenn der Dichter einmal des Geistes mächtig ist, wenn er die gemeinschaftliche Seele [...] *gefühlt* und sich zugeeignet, sie *vestgehalten*, sich ihrer versichert hat' [When the poet is once in command of the spirit, when he has *felt* and appropriated the common soul [...], has *held it fast*, assured himself of it] (MA, II, 77; AL, 277; my emphasis).

Die Bedeutung der Tragödien ...

This short text (MA, II, 114) may be a fragment of the projected 'introduction' to the Sophocles translations mentioned in three letters to Wilmans (MA, II, 924–27; AL, 215–17). For a more detailed discussion see Chapter 5 above. There are previous translations by Thomas Pfau, Jeremy Adler, Denise Naville, Jean-François Courtine, and Riccardo Ruschi.[1]

[1] The meaning of tragedies is most easily understood by means of paradox. [2] For everything elemental,[2] because all capacity is justly and equally apportioned, appears to be sure not in original strength, not really,[3] but properly[4] only in its weakness; so that the light of life and appearance quite properly[5] belong to the weakness of every whole.[6] [3] Now in the tragic the sign is in itself insignificant, without effect, but the elemental is straight out.[7] [4] For the elemental can properly appear only in its weakness; but insofar as the sign is in itself posited as insignificant = 0, the elemental, the hidden ground of every nature, can also present itself. [5] If Nature presents itself properly in its weakest endowment, then the sign when it presents itself in its strongest endowment = 0.

---

1   See respectively (1) *Essays and Letters on Theory* (Albany: State University of New York Press, 1988), p. 89; (2) AL, 316; (3) *Œuvres*, trans. by Philippe Jaccottet and others (Paris: Gallimard, 1967), p. 644; (4) *Fragments de poétique et autres textes* (Paris: Imprimerie nationale Éditions, 2006), pp. 363–64 — referred to below as 'P.', 'A.', 'N.' and 'Court.' — and (5) *Scritti di estetica*, 2nd edition, Testi e documenti, 144 (Milan: SE, 2004), p. 149.
2   elemental [Ursprüngliche]: cf. 'primal' (A.); or perhaps 'originary'. As Courtine's commentary suggests, this notion can be compared with the 'aorgic' aspect of nature discussed in *Die tragische Ode ...* (MA, I, 868–70; AL, 261–63). See also 'the power of nature' referred to in AO [1.14] and [3.1]. The notion is explained further in [4] below as 'the hidden ground of every nature'.
3   not really [nicht wirklich]: these words in the manuscript are omitted from the versions established by StA and KA, but included in FHA and MA, and in *Theoretische Schriften*, ed. by Johann Kreuzer; Philosophische Bibliothek, 509 (Hamburg: Meiner, 1998), p. 93. Cf. KA, II, 561.
4   properly [eigentlich]: cf. 'actually' (A.). The immediately following 'only' [nur] is similarly omitted in StA and KA.
5   quite properly [rechteigentlich]: following P. Cf. 'really and essentially' (A.); 'de manière tout à fait propre' (Court.); 'au vrai' (N.).
6   the light of life and appearance ... belong to the weakness of every whole [das Lebenslicht und die Erscheinung der Schwäche jedes Ganzen angehört]: rather than 'the light of life and the manifestation of weakness are part of every whole' (A.).
7   straight out [gerade heraus]: following A.; cf. 'right there' (Louth 1998: 77). Cf. also 'franchement à découvert' (Court.); 'ressort directement' (N.); rather than 'straightforward' (P.).

BIBLIOGRAPHY

Any websites mentioned were accessed on 3 July 2019 or after.

1. Dictionaries

The Brill Dictionary of Ancient Greek, by Franco Montanari, English Edition ed. by Madeleine Goh and Chad Schroeder (Leiden: Brill, 2015)
A Greek-English Lexicon, by Henry George Liddell and Robert Scott, 9th edn 1940, rev. by Henry Stuart Jones and others (Oxford: Clarendon Press, 1996)
Deutsches Wörterbuch von Jacob und Wilhelm Grimm, 16 vols (Leipzig: Hirzel, 1854–1961) <www.woerterbuchnetz.de//cgi-bin/WBNetz/wbgui_py?sigle=DWB>
Dictionnaire de la langue française, by E. Littré (Paris: Hachette, 1873–1874; supplement 1878), electronic version by François Gannaz <https://www.littre.org>

2. Primary sources: collections

Early Greek Philosophy, ed. and trans. by André Laks and Glenn W. Most, 9 vols, LCL 524-32 (Cambridge, MA: Harvard University Press, 2016)
The Hellenistic Philosophers, ed. and trans. by A. A. Long and D. N. Sedley, 2 vols (Cambridge: Cambridge University Press, 1987)
Ποίησις φιλόσοφος. *Poesis philosophica, Vel saltem, Reliquiæ poesis philosophicæ, Empedoclis, Parmenidis, Xenophanis, Cleanthis, Timonis, Epicharmi* [...], ed. by Henr. Stephanus [Henri II Estienne] ([Geneva]: 1573) <https://www.e-rara.ch/doi/10.3931/e-rara-6276>

3. Primary sources: Hölderlin

These sources are listed in chronological order, and attributed to an editor only where the German text is included.

HÖLDERLIN, FRIEDRICH, *Sämtliche Werke: Historisch-kritische Ausgabe*, ed. by Norbert von Hellingrath, Friedrich Seebaß and Ludwig von Pigenot, 6 vols (Munich: Müller, for vols I, IV and V; Berlin: Propyläen, for vols II, III and VI; 1913–23)
—— *Sämtliche Werke: Große Stuttgarter Ausgabe*, ed. by Friedrich Beißner, Adolf Beck and Ute Oelmann, 8 vols (Stuttgart: Kohlhammer, 1946–1985) <https://www.wlb-stuttgart.de/sammlungen/hoelderlin-archiv/sammlung-digital/zur-stuttgarter-hoelderlin-ausgabe-online>
—— *Œuvres*, trans. by Philippe Jaccottet and others (Paris: Gallimard, 1967)
—— *Sämtliche Werke: Historisch-kritische Ausgabe ('Frankfurter Ausgabe')*, ed. by D. E. Sattler, 20 vols with 3 supplements (Frankfurt a.M.: Stroemfeld, 1976–2008)
—— *Hymns and Fragments*, ed. and trans. by Richard Sieburth (Princeton, NJ: Princeton University Press, 1984)
—— *Essays and Letters on Theory*, trans. by Thomas Pfau (Albany: State University of New York Press, 1988)

―― *Sämtliche Werke und Briefe*, ed. by Michael Knaupp, 3 vols (Munich: Hanser, 1992–93)
―― *Sämtliche Werke und Briefe*, ed. by Jochen Schmidt, 3 vols (Frankfurt a.M.: Deutscher Klassiker Verlag, 1992–94)
―― *Theoretische Schriften*, ed. by Johann Kreuzer; Philosophische Bibliothek, 509 (Hamburg: Meiner, 1998)
―― *Tutte le liriche*, ed. and trans. by Luigi Reitani (Milan: Mondadori, 2001; repr. 2004)
―― *Poems and Fragments*, ed. and trans. by Michael Hamburger, 4th edn (London: Anvil Press Poetry, 2004; rev. 2007, repr. 2013)
―― *Scritti di estetica*, trans. by Riccardo Ruschi, 2nd edition, Testi e documenti, 144 (Milan: SE, 2004)
―― *Fragments de poétique et autres textes*, ed. and trans. by Jean-François Courtine (Paris: Imprimerie nationale Éditions, 2006)
―― *Hyperion or the Hermit in Greece*, trans. by Ross Benjamin (Brooklyn, NY: Archipelago Books, 2008)
―― *Odes and Elegies*, ed. and trans. by Nick Hoff (Middletown, CT: Wesleyan University Press, 2008)
―― *Essays and Letters*, trans. by Jeremy Adler and Charlie Louth (London: Penguin Books, 2009)
―― *Selected Poetry*, trans. by David Constantine (Hexham: Bloodaxe Books, 2018)
―― *Hyperion, or the Hermit in Greece*, trans. by Howard Gaskill (Cambridge: Open Book Publishers, 2019) <https://doi.org/10.11647/OBP.0160>

4. Other primary sources

ARISTOTLE, *Poetics*, ed. and trans. by Stephen Halliwell, in Aristotle, XXIII, LCL 199 (Cambridge, MA: Harvard University Press, 1995; corrected repr. 1999), pp. 1–141
BOILEAU [NICOLAS BOILEAU-DESPRÉAUX], *Œuvres*, ed. by Françoise Escal (Paris: Gallimard, 1966)
―― *Les Oeuvres de M. Boileau Despreaux, avec des éclaircissemens historiques. Nouvelle édition revue et corrigée*, 2 vols (Paris, 1735)
DIOGENES LAERTIUS, *Lives of eminent philosophers*, ed. and trans. by R. D. Hicks, 2 vols, LCL 184 and 185 (Cambridge, MA: Harvard University Press, 1925; repr. 1979–80)
HEGEL, GEORG WILHELM FRIEDRICH, *Phänomenologie des Geistes*, ed. by Hans-Friedrich Wessels and Heinrich Clairmont; Philosophische Bibliothek, 414 (Hamburg: Meiner, 1988)
―― *Phenomenology of Spirit*, trans. by Michael Inwood (Oxford: Oxford University Press, 2018)
HESIOD, ed. and trans. by Glenn W. Most, 2nd edn, 2 vols, LCL 57 and 503 (Cambridge, MA: Harvard University Press, 2018)
KANT, IMMANUEL, *Gesammelte Schriften*, Akademie-Textausgabe, 9 vols (Berlin: Reimer, 1902–17 and De Gruyter, 1923; repr. Berlin: De Gruyter, 1968)
―― *Kritik der reinen Vernunft*, ed. by Ingeborg Heidemann (Stuttgart: Reclam, 1966; repr. 1980)
[PSEUDO-]LONGINUS, *On the Sublime* [Περὶ ὕψους], ed. and trans. by W. H. Fyfe, rev. by Donald Russell, in Aristotle, XXIII, LCL 199 (Cambridge, MA: Harvard University Press, 1995; corrected repr. 1999), pp. 143–305
MARCUS AURELIUS ANTONINUS, *Ad se ipsum libri XII* [Τῶν εἰς ἑαυτόν], ed. by Joachim Dalfen, 2nd edn (Leipzig: Teubner, 1987)
―― *Meditations*, trans. by Martin Hammond (London: Penguin Books, 2006)
PINDAR, ed. and trans. by William H. Race, 2 vols, LCL 56 and 485 (Cambridge, MA: Harvard University Press, 1997; revised repr. 2012)

—— *Olympia, Pythia, Nemea, Isthmia* etc., 2 vols, ed. by Henr. Stephanus [Henri II Estienne] ([Geneva]: 1560)
PLATO, *Symposium*, trans. by Michael Joyce, in *The Collected Dialogues of Plato Including the Letters*, ed. by Edith Hamilton and Huntington Cairns; Bollingen Series, 71 (Princeton, NJ: Princeton University Press, 1961; repr. 1978), pp. 526–74
ROUSSEAU, JEAN-JACQUES, *Œuvres complètes*, ed. by Bernard Gagnebin and Marcel Raymond, 5 vols (Paris: Gallimard, 1959–1995)
SCHLEGEL, FRIEDRICH, 'Gespräch über die Poesie', in *Athenaeum*, ed. by August Wilhelm Schlegel and Friedrich Schlegel, 3 vols, 1798–1800 (Berlin; repr. Darmstadt: Wissenschaftliche Buchgesellschaft, 1992), III (1800), 58–128, 169–87
SOPHOCLES, ed. and trans. by Hugh Lloyd-Jones, 2 vols, LCL 20 and 21 (Cambridge, MA: Harvard University Press 1994; corrected repr. 1997–1998)
—— *Antigone*, ed. by Mark Griffith (Cambridge: Cambridge University Press, 1999)
—— *Oedipus Rex*, ed. by R. D. Dawe (Cambridge: Cambridge University Press, 1982; repr. 1986)

5. Secondary literature

Note that the *Hölderlin-Jahrbuch*, up to and including vol. 38 (2012–2013), can be accessed at <https://www.hoelderlin-gesellschaft.de/website/de/publikationen/jahresbuecher-digital/jahrbuecher-digital>

ALBERT, CLAUDIA. 1998. 'Allharmonie und Schweigen: Musikalische Motive in Hölderlins *Hyperion*', in Bay 1998, pp. 161–75
ANDRÉ, ROBERT. 2000. 'Hölderlins Auf-Gabe und die Ode "Blödigkeit"', in *Das Denken der Sprache und die Performanz des Literarischen um 1800*, ed. by Stephan Jaeger and Stefan Willer (Würzburg: Königshausen & Neumann), pp. 55–73
ARBURG, HANS-GEORG VON. 2009. '"Die bloße Vocalmusik ist eigentlich, was in den bildenden Künsten das Nackende ist": Pathosformeln zwischen Literatur, Musik und Malerei bei Wilhelm Heinse', in *Ekstatische Kunst — Besonnenes Wort: Aby Warburg und die Denkräume der Ekphrasis*, ed. by Peter Kofler; Essay & Poesie, 25 (Bozen: Edition Sturzflüge), pp. 145–64
ARNOLD, HEINZ LUDWIG (ed.). 1996. *Friedrich Hölderlin* (Munich: Edition Text + Kritik)
BACHMAIER, HELMUT. 1979. 'Theoretische Aporie und tragische Negativität: Zur Genesis der tragischen Reflexion bei Hölderlin', in *Hölderlin: Transzendentale Reflexion der Poesie*, ed. by Helmut Bachmaier, Thomas Horst and Peter Reisinger (Stuttgart: Klett-Cotta), pp. 83–145
BAEUMER, MAX L. 1966. *Heinse-Studien* (Stuttgart: Metzler)
BAGORDO, ANDREAS. 2012. 'Hölderlin und Sappho?', in *Hölderlin: Literatur und Politik*, ed. by Valérie Lawitschka; Turm-Vorträge, 7 (Tübingen: Hölderlin-Gesellschaft; Eggingen: Edition Isele), pp. 278–95
BARR, STEPHEN. 1965. *Experiments in Topology* (London: Murray)
BARTEL, HEIKE. 2000. *'Centaurengesänge': Friedrich Hölderlins Pindarfragmente*, Epistemata: Reihe Literaturwissenschaft, 318 (Würzburg: Königshausen & Neumann)
BASSERMANN-JORDAN, GABRIELE VON. 2008. '"Verborgenen Sinn enthält das Schöne!": Zur Liebes und Schönheitsthematik in den frühen Fassungen der *Hyperion*-Texte', in *Nur Narr? Nur Dichter? Über die Beziehungen von Literatur und Philosophie*, ed. by Roland Duhamel and Guillaume van Gemert (Würzburg: Königshausen & Neumann), pp. 165–83
BAUM, MANFRED. 1965. 'Hölderlins Pindar-Fragment "Das Höchste"', *Hölderlin-Jahrbuch*, 13 (1963–1964): 65–76

BAY, HANSJÖRG (ed.). 1998. *'Hyperion' — terra incognita: Expeditionen in Hölderlins Roman* (Opladen: Westdeutscher Verlag)

—— 2002. 'De revolutionibus: Bahnen und Bahnungen im Werk Hölderlins', *MLN*, 117: 599–633

—— 2003. *'Ohne Rückkehr': Utopische Intention und poetischer Prozeß in Hölderlins 'Hyperion'* (Munich: Fink)

BEAUFRET, JEAN. 1983. *Hölderlin et Sophocle*, 2nd edn ([Paris]: Gérard Monfort; ebook FeniXX, 2015, Kindle version retrieved from Amazon.co.uk)

BEISER, FREDERICK C. 2002. *German Idealism: The Struggle against Subjectivism (1781–1801)* (Cambridge, MA: Harvard University Press; repr. 2008)

—— 2004. 'The Limits of Enlightenment', in Wellbery and others, pp. 418–24

BEISSNER, FRIEDRICH. 1961. *Hölderlins Übersetzungen aus dem Griechischen*, 2nd edn (Stuttgart: Metzler)

BELFIORE, ELIZABETH S. 2012. *Socrates' Daimonic Art: Love for Wisdom in Four Platonic Dialogues* (Cambridge: Cambridge University Press)

BÉNATOUÏL, THOMAS. 2009. 'How Industrious can Zeus be? The Extent and Objects of Divine Activity in Stoicism', in Salles, pp. 24–45

BENN, M. B. 1959. 'Hölderlin and Sophocles', *German Life and Letters*, 12 (1958–1959): 161–73

—— 1962. *Hölderlin and Pindar*, Anglica Germanica, 4 (The Hague: Mouton)

BENNHOLDT-THOMSEN, ANKE. 1967. *Stern und Blume: Untersuchungen zur Sprachauffassung Hölderlins* (Bonn: Bouvier)

—— 1997. '"Andenken": L'importance de la topographie pour la poétique et la philosophie de l'histoire dans l'œuvre tardive de Hölderlin', trans. by Sylvie Kubisch and Beate Kendler, in *Bordeaux au temps de Hölderlin*, ed. by Gilbert Merlio and Nicole Pelletier (Bern: Lang), pp. 265–86

—— 1998. 'Dissonanzen in der späten Naturauffassung Hölderlins', *Hölderlin-Jahrbuch*, 30 (1996–1997): 15–41

—— 2002. '"Nachtgesänge"', in Kreuzer 2002, pp. 336–46

—— 2005. '"Wir müssen die Mythe (...) beweisbarer darstellen": Hölderlins moderne Rezeption der Antigone', in *Mythenkorrekturen: Zu einer paradoxalen Form der Mythenrezeption*, ed. by Martin Vöhler and Bernd Seidensticker; Spectrum Literaturwissenschaft, 3 (Berlin: De Gruyter), pp. 181–99

BENNHOLDT-THOMSEN, ANKE, and ALFREDO GUZZONI. 1999. *Analecta Hölderliana [sic]: Zu Hermetik des Spätwerks* (Würzburg: Königshausen & Neumann)

—— 2004. *Analecta Hölderliniana II: Die Aufgabe des Vaterlands* (Würzburg: Königshausen & Neumann)

—— 2007. *Analecta Hölderliniana III: Hesperische Verheißungen* (Würzburg: Königshausen & Neumann)

—— 2017. *Analecta Hölderliniana IV: Zur Dreidimensionalität der Natur* (Würzburg: Königshausen & Neumann)

BERTHEAU, JOCHEN. 2003. *Hölderlins französische Bildung*, Heidelberger Beiträge zur deutschen Literatur, 14 (Frankfurt a.M.: Lang)

BEYER, UWE. 1993. *Mythologie und Vernunft: Vier philosophische Studien zu Friedrich Hölderlin* (Tübingen: Niemeyer)

BIGGS, NORMAN. 1993. 'The Development of Topology', in Fauvel, Flood and Wilson, pp. 105–19

BILLINGS, JOSHUA. 2010. 'Hyperion's Symposium: an Erotics of Reception', *Classical Receptions Journal*, 2: 4–24

—— 2013a. 'Choral Dialectics: Hölderlin and Hegel', in *Choral Mediations in Greek*

Tragedy, ed. by Renaud Gagné and Marianne Govers Hopman (Cambridge: Cambridge University Press), pp. 317–38

—— 2013b. 'The Ends of Tragedy: Oedipus at Colonus and German Idealism', *Arion*, 21: 113–31

—— 2014. *Genealogy of the Tragic: Greek Tragedy and German Philosophy* (Princeton, NJ: Princeton University Press)

BINDER, WOLFGANG. 1963. 'Hölderlins Namenssymbolik', *Hölderlin-Jahrbuch*, 12 (1961–1962): 95–204

—— 1992. *Hölderlin und Sophokles: Eine Vorlesung von Wolfgang Binder gehalten im Sommersemester 1984 an der Universität Zürich*, ed. by Uvo Hölscher; Turm-Vorträge, 4 (Tübingen: Hölderlin-Gesellschaft)

BOMSKI, FRANZISKA. 2014. *Die Mathematik im Denken und Dichten von Novalis: Zum Verhältnis von Literatur und Wissen um 1800*, Deutsche Literatur Studien und Quellen, 15 (Berlin: De Gruyter)

BÖSCHENSTEIN, BERNHARD. 1959. *Hölderlins Rheinhymne*, Zürcher Beiträge zur deutschen Literatur- und Geistesgeschichte, 16 (Zurich: Atlantis)

—— 1989a. *'Frucht des Gewitters': Hölderlins Dionysos als Gott der Revolution* (Frankfurt a.M.: Insel)

—— 1989b. 'Gott und Mensch in den Chorliedern der Hölderlinschen *Antigone*' in 1989a, pp. 54–71

—— 1989c. '"Was nennest du Glück, was Unglück? ... mein Vater!": Heinse in Hölderlins Dichtung', in 1989a, pp. 91–113

—— 1989d. 'Zu Hölderlins Dionysos-Bild', in 1989a, pp. 12–29

—— 1995a. 'Göttliche Instanz und irdische Antwort in Hölderlins Übersetzungsmodellen: Pindar, Hymnen — Sophokles — Pindar, Fragmente', *Hölderlin-Jahrbuch*, 29 (1994–1995): 47–63 (also in 2006c: 49–62)

—— 1995b. 'Hölderlins *Oedipus* — Hölderlins *Antigonä*', in *Hölderlin und die Moderne: Eine Bestandaufnahme*, ed. by Gerhard Kurz, Valérie Lawitschka and Jürgen Wertheimer (Tübingen: Attempto), pp. 224–39

—— 1995c. 'Le renversement du texte: Hölderlin interprète de Pindare', *Littérature*, 99: 53–61

—— 1999. '"Brod und Wein": From the "Classical" First Version to the Later Revision', trans. by Georgia Albert, in Fioretos, pp. 321–39 (see 2006a)

—— 2000. '*Oedipus auf Kolonos* in Hölderlins Dichtung, Übersetzung und Tragödientheorie', *Hölderlin-Jahrbuch*, 31 (1998–1999): 162–67

—— 2002. 'Sophokles-Anmerkungen', in Kreuzer 2002, pp. 247–53

—— 2004. 'Hölderlin und Rousseau: Der Garten als Asyl und Elysium', *Hölderlin-Jahrbuch*, 33 (2002–2003): 118–21

—— 2006a. '"Brod und Wein": Von der "klassischen" Reinschrift zur späten Überarbeitung', in 2006c, pp. 26–48 (originally in *Hölderlin: Christentum und Antike*, ed. by Valérie Lawitschka; Turm-Vorträge, 3 (Tübingen: Hölderlin-Gesellschaft, 1991), pp. 173–200)

—— 2006b. '"... du scheinst ein rotes Wort zu färben?"': Hölderlin als Übersetzer des Sophokles", in 2006c, pp. 63–77

—— 2006c. *Von Morgen nach Abend: Filiationen der Dichtung von Hölderlin zu Celan* (Munich: Fink)

—— 2015a. 'Hölderlins Antigone als Antitheos', *Hölderlin-Jahrbuch*, 39 (2014–2015): 9–21

—— 2015b. 'Hölderlins *Antigonä*: Dichtung und Deutung "heiligen Wahnsinns"', in Doering and Kreuzer, pp. 113–25

BOTHE, HENNING. 1998. 'Jovialität: Anmerkungen zu Hölderlins Ode "Natur und Kunst oder Saturn und Jupiter"', *Hölderlin-Jahrbuch*, 30 (1996–1997): 226–34

Bowie, Andrew. 2003. *Aesthetics and Subjectivity: From Kant to Nietzsche*, 2nd edition (Manchester: Manchester University Press)
Bowie, Malcolm. 1978. *Mallarmé and the Art of Being Difficult* (Cambridge: Cambridge University Press; repr. 2008)
Brague, Rémi. 1994. 'Ein rätselhaftes Zitat über Aristoteles in Hölderlins "Anmerkungen über Oedipus [sic]"', in *Idealismus mit Folgen: Die Epochenschwelle um 1800 in Kunst und Geisteswissenschaften*, ed. by Hans-Jürgen Gawoll and Christoph Jamme (Munich: Fink), pp. 69–74
Brandt, Reinhard. 2002. 'Friedrich Hölderlin: "Der Zeitgeist"', in *Metamorphosen: Wandlungen und Verwandlungen in Literatur, Sprache und Kunst von der Antike bis zur Gegenwart*, ed. by Heidi Marek, Anne Neuschäfer and Susanne Tichy (Wiesbaden: Harrassowitz), pp. 223–30
Bréhier, Émile. 1970. *La théorie des incorporels dans l'ancien stoïcisme*, 4th edn (Paris: Vrin)
——1971. *Chrysippe et l'ancien stoïcisme*, 2nd edn (Paris: Presses Universitaires de France)
Bremer, Dieter. 1998. '"Versöhnung ist mitten im Streit": Hölderlins Entdeckung Heraklits', *Hölderlin-Jahrbuch*, 30 (1996–1997): 173–99
——2001. 'Hölderlin als Pindar-Übersetzer', in Lawitschka 2001, pp. 157–73
Bröcker, Walter. 1959. 'Zu Hölderlins Ödipus-Deutung', in *Martin Heidegger zum Siebzigsten Geburtstag*, ed. by Günther Neske (Pfüllingen: Neske), pp. 19–23
Brody, Jules. 1958. *Boileau and Longinus* (Geneva: Droz)
Brooke, Christopher. 2012. *Philosophic Pride: Stoicism and Political Thought from Lipsius to Rousseau* (Princeton, NJ: Princeton University Press)
Brouwer, René. 2014. *The Stoic Sage: The Early Stoics on Wisdom, Sagehood and Socrates* (Cambridge: Cambridge University Press)
Brunschwig, Jacques. 1994. 'The Stoic Theory of the Supreme Genus and Platonic Ontology', in *Papers in Hellenistic Philosophy*, trans. by Janet Lloyd (Cambridge: Cambridge University Press), pp. 92–157
——2000. 'Stoicism', in Brunschwig and Lloyd, pp. 977–96
Brunschwig, Jacques, and Sir Geoffrey E. R. Lloyd (eds). 2000. *Greek Thought: A Guide to Classical Knowledge* (Cambridge, MA: Harvard University Press)
Budelmann, Felix. 2000. *The Language of Sophocles: Communality, Communication and Involvement* (Cambridge: Cambridge University Press)
Burian, Peter. 2012. 'Polyphonic *Ajax*', in *A Companion to Sophocles*, ed. by Kirk Ormand (Chichester: Wiley-Blackwell), pp. 69–83
Cairns, Douglas. 2016. *Sophocles: Antigone* (London: Bloomsbury)
Cartledge, Paul. 1997. '"Deep Plays": Theatre as Process in Greek Civic Life', in Easterling, pp. 3–35
Cartwright, Julyan H. E. and Diego L. González. 2016. 'Möbius Strips before Möbius: Topological Hints in Ancient Representations', *Mathematical Intelligencer*, 38.2: 69–76
Castellari, Marco. 2016. '"Es klingt paradox": Hölderlin, Böhlendorff e il teatro moderno', *Studia theodisca: Hölderliniana*, 2: 119–44 <https://riviste.unimi.it/index.php/StudiaTheodisca/issue/view/947>
——2018. *Hölderlin und das Theater: Produktion — Rezeption — Transformation*, Philologus Supplemente, 10 (Berlin: De Gruyter)
Christen, Felix. 2007. *Eine andere Sprache: Friedrich Hölderlins 'Große Pindar-Übertragung'*, Sammlung Theorie, 7 (Basle: Engeler)
——2013. *Das Jetzt der Lektüre: Zur Edition und Deutung von Friedrich Hölderlins 'Ister'-Entwürfen*, edition TEXT, 10 (Frankfurt a.M.: Stroemfeld)
——2018. 'Die Freundlichkeit des Gedichts: Hölderlins Ode "Vulkan"' (unpublished manuscript)

CONSTANTINE, DAVID. 1986. 'Translation and Exegesis in Hölderlin', *Modern Language Review*, 81: 388–97
—— 1988. *Hölderlin* (Oxford: Clarendon Press; corrected repr. 1990)
—— 1996. 'Saying and Not-Saying in Hölderlin's Work', in *Taboos in German Literature*, ed. by David Jackson (Providence, RI: Berghahn), pp. 43–58
CORSSEN, META. 1949. 'Die Tragödie als Begegnung zwischen Gott und Mensch: Hölderlins Sophokles-Deutung', *Hölderlin-Jahrbuch*, 3 (1948–1949), 139–87
CSAPO, ERIC, and MARGARET MILLER. 1998. 'Democracy, Empire, and Art: Towards a Politics of Time and Narrative', in *Democracy, Empire, and the Arts in Fifth-Century Athens*, ed. by Deborah Boedeker and Kurt A. Raaflaub (Cambridge, MA: Harvard University Press), pp. 87–125
D'ANGOUR, ARMAND. 2006, 'Metre', in *The Edinburgh Companion to Ancient Greece and Rome*, ed. by Edward Bispham, Thomas Harrison, and Brian A. Sparkes (Edinburgh: Edinburgh University Press), pp. 489–94
—— 2011. *The Greeks and the New: Novelty in Ancient Greek Imagination and Experience* (Cambridge: Cambridge University Press)
DASTUR, FRANÇOISE. 2013. *Hölderlin: le retournement natal*, 2nd edn ([Paris]: Éditions Les Belles Lettres)
DEGNER, UTA. 2008. *Bilder im Wechsel der Töne: Hölderlins Elegien und 'Nachtgesänge'*, Germanisch-Romanische Monatsschrift, Beiheft 36 (Heidelberg: Winter)
DELEUZE, GILLES. 1969. *Logique du sens* (Paris: Éditions de Minuit)
—— 1990. *The Logic of Sense*, trans. by Mark Lester with Charles Stivale (London: Athlone Press; repr. 2004, London: Continuum)
—— 2002. 'Jean Hyppolite, *Logique et existence*', in *L'île déserte: Textes et entretiens 1953–1974*, ed. by David Lapoujarde (Paris: Éditions de Minuit), pp. 18–23 (originally in *Revue philosophique de la France et de l'étranger*, 144 (1954), 457–60)
DESTRÉE, PIERRE, and FRITZ-GREGOR HERRMANN (eds). 2011. *Plato and the Poets* (Leiden: Brill)
DETIENNE, MARCEL. 1996. *The Masters of Truth in Archaic Greece*, trans. by Janet Lloyd (New York: Zone Books; repr. 1999)
DETIENNE, MARCEL, and JEAN-PIERRE VERNANT. 1974. *Les ruses de l'intelligence: La mètis des Grecs* ([Paris]: Flammarion; repr. 2004)
DIECKMANN, HERBERT. 1966. 'Zur Theorie der Lyrik im 18. Jahrhundert in Frankreich, mit gelegentlicher Berücksichtigung der englischen Kritik', in Iser, pp. 73–112
DILCHER, ROMAN. 1995. *Studies in Heraclitus*, Spudasmata, 56 (Hildesheim: Olms)
DODDS, E. R. (ed.). 1959. *Plato, Gorgias: A Revised Text with Introduction and Commentary* (Oxford: Clarendon Press; repr. 1990)
DOERING, SABINE, and JOHANN KREUZER (eds). 2015. *Unterwegs zu Hölderlin: Studien zu Werk und Poetik* (Oldenburg: BIS-Verlag der Carl von Ossietzky Universität)
DONELAN, JAMES H. 2002. 'Hölderlin's Poetic Self-Consciousness', *Philosophy and Literature*, 26: 125–42
DUARTE, BRUNO. 2007. '"O toi parole de Zeus": Hölderlin et Sophocle', unpublished doctoral thesis, University of Strasbourg
DÜSING, KLAUS. 1981. 'Ästhetischer Platonismus bei Hölderlin und Hegel', in *Homburg vor der Höhe in der deutschen Geistesgeschichte: Studien zum Freundeskreis um Hegel und Hölderlin*, ed. by Christoph Jamme and Otto Pöggeler; Deutscher Idealismus, 4 (Stuttgart: Klett-Cotta), pp. 101–17
EASTERLING, P. E. (ed.). 1997. *The Cambridge Companion to Greek Tragedy* (Cambridge: Cambridge University Press; repr. 2005)
ECK, CAROLINE VAN, and OTHERS (eds). 2012. *Translations of the Sublime: The Early Modern*

Reception and Dissemination of Longinus' 'Peri Hupsous' in Rhetoric, the Visual Arts, Architecture and the Theatre (Leiden: Brill)

EIBL, KARL. 1983. 'Der Blick hinter den Spiegel: Sinnbild und gedankliche Bewegung in Hölderlins "Hälfte des Lebens"', *Jahrbuch der deutschen Schillergesellschaft*, 27: 222–35

ELDRIDGE, HANNAH VANDEGRIFT. 2015. *Lyric Orientations: Hölderlin, Rilke, and the Poetics of Community* (Ithaca, NY: Cornell University Press and University Library)

ENGEL, MANFRED. 1993. *Der Roman der Goethezeit: Anfänge in Klassik und Frühromantik — Transzendentale Geschichten*, Germanistische Abhandlungen, 71 (Stuttgart: Metzler)

FAUVEL, JOHN, RAYMOND FLOOD and ROBIN WILSON (eds). 1993. *Möbius and his Band: Mathematics and Astronomy in Nineteenth-century Germany* (Oxford: Oxford University Press)

FINK, MARKUS. 1982. *Pindarfragmente: Neun Hölderlin Deutungen*, Untersuchungen zur deutschen Literaturgeschichte, 32 (Tübingen: Niemeyer)

FIORETOS, ARIS (ed.). 1999. *The Solid Letter: Readings of Friedrich Hölderlin* (Stanford, CA: Stanford University Press)

FLEMING, PAUL. 2002. 'Das Gesetz: Hölderlin und die Not der Ruhe', trans. by Elke Siegel and the author, *Hölderlin-Jahrbuch*, 32 (2000–2001): 273–92

FORD, ANDREW. 2002. *The Origins of Criticism: Literary Culture and Poetic Theory in Classical Greece* (Princeton, NJ: Princeton University Press; repr. 2004)

FRANK, MANFRED. 1998. *'Unendliche Annäherung': Die Anfänge der philosophischen Frühromantik*, 2nd edn (Frankfurt a.M.: Suhrkamp)

FRANZ, MICHAEL 1987, 'Hölderlins Logik: Zum Grundriß von "Sein Urtheil Möglichkeit"', *Hölderlin-Jahrbuch*, 25 (1986–1987): 93–124

—— 1988. 'Die Schule und die Welt: Studien zu Hölderlins Pindarfragment "Untreue der Weisheit"', in Jamme and Pöggeler, pp. 139–55

—— 1991. 'Jupiter Befreier', *Hölderlin-Jahrbuch*, 27 (1990–1991): 152–54

—— 2002. 'Pindarfragmente', in Kreuzer 2002, pp. 254–69

—— 2005. 'Exkurs zu Ploucquets Logik', in *'... im Reiche des Wissens cavalieremente'? Hölderlins, Hegels und Schellings Philosophiestudium an der Universität Tübingen*, ed. by Michael Franz; Schriften der Hölderlin-Gesellschaft, 23/2 (Tübingen: Hölderlin-Gesellschaft; Eggingen: Edition Isele), pp. 527–34

—— 2012. *Tübinger Platonismus: Die gemeinsamen philosophischen Anfangsgründe von Hölderlin, Schelling und Hegel* (Tübingen: Francke)

—— 2013. '"... wenn die Dunkelheit einsickert ... ": Über die Unverständlichkeit in Hölderlins Dichtung', *Hölderlin-Jahrbuch*, 38 (2012–2013): 187–98

FREDE, DOROTHEA. 1993. 'Out of the Cave: What Socrates Learned from Diotima', in *Nomodeiktes: Greek Studies in Honor of Martin Ostwald*, ed. by Ralph M. Rosen and Joseph Farrell (Ann Arbor: University of Michigan Press), pp. 397–422

FREDE, MICHAEL. 1994. 'The Stoic Notion of *lekton*', in *Language*, ed. by Stephen Everson; Companions to Ancient Thought, 3 (Cambridge: Cambridge University Press), pp. 109–28

—— 2000. 'The Philosopher', in Brunschwig and Lloyd, pp. 3–19

FREY, HANS-JOST. 1990. 'Textrevision bei Hölderlin', in *Der unendliche Text* (Frankfurt a.M.: Suhrkamp), pp. 77–123

FRIEDRICH, JÜRG. 2007. *Dichtung als 'Gesang': Hölderlins 'Wie wenn am Feiertage ...' im Kontext der Schriften zur Philosophie und Poetik 1795–1802* (Munich: Fink)

FUHRMANN, MANFRED. 1966. 'Obscuritas: das Problem der Dunkelheit in der rhetorischen und literarästhetischen Theorie der Antike', in Iser, pp. 47–72

—— (ed. and trans.). 1982. *Aristoteles: Poetik* (Stuttgart: Reclam; repr. 1994)

—— 2003. *Die Dichtungstheorie der Antike: Aristoteles — Horaz — 'Longin'* (Düsseldorf: Artemis & Winkler)

GAIER, ULRICH. 1987. 'Hölderlins vaterländische Sangart', *Hölderlin-Jahrbuch*, 25 (1986–1987): 12–59
———1989. 'Hölderlins vaterländischer Gesang "Andenken"', *Hölderlin-Jahrbuch*, 26 (1988–1989): 175–201
———1994. '"... ein Empfindungssystem, der ganze Mensch": Grundlagen von Hölderlins poetologischer Anthropologie im 18. Jahrhundert', in *'Der ganze Mensch': Anthropologie und Literatur im 18. Jahrhundert*, ed. by Hans-Jürgen Schings (Stuttgart: Metzler), pp. 724–46
———1996. 'Hölderlins Ode über die Mythologie', in Kurz 1996, pp. 125–41
———1998. '"Mein ehrlich Meister": Hölderlin im Gespräch mit Heinse', in Theile, pp. 25–54
———2000. 'Neubegründung der Lyrik auf Heinses Musiktheorie', *Hölderlin-Jahrbuch*, 31 (1998–1999): 129–38
———2002a. 'Ein Faszikel Oden', in *'Wo sind jezt Dichter?': Homburg, Stuttgart 1798–1800*, Hölderlin Texturen, 4 (Tübingen: Hölderlin-Gesellschaft), pp. 315–20
———2002b. 'Wilhelm Heinse', in Kreuzer 2002, pp. 86–89
———2014a. '"Heiliger Plato": Platonismus in der Goethezeit', in 2014c, pp. 159–207
———2014b. 'Hölderlins Melancholie', in 2014c, pp. 27–129
———2014c. *Hölderlin Studien* (Eggingen: Edition Isele)
GASKILL, HOWARD. 1984. *Hölderlin's Hyperion* ([Durham]: University of Durham)
GHEERBRANT, XAVIER. 2017. *Empédocle: une poétique philosophique*, Kaïnon — Anthropologie de la pensée ancienne, 6 (Paris: Garnier)
GILL, CHRISTOPHER. 2013. *Marcus Aurelius, Meditations Books 1–6: Translated with an Introduction and Commentary* (Oxford: Oxford University Press)
GOLDHILL, SIMON. 1997a. 'The Language of Tragedy: Rhetoric and Communication', in Easterling, pp. 127–50
———1997b. 'Modern Critical Approaches to Greek Tragedy', in Easterling, pp. 324–47
———2002. *The Invention of Prose*, Greece & Rome: New Surveys in the Classics, 32 (Oxford: Oxford University Press)
GOLDSCHMIDT, VICTOR. 1977. *Le système stoïcien et l'idée de temps*, 3rd edn (Paris: Vrin)
GOURINAT, JEAN-BAPTISTE. 2000. *La dialectique des stoïciens* (Paris: Vrin)
GRAVES, ROBERT. 1958. *Greek Myths* (London: Cassell; repr. 1980)
GRODDECK, WOLFRAM. 1995. 'Hölderlin: Neue (und alte) Lesetexte', *Text: Kritische Beiträge*, 1: 61–76
———1996. 'Betrachtungen über das Gedicht "Lebensalter"', in Kurz 1996, pp. 153–65.
———1998. '"Hörst Du? horst Du? Diotima's Grab": Zur Aporie der Schriftlichkeit in den 'Hyperion'-Briefen', in Bay 1998, pp. 176–89
———2006. 'Über das "Wortlose" in Hölderlins Ode "Thränen"', *Deutsche Vierteljahrsschrift für Literaturwissenschaft und Geistesgeschichte*, 80: 624–39
———2007. 'Zahl, Maß und Metrik in Hölderlins Gedicht "Hälfte des Lebens"', in *Weiterlesen: Literatur und Wissen*, ed. by Ulrike Bergermann and Elisabeth Strowick (Bielefeld: Transcript)
———2008. *Reden über Rhetorik: Zu einer Stilistik des Lesens*, 2nd edn (Frankfurt a.M.: Stroemfeld)
———2012. *Hölderlins Elegie 'Brod und Wein' oder 'Die Nacht'*, edition TEXT, 8 (Frankfurt a.M.: Stroemfeld)
HADOT, PIERRE. 1998. *The Inner Citadel: The 'Meditations' of Marcus Aurelius*, trans. by Michael Chase (Cambridge, MA: Harvard University Press)
HALLIWELL, STEPHEN. 2011. 'Antidotes and Incantations: Is There a Cure for Poetry in Plato's *Republic*?', in Destrée and Herrmann, pp. 240–66

HAMACHER, WERNER. 2006. 'Parusie, Mauern: Mittelbarkeit und Zeitlichkeit, später Hölderlin', *Hölderlin-Jahrbuch*, 34 (2004–2005): 93–142
HAMILTON, JOHN T. 2003. *Soliciting Darkness: Pindar, Obscurity and the Classical Tradition*, Harvard Studies in Comparative Literature, 47 (Cambridge, MA: Harvard University Dept. of Comparative Literature)
—— 2008. *Music, Madness, and the Unworking of Language* (New York: Columbia University Press)
—— 2014. 'Ellipses of World Literature', *Poetica*, 46: 1–16
HAMLIN, CYRUS. 1999. 'The Philosophy of Poetic Form: Hölderlin's Theory of Poetry and the Classical German Elegy', in Fioretos, pp. 291–320
HANKE, THOMAS. 2015. 'Im Bunde der Dritte von vieren und Schelling außen vor: Hegels Konsequenzen aus seinem Wechsel nach Frankfurt', in *Der Frankfurter Hegel in seinem Kontext: Hegel-Tagung in Bad Homburg vor der Höhe im November 2013*, ed. by Thomas Hanke and Thomas M. Schmidt; Geist und Geschichte, 27 (Frankfurt a.M.: Klostermann), pp. 96–125
HARRISON, R. B. 1975. *Hölderlin and Greek Literature* (Oxford: Clarendon Press)
HÄRTL, HEINZ. 2000. 'Ein Briefwechsel Hölderlins mit Mehmel', *Text: Kritische Beiträge*, 6: 141–50
HARVEN, VANESSA DE. 2012. 'The Coherence of Stoic Ontology' (doctoral dissertation, University of California, Berkeley) <http://digitalassets.lib.berkeley.edu/etd/ucb/text/deHarven_berkeley_0028E_12503.pdf>
HENRICH, DIETER. 1992. *Der Grund im Bewußtsein: Untersuchungen zu Hölderlins Denken (1794–1795)* (Stuttgart: Klett-Cotta)
—— 1993. 'Eine philosophische Konzeption entsteht: Hölderlins Denken in Jena, *Hölderlin-Jahrbuch*, 28 (1992–1993): 1–28
HILLER, MARION. 2008. *'Harmonisch entgegengesetzt': Zur Darstellung und Darstellbarkeit in Hölderlins Poetik um 1800*, Hermaea, n. s. 118 (Tübingen: Niemeyer)
HOCK, ERICH. 1995. *'dort drüben, in Westphalen': Hölderlins Reise nach Bad Driburg mit Wilhelm Heinse und Susette Gontard*, 2nd edn, ed. by Alfred Kelletat (Stuttgart: Metzler)
HÖLSCHER, UVO. 1965a. *Empedokles und Hölderlin* (Frankfurt a.M.: Insel)
—— 1965b. 'Empedokles von Akragas: Erkenntnis und Reinigung', *Hölderlin-Jahrbuch*, 13 (1963–1964): 21–43
HOLT, PHILIP. 1999. '*Polis* and Tragedy in the *Antigone*', *Mnemosyne*, 52: 658–90
HONOLD, ALEXANDER. 2002. '"Der scheinet aber fast / Rükwärts zu gehen": Zur kulturgeographischen Bedeutung der '"Ister"-Hymne', *Hölderlin-Jahrbuch*, 32 (2000–2001): 175–97
—— 2005. *Hölderlins Kalender: Astronomie und Revolution um 1800* (Berlin: Vorwerk 8)
HORNBACHER, ANNETTE. 1995. *Die Blume des Mundes: Zu Hölderlins poetologisch-poetischem Sprachdenken* (Würzburg: Königshausen & Neumann)
—— 2001. '"Eines zu seyn mit Allem, was lebt ...": Hölderlins "intellectuale Anschauung"', in Lawitschka 2001, pp. 24–47
HÖSLE, VITTORIO. 2009. 'Poetische Poetiken in der Antike: Horaz' "Ars Poetica" und Pseudo-Longinos' Περὶ ὕψους', *Poetica*, 41: 55–74
HÜHN, HELMUT. 1997. *Mnemosyne: Zeit und Erinnerung in Hölderlins Denken* (Stuttgart: Metzler)
HUSS, BERNHARD, PATRIZIA MARZILLO and THOMAS RICKLIN (eds). 2011. *Para/Textuelle Verhandlungen zwischen Dichtung und Philosophie in der Frühen Neuzeit*, Pluralisierung & Autorität, 26 (Berlin: De Gruyter)
HYPPOLITE, JEAN. 1991. *Logique et existence: Essai sur la logique de Hegel*, 3rd edn (Paris: Presses Universitaires de France)

—— 1997. *Logic and Existence*, trans. by Leonard Lawlor and Amit Sen (Albany: State University of New York Press)

INDLEKOFER, BARBARA. 2007. *Friedrich Hölderlin: Das Geschick des dichterischen Wortes: Vom poetologischen Wandel in den Oden 'Blödigkeit', 'Chiron' und 'Ganymed'*, Basler Studien zur deutschen Sprache und Literatur, 89 (Tübingen: Francke)

IRWIN, JOHN T. 1994. *The Mystery to a Solution: Poe, Borges, and the Analytic Detective Story* (Baltimore, MD: The Johns Hopkins University Press; repr. 1996)

ISER, WOLFGANG (ed.). 1966. *Immanente Ästhetik — Ästhetische Reflexion: Lyrik als Paradigma der Moderne*, Poetik und Hermeneutik, 2 (Munich: Fink)

JAGO, MARK. 2018. *What Truth Is* (Oxford: Oxford University Press)

JAMME, CHRISTOPH, and OTTO PÖGGELER (eds). 1988. *Jenseits des Idealismus: Hölderlins letzte Homburger Jahre (1804–06)*, Neuzeit und Gegenwart, 5 (Bonn: Bouvier)

JAMME, CHRISTOPH, and ANJA LEMKE (eds). 2004. *'Es bleibet aber ein Spur / Doch eines Wortes': Zur späten Hymnik und Tragödientheorie Friedrich Hölderlins* (Munich: Fink)

KAHN, CHARLES H. 1979. *The Art and Thought of Heraclitus: An Edition of the Fragments with Translation and Commentary* (Cambridge: Cambridge University Press; repr. 2001)

—— 1996. *Plato and the Socratic Dialogue: The Philosophical Use of a Literary Form* (Cambridge: Cambridge University Press)

KASPER, MONIKA. 2000. *'Das Gesez von allen der König': Hölderlins Anmerkungen zum Oedipus und zur Antigonä*, Epistemate: Reihe Literaturwissenschaft, 265 (Würzburg: Königshausen & Neumann)

KEIL, WERNER. 1998. 'Heinses Beitrag zur romantischen Musikästhetik', in Theile, pp. 139–58

KERSLAKE, LAWRENCE. 2000. *Essays on the Sublime: Analyses of French Writings on the Sublime from Boileau to La Harpe* (Bern: Lang)

KILLY, WALTHER. 1961. 'Welt in der Welt: Friedrich Hölderlin', in *Wandlungen des lyrischen Bildes*, 3rd edn (Göttingen: Vandenhoeck & Ruprecht), pp. 30–52

KINGSLEY, PETER. 1995. *Ancient Philosophy, Mystery, and Magic: Empedocles and the Pythagorean Tradition* (Oxford: Clarendon Press; repr. 1996)

—— 1999. *In the Dark Places of Wisdom* (Shaftesbury: Element Books; repr. London: Duckworth, 2001)

—— 2002. 'Empedocles for the New Millennium', *Ancient Philosophy*, 22: 333–413

KNOX, BERNARD. 1964. *The Heroic Temper: Studies in Sophoclean Tragedy*, Sather Classical Lectures, 35 (Berkeley: University of California Press; repr. 1966)

—— 1998. *Oedipus at Thebes: Sophocles' Tragic Hero and His Time*, 2nd edn (New Haven, CT: Yale University Press)

KOCZISZKY, EVA. 2009. *Hölderlins Orient* (Würzburg: Königshausen & Neumann)

KOPPENFELS, MARTIN VON. 1996. 'Der Moment der Übersetzung: Hölderlins *Antigonä* und die Tragik zwischen den Sprachen', *Zeitschrift für Germanistik*, n. s. 6: 349–67

KRAYE, JILL. 2003. 'The Legacy of Ancient Philosophy', in *The Cambridge Companion to Greek and Roman Philosophy*, ed. by David Sedley (Cambridge: Cambridge University Press), pp. 323–52

KREUZER, JOHANN (ed.). 2002. *Hölderlin-Handbuch: Leben — Werk — Wirkung* (Stuttgart: Metzler)

—— 2003. 'Hölderlins Kritik der intellektuellen Anschauung: Überlegungen zu einem platonischen Motiv', in Mojsisch and Summerell, pp. 119–37

KURKE, LESLIE. 2013. *The Traffic in Praise: Pindar and the Poetics of Social Economy*, 2nd electronic edn; California Classical Studies, 1 (University of California, Berkeley) <https://escholarship.org/uc/item/29r3j0gm>

KURZ, GERHARD. 1975. *Mittelbarkeit und Vereinigung: Zum Verhältnis von Poesie, Reflexion und Revolution bei Hölderlin* (Stuttgart: Metzler)

———1988. 'Poetische Logik: Zu Hölderlins "Anmerkungen" zu *Oedipus* und *Antigone*', in Jamme and Pöggeler, pp. 83–101

———(ed.) 1996. *Interpretationen: Gedichte von Friedrich Hölderlin* (Stuttgart: Reclam)

———1998. 'Aus linkischem Gesichtspunkt: Zu Hölderlins Ansicht der Antike', in *Antiquitates Renatae: Deutsche und französische Beiträge zur Wirkung der Antike in der europäischen Literatur*, ed. by Verena Ehrich-Haefeli, Hans-Jürgen Schrader and Martin Stern (Würzburg: Könighausen & Neumann), pp. 177–90

———2002. 'Der Roman als Symposion der Moderne: Zu Friedrich Schlegels "Gespräch über die Poesie"', in Matuschek 2002b, pp. 63–79

———2015a. 'Hölderlin, Subjektivität und Moderne', in Doering and Kreuzer, pp. 97–112

———2015b. *Das Wahre, Schöne, Gute: Aufstieg, Fall und Fortbestehen einer Trias* (Paderborn: Fink)

LACOUE-LABARTHE, PHILIPPE. 1989. 'The Caesura of the Speculative', trans. by Robert Eisenhauer and Christopher Fynsk, in *Typography: Mimesis, Philosophy, Politics*, ed. by Christopher Fynsk (Cambridge, MA: Harvard University Press; repr. 1998, Stanford, CA: Stanford University Press), pp. 208–35

———1998. *Métaphrasis, suivi de Le théâtre de Hölderlin* (Paris: Presses Universitaires de France)

LAKS, ANDRÉ. 2001. '"Philosophie Présocratique": Remarques sur la construction d'une catégorie de l'historiographie philosophique', in *Historicization — Historisierung*, ed. by Glenn W. Most; Aporemata: Kritische Studien zur Philologiegeschichte, 5 (Göttingen: Vandenhoeck & Ruprecht), pp. 293–311

LAMPENSCHERF, STEPHAN. 1993. '"Heiliger Plato, vergieb ...": Hölderlins *Hyperion* oder Die neue platonische Mythologie', *Hölderlin-Jahrbuch*, 28 (1992–1993): 128–51.

LANGDON, HELEN. 2012. 'The Demosthenes of Painting: Salvator Rosa and the 17th century Sublime', in van Eck and others, pp. 163–85

LANGE, WILHELM. 1909. *Hölderlin: Eine Pathographie* (Stuttgart: Enke)

LAPLANCHE, JEAN. 1969. *Hölderlin et la question du père*, 2nd edn (Paris: Presses Universitaires de France)

LAWITSCHKA, VALÉRIE (ed.). 2001. *Hölderlin: Philosophie und Dichtung*, Turm-Vorträge, 5 (Tübingen: Hölderlin-Gesellschaft; Eggingen: Edition Isele)

LEMKE, ANJA. 2002. *Konstellation ohne Sterne: Zur poetischen und geschichtlichen Zäsur bei Martin Heidegger und Paul Celan* (Munich: Fink)

LINK, JÜRGEN. 1999. *Hölderlin-Rousseau: Inventive Rückkehr* (Opladen: Westdeutscher Verlag)

LITMAN, THÉODORE A. 1971. *Le Sublime en France (1660–1714)* (Paris: Nizet)

LITTLEWOOD, C. A. J. 2014. 'Hercules Oetaeus', in *Brill's Companion to Seneca: Philosopher and Dramatist*, ed. by Gregor Damschen and Andreas Heil (Leiden: Brill), pp. 515–20

LONG, ANTHONY A. 1996a. 'Heraclitus and Stoicism', in 1996c, pp. 35–57

———1996b. 'Stoic Readings of Homer', in 1996c, pp. 58–84

———1996c. *Stoic Studies* (Cambridge: Cambridge University Press)

———2011. 'Poets as Philosophers and Philosophers as Poets: Parmenides, Plato, Lucretius and Wordsworth', in Huss, Marzillo and Ricklin, pp. 293–308

LÖNKER, FRED. 1989. '"Unendliche Deutung"', *Hölderlin-Jahrbuch*, 26 (1988–1989): 287–303

LOUTH, CHARLIE. 1998. *Hölderlin and the Dynamics of Translation*, Studies in Comparative Literature, 2 (Oxford: Legenda)

———2000. 'The Question of Influence: Hölderlin's Dealings with Schiller and Pindar', *Modern Language Review*, 95: 1038–52

———2004. 'Reflections: Goethe's "Auf dem See" and Hölderlin's "Hälfte des Lebens"', *Oxford German Studies*, 33: 167–75

———2015. '"jene zarten Verhältnisse": Überlegungen zu Hölderins Aufsatz-bruchstück *Über Religion / Fragment philosophischer Briefe*', *Hölderlin-Jahrbuch*, 39 (2014–2015): 124–38

LÜDERS, DETLEV. 1968. 'Die Welt im verringerten Maasstab': Hölderlin-Studien (Tübingen: Niemeyer)

MACINTOSH FIONA. 2009. Sophocles: Oedipus Tyrannus (Cambridge: Cambridge University Press)

MARTENS, GUNTER. 2008. 'Hölderlins Poetik der Polyphonie: Ein Versuch, das Hymnenfragment "Die Nymphe. / Mnemosyne." aus den Handschriften zu deuten', in *Hölderlin: Sprache und Raum*, ed. by Valérie Lawitschka; Turm-Vorträge, 6 (Tübingen: Hölderlin-Gesellschaft; Eggingen: Edition Isele), pp. 9–45

MATUSCHEK, STEFAN. 2002a. 'Die Macht des Gastmahls: Schlegels "Gespräch über die Poesie" und Platons *Symposion*', in 2002b, pp. 81–96

—— (ed.). 2002b. *Wo das philosophische Gespräch ganz in Dichtung übergeht: Platons Symposion und seine Wirkung in der Renaissance, Romantik und Moderne*, Jenaer germanistische Forschungen, n. s. 13 (Heidelberg: Winter)

MATZNER, SEBASTIAN. 2016. *Rethinking Metonymy: Literary Theory and Poetic Practice from Pindar to Jakobson* (Oxford: Oxford University Press)

MAURER, KARL. 1979. 'Boileaus Übersetzung der Schrift Περὶ ὕψους als Text des Französischen 17. Jahrhunderts', in *Le Classicisme à Rome aux Iers siècles avant et après J.-C.*, ed. by Hellmut Flashar; Entretiens sur l'Antiquité Classique, 25 (Geneva: Fondation Hardt), pp. 213–62

MENNINGHAUS, WINFRIED. 1987. *Unendliche Verdopplung: Die frühromantische Grundlegung der Kunsttheorie im Begriff absoluter Selbstreflexion* (Frankfurt a.M.: Suhrkamp)

—— 1991. 'Dichtung als Tanz: Zu Klopstocks Poetik der Wortbewegung', *Comparatio: Revue internationale de littérature comparée*, 2/3 (1990–1991): 129–50

—— 1994. '"Darstellung": Friedrich Gottlieb Klopstocks Eröffnung eines neuen Paradigmas', in *Was heißt 'Darstellen'?*, ed. by Christiaan L. Hart Nibbrig (Frankfurt a.M.: Suhrkamp), pp. 205–28

—— 2005. *Hälfte des Lebens: Versuch über Hölderlins Poetik* (Frankfurt a.M.: Suhrkamp)

MEYER, SUSAN SAUVÉ. 2009. 'Chain of Causes: What is Stoic Fate?', in Salles, pp. 71–90

MILLER, JON. 2015. *Spinoza and the Stoics* (Cambridge: Cambridge University Press)

MÖGEL, ERNST. 1994. *Natur als Revolution: Hölderlins Empedokles-Tragödie* (Stuttgart: Metzler)

MOJSISCH, BURKHARD, and ORRIN F. SUMMERELL (eds). 2003. *Platonismus im Idealismus: Die platonische Tradition in der klassischen deutschen Philosophie* (Munich: Saur)

MONTGOMERY, MARSHALL. 1923. *Friedrich Hölderlin and the German Neo-Hellenic Movement, Part I: From the Renaissance to the Thalia-Fragment of Hölderlin's 'Hyperion' (1794)* (London: Milford)

MOST, GLENN W. 1999. 'The Poetics of Early Greek Philosophy', in *The Cambridge Companion to Early Greek Philosophy*, ed. by A. A. Long (Cambridge: Cambridge University Press), pp. 332–62

—— 2010. 'Hellenistic Allegory and Early Imperial Rhetoric', in *The Cambridge Companion to Allegory*, ed. by Rita Copeland and Peter T. Struck (Cambridge: Cambridge University Press), pp. 26–38

—— 2011. 'What Ancient Quarrel between Philosophy and Poetry?', in Destrée and Herrmann, pp. 1–20

NÄGELE, RAINER. 1999. 'Ancient Sports and Modern Transports: Hölderlin's Tragic Bodies', in Fioretos, pp. 247–67

—— 2004. 'Poetic Revolution', in Wellbery and others, pp. 511–16

—— 2005. *Hölderlins Kritik der poetischen Vernunft* (Basle: Engeler)

NEYMEYR, BARBARA, JOCHEN SCHMIDT and BERNHARD ZIMMERMANN (eds). 2008. *Stoizismus in der europäischen Philosophie, Literatur, Kunst und Politik: Eine Kulturgeschichte von der Antike bis zur Moderne*, 2 vols (Berlin: De Gruyter)

NIGHTINGALE, ANDREA WILSON. 1995. *Genres in Dialogue: Plato and the Construct of Philosophy* (Cambridge: Cambridge University Press)

OSTWALD, MARTIN. 2009. 'Pindar, *Nomos*, and Heracles [...]', in *Language and History in Ancient Greek Culture* (Philadelphia: University of Pennsylvania Press), pp. 94–124 (originally in *Harvard Studies in Classical Philology*, 69 (1965), 109–38)

OUDEMANS, TH. C. W., and A. P. M. H. LARDINOIS. 1987. *Tragic Ambiguity: Anthropology, Philosophy and Sophocles' 'Antigone'*, Brill's Studies in Intellectual History, 4 (Leiden: Brill)

PERGER, MISCHA VON. 2004. '"Die ästhetischen Ideen": Hölderlins Plan, mit Hilfe Platons das Schöne zu analysieren', in *Das antike Denken in der Philosophie Schellings*, ed. by Rainer Adolphi and Jörg Jantzen; Schellingiana, 11 (Stuttgart: frommann-holzboog), pp. 637–61

PICKOVER, CLIFFORD A. 2006. *The Möbius Strip: Dr. August Möbius's Marvelous Band in Mathematics, Games, Literature, Art, Technology, and Cosmology* (New York: Thunder's Mouth)

PÖGGELER, OTTO. 1988. 'Einleitung', in Jamme and Pöggeler, pp. 9–52

—— 1993. *Hegels Idee einer Phänomenologie des Geistes*, 2nd edn (Freiburg: Alber)

—— 2004. *Schicksal und Geschichte: Antigone im Spiegel der Deutungen und Gestaltungen seit Hegel und Hölderlin* (Munich: Fink)

PORTER, JAMES I. 2016. *The Sublime in Antiquity* (Cambridge: Cambridge University Press)

POURCIAU, SARAH. 2015. 'Passing Through Infinity: Kleist's Marionettentheater, Kantian Metaphor, and the Spherical Geometry of Grace', *Poetica*, 47: 51–82

PRIMAVESI, OLIVER. 2005. 'Theologische Allegorie: Zur philosophischen Funktion einer poetischen Form bei Parmenides und Empedokles', in *Wissensvermittlung in dichterischer Gestalt*, ed. by Marietta Horster and Christiane Reitz; Palingenesia, 85 (Stuttgart: Steiner), pp. 69–93

—— 2007. 'Zur Überlieferung und Bedeutung des Empedokleischen Titels "καθαρμοί"', in *Katharsis vor Aristoteles*, ed. by Martin Vöhler and Bernd Seidensticker (Berlin: De Gruyter), pp. 183–225

—— 2008. 'Empedocles: Physical and Mythical Divinity', in *The Oxford Handbook of Presocratic Philosophy*, ed. by Patricia Curd and Daniel W. Graham (Oxford: Oxford University Press), pp. 250–83

—— 2011a. 'Henri II Estienne on Greek Philosopher Poets: An Epistle Dedicatory as a Model of Early Modern Paratextuality', in Huss, Marzillo and Ricklin, pp. 155–78

—— 2011b, 'Henri II Estienne über philosophische Dichtung: Eine Fragmentsammlung als Beitrag zu einer poetologischen Kontroverse', in *The Presocratics from the Latin Middle Ages to Hermann Diels*, ed. by Oliver Primavesi and Katharina Luchner (Stuttgart: Steiner), pp. 157–96

—— 2013. 'Aristoteles *Poetik* 1: die Poetizität philosophischer Texte und die Unterscheidung zwischen Metrum und Rhythmus', in *Argument und literarische Form in antiker Philosophie*, ed. by Michael Erler and Jan Erik Heßler; Beiträge zur Altertumskunde, 320 (Berlin: De Gruyter), pp. 239–88

—— 2014. 'Empedokleisches im "Tod des Empedokles": Ein neuentdeckter Text des Vorsokratischers und Hölderlins Trauerspiel', in *Hölderlin in der Moderne: Kolloquium für Dieter Henrich zum 85. Geburtstag*, ed. by Friedrich Vollhardt (Berlin: Erich Schmidt), pp. 13–41

RAULET, GÉRARD. 1996. '"Natur und Kunst, oder Saturn und Jupiter": Mythos und Moderne bei Friedrich Hölderlin', in *'Unvollständig, krank und halb?': Zur Archäologie moderner Identität*, ed. by Christoph Brecht and Wolfgang Fink (Bielefeld: Aisthesis), pp. 17–24

REITANI, LUIGI. 1999. 'Spiel oder Ziel: Zur Problematik einer (un?)kritischen Emendation in Hölderlins "Ganymed"', *Text: Kritische Beiträge*, 5: 105–08

——2015. 'Die terra incognita des Romans: Hölderlins *Hyperion* im Rahmen der Kulturdebatte des 18. Jahrhunderts', in Doering and Kreuzer, pp. 27–42
ROCHE, MARK WILLIAM. 1987. *Dynamic Stillness: Philosophical Conceptions of 'Ruhe' in Schiller, Hölderlin, Büchner and Heine*, Studien zur deutschen Literatur, 92 (Tübingen: Niemeyer)
——2002. 'Allusions to and Inversions of Plato in Hölderlin's *Hyperion*', in *Literary Paternity, Literary Friendship: Essays in Honor of Stanley Corngold*, ed. by Gerhard Richter; University of North Carolina Studies in the Germanic Languages and Literatures, 125 (Chapel Hill: University of North Carolina Press), pp. 86–103
ROMILLY, JACQUELINE DE. 1968. *Time in Greek Tragedy* (Ithaca, NY: Cornell University Press)
ROSENFIELD, KATHRIN H. 2003. *Antigone — de Sophocle à Hölderlin: La logique du 'rythme'* (Paris: Éditions Galilée)
RYAN, LAWRENCE. 1960. *Hölderlins Lehre vom Wechsel der Töne* (Stuttgart: Kohlhammer)
——1963. 'Hölderlins Dichtungsbegriff', *Hölderlin-Jahrbuch*, 12 (1961–1962): 20–41
——1965. *Hölderlins 'Hyperion': Exzentrische Bahn und Dichterberuf*, Germanistische Abhandlungen, 7 (Stuttgart: Metzler)
——1973. 'Zur Frage des "Mythischen" bei Hölderlin', in *Hölderlin ohne Mythos*, ed. by Ingrid Riedel (Göttingen: Vandenhoeck & Ruprecht), pp. 68–80
——1988. 'Hölderlins Antigone: "Wie es vom griechischen zum hesperischen gehet"', in Jamme and Pöggeler, pp. 103–21
——1990. Review of Constantine 1988 and of *Friedrich Hölderlin: Essays and Letters on Theory*, ed. and trans. by Thomas Pfau (Albany: State University of New York Press, 1988), *German Quarterly*, 63: 557–59
——2002. 'Hyperion oder Der Eremit in Griechenland', in Kreuzer 2002, pp. 176–97
——2006. '"Vaterländisch und natürlich, eigentlich originell": Hölderlins Briefe an Böhlendorff', *Hölderlin-Jahrbuch*, 34 (2004–2005): 246–76
SALLES, RICARDO (ed.). 2009. *God and Cosmos in Stoicism* (Oxford: Oxford University Press)
SANTOS GOMES, MÁRCIO DOS. 2004. 'Die ontologische Zirkularität: Hölderlins Vorsokratiker-Rezeption und ihr Einfluss auf seine Poetologie', doctoral dissertation, University of Jena <https://www.db-thueringen.de/receive/dbt_mods_00001982>
SASSI, MARIA MICHELA. 2015. 'How Musical was Heraclitus' Harmony? A Reassessment of 22 B8, 10, 51 DK', *Rhizomata*, 3: 3–25
——2018. *The Beginnings of Philosophy in Greece*, trans. by Michele Asuna (Princeton, NJ: Princeton University Press)
SATTLER, D. E. (ed.). 1996a. 'Friedrich Hölderlin: "Nachtgesänge" & Pindar-Kommentare', in Arnold, pp. 145–58
——1996b. 'Synthesis: Versuch einer dritten Vermittlung', in Arnold, pp. 159–74
SCHMID, HOLGER. 2002. 'Wechsel der Töne', in Kreuzer 2002, pp. 118–27
SCHMIDT, JOCHEN. 1978. *Hölderlins später Widerruf in den Oden 'Chiron', 'Blödigkeit' und 'Ganymed'*, Studien zur deutschen Literatur, 57 (Tübingen: Niemeyer)
——1981. 'Hölderlins idealistischer Dichtungsbegriff in der poetologischen Tradition des 18. Jahrhundert', *Hölderlin-Jahrbuch*, 22 (1980–1981): 98–121
——1983. 'Sobria ebrietas: Hölderlins "Hälfte des Lebens"', *Hölderlin-Jahrbuch*, 23 (1982–1983): 182–90
——1990. *Hölderlins geschichtsphilosophische Hymnen: 'Friedensfeier' — 'Der Einzige' — 'Patmos'* (Darmstadt: Wissenschaftliche Buchgesellschaft)
——1996. 'Hölderlins dichterische Rezeption der stoischen Ethik und Naturphilosophie', in Arnold, pp. 33–50
——2003. 'Geschichtsphilosophische Poetologie: Hölderlins Ode "Natur und Kunst oder Saturn und Jupiter"', in *Poetologische Lyrik von Klopstock bis Grünbein: Gedichte und Interpretationen*, ed. by Olaf Hildebrand (Cologne: Böhlau), pp. 83–97

——2008a. 'Die poetologische Transformation der stoischen Euthymie: Marc Aurel und Hölderlins Ode "Dichtermut"', in Neymeyr, Schmidt and Zimmermann, II, 951–62
——2008b. 'Stoischer Pantheismus als Medium des Säkularisierungsprozesses und als Psychotherapeutikum um 1800: Hölderlins *Hyperion*', in Neymeyr, Schmidt and Zimmermann, II, 927–50
SCHOFIELD, MALCOLM. 1988. 'The Retrenchable Present', in *Matter and Metaphysics: Fourth Symposium Hellenisticum*, ed. by Jonathan Barnes and Mario Mignucci; Elenchos, 14 (Naples: Bibliopolis), pp. 329–74
SCHÖNBERGER, OTTO (ed. and trans.). 1988. *Longinus: Vom Erhabenen* (Stuttgart: Reclam)
SEGAL, CHARLES. 1981. *Tragedy and Civilization: An Interpretation of Sophocles* (Cambridge, MA: Harvard University Press)
——1995. *Sophocles' Tragic World: Divinity, Nature, Society* (Cambridge, MA: Harvard University Press)
SEIDENSTICKER, BERND. 2005. 'Peripetie und tragische Dialektik: Aristoteles, Szondi und die griechische Tragödie', in *Über das Vergnügen an tragischen Gegenständen: Studien zum antiken Drama* (Munich: Saur), pp. 279–308
SEIFERT, ALBRECHT. 1982. *Untersuchungen zu Hölderlins Pindar-Rezeption*, Münchner Germanistische Beiträge, 32 (Munich: Fink)
——1983. 'Die Rheinhymne und ihr Pindarisches Modell: Struktur und Konzeption von Pythien 3 in Hölderlins Aneignung', *Hölderlin-Jahrbuch*, 23 (1982–1983): 79–133
——1988. '"Die Asyle": Überlegungen zu einer Interpretation des Hölderlinschen Pindarfragments', in Jamme and Pöggeler, pp. 173–78
——1998. 'Die Spuren der Alten Zucht: Hölderlins Pindarfragment "Die Asyle"', in Albrecht Seifert, *Hölderlin und Pindar*, ed. by Anke Bennholdt-Thomsen; Schriften der Hölderlin-Gesellschaft, 22 (Eggingen: Edition Isele), pp. 11–123
SELLARS, JOHN. 2007. 'Aiôn and Chronos: Deleuze and the Stoic Theory of Time', *Collapse*, 3: 177–205
——2009. *The Art of Living: The Stoics on the Nature and Function of Philosophy*, 2nd edn (London: Duckworth)
SIEKMANN, ANDREAS. 1980. 'Die ästhetische Funktion von Sprache, Schweigen und Musik in Hölderlins *Hyperion*', *Deutsche Vierteljahrsschrift für Literaturwissenschaft und Geistesgeschichte*, 54: 47–57
SOURVINOU-INWOOD, CHRISTIANE. 1989. 'The Fourth Stasimon of Sophocles' *Antigone*', *Bulletin of the Institute of Classical Studies*, 36: 141–65
STAIGER, EMIL. 1961. 'Hölderlin: Drei Oden', in *Meisterwerke deutscher Sprache aus dem neunzehnten Jahrhundert*, 4th edn (Zurich: Atlantis), pp. 15–56
STANITZEK, GEORG. 1989. *Blödigkeit: Beschreibungen des Individuums im 18. Jahrhundert*, Hermaea, n. s. 60 (Tübingen: Niemeyer)
STEIMER, HANS GERHARD. 2004. 'Säulenwälder: Bildvortrag zu Hölderlins Gedicht "Lebensalter"', *Hölderlin-Jahrbuch*, 33 (2002–2003): 193–229
STEINMETZ, PETER. 1994. 'Die Stoa', in *Die Philosophie der Antike*, ed. by Hellmut Flashar, IV: *Die Hellenistische Philosophie* (Basle: Schwabe), pp. 491–716
STEWART, IAN. 1993. 'Möbius's Modern Legacy', in Fauvel, Flood and Wilson, pp. 121–60
STIENING, GIDEON. 2005. *Epistolare Subjektivität: das Erzählsystem in Friedrich Hölderlins Briefroman 'Hyperion oder der Eremit in Griechenland'* (Tübingen: Niemeyer)
STIERLE, KARLHEINZ. 1979. 'Die Identität des Gedichts: Hölderlin als Paradigma', in *Identität*, ed. by Odo Marquard and Karlheinz Stierle; Poetik und Hermeneutik, 8 (Munich: Fink), pp. 505–52
——1989. 'Die Friedensfeier: Sprache und Fest im revolutionären und nachrevolutionären Frankreich und bei Hölderlin', in *Das Fest*, ed. by Walter Haug and Rainer Warning; Poetik und Hermeneutik, 14 (Munich: Fink), pp. 482–525

STRACK, FRIEDRICH. 2013. *Über Geist und Buchstabe in den frühen philosophischen Schriften Hölderlins* (Heidelberg: Manutius)
STRAUSS, LUDWIG. 1927. 'Hölderlins Anteil an Schellings frühem Systemprogramm', *Deutsche Vierteljahrsschrift für Literaturwissenschaft und Geistesgeschichte*, 5: 679–734
—— 1963. 'Friedrich Hölderlin: "Hälfte des Lebens"', in Ludwig Strauß, *Dichtungen und Schriften*, ed. by Werner Kraft (Munich: Kösel), pp. 478–512 (originally in *Trivium*, 8 (1950), 100–27)
STRIKER, GISELA. 1996. 'Ataraxia: Happiness as Tranquillity', in *Essays on Hellenistic Epistemology and Ethics* (Cambridge: Cambridge University Press), pp. 183–95
SUMMERELL, ORRIN F. 2003. 'Perspektiven der Schwärmerei um 1800: Anmerkungen zu einer Selbstinterpretation Schellings', in Mojsisch and Summerell, pp. 139–73
SZONDI, PETER. 1975. *Einführung in die literarische Hermeneutik*, ed. by Jean Bollack and Helen Stierlin (Frankfurt a.M.: Suhrkamp)
—— 1978a. 'Gattungspoetik und Geschichtsphilosophie: Mit einem Exkurs über Schiller, Schlegel und Hölderlin', in 1978b, I, 367–412
—— 1978b. *Schriften*, ed. by Jean Bollack and others, 2 vols (Frankfurt a.M.: Suhrkamp)
—— 1978c. 'Überwindung des Klassizismus: Der Brief an Böhlendorff vom 4. Dezember 1801', in 1978b, I, 345–66 (originally in *Euphorion*, 58 (1964), 260–75)
—— 1978d. 'Versuch über das Tragische', in 1978b, I, 149–260 (originally *Versuch über das Tragische*, 2nd edn (Frankfurt a.M.: Insel, 1964))
TAMINIAUX, JACQUES. 1995. *Le théâtre des philosophes: La tragédie, l'être, l'action* (Grenoble: Millon)
TANG, CHENXI. 2007. 'The Tragedy of Popular Sovereignty: Hölderlin's "Der Tod des Empedokles"', *Deutsche Vierteljahrsschrift für Literaturwissenschaft und Geistesgeschichte*, 81: 346–68
—— 2008. *The Geographic Imagination of Modernity: Geography, Literature, and Philosophy in German Romanticism* (Stanford, CA: Stanford University Press)
—— 2010. 'Re-imagining World Order: From International Law to Romantic Poetics', *Deutsche Vierteljahrsschrift für Literaturwissenschaft und Geistesgeschichte*, 84: 526–79
TAPLIN, OLIVER (trans.). 2015. *Sophocles: Four Tragedies* (Oxford: Oxford University Press)
TAUSCH, HARALD. 2016. 'Palmyra in Wissenschaft und Literatur um 1800: Winckelmann, Herder, Hölderlin und Goethe', *Germanisch-romanische Monatsschrift*, 66: 269–93
THEILE, GERT (ed.). 1998. *Das Maß des Bacchanten: Wilhelm Heinses Über-Lebenskunst* (Munich: Fink)
THEUNISSEN, MICHAEL. 2000. *Pindar: Menschenlos und Wende der Zeit* (Munich: Beck)
THOM, JOHAN C. 2005. *Cleanthes' 'Hymn to Zeus': Text, Translation, and Commentary*, Studien und Texte zu Antike und Christentum, 33 (Tübingen: Mohr Siebeck)
TILL, DIETMAR. 2006. *Das doppelte Erhabene: Eine Argumentationsfigur von der Antike bis zum Beginn des 19. Jahrhunderts*, Studien zur deutschen Literatur, 175 (Tübingen: Niemeyer)
—— 2012. 'The Sublime and the Bible: Longinus, Protestant Dogmatics, and the "Sublime Style"', in van Eck and others, pp. 55–64
TOTSCHNIG, WOLFHART. 2013. 'Bodies and Their Effects: The Stoics on Causation and Incorporeals', *Archiv für Geschichte der Philosophie*, 95: 119–47
UGOLINI, GHERARDO. 1995. *Untersuchungen zur Figur des Sehers Teiresias*, Classica Monacensia, 12 (Tübingen: Narr)
VERNANT, JEAN-PIERRE. 1988. 'Ambiguity and Reversal: On the Enigmatic Structure of *Oedipus Rex*', in Vernant and Vidal-Naquet, pp. 113–40
VERNANT, JEAN-PIERRE, and PIERRE VIDAL-NAQUET. 1988. *Myth and Tragedy in Ancient Greece*, trans. by Janet Lloyd (New York: Zone Books)
VÖHLER, MARTIN. 1993a. 'Hölderlins Arbeit am Titanenmythos', in *Symbolae Berolinenses für Dieter Harlfinger*, ed. by Friederike Berger and others (Amsterdam: Hakkert), pp. 421–37
—— 1993b. 'Hölderlins Longin-Rezeption', *Hölderlin-Jahrbuch*, 28 (1992–1993): 152–72

——1997. 'Danken möcht' ich, aber wofür?': Zur Tradition und Komposition von Hölderlins Hymnik (Munich: Fink)
——2002. 'Frühe Hymnen', in Kreuzer 2002, pp. 290–308
——2005. Pindarrezeptionen: Sechs Studien zum Wandel des Pindarverständnisses von Erasmus bis Herder, Bibliothek der klassischen Altertumswissenschaften, n. s. 2, 117 (Heidelberg: Winter)
WARMINSKI, ANDRZEJ. 1987. Readings in Interpretation: Hölderlin, Hegel, Heidegger (Minneapolis: University of Minnesota Press)
——1999. 'Monstrous History: Heidegger reading Hölderlin', in Fioretos, pp. 201–14
WEINRICH, HARALD. 1987. 'Zur Definition der Metonymie und zu ihrer Stellung in der rhetorischen Kunst', in Text-Etymologie: Untersuchungen zu Textkörper und Textinhalt, ed. by Arnold Arens (Stuttgart: Steiner), pp. 105–10
WELLBERY, DAVID E. and OTHERS (eds.). 2004. A New History of German Literature (Cambridge, MA: Belknap Press)
WETZELS, WALTER D. 1973. Johann Wilhelm Ritter: Physik im Wirkungsfeld der deutschen Romantik, Quellen und Forschungen zur Sprach- und Kulturgeschichte der germanischen Völker, n. s. 59 (Berlin: De Gruyter)
WILAMOWITZ-MOELLENDORFF, ULRICH VON. 1925. 'Kleanthes: Hymnus auf Zeus', in Reden und Vorträge, 4th edn, 2 vols (Berlin: Weidmann, 1925–26), I, 306–32
WITTSTOCK, ALBERT (trans.). 1949. Marcus Aurelius Antoninus: Selbstbetrachtungen (Stuttgart: Reclam; repr. 2015)
ZUBERBÜHLER, ROLF. 1969. Hölderlins Erneuerung der Sprache aus ihren etymologischen Ursprüngen, Philologische Studien und Quellen, 46 (Berlin: Eric Schmidt)
ZUNTZ, GÜNTHER. 2005. Griechische philosophische Hymnen, ed. by Hubert Cancik and Lutz Käppel; Studien und Texte zu Antike und Christentum, 35 (Tübingen: Mohr Siebeck)

Supplementary references (added to the 2021 edition)

HÖLDERLIN, FRIEDRICH, Prose, teatro e lettere, ed. by Luigi Reitani, trans. by Mauro Bozzetti and others (Milan: Mondadori, 2019) — This second volume of Reitani's Hölderlin edition includes his new reconstruction of the drafts of the Empedocles drama (in German and Italian translation), and in some cases newly edited versions of the theoretical essays (in Italian only).

Secondary literature

CHRISTEN, FELIX. 2020. 'Die Freundlichkeit des Gedichts: Hölderlins Ode "Vulkan"', in Friedrich Hölderlin, Neun 'Nachtgesänge': Interpretationen, ed. by Roland Reuß with Marit Müller; edition TEXT, 19 (Göttingen: Wallstein Verlag), pp. 139–56 — The reference at p. 133 n. 46 above to Christen 2018 should now be to pp. 155–56 of this published version.
LEWIS, CHARLES. 2020. 'Between Fate and Skill: Translating Hölderlin's Term "Geschik"', Studia theodisca, 27: 5–24 <https://doi.org/10.13130/1593-2478/14562> — Contains a fuller discussion of the question considered at pp. 136–37 above.

C.L., April 2021

INDEX

Adler, Jeremy 57 n. 1, 63 n. 19, 85, 113, **122 nn. 5 &
    7**, 147, 185
Adorno, Theodor 1
aiōn **49–52**, 54, 130 n. 34
Albert, Claudia 112 n. 25
ambiguity 20, 33, **35–36**, **45–46**, 96, 129, 133 nn. 45 &
    46, 137, 139, **141–43**
André, Robert 32 n. 64, 33 n. 67
Apollo **20**, **27**, 30 n. 60, 55, **135**, 158 n. 4, 175 n. 37
Arburg, Hans-Georg von 115 n. 34
Aristotle 2, 5, **10**, 11 n. 14, 64 n. 24, **91–92**, 116 n. 36,
    165 n. 6, **166 n. 7**, 175 n. 34, 181 n. 27

Bacchus 28, 55, **74–75**, **125**, 175 n. 42, 176 nn. 42 &
    43, 183 n. 43
Bachmaier, Helmut 107 n. 13
Baeumer, Max L. 114 n. 31
Bagordo, Andreas 111 n. 23
Barr, Stephen 61 n. 15
Bartel, Heike 113, 114 n. 28, 115, 122 n. 4, 123 n. 10,
    126 n. 18, 128 n. 24, 129 n. 30, **139**, 142 n. 71
Bassermann-Jordan, Gabriele von 12 n. 20
Batteux, Charles 4 n. 10, **89**, 93, 96 n. 35
Baum, Manfred 124 n. 12
Bay, Hansjörg 18 n. 33, 22 n. 43, 157 n. 41
Beaufret, Jean **149**, 150 n. 12
Beiser, Frederick C. 2 n. 6, 12 n. 20
Beißner, Friedrich 182 n. 38
Belfiore, Elizabeth S. 14 n. 23, 19 n. 35, 20 n. 40
Bénatouïl, Thomas 32 n. 66
Benn, M. B. 156 n. 25, 157 n. 36, 167 n. 17
Bennholdt-Thomsen, Anke 27 n. 53, 37 n. 1, 72 n. 35,
    73 n. 36, 87 n. 17, 99 n. 47, 133 n. 47, 173 n. 22,
    174 n. 25, **175 nn. 32, 36 & 37**
Bennholdt-Thomsen and Guzzoni ('Analecta') 33 n. 67,
    74, 99 n. 47, 109 n. 18, 110 nn. 19 & 20, 125 n. 15,
    126 n. 18, 133 n. 47, 136 n. 54, 157 n. 39, 167 n. 19,
    171 nn. 2 & 5, **179 n. 13**, 180 n. 19
Bertheau, Jochen 87 n. 17, 174 n. 24
Beyer, Uwe 38 n. 6
Biggs, Norman 60 nn. 11 & 12
Billings, Joshua 12 n. 20, **16**, 79 n. 54, **86 n. 11**,
    150–51, 153 n. 3, 155 n. 21, 161 n. 33, 166 n. 8,
    172 n. 12, 180 n. 20, 181 n. 28, 184 nn. 52 & 56
Binder, Wolfgang 38 n. 6, 41 n. 21, 154 nn. 10 &
    14, 155 n. 19, 156 n. 25, 166 n. 9, 167 n. 14,

171 nn. 3, 4, 5 & 6, 172 n. 12, 174 nn. 23 & 26,
    175 n. 33, **178 n. 7**, **179 n. 13**
Boileau, Nicolas 4, 83, 86, **87–93**, 95, 96, **97–99**
Bomski, Franziska 3 n. 8, 59 n. 8
Böschenstein, Bernhard 3, 4 n. 11, 27 n. 53, 53 n. 54,
    74, 83 n. 4, 90 n. 23, 93 n. 32, 96–97 n. 39,
    116 n. 35, **123**, 127 n. 22, 131, 150 n. 10,
    171 nn. 3 & 4, 172 n. 12, 173 nn. 22 & 23,
    176 nn. 39, 40, 43 & 44, 181 n. 28, 182 n. 41,
    183 nn. 43 & 49
Bothe, Henning 38 n. 6, 41 n. 23, 53 n. 53
Bowie, Andrew 1 n. 2
Bowie, Malcolm 133 n. 44
Brague, Rémi 91 n. 27, 166 n. 7
Brandt, Reinhard 39 n. 14, 55 n. 59
Bréhier, Émile 38 n. 8, 47 n. 39, 77
Bremer, Dieter 2 n. 6, **12**, 19 n. 35, 20 n. 39, 39 n. 11,
    122 n. 6, 127 n. 21
Bröcker, Walter 168 n. 23
Brody, Jules 87 n. 15, **89 n. 20**, 92 n. 28, 95 n. 34,
    98 n. 41
Brooke, Christopher 2 n. 6, 39 n. 13, 53 n. 53
Brouwer, René 32 n. 66
Brunschwig, Jacques 47 n. 39, 48 n. 40, 76 n. 46
Budelmann, Felix 153 n. 1
Burian, Peter 5, 177 n. 47

Cairns, Douglas 176 n. 42, 177 n. 46, 182 n. 39
Cartledge, Paul 153 n. 4
Cassas, Louis-François 99 n. 46
Castellari, Marco 76 n. 45, 87 n. 17, 137 n. 58,
    147 n. 3, 149 n. 8, 155 n. 24, 183 n. 50
centaurs 122, **123**, 124, **125–27**, 131–32
Christen, Felix 122 n. 6, 127 n. 20, **133 n. 46**,
    135 n. 52
Chrysippus 33 n. 69, 48, 51, 142–43
Cicero 9 n. 3, 40, 47 n. 38, 142
Cleanthes **2**, 11 n. 13, **33**, 36, **37–39**, **42–46**, 54, 55
Constantine, David 18 n. 33, 117 n. 38, 122 n. 7, 147,
    158 nn. 2 & 5
Corneille, Pierre 92–93
Corßen, Meta 93 n. 30, 156 n. 25, 166 nn. 9, 10 & 11,
    167 n. 16, 171 nn. 2, 3 & 4, 173 n. 19, 174 n. 23,
    177 n. 46, **181 n. 33**, 182 n. 34
Courtine, Jean-François 123 n. 9, 147, 150 n. 9,
    155 n. 20, 185

Cronus **33–36**, 37, **40–47**, 54–55, 72
Csapo, Eric 155 n. 19, **167 n. 21**
Cudworth, Ralph 39

D'Angour, Armand 118 n. 42, 155–56 n. 25, 167 n. 21
Dastur, Françoise 150 n. 9
Degner, Uta 132 n. 42, 133 n. 46
deinos 5, **93 n. 30**, 151, **165 n. 2**
Deleuze, Gilles 23 n. 45, 72, **75–79**, 82
Detienne, Marcel 10 n. 9
Detienne and Vernant **126 n. 18**, 139 n. 64, 140 nn. 66, 67 & 68
Dieckmann, Herbert 89 n. 22, 93
dikē 43 n. 28, **139–40**, 143
Dilcher, Roman 38 n. 8
Diogenes Laertius 32 n. 66, **39**, **40 n. 15**, 47 n. 38, 142–43
Dionysus *see* Bacchus
Dodds, E. R. 124 nn. 12 & 14
dolphins 112–13, **114–16**
Donelan, James H. 58 n. 6, 64 n. 25
Duarte, Bruno 91–92 n. 27, 166 n. 7
Düsing, Klaus 12 n. 20, **13**, 17 n. 28

Eibl, Karl **110**, **111 n. 23**
Eldridge, Hannah Vandegrift 58
Empedocles 2, **9–11**, 17, **38–39**, 73, 74, 76, 89 n. 22
Engel, Manfred 22 n. 43, 23 n. 45
Estienne, Henri 11, 17, 33, 39, 123 n. 9

Fédier, François 147, 149
Fichte, Johann Gottlieb 1, **11**, 15 n. 25
Fink, Markus **113**, 121 n. 3, 122 n. 7, **126–27**, 128 nn. 24 & 27, 129, **141**, 142 n. 70, 168 n. 23
Fleming, Paul 122 n. 7, 128 nn. 26 & 27, 167 n. 17
Frank, Manfred 1, 15 n. 25
Franz, Michael 12 n. 20, 33 n. 67, 40 n. 18, 41 n. 20, **57 n. 1**, 122 n. 4, 128 n. 24
Frede, Dorothea 13–14
Frede, Michael 9 n. 5, 49 n. 43, 76 n. 47, 77 n. 48
Frey, Hans-Jost 32 n. 65, 34 n. 70, 113 n. 27, 131 n. 37
Friedrich, Jürg 15 n. 26, 62 n. 18
Fuhrmann, Manfred 64 n. 24, 85 n. 8, 87 n. 13, 98 n. 43, 175 n. 34

Gaier, Ulrich 12 n. 20, **23 nn. 44 & 45**, 28, 38 n. 6, 41 n. 19, 46 n. 36, **53**, 55, 58 n. 6, 64 n. 25, 88 n. 19, **114**, 154 n. 15, 179 n. 16
Gasché, Rudolph 96 n. 39
Gaskill, Howard 18 n. 34, 21 n. 42
German Romantics 9 n. 4, 81
Gheerbrant, Xavier 10 n. 6
Gill, Christopher 51
Goldhill, Simon 9 n. 3, 150, 166 n. 8
Goldschmidt, Victor 48 n. 42, **49–50**, **52**
Gourinat, Jean-Baptiste 76 n. 47, 142 n. 72

Groddeck, Wolfram 4 n. 13, 21 n. 41, 85 n. 8, 87 n. 13, 98 n. 43, **99**, 103 n. 6, **118 n. 41**, 121 n. 3, **131 n. 38**, 133 n. 45, 134 n. 48, **137 n. 59**
Guzzoni, Alfredo *see* Bennholdt-Thomsen and Guzzoni

Hadot, Pierre 25, **51**, 52 n. 50
Halliwell, Stephen 9 n. 2, 64 n. 24
Hamacher, Werner 117 n. 37
Hamann, Johann Georg 166 n. 7
Hamburger, Käte 59 n. 8
Hamburger, Michael 35, **45 n. 32**, 110 n. 19, 116 n. 35, 117 n. 38, 134
Hamilton, John T. 59 n. 7, 87 n. 16, 89 n. 22, **90 n. 24**, 96 n. 36
Hamlin, Cyrus 64 nn. 21 & 23
Hanke, Thomas 12 n. 16, 82 n. 59
Harrison, R. B. 96 n. 35, 173 n. 22, 176 n. 43, 177 n. 47, 182 n. 41
Härtl, Heinz 135 n. 51
Harven, Vanessa de 47 n. 39, 48 n. 41
Hederich, Benjamin 40 n. 18
Hegel, Georg Wilhelm Friedrich 1, **11–12**, 72, **79–82**, 132 n. 43
Heidegger, Martin 1
Heinse, Wilhelm 110 n. 20, **114–16**
Hellingrath, Norbert von 93 n. 31, 123 n. 8, 155 n. 20, 171 n. 3
hen diapheron heautōi 2 n. 6, **19**, 20, **24**
hen kai pan 2, **14**, 18, 20, 23 n. 45, **24**, 39 n. 14, 41
Henrich, Dieter 11–12, 15 n. 26, 62 n. 18
Heracles **74–75**, 76 n. 46, **124–25**, **131–32**, 135, 140
Heraclitus 2 n. 6, 11 n. 13, **19–20**, 38, 39 n. 11, 44, 50 n. 47, 168 n. 24
Hercules *see* Heracles
Herder, Johann Gottfried 103 n. 6
Hesiod 36 n. 74, 40, 122 n. 4, 140
Hiller, Marion 96 n. 39, 101 n. 1, 118 n. 42
Hock, Erich 114 n. 31, 115 n. 32
Hölderlin, Friedrich:
    alternation of tones 41, **57–72**, 73, 76, **77–78**, 91, 107, 112, 114, 119, 131, 155 n. 17
    ancient and modern tragedy 5–6, 117–18, 122, 133–34, **135–38**, 149–51, **178–81**
    anti-tragic, the 1, 3, 112, 122, **124–30**, 133, 138, 168 n. 23
    calculable law 3–4, **57–58**, 87 n. 14, 88, 94, 118, 131, 140 n. 68, **153–57**, **169–70**
    and Goethe 88
    and Hegel 11–12, **79–80**, 82, 124 n. 11, 132 n. 43
    mental state **23**, 27, 79
    and Platonism 1–2, **12–22**, 23, 27, 74
    and Schiller 12, 37, **54**, 55 n. 57, 84 n. 6
    see also Hölderlin (letters): to Schiller
    and Stoicism 1–3, **23–36**, **37–46**, 52, 54, 55–56, 74–75, 76, 77, 130 n. 34, 142–43

and Susette Gontard 27, 110, **114–15**, 116
Wechsel der Töne, *see* alternation of tones
Hölderlin (letters):
  to Böhlendorff 5, 103, **109**, 117, **135–37**, 174 n. 24,
    177 n. 47, 179–80 n. 18, 181 n. 30
  to brother 12 n. 15, **16**, 60 n. 13, 106 n. 12,
    114 n. 30
  to Ebel 175 n. 33, 182 n. 40
  to Mehmel 125 n. 16, 134 n. 48, 135, **137–38**,
    165 n. 6
  to mother 3, 25 n. 49, **28 n. 57**, **86 n. 11**, 153 n. 2
  to Neuffer 12 n. 20, **23 n. 44**, 64 n. 22, 153–
    54 n. 7, 156 n. 26
  to Niethammer 12 n. 19, 15 n. 24
  to Schelling 175 n. 33
  to Schiller **15–16**, 16–17 n. 28, 18 n. 32
  to sister 26 n. 52, 134 n. 49
  to Wilmans 5 n. 14, 32 n. 65, 96, 98, 103 n. 5,
    110 n. 22, 121 n. 3, **147**, 151, 178 n. 10, **185**
Hölderlin (poetic works):
  'An die Madonna' 109–10
  'An die Parzen' 30 n. 58, 55 n. 59
  'An Eduard' 28, **29**, **36**, **46**, **47 n. 37**, 55 n. 59,
    121 n. 3, **136 n. 55**
  'An unsre großen Dichter' 45
  'Andenken' 52–53
  'Blödigkeit' 28, **31–33**, 35, 58, **99–100**, 130 n. 36,
    134–35, **136–37**, **138**, 160 n. 24
  'Brod und Wein' 74, 103, 116, 134 n. 48
  'Chiron' 58 n. 4, 75 n. 41, 123, 130 n. 35, **131–33**,
    134, 136, 138, 143, 151
  'Dem Sonnengott' 55 n. 59
  'Der Archipelagus' 50 n. 47, 114 n. 28
  'Der blinde Sänger' 58 n. 4, 131 n. 40, 133
  'Der Einzige' 37 n. 2, **75**, 178 n. 4
  'Der Ister' 135 n. 52
  'Der Rhein' **3–4**, 53 n. 52, 116
  'Der Zeitgeist' 41 n. 22, 55 n. 59
  'Dichterberuf' 45 n. 33, 55
  'Dichtermuth' (first version) 24 n. 46, 28, 30 n. 59,
    58
  'Dichtermuth' (second version) **28–31**, 32 n. 65,
    33, 37, 46 n. 35, 47 n. 37, 50 n. 47, 55, 58,
    130 n. 36, 138
    see also 'Blödigkeit', 'Muth des Dichters'
  'Die Dioskuren' 121 n. 3, 136 n. 55
  'Die Muße' 72 n. 35, 109 n. 17
  'Die Nymphe' 117
  'Diotima' (ode) 111 n. 24
  'Elegie' 134 n. 49
  Empedocles (tragedy) 6, 11, 17, 38, 40 n. 15, 41,
    72, 73, **74**, **76**, 101 n. 3, 103, 105, 147 n. 3,
    165 n. 5, 174 n. 30
  'Empedokles' (ode) 73–74
  'Ermunterung' 27 n. 54, 34 n. 70, 55
  'Friedensfeier' 41, **53**
  'Ganymed' **132**, **133 n. 46**, 136, 138, 151, 184 n. 56

  'Griechenland' 74
  'Hälfte des Lebens' 99, **110–11**, 115 n. 33, 117–18,
    122 n. 4, **134**
  'Heidelberg' 12
  Hyperion 2, 3, **12–13**, **16–22**, **23–25**, 26, 37, 52, 80,
    111, 113 n. 26, 114, 121, 180 n. 20
    penultimate version **13–14**, 15, 17, 18, 21, 22, 23,
      24, 59, 157 n. 41
    Thalia fragment 12 n. 20, 17 n. 29, 59, 157 n. 41
  'Kolomb' 126 n. 18
  'Lebensalter' 98–99
  'Lebenslauf' 20, 74, 134 n. 49
  'Mein Eigentum' **26–27**, 28 n. 57, 50 n. 47, 53,
    129 n. 32
  'Menons Klagen um Diotima' 64 n. 21, 110, 134 n. 49
  'Mnemosyne' 53, **117**, 118 n. 41
  'Muth des Dichters' 28, 30 n. 59, 32 n. 65
  Nachtgesänge 6, 28, 98, 110, 121–22, 123, **130–38**,
    143, 151
  'Natur und Kunst oder Saturn und Jupiter' 2 n. 4,
    28, **29**, **33–36**, **37–46**, 50, 53 n. 53, 55, 72, 104,
    176 n. 38
  Προς εαυτον **25**, 26 n. 52, 37 n. 2
  'Sonnenuntergang' 30 n. 60
  'Thränen' 131 n. 38, 137 n. 59
  'Vulkan' 99, **133 nn. 46 & 47**, 136, 151
Hölderlin (theoretical works):
  Being and Judgment **14–16**, 59, 62, 78, 167 n. 17,
    178 n. 6
  Das lyrische dem Schein nach idealische Gedicht …
    66 n. 28, 107 n. 14, 130 n. 34
  Das untergehende Vaterland … 101 n. 3
  Die Bedeutung der Tragödien … 4, **101–20**, **185**
  Die Empfindung spricht … 65 n. 26, 155 n. 17
  Die tragische Ode … 72, **73**, 101 n. 3, **105**, 158 n. 2,
    165 n. 5, 185 n. 2
  fragment on religion 154 n. 13, 157 n. 40
  Fragment philosophischer Briefe, *see* fragment on
    religion
  Frankfurter Aphorismen, *see* seven maxims or
    aphorisms
  'Grund zum Empedokles' *see Die tragische Ode …*
  Löst sich nicht … 119 n. 43
  Master's exercises *see* specimina
  Pindarfragmente 6, 101, 112, **121–22**, **123–30**, 131,
    133, 138, 139, 141
    'Das Alter' 123 n. 9, 126
    'Das Belebende' **123**, **124–25**, 139
    'Das Höchste' 122 n. 5, 123 n. 9, **124–25**, 128,
      129, **130**, 131, 139–40, **141**, 167 n. 17,
      168 n. 23, 178 n. 2
    'Das Unendliche' 121, 123 n. 9, **139–43**
    'Die Asyle' 26 n. 52, 54 n. 55, 75 n. 43, 112,
      121 n. 3, 122 n. 5, 125 n. 17, 126, **128–30**,
      167 n. 17, 168 n. 23
    'Untreue der Weisheit' **112–13**, 122 nn. 5 & 6,
      123, **125–26**, **127**, 130 n. 35, 139

'Vom Delphin' 112–14, 115, 116, 122 nn. 4 & 5, 126, 127, 128
'Von der Ruhe' 26 n. 52, 112, 123 n. 9, 126, 127–28
'Von der Wahrheit' 112, 123 n. 9, 126
seven maxims or aphorisms 4 n. 12, 84, 89, 138 n. 60
Seyn, Urtheil, Möglichkeit, see Being and Judgment
Sophokles-Anmerkungen 3, 4–5, 6, 45, 58, 73, 74, 83–97, 99, 101, 102–03, 105, 110, 112–13, 118, 121–22, 125, 126, 127, 128, 129, 131, 132 n. 43, 134, 135, 136, 147–51, 153–84
specimina 87 n. 14, 90, 92 n. 29, 94–95 n. 33, 156 n. 27
tone tables 3, 41, 57–59, 63, 65–66, 67–72, 119 n. 43, 131
Urtheil und Seyn, see Being and Judgment
Wenn der Dichter … 68 n. 32, 153 n. 6, 155 n. 17, 184 nn. 54 & 57
Hölderlin (translations):
 of Pindar 26 n. 52, 38 n. 5, 121, 122, 123 n. 9, 127, 129 n. 29, 139
 of Sophocles 4, 5–6, 79, 83, 84 n. 4, 87, 93 n. 30, 98, 101, 121, 122, 147, 148, 149, 151
 see also Hölderlin (theoretical works): *Sophokles-Anmerkungen*
Hölscher, Uvo 2 n. 6, 38, 39 nn. 11 & 14
Holt, Philip 177 nn. 46 & 48
Honold, Alexander 38 n. 6, 41 n. 19, 59 n. 7, 125 n. 15
Horace 11 n. 14, 17
Hornbacher, Annette 12 n. 17
Hösle, Vittorio 98 n. 43
Hühn, Helmut 91 n. 27, 93 n. 30, 105, 125 n. 16, 155 n. 20, 168 n. 23
Hyppolite, Jean 79, 82

Indlekofer, Barbara 30 n. 59, 31 n. 63, 58 n. 4, 99 n. 48, 131 n. 40, 133 nn. 45 & 46, 141 n. 69
Irwin, John T. 75–76 n. 44, 78, 165 n. 3

Jacobi, Friedrich Heinrich 2, 39 n. 14, 103 n. 6
Jago, Mark 142 n. 72
Jupiter *see* Zeus

Kahn, Charles H. 9 n. 3, 11 n. 13, 14, 19 n. 35, 20 nn. 37 & 38, 38 n. 8, 44 n. 30
Kant, Immanuel 13, 15 n. 25, 54–55, 78, 81, 85, 139 n. 64, 150, 167 n. 21, 168 n. 25
Kasper, Monika 94 n. 33, 118 n. 42, 156 n. 28
Keil, Werner 115 n. 34
Kerslake, Lawrence 87 n. 15
khronos 36, 40, 46, 48, 49, 50–52, 130 n. 34
Killy, Walter 123 n. 10
Kingsley, Peter 10 nn. 6, 7 & 9
Kleist, Heinrich von 3, 59 n. 8

Klopstock, Friedrich Gottlieb 96, 155 n. 24
Knox, Bernard 153 n. 1, 156 n. 26, 158 n. 1, 165 nn. 2 & 3, 167 n. 20, 168 nn. 21 & 24
Kociszky, Eva 96 n. 38, 99 n. 46, 135 n. 53
Koppenfels, Martin von 150 n. 9, 151 n. 13, 182 n. 34
Kraye, Jill 10 n. 8, 11 n. 13
Krell, David Farrell 11 n. 11, 96 n. 39
Kreuzer, Johann 15 n. 26, 57 n. 3, 126 n. 20, 185 n. 3
Kronos *see* Cronus
Kurke, Leslie 5, 6, 122 n. 5, 137 n. 57, 166 n. 8, 180 n. 21, 181 n. 31
Kurz, Gerhard 9 nn. 3 & 4, 16–17 n. 28, 73, 93, 94 n. 33, 97, 184 nn. 53, 54 & 56

Lacoue-Labarthe, Philippe 97 n. 39, 150 n. 9, 151
Laks, André 9 nn. 5 & 6, 11 n. 13, 44 n. 30, 153 n. 1
Lampenscherf, Stephan 12 n. 20, 17 n. 28
Langdon, Helen 89 n. 22
Lange, Wilhelm 57 n. 3
Laplanche, Jean 114
Lardinois, A. P. M. H. 125 n. 15, 165 n. 2
Lemke, Anja 103 n. 7, 118 n. 42, 119 n. 43
Lessing, Gotthold Ephraim 2
Link, Jürgen 25 n. 48, 38 n. 7, 53 n. 53, 156 n. 32
Listing, J. B. 60
Litman, Théodore A. 87 n. 15
Littlewood, C. A. J. 75 n. 42
Long, Anthony A. 9 n. 6, 38, 40 n. 18, 43 n. 27, 44 n. 30, 45 n. 31, 48 n. 42, 49
Longinus, Cassius 98, 99
[Pseudo-]Longinus *see On the Sublime*
Lönker, Fred 117 n. 37, 158 n. 4
Louth, Charlie 12 n. 18, 57 n. 1, 58 n. 6, 61 n. 16, 96, 107 n. 13, 110 n. 21, 111 n. 23, 117 n. 37, 122 nn. 5, 6 & 7, 123 n. 10, 127 n. 22, 132, 154 n. 13, 165 n. 2, 179 n. 16
Lüders, Detlev 168 n. 23

Macintosh, Fiona 167 n. 15
Marcus Aurelius 3, 25–26, 31, 32, 37, 41 n. 24, 47, 49–52, 54, 160 n. 21
Marmontel, Jean-François 88
Martens, Gunter 37 n. 1, 58 n. 6
Matuschek, Stefan 9 n. 3
Matzner, Sebastian 62 n. 17, 161 n. 33
Maurer, Karl 87 n. 15, 98 n. 41
Menninghaus, Winfried 59 n. 7, 111, 155 n. 24, 165 n. 1
mētis 126, 139–40, 143
Meyer, Susan Sauvé 32 n. 66, 40 n. 16
Miller, Jon 2 n. 6
Miller, Margaret 155 n. 19, 167 n. 21
Möbius, A. F. 60
möbius strip 3, 58–61, 62 n. 18, 67–72, 78, 82
Mögel, Ernst 38 n. 6, 46 n. 36, 101 n. 3, 103, 104, 108–09

Montaigne, Michel de 2 n. 5
Montgomery, Marshall 2 n. 3, 87 n. 14
Most, Glenn W. 9 nn. 1 & 6, 11 n. 13, 38 n. 9, 40 n. 18, 44 n. 30, 153 n. 1

Nägele, Rainer 58 n. 5, 62, 96 n. 39, 153 n. 3, 154 n. 10
Naville, Denise 185
Nightingale, Andrea Wilson 1, 9
Novalis 1, 3, 59 n. 8

On the Sublime 4, 83, 84–85, 86–92, 93, 95 n. 33, 97–98, 99, 133, 138 n. 60
One and All, *see hen kai pan*
Ostwald, Martin 124 n. 14
Oudemans, Th. C. W. 125 n. 15, 165 n. 2

Palmyra 98–99
Parmenides 9–10
Perger, Mischa von 12 n. 20
Perrault, Charles 87, 96
Pfau, Thomas 137, 147, 185
philosophy:
  and poetry 1–3, 9–36, 37–46, 54, 55–56, 74, 75–76, 79–80, 82, 84, 132, 142–43, 154 n. 15, 169, 175 n. 34
  see also Aristotle, Chrysippus, Cleanthes, Empedocles, Fichte, Hegel, Heraclitus, Kant, Marcus Aurelius, Plato, Schelling, Seneca, Spinoza
Pickover, Clifford A. 59 n. 9, 60 nn. 11 & 14, 61 n. 15
Pindar 87, 89, 95 n. 33, 96
  fragments 122, 123 n. 9
  see also Hölderlin (theoretical works): *Pindarfragmente*
  victory odes x, 3–4, 5, 6, 95 n. 33, 122, 126 n. 18, 129, 133 n. 47, 135, 137 n. 57, 180 n. 21
  see also Hölderlin (translations): of Pindar
Plato 2, 9, 10, 13–14, 19–20, 76, 124, 140
  see also Hölderlin: and Platonism
Pöggeler, Otto 79 n. 53, 85 n. 10, 179 n. 16
Porter, James I. 4, 85 n. 8, 87 nn. 13 & 15, 92 n. 28, 98 n. 43
Pourciau, Sarah 3 n. 8, 59 n. 8
Primavesi, Oliver 10 nn. 6, 8, 9 & 10, 11, 17 n. 31, 39 nn. 11 & 14

Rapin, René 98 n. 41
Raulet, Gérard 38 n. 6, 41 n. 23
Reitani, Luigi 17 n. 29, 20 n. 39, 31 n. 62, 32 n. 65, 37 nn. 1, 2 & 3, 38 n. 6, 43, 45 n. 32, 55, 99 n. 46, 110 n. 19, 117 n. 38, 133 n. 46, 134 n. 48
Robinet, Jean-Baptiste 91 n. 27, 166 n. 7
Roche, Mark William 12 n. 20, 22, 24 n. 47
Romilly, Jacqueline de 168 n. 24
Rosenfield, Kathrin H. 117 n. 37, 151 n. 15
Rousseau, Jean-Jacques 53, 128

Ruschi, Riccardo 147, 185
Russell, Donald 98 n. 43
Ryan, Lawrence 3, 4 n. 11, 18 nn. 33 & 34, 21 n. 42, 22, 38 n. 6, 41 nn. 23 & 24, 57–58, 61–62, 63, 64 n. 21, 65 n. 26, 68 n. 31, 71 n. 33, 73, 78, 101 n. 1, 107, 118–19, 130 n. 34, 137, 150, 173 n. 18

Saint-Mard, Rémond de 93
Santos Gomes, Márcio dos 20 n. 39, 39 nn. 11 & 14
Sappho 111, 131 n. 38
Sassi, Maria Michela 9 nn. 1 & 5, 10 nn. 9 & 10, 20 n. 38
Sattler, D. E. 130 n. 35
Saturn *see* Cronus
Schelling, Friedrich Wilhelm Joseph 11, 12, 15, 16, 62 n. 18, 79
Schiller, Friedrich 1, 88 n. 19
  see also Hölderlin: and Schiller
Schlegel, Friedrich 1, 9 n. 4, 54–55, 59, 83, 84
Schmid, Holger 58 n. 6
Schmidt, Jochen 2, 17, 21 n. 42, 24 n. 47, 27 nn. 53 & 54, 28, 31 nn. 61 & 62, 32, 37–38, 41 nn. 21 & 24, 46 n. 36, 55 n. 58, 75 nn. 41 & 43, 84, 85 n. 7, 91 n. 27, 93 n. 32, 96 nn. 35 & 38, 99 n. 47, 103 n. 6, 104, 109, 110 n. 20, 122 n. 5, 125 n. 15, 130, 131 nn. 40 & 41, 132, 133 n. 47, 134 n. 48, 137 nn. 58 & 59, 149 n. 7, 153 n. 1, 155 nn. 16, 17 & 20, 166 nn. 7, 9 & 11, 169 nn. 3 & 7, 173 n. 21, 176 n. 40, 177 n. 47, 178 n. 4, 181 n. 32, 182 n. 42
Schofield, Malcolm 48 n. 40, 49 n. 43
Schönberger, Otto 88
Sedley, D. N. 38, 43 n. 27, 44 n. 30, 45 n. 31, 48 n. 42, 49
Segal, Charles 5, 136, 158 n. 4, 159 n. 11, 165 n. 6, 167 n. 21, 177 n. 47
Seidensticker, Bernd 172 n. 13
Seifert, Albrecht 3–4, 23 n. 44, 25 n. 48, 84, 85 n. 7, 87 nn. 14 & 15, 89 n. 22, 121 n. 3, 122 n. 5, 128 nn. 24 & 26, 129, 130 nn. 33 & 35
Sellars, John 25 n. 51, 48 n. 42, 49, 51
Seneca 2 n. 5, 24 n. 47, 37, 38 n. 9, 41, 51, 75
Sextus Empiricus 76
Shelley, Percy Bysshe 20 n. 36
Sieburth, Richard 53 n. 52, 117 n. 38
Siekmann, Andreas 112 n. 25
Sikes, Elizabeth B. 96 n. 39
Sömmerring, Samuel Thomas 114
Sourvinou-Inwood, Christiane 175 nn. 31 & 32, 176 n. 42
Spinoza, Baruch 2, 24 n. 47, 54–55
Staiger, Emil 35 n. 71, 38 n. 6, 45 n. 32, 46 n. 36
Stanitzek, Georg 31 n. 64
Steimer, Hans Gerhard 99
Steinmetz, Peter 42 n. 26, 43 n. 27, 140 n. 67
Stephanus *see* Estienne

Stewart, Ian 60 n. 14
Stierle, Karlheinz 54 n. 54, 88 n. 19, 179 n. 16
Strack, Friedrich 12 n. 17, 15 nn. 24, 25 & 26, 62 n. 18
Strauß, Ludwig 12 n. 19, **134 n. 49**
Striker, Gisela 24 n. 47
Summerell, Orrin F. 13 n. 21
Swift, Jonathan 83
Szondi, Peter **5 n. 15**, 38 n. 6, 41, 58 n. 6, 64 n. 22, 107 nn. 13 & 15, **137**

Taminiaux, Jacques 97 n. 39, 166 n. 7
Tang, Chenxi 36 n. 72, 38 n. 6, 45 n. 33, **53–54 n. 54**, **73 n. 36**, 78 n. 51
Taplin, Oliver 158 n. 1, 160 n. 27, 161 n. 32, 162 n. 40, 167 n. 12
Tausch, Harald 99 nn. 46 & 47
Themis **129**, 140 nn. 66 & 67
Theunissen, Michael 122 n. 5, 126 n. 18
Thom, Johan C. 37 n. 4, 38 n. 8, 44 nn. 29 & 30, 45 n. 31
Till, Dietmar 85 n. 8, 92 n. 28
Totschnig, Wolfhart 47 n. 39, 48 n. 40, 77 nn. 48 & 49
Tübingen *Stift* 9 n. 3, 11, 39, 40 n. 18

Ugolini, Gherardo 118 n. 42, 157 n. 37

Vernant, Jean-Pierre 117, **150**, 153 n. 1, **165 nn. 2 & 3**, 166 n. 8, 181 n. 31
see also Detienne and Vernant
Vöhler, Martin 4 n. 10, 41 n. 19, **72 n. 35**, **84**, 87 n. 14, 89 nn. 21 & 22, 91, 96 n. 37, 127 n. 21
Volney, Constantin-François de 99

Warminski, Andrzej **59**, 62 n. 18, **68 n. 32**, 94 n. 33, 135 n. 53, 156 n. 28
Weinrich, Harald 62 n. 17
Wetzels, Walter D. 81 n. 56
Wilamowitz-Moellendorff, Ulrich von **42–43**, 140 n. 67
Winckelmann, Johann Joachim 91 n. 27, 166 n. 7
Wittstock, Albert 31 n. 62, 50 n. 47
Wood, Robert 99 n. 46

Zeus 2, 32, **33–36**, **37–47**, **54–56**, 72–73, 74, 75, 124 n. 14, 129 n. 30, 131, 135, 136 n. 55, **140**, 143, 151, 171, 173 n. 19, **175**, 176 n. 38, **179**
Zuberbühler, Rolf 134 n. 48, 137 n. 57
Zuntz, Günther 42 n. 26, 43 n. 27, 44 n. 30

www.ingramcontent.com/pod-product-compliance
Lightning Source LLC
LaVergne TN
LVHW061250060426
835507LV00017B/2003